# The First GENERATION

A Half Century of
Pioneering in Perry, Oklahoma.

 *The Oklahoma Legacies Series*

# The First GENERATION

A Half Century of
Pioneering in Perry, Oklahoma.

*Our Best Wishes*

## By Fred G. Beers

 *The Oklahoma Legacies Series*

Published by The Charles Machine Works, Inc.

Library of Congress Card Catalog Number: 91-061776

ISBN: 0-913507-22-9

Ditch Witch is a registered trademark
    Of The Charles Machine Works, Inc.

# CONTENTS

Preface . . . . . . . . . . . . . . . . . . . . . . . . . . . . . . . . . *vii*

Acknowledgments . . . . . . . . . . . . . . . . . . . . . . . . . . . . *.xi*

**PART I: PERRY'S INFANCY** . . . . . . . . . . . . . . . . . . . . . 1
1.  The Pioneer Spirit . . . . . . . . . . . . . . . . . . . . . . . 3
2.  Some Background . . . . . . . . . . . . . . . . . . . . . . . 7
3.  The Run . . . . . . . . . . . . . . . . . . . . . . . . . . . 12
4.  Orlando Walkling . . . . . . . . . . . . . . . . . . . . . . . 34
5.  C.T. Talliaferro . . . . . . . . . . . . . . . . . . . . . . . . 39
6.  James A. Lobsitz . . . . . . . . . . . . . . . . . . . . . . . 42
7.  After the Run . . . . . . . . . . . . . . . . . . . . . . . . . 45

**PART II: 1900 TO 1920** . . . . . . . . . . . . . . . . . . . . . . 59
8.  Malzahns Come to Perry . . . . . . . . . . . . . . . . . . . 61
9.  The Library and the Opera House . . . . . . . . . . . . . 66
10.  Churches and Schools . . . . . . . . . . . . . . . . . . . . 79
11.  Mr. Hovey and Some Others . . . . . . . . . . . . . . . . 91
12.  The Famous Store . . . . . . . . . . . . . . . . . . . . . . 97
13.  The Cyclone of 1912 . . . . . . . . . . . . . . . . . . . . .101

**PART III: THE 1920s** . . . . . . . . . . . . . . . . . . . . . . . .119
14.  Life After World War I . . . . . . . . . . . . . . . . . . . .121
15.  The Malzahn Brothers . . . . . . . . . . . . . . . . . . . .126
16.  Uncle Christ . . . . . . . . . . . . . . . . . . . . . . . . . .129
17.  Charlie and Bertha Malzahn . . . . . . . . . . . . . . . . .131
18.  Young Ed Malzahn . . . . . . . . . . . . . . . . . . . . . .136
19.  Henry S. Johnston . . . . . . . . . . . . . . . . . . . . . .143
20.  Manuel Herrick . . . . . . . . . . . . . . . . . . . . . . . .151
21.  Eddie, Kate and the Kumback . . . . . . . . . . . . . . . .160
22.  WKL and the *Perry Journal* . . . . . . . . . . . . . . . . .169
23.  Lions and Rotarians . . . . . . . . . . . . . . . . . . . . . .173
24.  The Wrestling Capital . . . . . . . . . . . . . . . . . . . . .176

*PART IV: THE 1930s* . . . . . . . . . . . . . . . . . . . . . .197
25.  Facing the Depression . . . . . . . . . . . . . . . . . .199
26.  Charlie's Machine Shop . . . . . . . . . . . . . . . .202
27.  Marty, Shorty and Kirby . . . . . . . . . . . . . . . .208
28.  Cap Swift and Friends . . . . . . . . . . . . . . . . .210
29.  Professor Radgowsky . . . . . . . . . . . . . . . . . .214
30.  The Poor Boys Club . . . . . . . . . . . . . . . . . .219
31.  Mickey and Eleanor Visit . . . . . . . . . . . . . . . .229
32.  The Exchange Bank Holdup . . . . . . . . . . . . . . .233
33.  The First National Bank . . . . . . . . . . . . . . . .243

*PART V: THE 1940s* . . . . . . . . . . . . . . . . . . . . .259
34.  The 1940s Arrive . . . . . . . . . . . . . . . . . . . .261
35.  The Ditch Witch Era Dawns . . . . . . . . . . . . . . .264
36.  Why Is It "Ditch Witch?" . . . . . . . . . . . . . . . .276
37.  Geronimo and Other Products . . . . . . . . . . . . .279
38.  CMW Finds New Ways . . . . . . . . . . . . . . . . . .283
39.  Around the Square in 1940 . . . . . . . . . . . . . . .295
40.  The Cherokee Strip Museum . . . . . . . . . . . . . .314
41.  Wistful Local Legends . . . . . . . . . . . . . . . . .322
42.  Perry at Fifty Years . . . . . . . . . . . . . . . . . . .329
43.  Appendix . . . . . . . . . . . . . . . . . . . . . . . .347

      Index . . . . . . . . . . . . . . . . . . . . . . . . . . .353

# PREFACE

In 1902, when a family of blacksmiths began to forge a new business that would become an amazing, world-class industry, Perry was already the bustling young queen of the prairie. The spunky little city and the innovative firm whose Ditch Witch equipment is now used worldwide grew up together. Adding zest to the pioneering years was a colorful mixture of personalities drawn to the Oklahoma Territory by the Cherokee Strip Land Run of 1893.

This book is a collection of stories about the first half-century of both Perry and the Charles Machine Works, Inc., which is the official name of the Ditch Witch company. Both are unusual in many ways, largely because of the people who made them work. Perry's saga begins with that incredible run for free land and continues through 1943, with a minor excursion at either end.

This is not a history of Perry in the conventional sense. Several such volumes already are on the shelves of Oklahoma libraries. They contain excellent, detailed accounts of the establishment and development of this community and the surrounding area. Oklahoma museums, particularly the one in Perry, have many fascinating artifacts and documents about this exciting part of America. We commend all of them to you.

This one is more a celebration of some of the people who made the lively first half-century possible. The truth is that Perry has had more than her share of colorful and significant residents. This book profiles a generous sampling of them.

So, this is not an all-encompassing story, just a loving look back at Perry and CMW during the years they were growing up on the prairie. The writer also grew up here. He spent twenty-five years as editor of the local newspaper and then twenty more as an employee of CMW, primarily in the Graphic Communications Department. He has heard about and seen many of the good and bad parts of the city, but not all of them. He loves the place, as you will see.

After a period of research in preparation for this book, he has a new sense of appreciation for the pioneer settlers who came here in the early days. Pondering the hardships they endured and the obstacles they had to overcome in carving a social order out of the wilderness, he stands genuinely in awe of their spirit and determination.

Information came from many sources. Where possible it was obtained through first-person accounts of people who were there when the event at hand occurred. The number of true pioneers is diminishing, however, so we now must rely on such things as letters, diaries, old newspapers and tales passed along by second and third generation family members. Help came from many sources and every bit of it was freely given when requested. Sincere thanks to all who assisted.

Some of the recollections may be slightly flawed. Time does that, but the stories are not knowingly romanticized or embellished. They really do not need to be. Think of them as snapshots from the prairie. Not the kind on film, just some random views from the gallery of the mind.

Growing up in Perry America, as we like to call it, was a unique privilege for relatively few young people as well as young businesses. Since this is, after all, a small town, the total number of children who have been born here is not very large. Then you have to subtract those native-borns who did not stick around through adolescence. It follows that those who did their growing up in Perry were relatively few in number. Of course, they were the lucky ones.

The same applies to businesses and industries that started here. For them was reserved the special joy, the close family feeling of a small town upbringing.

Ed Kelley, managing editor of the Oklahoma City *Daily Oklahoman* and a 1971 graduate of Perry High School, recently remarked: "I've heard it said that if everybody in this world who once lived in Perry would stand up and be counted, it would total more than one million people. That may be an exaggeration, but even if it is, it does show that the world is not such a bad place after all."

At any rate, a lot of folks have passed through here and we're thankful for all who stayed. Most of them are grateful, too.

Census figures for Perry have shown modest population increases through the years, not as great as civic boosters would like, but generally it's been on the plus side after the initial boom. Here's the rundown:

| 1893 | — | 40,000 (Est. First Day) |
|------|---|-------------------------|
| 1897 | — | 4,000 (Est.) |
| 1900 | — | 3,351 (U.S. Census) |
| 1907 | — | 2,881 (Est.) |
| 1920 | — | 3,154 (U.S. Census) |
| 1930 | — | 4,206 (U.S. Census) |
| 1940 | — | 5,045 (U.S. Census) |
| 1950 | — | 5,137 (U.S. Census) |
| 1960 | — | 5,210 (U.S. Census) |
| 1970 | — | 5,341 (U.S. Census) |
| 1980 | — | 5,783 (U.S. Census) |
| 1990 | — | 4,978 (U.S. Census) |

A great effort was made in 1940 to count everyone possible. Civic leaders badly wanted to ease past the 5,000 level so Perry's official status could be upgraded from "town" to "city." It sounds so much bigger. That goal was achieved, and the number hovered between 5,000 and 6,000 until the 1990 census. That tally has been disputed by city officials. They have asked for a recount.

It is said there is something "different" about a native-born Perryan. Visitors and new residents often say that, and they usually make it sound complimentary. The differences are not as pronounced as they used to be. Those with the most legitimate claim to uniqueness were those who took part in the Cherokee Strip Land Run on September 16, 1893. Few, if any, of them remain.

Their offspring are prairie blue bloods, comparable in a way to the Daughters and Sons of the American Revolution, so you could say they are "different" because they constitute a rare breed. They are rightfully held in high esteem. But time is decimating their number, and so the mantle of "first family" is being draped around those who simply were born here, whatever the year.

Some people also claim, perhaps with tongue in cheek, that an invisible barrier separates Perry natives and those who came from somewhere else. After about forty years of living here, they say, a newcomer begins to feel "accepted." If that is so, the reason may be a legacy from the land run era. Then newcomers were required to "prove up" the real estate they claimed by living on it for a period of years before receiving a government deed. They did not automatically become land owners just because they arrived here.

In the meantime, however, while "proving" themselves, they enjoyed all the benefits and privileges of living in this blessed area. That's still sort of how it is with new arrivals today. They are welcomed with open arms while we native Perryans get to know them, and we always hope they stay here forever. Every one of them who moves on is missed.

This is a community with great neighborly feeling. When misfortune befalls someone, help and understanding invariably are provided by people they may not even know. Should a farmer become disabled during planting season or at harvest time, he will find his place swarming with volunteers getting the job done.

If a family's home is damaged by fire or the elements, others will quickly organize the collection of food, clothing or whatever is needed to sustain them. Loss of a loved one also produces great compassion. Likewise, when someone's son, daughter or grandchild earns an honor or an award, we all feel a sense of pride. Such things may be typical of small towns generally, but none of the others has more of it than this little city.

Perry is not perfect, but as a lyricist once put it, everything is beautiful in its own way. That applies to little towns still growing up on the prairie.

*—fgb*

# $A$CKNOWLEDGMENTS

Many people contributed information, photographs and special kinds of assistance to make this book possible. Their help is gratefully acknowledged, even though such a general statement admittedly is inadequate. Contributions came from so many sources, it is physically impossible to name each one.

The writer is indebted to all who provided ideas and material, including family members, friends, colleagues in the Charles Machine Works Graphic Communications Department, new acquaintances and those who simply expressed encouragement and interest.

The motivation provided by Ed Malzahn, president of CMW, is responsible for this undertaking. He has been generous in his understanding and assistance in every way. The story of his company and its employees, his family and the other people of this community through the years is a great folk tale in the classic "American ingenuity" tradition. Working on it has been a wonderfully fulfilling experience.

Doris Dellinger was most helpful in editing the manuscript, compiling the index and suggesting sequential order of material. The cover design and other original art work are by Tiffany Sewell Hogan, talented granddaughter of Ed and Mary Malzahn. Among many others, these also provided special assistance:

Wesley Aldrich and the family of Gene Aldrich, Roy Baker, Laura Beers, Fred W. Beers, Lawrence Beier, Karen Bigbee of Perry Carnegie Library, Rudy Bittle of Frontier Printers, Inc., Juanita Bolay, Kaye Bond of the Cherokee Strip Museum in Perry, Kenneth Coldiron, Paul W. Cress, Robert H. Donaldson Jr., Robin Wilson Dorl, Lucille Foster, Ruth Esther Willett Lanza, Wilbur G. Mouser, Barbara Rupp, Glenn Shirley, Genevieve Willett Slade, Myrna Stoops, Milo W. Watson, Elizabeth Willems and Glenn A. Yahn.

Source material referenced includes: "Okie Jesus Congressman," by Gene Aldrich; "Early Day History of Perry, Oklahoma," by Judge E.W. Jones; "Perry, Pride of the Prairie," by

Robert Cunningham; "The Beginning of Perry, Oklahoma," by Ethel Knox; "The McCandless House" (term paper) by Susan Beers Bieberdorf; "History of Noble County, Oklahoma," published by the Noble County Genealogical Society; files of *the Perry Daily Journal*; and the 1988 Noble County Yesteryear Calendar published by the Noble County Historical Society.

Many photos were provided by the Oklahoma Historical Society from the collection at the Cherokee Strip Museum in Perry. Photos from several private collections also were generously shared. In some cases it was difficult to identify all individuals shown in the photos, but many long-time residents of this community helped by furnishing names, dates and places.

Every effort was made to verify information, including photo captions, used throughout this book, but we must acknowledge that errors are probably inevitable despite the most meticulous attempts to avoid them.

Thanks to each and every one, including all those not named above, who helped in this endeavor. Bringing it to completion, through the stages of concept, research, interviewing, writing and publication, has been a labor of love.

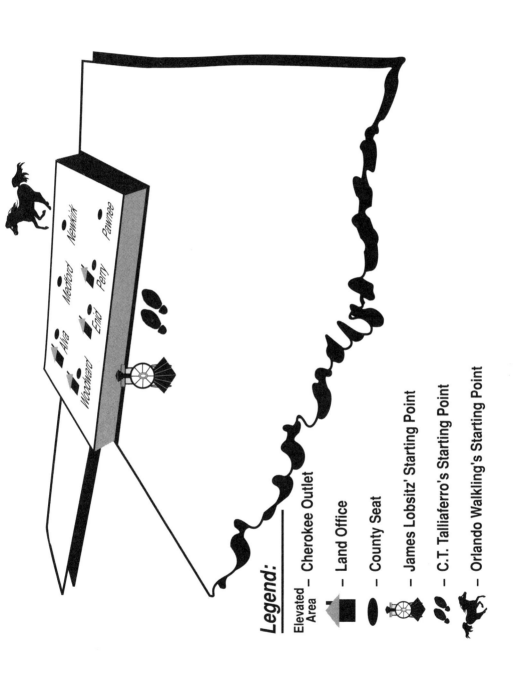

*Legend:*

Elevated Area — Cherokee Outlet

— Land Office

— County Seat

— James Lobsitz' Starting Point

— C.T. Talliaferro's Starting Point

— Orlando Walkling's Starting Point

Alva  Woodward  Medford  Enid  Perry  Newkirk  Pawnee

# PART I: PERRY'S INFANCY

# 1

# *T*HE PIONEER SPIRIT

Oklahoma was the only state settled almost entirely by land runs. It started fast and grew fast. So, it's been said, that accounts for the present inhabitants' impatience to get things done.

The Cherokee Strip was born in a land rush frenzy on a hot and dusty September afternoon in 1893. Perry was considered the "queen city" of the Strip. It has survived almost a hundred years of men's follies, Nature's foibles, economic failures and social furors, yet it remains vigorous and forward-looking. Why? Many small towns with similar foundations withered and died long ago. Let's look for reasons.

Perry began in a spectacular way that will not be witnessed again. It sprang forth more or less fully grown in a single day on September 16, 1893, when the Cherokee Strip was opened to non-Indian settlers by the United States government. The signal for the run was a gunshot provided by the Army—literally a big bang. Men were offered whole quarter-sections of land—160 acres per parcel—simply by staking a claim on the property and remaining there long enough to "prove it up."

Perhaps it was the hardiness of those pioneer men, women and children that has given Perry the backbone to endure despite recurring waves of difficulties that have harassed the little prairie city through the years.

Consider how the area developed. From the beginning, the economy was agrarian-based. Families relied on livestock and produce from the land for their existence, though unpredictable and often severe weather conditions reduced hard-muscled farmers to bent and weary figures. Crops and herds perished in prairie wind storms, torrential rains, prolonged drought and unforgiving winters. Uncertain markets were a certainty. Despite that pervasive specter, they stuck with the land year after year, drawing from a limitless reservoir of optimism that sometimes seemed to have no basis at all.

The run brought more than its share of those who came not to claim soil for farming but to begin life anew as lawyers, doctors, merchants, newspapermen, educators, preachers, land agents, officers of the law and assorted others, even some scoundrels who chose to live outside the law. Not all of them were paragons. Most were young and adventurous. It was an interesting mixture of humanity.

Those who had the tenacity to battle adversity after the opening must have been equipped with a rare, God-given determination that enabled them to wrest a livelihood from the prairie. They cared for each other in the unique, compassionate way that binds those who have suffered common hardships.

Those traits are the heritage of today's Perry community and as much as anything they answer the question: what is so special about Perry, Oklahoma?

Perry emerged from the 1893 land rush into a post-run period of building homes, farmsteads, businesses, schools and churches, attracting still more newcomers as others learned about the frenzied development here. The new community also lost some who quickly tired of primitive frontier life. It was a time of get-rich-quick for land speculators and a few others, but most of the homesteaders had to learn to accept daily agonies and deprivations.

The post-run period was followed by a time of great development as some farms and ranches consolidated, businesses became more stable and "up to date" after the early days, municipal governments carried out their responsibilities and local politics began emerging.

Oil reserves were discovered and pumped from the ground, strong individuals from rural and urban communities began shaping the area's destiny, and the Charles Machine Works, Inc. had its beginning in a blacksmith shop operated by a German immigrant and his two sons.

As the decade of the 1920s approached, Perry joined hands with the rest of America to do its part in the War to End All Wars, sending dozens of its strong young men into military service. Some who answered the call paid the supreme sacrifice on European battlefields, but most returned to the little prairie city after the

Armistice was signed in 1918. They brought with them a renewed vigor and vision that enabled the pattern of growth to be resumed.

The nation's economy, strengthened by wartime industrial development, quickly surged to unprecedented heights, and Perry joyously shared in the momentous growth—and the disastrous crash which signaled its demise at the end of the decade.

The 1930s dawned and depression gripped the U.S., along with virtually the entire world. Perry knew hard times again. Banks struggled and some floundered. Foreclosures drove many farmers and businessmen away. Unprecedented drought created an epic Dust Bowl that rendered cropland useless and relentless prairie winds compounded the misery.

It was a time of darkness, despair and doubt, trying men's souls, but a few bright rays emerged through the gloom. Toward the end of the decade Perry was awarded a political plum—a State Highway Department division office, one of only eight in all of Oklahoma. It assured the area of a major employer.

During the same period, a new U.S. Post Office was built on the courthouse square and the city became the beneficiary of federal largess through such depression-spawned agencies as the CCC (Civilian Conservation Corps) and the WPA (Works Project Administration). Among other things, Perry received a fine new park (still called the CCC Park), several school buildings, a large armory and the Perry school stadium, regarded as the state's finest at the time it was completed in 1939.

The economy was showing positive signs of recovery as that decade ended, but the war in Europe grew more ominous daily. In 1940, the 45th National Guard division was mobilized for federal service and dozens of young Perry area men were shipped to Fort Sill for active duty.

World War II ensnared the U.S. when Pearl Harbor was bombed by the Japanese in a surprise attack on the morning of Sunday, December 7, 1941, and it marked a loss of innocence for the nation as a whole. Perry experienced the wartime tragedies of the death and maiming of many of its finest young people.

The massive war effort required those on the home front to deal with shortages of just about everything. Still the community continued the process of surviving and evolving, eventually coming to grips with preparations for growing and rebuilding in the post-World War II era.

In the latter half of the 1940s, the Charles Machine Works began experimenting with the prototype of a new small trencher which became known by the trade name Ditch Witch.

In more recent decades Perry has continued to prove itself a survivor while some communities have literally faded into oblivion. The State Highway Department (now the Department of Transportation) division office remains a vital part of the community and other employers are developing promising new businesses and industries to add to those that have been able to endure.

Farmers must still battle the elements, government programs and other challenges, and many small operators have sold out to multi-farm operators. Perry has two outstanding banks and a stable, though reconfigured, retail business community. A daily newspaper and an AM/FM radio station are major communications media, perhaps unique among towns this size.

Shining brightest of all, however, and unquestionably the reason Perry has endured, is the Charles Machine Works, Inc., manufacturer of Ditch Witch products, an internationally marketed line of medium construction equipment. CMW is a compelling story all by itself, but its history is so interwoven with that of Perry that it is impossible to discuss one and not the other.

Perry has always had its share of rich personalities. Some of the earliest among them might be called mavericks, rebels or worse today, but they were regarded in earlier times only as eccentrics, maybe a little strange because they heard the tattoo of a different drummer. Some of that strain continues to the present day, giving the community another facet that enriches it in a unique way.

As we go through these pages, some of the stories encapsulated in the preceding paragraphs will be dealt with in slightly more detail, perhaps enabling an understanding of what it is that makes Perry, Oklahoma, something special. The people who came here in 1893, those who followed, and the way all of them responded to the circumstances of their times...that is the story of this community and the focus of this book.

# 2

# SOME BACKGROUND

On June 30, 1893, an armed holdup on a northbound Santa Fe train clanking through what was to become North-Central Oklahoma was nipped aborning when the conductor, Al Glazier, overpowered a husky gunman, barely seventeen years old. The locomotive was lumbering across a wooden bridge on Black Bear Creek en route to Kansas.

This was the Cherokee Outlet in Oklahoma Territory some two and a half months before it was opened to non-Indian settlers. Many still regarded it as wild country, and rightfully so.

The would-be robber was supposed to have met three accomplices on the train, but unfortunately the youth was confused. He boarded one day earlier than the date he and his older confederates had agreed upon, and so he had to pull the job alone. He was very inexperienced at train robbing. Less than a month later he was declared insane and committed to an asylum.

It was the first public awareness of Manuel Herrick, whose parents believed him to be the reincarnation of Jesus Christ.

Despite this early setback, Manuel later served a term in Congress as a member of the Oklahoma delegation in the U.S. House of Representatives. There, in the company of other eccentrics, his behavior was still sufficiently bizarre to merit national attention.

Manuel Herrick was just one of the players in the comedy and the drama that accompanied the birth and development of Perry, Oklahoma, heralded as the queen city of the Cherokee Outlet. It is quite possible that no other frontier city ever had as many legendary, interesting people in its history.

❧

The first recorded white man in what is now Noble County was Lt. James B. Wilkinson, who camped on October 26, 1808, in the Bressie Flats, northeast of Perry's present location. A few years later, on November 25, 1832, a troop of military dragoons passed through this area led by Capt. Nathan Boone, youngest son of legendary frontiersman Daniel Boone. The dragoons were a newly formed unit brought together at the request of the secretary of war.

Little more is known about the experiences of those two men in this area besides the fact that they were here.

When the Cherokee Indians were unwillingly moved overland by the U.S. government to their new home early in the nineteenth century, the Trail of Tears ended in the northeast corner of Indian Territory, which ultimately became part of the state of Oklahoma. There they were granted approximately seven million acres in exchange for their lands in Arkansas and east of the Mississippi River.

The Cherokees requested an outlet to the Western game country on May 8, 1818. They were given a fifty-seven-mile wide area extending west from the border of their land to the 100th meridian as a passage to the buffalo hunting grounds. Although this strip of land officially was called the Cherokee Outlet, it became popularly known as the Cherokee Strip. The Cherokees rarely used it as a gateway to the buffalo ranges because many of the herds already had been destroyed. Better hunting awaited the tribe in their northeast territorial preserve, adjoining the Outlet on the east.

During the Civil War, some of the Cherokees sided with the Confederacy. As a result, the federal government later punished the entire tribe by reducing its land. On July 19, 1866, the Cherokees agreed to the settlement of "friendly" Indians in the Outlet west of the 96th meridian. The Osage, Kaw, Ponca, Pawnee, Nez Perce, Otoe-Missouria and Tonkawa tribes eventually were moved into the eastern part of the Strip, separating the Cherokees from their outlet. The Otoe-Missouria tribe arrived in the area from Nebraska fifteen years later, on October 23, 1881. Their new home was on the Otoe reservation in the Red Rock area, northeast of the land where Perry would rise.

After the war, Texas cattlemen drove huge herds to the rail-heads in Kansas for shipment to the meat-hungry cities in the North. Three of the cattle trails—the Chisholm, Great Western and

West Shawnee—came through the Strip. Noting the excellent grassland in the area, the so-called cattle kings formed the Cherokee Strip Live Stock Association to lease the land from the Cherokees. Cattle were fattened there for market before being moved on to be sold in Kansas.

Pressure to open the Strip to homesteaders began building. Many would-be settlers could not wait for permission and moved into the area illegally. They were called "Boomers" because they were "booming," or promoting, the release of these lands to non-Indians. As their number increased, U.S. Cavalry was sent from Kansas on December 12, 1884, to oust a camp of Boomers from an area south of the present town of Morrison.

The Santa Fe Railroad extended its branch line south from Arkansas City, Kansas, to Purcell, Oklahoma, in 1887, completing the line to Gainesville, Texas, through Noble County. Cattle drives from Texas to Missouri and Kansas were increasing. A Santa Fe way station was established one mile south of the present location of Perry. It consisted primarily of a large coal chute and a water tank. A telegraph office was added in 1888. The station originally was named Mendota but on January 27, 1889, the name was changed to Wharton. In a few years, after the land rush, a Perry vs. Wharton battle became extremely heated, with the Santa Fe Railroad spang in the middle.

President Benjamin Harrison appointed the Jerome Commission to negotiate with the Indians, and in 1889 the commission offered the Cherokees $1.25 an acre to purchase the land. The tribe refused. They were then receiving $200,000 in annual rental fees from cattlemen. A group of ranchers offered to buy the land for $3 an acre if the Cherokees could obtain government approval, but they could not.

On February 17, 1890, Harrison forced the matter by issuing a proclamation banning use of the land for grazing. He ordered cattlemen to leave the Outlet by October 1. It was seen as part of the strategy to force the Cherokees to offer the area for settlement. When the October 1 deadline passed, some occupants and livestock remained in the Outlet illegally. Troops were issued "war orders" on December 31, 1890, to proceed into the area and remove them.

Thus denied any revenue from the land, the Cherokees reluctantly agreed to sell the 6,220,854 acres on December 19, 1891, for $8,595,736—about $1.40 per acre. Added to this was more land obtained by allotments from the Pawnee and·Tonkawa tribes, bringing the total to nearly six and a half million acres.

Later an amount approximately doubling the original payment was granted to the tribe as compensation for a value increase in Western lands.

Legislation known as the Organic Act was approved by Congress in 1890, and on May 2 that year President Harrison signed the measure. It permitted the creation of Oklahoma Territory. A little more than one year later—on May 20, 1891—individual members of the Otoe-Missouria tribe began receiving allotments of land. Helen Clarke, an Indian agent, was sent here by the U.S. Interior Department for that purpose.

Outlaws knew this area well. The Dalton Gang held up the Texas Express train at Wharton on May 9, 1891, and Wells Fargo calculated losses at $1,745. The gang escaped into the Osage Reservation. The Daltons struck again on June 1, 1892, robbing a train at Red Rock. U.S. Marshal E.D. Nix and 1,000 deputies were commissioned to police the area and maintain order.

The opening of this area to settlement, long viewed as inevitable, was finally assured on January 23, 1893, when the U.S. Senate ratified an agreement for the purchase of the Cherokee Outlet from the Cherokee nation. A few weeks later, on March 3, Congress completed the enactment of legislation required for opening the Outlet to homesteaders. It was an historic day, heralding an unprecedented rush for some of the choice land in the U.S.

On August 19, 1893, President Grover Cleveland designated September 16 of that year as the date of the homesteaders' land rush into the Cherokee Outlet. With the exception of some parcels of Indian land and the Fort Supply military reservation, the entire Outlet was to be made available for settlers. It was not intended to be totally "free" land. Congress legislated fees ranging from $1.25 per acre in the western area to twice that amount in the east.

However, Dennis T. Flynn, an Oklahoma Territorial delegate to Congress, led a fight to eliminate the fees, and eventually he was successful. The so-called "Free Homes" bill thus saved Oklahoma farmers more than fifteen million dollars.

As noted, the Strip was fifty-seven miles wide, stretching south from the Kansas border to a line running north of Stillwater and Orlando, and two hundred miles long from the Texas line to the

Cherokee reserve in Northeastern Oklahoma. The Panhandle ("No Man's Land") was not included. The Strip comprised approximately one-fifth of the present state of Oklahoma. The counties were Noble, where Perry was located, plus six others: Woodward, Woods, Garfield, Grant, Kay and Pawnee. Perry and Noble County were considered the pick of the litter.

Counties at that point were designated only by a letter of the alphabet. Noble County was "P" county. The others were K, L, M, N, O and Q.

The Cherokee Outlet was just one of five land runs staged by the government to settle Oklahoma, but it was far and away the biggest and most hotly contested. The first of the runs was on April 22, 1889, in Old Oklahoma, followed by Sac and Fox, Iowa and Shawnee-Potawotomi lands, September 23, 1891; Cheyenne-Arapaho, April 19, 1892; Cherokee Outlet, September 16, 1893; and Kickapoo Country, May 1895. The Kiowa-Comanche-Apache Reservation was opened by lottery in 1901.

The three runs that preceded the Cherokee Strip opening were significant in their own way, and the other run and the lottery that followed it were quiet and almost anti-climactic by comparison.

This was the big one. This was the greatest, wildest, most frenzied land lottery ever held. The sheer drama of the event is monumental. Its equal will never be seen again.

# 3

# *T*HE RUN

A part-Indian, twenty-five-year-old cowboy named Orlando Walkling reined in the high-spirited horse under him and tried as best he could to gentle the animal, but it was wasted effort. They were mere specks bobbing in a choking cloud of dust raised by more than thirty thousand men, women and children, some mounted, some in horse-drawn buggies and wagons. All of them were waiting for the sound of a gunshot to signal the start of the greatest land rush the world had ever seen.

It was a few minutes before noon on Saturday, September 16, 1893, and the Cherokee Strip in Oklahoma Territory was about to be thrown open to homesteaders by the U.S. government. Walkling and the swarming company of humanity and animals around him were massed along the southern border of Kansas, in the Arkansas City area, looking south into the virgin territory. They formed the northern line of the land seekers.

Some fifty-seven miles to the south, along a line passing near Stillwater and Orlando and extending west to the Texas border, another wave awaited the same signal before surging northward into the Strip. Among them were James Lobsitz, thirty-nine years old, a small but wiry merchant from Edmond, preparing to ride a train into the territory; and C.T. Talliaferro, a young black not quite twenty-one and just recovering from malaria, who was going to make the run on foot.

Walkling, Lobsitz and Talliaferro were only three of the estimated 100,000 people from more than half the states in the Union who had gathered that day. They were lured there by the opportunity to claim 40,000 homesteads of 160 acres each—one-quarter of a section—or perhaps a townsite lot on the prairie. More than six million acres of the choice land of the Midwest was up for grabs.

In a few years the territory would become part of the new state of Oklahoma.

It was a time of extreme financial depression throughout the nation. Many of those poised to take part in the run hoped fervently that they would find riches in this bounteous land.

❧

The Cherokee Strip more than equals the combined acreage of the District of Columbia, Rhode Island, Delaware and Connecticut. It contains 400 square miles more than the state of New Hampshire. It is larger than Massachusetts by 1,277 square miles. It is a trifle more than one-seventh the size of Missouri and only a little less than one-eighth as large as Kansas. Its magnitude and potential stirred the dreams and aspirations of an entire nation.

In order to make the run into the Strip, prospective homesteaders were required to register at one of nine booths provided by the government. Land Office officials intended to do what they could to eliminate illegal early entry by the "Sooners." These were the over-eager settlers who crossed the border before the designated time and hid in heavily wooded areas or creek bottoms, waiting for the official signal.

Sooners had plagued each of the three previous openings, and they continued to be a problem in the Strip despite the use of registration booths and the presence of the military. Not enough soldiers were on hand to deal with the large number of Sooners, so many of them succeeded in getting claims.

Some thirteen years earlier, another group of pioneers known as "Boomers" had followed Capt. David Payne in attempting to settle the unassigned lands in the territory without government permission. They were given that name because they were "booming," or promoting, the opening of Indian lands in Oklahoma to white settlement. The nickname Sooner, which was almost an epithet to the homesteaders, became the nickname of Oklahomans in general many years later.

A strip of land one hundred feet wide, just inside the line, was opened as a zone where the settlers could camp. Confusion mounted daily in direct proportion to the pressure imposed by the approaching deadline. Rumors of all kinds swept swiftly through every assembled group, and each story became a little wilder than the one before.

The registration booths were located north of Stillwater, north of Orlando, north of Hennessey, south of Goodwin and a mile north of Higgins, Texas, at Kiowa, Kansas, south of Cameron, Kansas, near Caldwell, Kansas, and south of Arkansas City. Orlando was twelve miles south of the Perry townsite and Stillwater was almost due east of Orlando.

All the booths—five on the northern border of the Outlet and four on the southern border—were opened for registration on September 11. They were kept open from 7 a.m. to 6 p.m. each business day, with forty-five clerks from the General Land Office in charge, but they could not handle the load.

On September 14, the fourth day of registration, the Orlando booth issued certificate No. 14,892. The booth at Arkansas City wrote out certificate No. 12,370 on that same day, and on September 15 the Stillwater booth issued certificate No. 10,892. Settlers could receive either a homestead or town lot certificate, or both. They were required to return the certificates to one of the four Land Office booths in the Strip after staking a claim. The booths were located at Perry, Enid, Alva and Woodward.

More than 100,000 individuals received certificates, while only 40,000 homesteads were available. It was obvious that many contests were going to develop after the run. Many of the valid certificates were bought and sold in defiance of the law, but fraudulent certificates also were plentiful. A large number of these fake documents were bought, often knowingly.

Registration lines were still blocks long at noon on the day of the run, and at that point someone made the decision that it was not necessary to register. Many had waited as long as three days without receiving a certificate, and they were angry. Gamblers moved through the crowd to provide entertainment of sorts. A glass of water cost five cents and dry sandwiches brought in from nearby cities were sold at greatly inflated prices. Despite the grumbling, there were plenty of takers and the entrepreneurs who provided those services profited greatly.

Women especially suffered in the primitive conditions and the heat. Many of them became ill and were unable to make the run.

Cowboys and most of the other men who made their living by farming or ranching wore heavy apparel and were acutely aware of the heat. Trousers and shirts were usually made of wool and a cotton neckerchief was worn knotted around the neck to absorb perspiration, or to be pulled up around the face to cover the nose when the red dirt was blowing. When mounted on horseback, the men wore buckskin gloves and boots. Heavy leather chaps were worn by cowboys when working cattle to protect their legs from thorns and underbrush. Unlike the cowboys now known through books and movies, few of them carried a pistol strapped around their waist. Not many could afford the ammunition.

The settlers were provided with maps of the Strip showing the land to be homesteaded, but not everyone could interpret the section and township markings. Studying these maps gave them something to do while awaiting the starting gun.

&.

The settlers' camps along the line were ripe for rumors of any kind. Some of the stories that swirled from tent to tent even had a grain of truth, but many were perhaps designed to discourage the fainthearted from taking part in the run. It was known, for example, that many Sooners already were in the Strip. They were said to have been placed there by wealthy cattle barons and others to seize the townsite of Perry, which had been proclaimed the choice location in the entire Outlet. The Sooners supposedly were to hold the lots until they could be taken over by confederates who came in legally and could not be challenged.

At Arkansas City, thousands of homesteaders were prepared to make the run on trains. They were terrorized by tales that horsemen, who would arrive in the Strip before them, planned to burn the railroad bridges and prevent the trains from moving south. As if to counter this, rumors flew that horses being readied for the race were dying of poison administered in retaliation by the train passengers.

Some of the settlers at Arkansas City decided they would have a better chance at claims by entering from the south line and went by train to Orlando. There they heard that a large band of Iowa and Pawnee Indians had been employed by outlaws to make the race from Orlando and massacre homeseekers. The frightened pioneers took the next train back to Arkansas City and considered themselves lucky. The story created so much laughter there that they quit telling why they returned to Kansas.

The weary settlers heard that trains would not be permitted to make the run, or that trains would be limited to a speed of five miles per hour. Another story said only wagons drawn by a team of white horses and driven by red-headed girls could participate.

Banks at Guthrie, the territorial capital, remained closed on opening day because of a rumor that the notorious Dalton Gang of outlaws intended to rob them while attention was focused on the run. Forty special policemen were on duty to guard against this possibility.

ૐ

On the morning of September 16, 1893, an end to all the waiting and frustration seemed to be at hand. The homesteaders were sweltering on a day when the heat and drought felt more like mid-August. Thermometers throughout the Strip and in Southern Kansas registered up to 109 degrees. The men were caked with dust and sweat, weary from waiting in endless lines, and short-tempered with the rest of the world. Still, a sense of jubilant anticipation subordinated all of these problems, and their minds struggled to grasp the epic panorama spreading around them. Some had a sense of the historic moment, but most were doing their best to focus on the job at hand—making a dash for the new land.

As the climactic hour approached, Army officers stationed their soldiers along the line at six hundred-yard intervals. They were ordered to have carbines at the ready to give the starting signal precisely at high noon, when a bugle would be blown.

Skittish horses, some of them among the best racing animals in the country, knew they were in for an adventure and were as highly charged as their riders. Mingled with them were hardened little cow ponies—some of these proved better suited for the run than the racing stock—along with small buggies, large, heavily loaded wagons, bicyclists and a surprisingly large number of dismounted men, all of them ready to break from the pack at the signal. It was impossible to maintain an orderly line despite the most determined efforts.

Passenger trains crammed with homesteaders also stood by on the Santa Fe and Rock Island tracks, and the heat from their

locomotives may have added a few degrees to the ambient tempera-
ture. It was the first time trains had been used in an Oklahoma land
run, and the plush, green cushioned seats were understandably
greatly in demand. When the supply of seats was exhausted, tickets
were sold for men and women who were willing to ride atop the
coaches, between them, and even on the rods underneath. These
were desperate people longing for a chance to carve out a better
life on the prairie. They could afford to ride into the Strip on a
commercial conveyance.

Trains were limited to a speed of fifteen miles per hour to avoid
an unfair advantage. The morning of the run ten trains with ten box
cars each were at Arkansas City; thirty-nine cars with a large Mallet
engine were at Hennessey; and forty-two cars with three engines
were at Orlando.

An estimated 5,000 made the run aboard trains entering from
the north and south lines. Just behind the passenger trains were
freight trains piled high with household goods, provisions and
lumber.

❧

Orlando Walkling nudged his horse into position in the northern line, James Lobsitz boarded the train at Orlando and C.T.
Talliaferro, nearby, stretched his legs to prepare for the run. They
were unknown to one another, mere faces in the crowd, as the
midday sun neared its zenith. The three of them and some 40,000
others would spend the night in or near the townsite of Perry, and
their lives would be entwined forever after.

A tense silence began spreading as high noon approached. Only
a horse's nervous whinny or the braying of a mule was audible. Men
gazed straight ahead, waiting for the crack of a carbine to signal
the start of the run. But at Arkansas City, eleven minutes before
noon, a pistol shot sent 5,000 horses charging into the Strip. At
Hennessey, on the southern line, someone fired a gun five minutes
early and the surrounding crowd surged forward unrestrained.

Troops at both locations attempted to stop them, but there was
no turning back. Realizing the futility of the situation, all were
permitted to begin the run.

Suddenly, the almost treeless plains were alive with shouting
men, thundering wagons, cracking whips, shrieking locomotive

whistles, barking dogs and plunging animals, a tidal wave of humanity churning inside a cloud of dust, sweeping toward Perry and the adjoining countryside. Good men and thieves, some with property and wealth elsewhere, others with only the coarse clothing on their back, merchants, adventurers...a "motley crew," one newspaper called them, but all flailing away at the same goal —homesteads in the Cherokee Strip.

In two hours the prairie was quiet again, but teeming with people spilling over the landscape. The land had been claimed and non-Indian settlers were legally camped where farms, towns, schools, churches and the other symbols of frontier life would soon appear.

The 160-acre tracts and the townsite lots were to belong to the persons who first laid claim to them. This was done by driving a stake into the ground and then filing an official notice of the claim at one of the four Land Offices. It was not a simple task at all and many spirits were broken by the difficulties of staking and holding a claim in the Outlet.

Observers estimated that from 30,000 to 50,000 came into the territory from Arkansas City, 7,000 from Stillwater, 25,000 from Orlando and 50,000 from other points along the boundary. By fifteen minutes past noon, more than 2,000 Sooners were staking off lots in Perry. Tents were quickly put up, and it took only a short time to start the operation of blacksmith shops, law offices, saloons, restaurants, dance halls and other businesses. H.L. Boyes and L.D. Treeman established the city's first bank, the Farmers & Merchants, on opening day. Perry was bustling from the beginning.

❧

By nightfall Perry appeared to be strung out over all the face of the earth. It was the favored destination for those who came in on the Santa Fe Railroad from the south. Medford and Pond Creek were said to be the chief stopping places for the hundreds who made the race from Kansas on the Rock Island line. An Arkansas City newspaper stated that 25,000 men and women, "with a goodly number of boys and girls," started the race toward Perry from Orlando, the closest point of entry. Hundreds more came from other directions.

Most estimates place the number of people in Perry that first night at 40,000. The actual count will never be known, but there is unanimous agreement that the number, whatever it may have been, was far too many for the available lots. Half a dozen claimants were camped on virtually each one. All of this seems to reinforce the pre-run predictions that the Perry area, for whatever reasons, was the choice location for nearly half the 100,000 Cherokee Strip homesteaders.

Flaming torches and camp fires provided light after sundown. Tents and crude shelters were hastily erected, and the location of several temporary saloons soon became known to all.

When daylight arrived, chaos reigned. Boundaries were obscured or disputed. It was a city of hole-in-the-ground dugouts, tents, crude shacks and canvas covers strewn about as if dumped there. No one paid attention to streets and alleys, park sites or government reserves. Such things were indicated on townsite maps but other markers were simply obliterated by the swarm of people.

Government Acre, actually a five-acre tract in the center of Perry's business district reserved for the Post Office and court-house, was occupied by squatters on opening day. Hundreds of businessmen located on the four sides, facing the street. They had been misled by an anonymous mercenary who spread the word that the "Acre" was open for settlement rather than block "B," just south of it. Soldiers kept block "B" clear of lot claimants until certain favored ones were said to have been located. Then the balance was turned over for public settlement and an order was posted showing the Government Acre was reserved.

The dismayed squatters were ordered off the Acre by a federal agency in Washington, and early in October, nearly a month after the opening, they were forced to vacate at the point of bayonets. Despite an ensuing court battle, the squatters lost.

On October 24, after the settlers were cleared out, the Land Office was moved from Hell's Half Acre to Government Acre. The location was just north of the present Perry Carnegie Library. A semblance of order began in Hell's Half Acre when the Land Office building was moved away from there.

Government Acre today is Perry's attractive courthouse park, but for the first year after the settlers were removed it was a dusty, windswept expanse. Old buffalo wallows on the east side of the

Acre had to be filled in before the first courthouse, a wooden building, could be erected. Only the Land Office on the west side and a small frame Post Office building at the southwest corner occupied the area at first. The Post Office, which had been established on August 25 prior to the run, was later moved to the northwest corner. For a time the area was known as Central Park.

Each county seat town in the Strip was laid out around a central square at the direction of the secretary of the interior, Hoke Smith. That was the custom in most Southern towns of the U.S. Many regard the style as a statement of culture and gentility, providing a green area in the heart of a business district and a comfortable gathering place for the community. The Central Park square in Perry was rough and dusty at the beginning, but it has been carefully maintained through the years. First-time visitors to the city usually comment on its lush beauty.

On Sunday, the day after the run, worshipers were called together by Rev. Simon P. Meyers, a Presbyterian missionary who had made the run from the Orlando line. He delivered the first sermon in Perry in J.W. Young's unfinished hardware building on the north side of the square. Beer kegs, emptied by the record consumption of the preceding day, and boards from building material at the site were used to seat the congregation. Services were held there for two Sundays, but for the next few weeks the group met in a grocery store on the west side of the square.

They soon raised funds for a tent which was raised at Eighth and E Streets, the present site of the Presbyterian Church. When cold weather arrived, the congregation moved to the Woodward building on the north side of the Merchants Hotel, on Seventh Street between D and E Streets, until a frame building could be erected to replace the tent. The Rev. Meyers, dean of the ministry in Noble County, had staked his claim on a good quarter section three miles southwest of Perry.

The original townsite of Perry was bounded by F Street and South Boundary on the north and south, and by East Boundary and Ninth Streets on the east and west. It was comprised of 320 acres, the maximum allowed for any town in the Strip, with 635 residential lots measuring fifty x 162 1/2 feet, 460 business lots with twenty-five-foot fronts, plus city parks and school reserves.

With an estimated 40,000 people in Perry at three o'clock on the afternoon of the opening, it was obvious that the original townsite was too small, limited to 320 acres as it was by government decree. The settlers were spread out over the original townsite. The solution was to create four new suburban towns adjoining the original townsite of Perry, each with 160 acres and separate governments. The additions, or sub-divisions, were named North Perry, West Perry, South Perry and Old Wharton. This provided 2,145 additional residential lots.

Each of the four new communities decided to abandon their original plans of separate identities and elected to join forces with Perry. All were absorbed in the year following the opening by extension of the original town's corporate limits.

Such growth was not without severe trauma. Henry Lynn had settled on the quarter section of land lying just north of the city of Perry and succeeded in filing on the claim the afternoon of the run. A number of men, perhaps several hundred, also settled on the same land and claimed it as a part of the town of Perry.

By Monday noon following the opening, several hundred people were settled on Lynn's quarter section. It appeared there were at least 2,000 inhabitants of the suburban town of "North Perry." These townsite settlers made application to Secretary of the Interior Smith, asking the township trustees to take charge of the town and the right to settle it as a town.

In October, the territorial governor, W.C. Renfrow, recognized that more than 2,500 people were occupying and claiming town lots, and so declared Perry to be a city of the first class.

According to a story in *the Daily Oklahoman* on January 13, 1894, concerning the North Perry controversy, the fight between the homesteader, Mr. Lynn, and the townsite settlers was heated and both sides engaged able counsel to represent them.

The case was decided in Mr. Lynn's favor on January 6, 1894, by Register J.E. Malone of the Perry Land Office. However, the townsite people claimed they had no notice from officials of the Land Office regarding the trial, and they were angry. Protest meetings were held during which "red hot resolutions" were passed denouncing Mr. Lynn and Register Malone in severe terms.

"North Perry has several hundred good residents," *the Oklahoman* reporter wrote, "and hundreds of the best people in town reside there. Henry Lynn, however, is the happiest man in Oklahoma. He has gone to Washington to have the papers approved, and will come back the proud owner of a beautiful town all his own."

The final outcome of that story is provided by Judge E.W. Jones in the February 8, 1912, edition of his *Perry Republican*. According to that account, Mr. Linn (as Judge Jones spelled it) was a speculative genius, "a genuine Oklahoma rustler, and had been through the mill in the land openings for years prior to that of the Strip."

"The case was fought to the departments at Washington with the result of the settlers winning after three or four years of expensive litigation....Had he (Lynn) won this case, it would have made him a handsome fortune as North Perry has since grown to be the fashionable portion of the city.

"After losing his contest, with his nerve his solitary asset, Linn drifted on farther west and when last heard of was exploiting a gold dredging scheme in the rivers of Idaho," the newspaper reported.

Another claimant for that quarter-section was a Miss Burke, but her part in the battle attracted little attention as she never developed any strength in the litigation.

Northeast Perry was homesteaded by "Billy" McCoy, one of the clerks in the local Land Office. His contest was short-lived, however, and the claimants prevailed in a matter of months. Mr. McCoy was from Milwaukee and after the boom days of the town subsided he went back there to take his place on the police force, which he had resigned to come to Perry.

John Malone, brother of the register of the Land Office, was the contestant in Northwest Perry. The settlers defeated him in this fight, and he suffered a nervous breakdown. He was declared insane and committed to an asylum in Jacksonville, Illinois, where Oklahoma mental patients were treated. Mr. Malone died there.

The contest over West Perry was a battle royal, again according to Judge Jones' *Perry Republican*. The newspaper described it like this:

"Henry Bowie, one of the real characters of the early days, filed his entry on the quarter-section and against him were a thousand lot claimants. Bowie had come here from Texas. He was a direct descendant from the illustrious defender of the Alamo. The contest for West Perry continued for several years but Bowie lost and like Henry Linn, down and out, wended his way back to his old home in Texas."

Continuing with his personal recollection of the early days, Judge Jones wrote:

"South Perry was the battlefield where various and sundry characters made their mark in early-day history. Chas. E. (Doc) Reed, a veterinarian and practical horseman; Chas. (Buffalo) Jones, pioneer and plainsman, later game warden of the Yellowstone Park, a friend of President Teddy Roosevelt and breeder of the catalo, a cross of the domestic cow and the buffalo; John McClintic, now in business in Oklahoma City; 'Jack' Combs, soldier of fortune, who died a few years ago in Kiowa County; all were contestants for the homestead right while against them were arrayed hundreds of settlers seeking town lot titles.

"This was the last of the townsite additions to be adjudicated and resulted in Doc Reed winning against all claimants, the first time in the history of land openings of a homesteader winning against the settlers. Reed was a reckless fellow, of not too pleasant disposition when sober, which was with him periodically, and he had but few friends at the finish of his local career, realizing comparatively nothing after having his claim to the land recognized. The record of the 'run' made by himself and 'Buffalo' Jones as recited in the records of the Land Office would make several chapters of the spectacular history of Perry. Their relays, change of horses and break neck speed, demonical riding and driving coming from Orlando over the rough country make a story of dime novel interest."

Judge Jones left a wealth of information about the early days of Perry in the columns of his newspaper and in a reflective collection of essays published in 1931, entitled "Early Day History of Perry, Oklahoma."

Although few were aware of it, the government townsite for Perry had not been completely surveyed. It was a mile long from east to west and half a mile wide.

The Land Office, where claimants were to register their property, was a half block east of the east side of the square. Land attorneys and agents descended on the site to assist the homesteaders and negotiate for fees. Tents serving as offices were crammed tightly together and movement around them was difficult. It was estimated that 500 lawyers were in Perry the first few weeks. Some were described as "sharks, jacklegs, pettifoggers and low down police court advocates who disgrace the profession."

Many of them were reputable attorneys, but the others were a disturbing element until most of them were invited to leave.

Homesteaders quickly learned that making the run was only the start of their travail. After driving their stake in the quarter-section or townsite lot they wanted, the next step was to file a claim at the Land Office. To do that meant leaving the property unattended, available to claim jumpers, so someone had to be on guard at the site. Many disputes arose and fierce battles were fought before either party could reach the Land Office. Shots were fired in the absence of enough troops or marshals to patrol the entire area.

Shelter of some sort had to be provided for the family, if only a tent or a dugout.

Long lines at the Land Office discouraged many of the homesteaders, and some gave up after waiting days in the heat and dust. Settlers were required to pay a ten-dollar fee to register. They also had to live on the land for five years before receiving title to it. Some cynics said that the government was betting 160 acres of land against ten dollars that one could not live on it for five years. Quite often the government won.

During the first few days after the opening, crowds estimated at from 10,000 to 12,000 milled around the Land Office building. The homesteaders came up with their own plan of numbering to facilitate the process. The line, starting with the man who had the next turn to file, was divided into ten-man groups, or companies. One in each company was designated a captain, and they calculated when their turn to file would come up. They were then free to go home and await that special day. When newcomers arrived, they were also grouped and numbered.

The Land Office processed an estimated 125 filings each day. The Perry land district had 6,200 claims and at least 3,000 contests. The court was able to dispose of approximately 900 a year.

Not all the land was taken on the first day of the run, nor even for a few years afterward. A few claims were abandoned and some were sold for bargain prices by disillusioned homesteaders.

The area surrounding the Land Office became host to some of the worst elements of the new city and was quickly dubbed "Hell's Half Acre." Some 110 saloons and gambling houses were in operation in a matter of days.

One visiting reporter described it thus:

"Probably on account of its youth, and consequent vitality, this particular Half Acre, during the short weeks that it existed in all its pristine beauty and unchecked exuberance, discounted anything in history either sacred or profane. Here assembled the choicest desperados of the West, its most dissolute women, its most disreputable characters, and the scum of half a dozen states. It deserved its name."

After a month, the Land Office was moved to the courthouse square, where squatters were being forced to clear out by the government. With the loss of the Land Office from Hell's Half Acre, the lawyers also relocated and business rapidly dwindled for the saloons and dance halls that had flourished there.

Among the first settlers to reach the townsite of Perry was Jack Tearney, formerly of Guthrie, who arrived from Orlando in what was believed to be record time—thirty-one minutes. He had the Blue Bell Saloon operating by four p.m. on September 16. Beer sold for one dollar a bottle due to the scarcity of water, and 38,000 glassfuls were sold that first day. The price was cut to fifty cents per bottle the next day and water was five cents a glass or five dollars a barrel. The water quality was not good, and the lack of it nearly proved a disaster.

The Buck Horn Saloon was established in a tent near the Land Office within an hour of the opening. It earned a fortune for its owners in short order. The tent gave way to a wooden building and the name was changed to Honk a Tonk Saloon with Joe and Ted Hill as managers. It combined a dance hall and gambling house.

Judge Jones, a pioneer Perry newspaperman as well as a county judge, wrote a history of that period in 1931 with these comments:

"The nearest point to enter from legally was from the south side at Orlando and a few miles east. The first persons arriving from this line, about twelve miles, were surprised to find the townsite covered with settlers. Evidently the overly anxious, or overly smart, lot seekers, who had started before noon or who had lain in the bed of Cow Creek near the new city until noon and then within fifteen or twenty minutes had their lots staked for ownership.

"It was a seething mass of humanity from a half mile south of the Government Acre, now the courthouse park, the center of the city, to more than a half mile north and west."

On that first day after the run, and for months to follow, the fare at mealtime was plain for most folks. A few families brought in chickens, and cows were quickly provided for milk and meat. Most housewives had flour and other cooking necessities, but the menu was monotonous at best. The new homesteaders ate a lot of corn bread and gravy, sometimes adding sorghum molasses. Another staple was turnips.

Restaurant menus featured ham and eggs with crackers and coffee as a standard meal for the first few days. They also had turnips, corn bread and gravy. Dining out, for those who could afford it, was not that much of a treat. Most of the restaurant patrons were men whose wives had not yet joined them in the frontier community.

Tales of tragic, comic, even bizarre happenings were related by the homesteaders. Jacob Sorenson of Michigan became so depressed over the hopelessness of holding his lot against claim jumpers that he cut his throat from ear to ear, just two days after the run. His sense of futility was shared by many to a lesser degree as they fought to hang on to what they believed was legally theirs.

Amid the thousands of tents, many wooden store buildings and homes quickly began appearing. Activity was intense all over the new area. As material was hauled to construction sites from the railroad supply dumps, homesteaders formed long lines at the Land Office to file their claims.

Pervading everything was the heat and dust. The tramp of thousands of pairs of human feet and uncounted horses' hooves had whipped up an almost unbearable, suffocating haze of red dust and prairie sand. Everything seemed to be covered. Men went to the creek to wash their clothes and hang them out to dry while friends guarded their lots.

It was said that in the Government Acre area the dust was so bad that visibility was limited to twenty feet for three weeks after the run.

જ઼

Perry was located on the main line of the Santa Fe Railroad, but it was not a stopping point for passenger or freight trains for nearly a year after the opening. Instead, the trains stopped at Wharton, the old cattle shipping station, one mile south of town.

The townsite of Perry was platted by the government before the run and designated as the location of the Land Office as well as the county seat of "P" (later Noble) County. Cattle barons had leased the land in this area prior to the opening for grazing herds on the way to Northern markets. Wharton was one of the important shipping stations.

Certain prominent Indians had selected allotments around the shipping stations in the Strip, anticipating that they would be principal towns, according to the late Henry S. Johnston, an early-day Perry attorney who later became governor of Oklahoma. Arnett, four miles north of Perry, also was a Santa Fe Railroad switch, and the Cherokees had taken allotments around it.

Townsite locators refused to select either Wharton or Arnett and made a new location at Perry.

"It seemed to disturb the railroad that the new metropolis was not to be located on, or even adjacent to, one of these allotments," Johnston said. "As a result, trains did not stop at the new town of Perry until the spring of 1894, and then only when compelled to by federal statute. A plain wooden depot was placed on the townsite."

Townsites in which the railroad was interested had free water, supplied by trains with tank cars. Government townsites of Perry, Enid and Pond Creek were boycotted by the railroads and were forced to depend on shallow wells and stale streams as a source of drinking water.

Perry's difficulties with the railroad persisted into the following year. On January 13, 1894, *the Daily Oklahoman* wrote:

"Wharton is no more. It is now Perry. Since the opening the railroad people knew no Perry, but through the influence of the railroad committee of Perry's board of trade the station of Wharton has been changed to Perry by officials of the Santa Fe Railroad. The railroad people will not say whether they will move the depot to the town proper or not. As it now stands the station is 1,200 yards from Perry. And it looks as if it will remain that distance for a while at least. The railroad people are erecting a new freight depot, and have added many hundred yards of tracks at the old station, all of which does not indicate that Perry will have a depot in town."

During the standoff between the railroad and Perry, homesteaders were going thirsty. Most of them could not afford to pay five cents a glass for water, so shallow wells were dug in town. One of them was eliminated when two sacks of salt were poured into it during the night in order to increase the sale of water by the cup.

This prompted a rumor that water around Perry was salty and several settlers moved on. The number of those remaining was still larger than the town's facilities could support.

Wrote a *Wichita Eagle* reporter:

"Rainmaker Jewell, at Pond Creek, is trying his best to coax rain from the sky, and his efforts are supplemented by prayers of the settlers. So far, all efforts have been unsuccessful. The exodus of homeseekers continues. A thousand pass through here on their way north, and an equally large number left the Strip via Caldwell (Kansas)."

Five days after the opening, a general rain soaked the Cherokee Strip. At least for a time, the dust settled and the desperate need for drinking water was eased. More wells were being dug, some to a depth of one hundred feet to test the potential supply. Good water eventually was found at thirty feet, enough of it to check the alarming flight of settlers leaving the Strip.

ૐ

Perry seemed to be the darling of the press corps which covered the opening. Most of the major newspapers from throughout this section of the country dispatched correspondents to the territory. The stories they sent back to their editors were filled with glowing adjectives describing the wonderful things they saw and heard. They did not pretend to hide their enthusiasm for Perry.

Some examples:

"Here is the town of towns in the recently opened Cherokee Strip, or anywhere else in the Western country for that matter. The original Oklahoma cities, which were regarded as marvels in nineteenth century progress, were simply not in it with Perry. At the age of two months she is bigger, richer, she is livelier and wider awake, she has more vim and go in her to the square inch than either Guthrie or Oklahoma City had to the square foot when they were six months old—possibly more than both of them combined." (*Kansas City Times*.)

"Perry is truly a wonder for a baby two weeks old. As one enters, it bears a striking resemblace to Wellington the day after the cyclone. Everything is topsy turvy looking from the train, and one does not begin to notice any sort of order until he drives leisurely into the city where he then observes wide and straight streets. The building of Perry is like the building of Babel so far as confusion of tongues and everything else is concerned. The Sabbath did not deter them from building, and the noise of hammers could be heard in every direction. The rapidity with which they put up buildings there is truly phenomenal.

"Two weeks ago there was but one frame building in Perry, the Land Office. Now about two-thirds of the town consists of frame buildings, and it is estimated that in two weeks every tent will be folded up and laid away for the next opening." (*Wichita Eagle.*)

"It is a good town, this town of Perry. Everybody says so. All the original Oklahoma spirit is here, but it has increased in sparkle and activity with age. Any of the three bankers will tell you there is more wealth represented here than in any city of the same age ever founded in the West. It is a good place to invest, too. Rough one-story buildings on twenty-five-foot lots about the square, just big enough for an office, rent for ten dollars a month. Barrels of money have been made in real estate. Mayor Brogan pointed out a corner he bought for twenty-five dollars, sold in two or three days for $500, and which now would bring $1,500 if it were put on the market. Lots in the business district range from $600 to $2,000 and residences from $100 to $1,000." (Source unknown.)

"One cannot get away from the racket of carpenters anywhere in residence or business sections. And it is little wonder when it is known that the town has twenty-eight big lumber yards, and all seem to be doing a rushing business. Then just think of sixty-two grocery stores in a town two months old." (*Wichita Eagle.*)

"When Cow Creek is not dry it meanders along the south borders of the city in a northeasterly direction. South of it are picturesque bluffs. North of it is Perry and additions, the ground sloping down gradually, but giving excellent drainage. Grading of streets will be an easy matter here. North and west are very sightly places, the view commanding miles of country north, east and west. Drive out from the heart of Perry a mile in any direction and homes are in process of erection. The fact of the matter is, there is money in Perry. It is seen not only in her business section, but her residence section." (*Kansas Observer.*)

"While Perry's tough section is of a red-hot, rip roaring character, it is only a small part of the town. There is a greater and better section where pluck, push, enterprise, energy and capital have combined to set the city rolling at almost startling velocity. Affairs have quieted a good deal since the first two weeks, but she is still forging ahead. At morning stands a vacant lot. At night the framework of a house or store has been put there. Another day it is enclosed, and another the stock is being moved in, even with the latherer and plasterers still at work. It is whoop and holler everywhere. And if Perry keeps this up much longer she will have every other Oklahoma city by both the hair and the heels." (Source unknown.)

❧

Other townsites were established in Noble County by early settlers, and some even prior to the run. More than thirty such communities have had U.S. Post Offices in this county through the years, but only Perry, Morrison, Billings, Red Rock and Marland still exist. Even the exact location of some of the others is unknown to today's generation.

Very soon after the run, a man named Dick White, who had a claim just north of Red Rock Creek, about four miles south and one east of the present Billings townsite, received permission to establish a Post Office on his land. A small townsite was laid out and named Whiterock.

The community became so rich in the production of livestock, wheat and other farm products that the Rock Island Railroad running through Enid built a spur to haul them to market. Later the Santa Fe projected a line from Wellington, Kansas, through Blackwell in a bid to capture part of the business. In time, the railroads compromised, with Santa Fe retaining the northern portion of the territory.

A man named Billings saw the importance of a townsite on the right of way, so one was laid out and invitations for a "grand opening" were issued. A barbecue was provided, and town lots were sold to hundreds of prospects who attended the celebration.

Red Rock's beginning was as a station established by the Santa Fe with stock yards to accommodate the livestock industry of ranchers and cattlemen in Red Rock Valley. It was later surveyed into a townsite and grew to be an important trading point for that section, which was a range center where thousands of cattle were shipped to market in the autumn after pasturing on ranges in the spring and summer.

The largest shippers were the Pryor, Witherspoon and 101 Ranches. The latter, established by George Miller and his sons, Joe, George Jr. and Zack, expanded until it commanded international recognition. This activity included the removal and settlement on their respective allotments of the Otoe-Missouria tribe on the southern half and the Poncas on the northern half of the reservations established by the government.

From the starting line four miles north of Stillwater on September 16, 1893, about 7,000 homeseekers surged northward into the Strip. Many secured land in and about Morrison. Some had been living at Boomer Camp near the line as a well-established community for several years in preparation for the opening.

The Boomers even had their own cheese factory. Some of the pioneers in that vicinity included Uncle Jack Testerman and family, C.N. Hetherington (called "Whispering Charlie"), Will McCurry, Charles Prather, Jack Crane, J.T. Perryman, J.H. Morrison (who gave forty-five acres of his claim for a townsite, and for whom the town is named), C.W. Swearingen and Sam Cunningham.

Following are all Noble County towns that have been officially recognized. Dates shown refer to establishing and closing of Post Offices. Changes in town names also are indicated:

Antrim 1898-1904
Arnold 1893-1894/Whiterock 1894 to 1915
Autry 1893-1894/Morrison 1894 to present
Billings 1894 to present
Black Bear 1894
Bliss 1898-1922/Marland 1922 to present
Bowdenton 1894-1897
Bressie 1904 to 1915
Burton 1894-1900
Chiquita 1895-1898
Compton 1894-1903
Day 1899-1905
Harperville 1894-1900
Lela 1895-1954
McKinney 1893-1897/Ceres 1897-1915
Magnolia 1890-1892/Red Rock 1892 to present
Mateer 1899-1903/Lucien 1903 to present

Pedee 1894-1904
Perry 1893 to present
Polo 1894-1904
Redrock 1881-1892/Otoe 1892-1917
Richburg 1893-1904
Sumner 1894-1957
Three Sands 1923-1957
Topeka 1894-1895

≥≥

The tremendous reception accorded Perry gave it an advantage over the other county towns that came and went through the years. The Santa Fe Railroad's preference for Wharton might have made it a contender for the courthouse, but Perry eventually won out even though it meant doing without a depot and direct telegraph facilities for a time.

Perry was named in honor of J.A. Perry, one of the members of the Townsite Commission appointed by the U.S. government. It was this commission which moved the location of Perry one mile north of Wharton and thus placed a portion of the townsite in Cow Creek.

Noble County was named in honor of John M. Noble of St. Louis, secretary of the Department of the Interior under President Harrison. The new name was chosen on November 6, 1894, when the first county election was held, and replaced the earlier letter designation "P". It was reported at the time that many of the settlers came here from Noble County, Ohio, and that helped influence their selection.

≥≥

Orlando Walkling's pony carried him quickly from the northern line to a spot south of Honeywell, Kansas, on the day of the run. There he decided to stake his claim, and some of the brutal reality of the opening became all too clear to him.

"Dead men and dead horses was all over the place when I put down my claim on the Cherokee Strip," he later told friends. "It didn't matter who got there first. The biggest bully or the fastest gun got the claim. There was one bully guy named Nelson. He killed six men to get a claim. And there was women hurt, too."

Walkling left his claim to file on it at the Perry Land Office. When he arrived in town he found a big cloud of dust, a lot of tents and covered wagons, and thousands of people ahead of him. Giving up on winning a homestead, he traded a horse to a man for a place seven miles east of Perry and eventually developed a large fruit and dairy farm along with a herd of goats. Later he operated a meat market in Perry.

C.T. Talliaferro reached the area north of Perry on foot the afternoon of the run, but his dream of claiming a 160-acre homestead also was not to come true. He wound up in one corner of a quarter-section while another man was in the opposite corner. Mr. Talliaferro gave up the contest and was rewarded by the other man for doing so.

He came to the Perry townsite and, with a fifty-cent loan to buy his start-up inventory, went into business as a peanut vendor. He became one of the town's most admired citizens and was a leader of the black community for many years.

James A. Lobsitz left the Santa Fe train at the Perry townsite on the day of the opening. He was a small Jewish man, a merchant, not a cowman or a farmer. He was one of those innocent victims of a costly hoax, those who were told that the courthouse park acreage was open to settlers looking for business lots. A month later they were driven off by troops using fixed bayonets.

Within a few weeks, however, Mr. Lobsitz had established the Famous Department Store with a partner, Hugh McCredie. The business was to become the largest family-owned retail firm in the new city, and Mr. Lobsitz played a major role in the development of this area.

None of these three men won a piece of land in the Cherokee Strip run, but in oddly different ways they achieved more "success" than they could have imagined. There were at least 100,000 stories in the Cherokee Outlet that day. These are just three of them.

# 4

# ORLANDO WALKLING

Orlando Walkling could have been forgiven for asking that this be carved on his tombstone: "See. I told you it was good for you."

He was talking about goat's milk and it would have been hard to argue with his testimony on the subject. He died at the age of 106 after a lifetime of proclaiming its virtues. For many of those 106 years he personally drank two quarts of it each day. He may have been the last surviving homesteader of the September 16, 1893, Cherokee Strip run. Something certainly deserves credit for his long and vigorous life.

His spare frame was always trim. Looking at him, you could sense a reservoir of energy like a taut, coiled spring, and indeed he was physically active and mentally alert almost to the very end. His face was deeply etched by years of facing the prairie sun and wind, and his shoulders drooped from a load of toil like that which claimed so many of his frontier friends. Although he outlived them all, in many ways he typified the spirit and character of everyone who settled the Strip.

Walkling peered at the world through eyes shaded by a broad brimmed Western hat and he strode among us in stockmen's boots and bib overalls. He was happiest when doing something with his hands, but next to that he loved to tell about the 1893 adventure that brought him to Perry, and the hard years that followed. Fortunately he took the time to jot down many of his colorful recollections.

Walkling lived in Perry or this immediate area from the time of the run until March 1942, when he and his wife moved to Modesto, California. There he remained until his death on February 10, 1974. He always regarded Perry as home, however, and carried on an extensive correspondence with friends here. He came back to Oklahoma only once or twice. The last trip was in September 1968, the year of his one hundredth birthday, and he celebrated it by walking—unassisted—around the Perry square as honorary marshal of the Cherokee Strip celebration parade. He was a proud and happy man.

John Divine, who was manager of the Chamber of Commerce at the time, was astonished at Walkling's physical condition.

"We had made arrangements for an open-top car to drive Mr. Walkling around the square," Divine said. "When Orlando found that out, he would have none of it. He insisted on walking the entire distance, and he set a fast pace for everyone behind him."

ॐ

The letters, essays and dialogues he bequeathed to subsequent generations comprise one of the most interesting volumes of information available about the early days in Perry and Noble County. Fantasizing with a composite of those sources, here are some of the things he might like us to know today. Listen, and the voice of Orlando Walkling still speaks to us:

"I was born January 2, 1868, as near as I know, at a Shawnee camp in Kansas. My mother was a Shawnee Indian and my father was an Englishman, name of Orlando Walkling. My real name is Skapocaset. That's Shawnee for 'To Be a Big Chief.' I kept that name until the age of sixteen, when I took my father's name. I never saw him to remember him, but I do know there was a fuss when his mother and brother came from England and found him married to an Indian. They thought it was awful and treated my mother terrible. She taught me to tan hides, make rope and do leathercraft.

"The Cherokee Strip run on September 16, 1893, was the greatest adventure of my life. It also was the biggest horse race of all time. I rode a fast pony from the north line (Kansas) and staked a claim just south of Honeywell, Kansas. When I came to the land office in Perry to file on it, I found a big cloud of dust, a lot of tents and covered wagons and many thousands of people ahead of me.

"The Land Office and Post Office were little temporary buildings. People were fighting over the lots and the few accommodations. My turn to file wouldn't come for months and I had no money. I found that my place south of Honeywell was filed on long before my turn came, so I traded a horse to an old man for a place seven miles east of Perry. I got married three years later and my wife, Lavinia, and I developed the land into a real wonderful fruit and dairy farm.

"There were lots of badmen around here in the early days. Some of the lawmen they sent to get them weren't much better. Bill Doolin was a famous outlaw, and he had a gang of men. There was a $5,000 reward on Doolin's head. One day I was sitting with a man outside a store near Stillwater. I didn't know he was Doolin at the time, but he was my friend. He got me a job when I needed it bad.

"A buckboard pulled up and these two marshals got out and went into the store. They said they was hunting Bill Doolin. Then Doolin got up and said to the marshals: 'You fellas treat me to some tobacco and I'll help you hunt.' Sure enough, they gave him some. Then they all got in the wagon and drove off. When they were gone, the store owner and his daughter had a big laugh.

"When I asked why, the store owner said: 'Shucks, that was Doolin the marshals gave the tobacco to.'"

"Of course, there was no depot or even side tracks on the Santa Fe Railroad line in Perry. They had built the depot and water tank south of town, at Wharton, thinking that's where the town would be. All kinds of merchandise was arriving by rail each day, and they just had to pile it up on the right of way for miles in both directions until somebody came to haul it off. Some of those piles were as high as telegraph wires. A lot of it was saloon stocks and fixtures. We had about 110 saloons in Perry right after the run. They were popular places. I'm proud to tell you that I never tasted whiskey in my life. Never drank coffee or smoked a cigaret, either.

"Land attorneys started up in the back of a wagon. Doctors' offices, cafes and lumber yards opened up in small tents. There was more traffic of people going back and forth to the railroad freight piles than on the main street of a big city. I had a team and got several jobs hauling freight from old Wharton.

"I sold my place in line at the Post Office for ten dollars once, and several other times for five dollars. The line would wrap around the square twice. Men who had money and were not able to stand in line would pay me to step out of line and give them my place. There was only one man in the little house. He would hand the mail out through a small window.

"As the town got organized I got a job on the street. The first street commissioner's name was 'Buck.' I think I plowed the first furrows to mark off Sixth Street. Everything north of D Street was a prairie dog town.

"Our first house on that 160 acres east of town was a log cabin. I planted peach trees and began acquiring more land. In time I had about a thousand acres out there, shipping fifty-five carloads of peaches and canning 85,000 barrels. It was one of the first canning factories in the West. The cans were soldered by hand and my wife and I boarded most of the workers.

"No telling how many peaches, plums, grapes, berries, apples and pears we raised and sold locally and at Stillwater, Red Rock and Billings. We had one good crop of fifteen acres of tomatoes. Canned all of them, then two or three years of drought and late freeze commenced to kill them.

"One day when I was just standing on a railroad platform in Perry, a Salvation Army woman handed me a bundle. There were twins wrapped up in there, a boy and a girl, and she just left me with them. My wife and I adopted them and we also reared six foster children until they finished their schooling. After thirty years working that ranch, we moved into Perry.

"I started a market and a little later bought the Delma Hotel. This was a two-story frame building on the alley behind Joe's Smoke House. My market was on the ground floor and the hotel was upstairs. We still raised fruit and vegetables east of town, and I had a herd of goats by then. A lot of women used goat's milk to nurse their babies. It was healthy for everybody and I always tried to persuade people to drink it. I had two quarts of goat's milk a day for many years and it made me strong.

"We extended credit to a lot of folks during the depression. I knew all the people, since I came here at the opening, and many had worked for me. Times were hard, jobs were scarce and money was hard to get, so I took promises and let people have what they wanted. Otherwise they wouldn't have been able to feed their families. I had butchered and sold my 500 head of cattle and sold all the wood and fence posts I could get from the land. In March of 1942 I was seventy-four years old and dead broke. I could no longer pay the wholesale firms I dealt with, so I closed up, paid all the bills I owed, including $175 my boy owed the city by working it out on the streets, and my wife and I moved out west to Modesto, California.

"The first time I made a trip to California I was by myself on a boxcar load of nanny goats, which I planned to sell. I squeezed between the animals to milk them and handed the conductor my ticket through the railings.

"When my wife and I moved to Modesto, I got a job in the slaughter house and she in a cannery. We bought two lots and started a business called 'Dad's Poultry Market.' My dear wife died in 1955. I married again a few years later when I was ninety and she was sixty-seven, but I lost her, also. I turned a hobby, making lariats and bullwhips, into a mail order business and it helped me pay the bills. I also made and sold a lot of moccasins, tomahawks, headbands and canes. Never in my entire life did I have to take welfare or charity.

"I'm thankful not only for all the good things that have happened, but also for the bad. The bad helped me appreciate the good. The people in Perry were my friends, and I was lonely for them every day after leaving there. Perry is where I really learned how to live. It's still the 'Queen City' of the Cherokee Strip."

ਟ**ੂ**

Orlando Walkling died February 10, 1974, a month after suffering a stroke. He had outlived two wives, two adopted children and all of the hundreds of homesteaders who came to the Perry/Noble County area at the opening of the Cherokee Strip on September 16, 1893.

# 5

# *C*.T. TALLIAFERRO

A substantial number of blacks took part in the Cherokee Strip run, but few were able to establish successful homesteads. Clem Tasmania Talliaferro was among those who tried but failed. Instead, he became a respected citizen, merchant and a leader of his people in the Perry community.

Tally, as he was called by most people, was nine days shy of his twenty-first birthday when he made the run. Perhaps his age would have denied him a claim anyway, but he had the misfortune to land on a corner of a quarter section north of Perry where another man also wound up. Tally accepted a reimbursement from the other man in exchange for leaving and returned to the townsite of Perry.

Mr. Talliaferro made the run on foot, starting from the southern line at Orlando. He had only recently recovered from a debilitating bout with malaria and was not strong despite his youth. Somehow he covered the twelve-mile distance only to become one of the numerous losers in the race for homes in the new territory.

In Perry, he borrowed fifty cents' worth of peanuts, roasted them and set up a vending stand to earn a living among the somewhat wild but hungry inhabitants of the infant community. Proceeds from the first day's sale enabled him to buy a bit of fresh fruit to add to his inventory. He continued to grow in that fashion for the next several days until enough capital had been accumulated to buy a lot on Government Acre, where the Post Office now stands. His first store there consisted of burlap bags strung over a few poles.

Like dozens of other would-be merchants, he was the victim of a cruel hoax. Government Acre was reserved for the courthouse and Post Office and parcels of it were not for sale at any price, despite rumors to the contrary. A month after the opening, troops drove settlers off the block. Tally and the others had to move. It was one of the harsh tragedies of the opening.

The Langston area in Logan County, on the south border of the Strip, was home to a large community of blacks before the run. A group of them had made plans to establish an all-black community in the Cherokee Strip. Their goal was to settle Perry and call it Liberty. The whites could have Wharton. Violence was not planned or anticipated. The plan was abandoned because not enough blacks succeeded in getting lots in Perry. C.T. Talliaferro was one of the few who did, although he failed to get a quarter-section.

Tally operated a grocery and general store from various locations until 1915 when he built a two-story twenty-five-foot front brick structure. His building was on Sixth Street off the northeast corner of the square in part of the area now occupied by the Exchange Bank & Trust Co.

He was a rarity for that time, a Negro college graduate. Soft-spoken, gentle and concerned for the black families of this area, he was highly regarded by all. He devoted a great deal of time and effort to encouraging young black boys and girls in intellectual pursuits. Although never wealthy, he provided books for young people and urged them to "look at the pictures," hoping they would become curious enough to learn how to read the text.

Mr. Talliaferro was regarded as a scholar and an orator as well as a linguist. From his customers he learned fragments of Spanish, French, German, Otoe Indian and even Greek and Latin. He was a leader in the African Methodist Episcopal Church and Prince Hall Lodge, and the black community in general.

A local paper reported on September 22, 1902, that the black people of Perry celebrated Emancipation Day in spite of a heavy downpour of rain. After a "speaking" at the courthouse, a banquet was served at "Talliaferro Hall," which was not otherwise identified as to location. It may have been on the upper floor of Mr. Talliaferro's general store.

The Perry Chamber of Commerce honored him as the first recipient of a lifetime membership.

Born September 25, 1872, in Brownsville, Tennessee, he entered Roger Williams University in Nashville at the age of sixteen. Four years later he earned a bachelor's degree and taught school that summer in Arkansas. Tally contracted malaria and returned home, he thought to die, but recovered and moved on to

Minnesota. A doctor there advised him to go West, and he boarded a train with that in mind. En route, he heard about the Cherokee Strip land rush and decided farming might be the healthful outdoor kind of life he needed. He left the train in Fort Worth, Texas, and headed back north to Oklahoma in time for the opening.

His first wife, Lillie, was from Natchez, Mississippi. They were married in 1895, and she died in 1942. Six years later Tally married a former Los Angeles school teacher.

After Mr. Talliaferro's death, his store building was sold in August 1960 to make way for construction of the new bank. That deleted the last visible sign of Tally's lifetime here. The positive impact he had on young people and adults of the black community would be impossible to measure. His influence doubtless is still being exerted through them somewhere today.

# 6

# J AMES A. LOBSITZ

James Lobsitz had his eye on a business lot in Perry and staked a claim on Government Acre. Along with several dozen others, he learned shortly that he had no right to be there. It was a government preserve, set aside for the county courthouse and the Perry Post Office. The settlers protested, but within a month of the opening they were forced off the five-acre tract by soldiers with fixed bayonets.

Mr. Lobsitz was operating a general merchandise store in Edmond when he made the decision to come to the new territory. He rode in on the first Santa Fe train that left Orlando at noon on the opening day. He was seated next to a very large, overweight woman. When the train slowed up at the approach to Perry, Mr. Lobsitz found the aisle blocked by his traveling companion. He decided the only way out was to squirm through a train window. He hit the ground running and covered the last few yards on foot.

Finding some lots that apparently had not been taken, he stepped off one hundred feet and drove his stake into the ground. He squatted there until three o'clock in the afternoon. When no one tried to contest his claim, he began making inquiries and learned that he was on the untouchable Government Acre, along with several others.

Although thwarted in his first attempt to open a business here, he succeeded at a new location on south Seventh Street, a half-block off the southwest corner of the square. With a partner, Hugh McCredie, he opened the Famous Department Store. It became the largest family-owned retail business in Perry.

Mr. Lobsitz moved a few weeks later to the south side of the square. Not long after that he relocated the store one door west, and in 1908 he erected and occupied a two-story building for the Famous just west of there. These frequent moves prompted an

early-day Perry editor to remark jokingly: "The moves of Jim Lobsitz...in Block B would make it the original 'Tourist Park' whether
from expansion of business or 'cheaper to move than pay rent.' It
has been hard to follow the travels of Jim...before (he) really got
'sot on his eggs'."

The Famous store building is now occupied by Leroy Rolling's
LJR Enterprises, a home decorating and gift store.

Jim Lobsitz wasted no time in assuming a leadership role in the
Perry community. He had been a member of the Edmond school
board before coming here and served in that same capacity in Perry
from 1894 to 1898. He was a member of the city council 1899-1906,
mayor of Perry 1909-11, again served on the school board 1913-15,
and was elected to a two-year term as Noble County treasurer in
1929.

Mr. Lobsitz energetically shouldered one major civic responsibility after another. He provided leadership for many of the
important early developmental movements in Perry. For one good
example, he is credited more than any other person with bringing
the Arkansas Valley Railroad (later Frisco) to Perry around the turn
of the century.

He was a member of the Masonic Lodge, Order of the Eastern
Star, Knights of Pythias, Perry Golf and Country Club and the
Chamber of Commerce.

He also was a member of Temple B'nai Israel in Oklahoma City,
but regularly attended worship services at the Perry First Presbyterian Church. He served several years there as chairman of the
board of trustees. The church knew him as a liberal contributor
through the years. His funeral services were held at the church
with the minister, Rev. David Thomas, officiating, assisted by Rabbi
Blatt of the temple in Oklahoma City.

Mr. Lobsitz was born November 1, 1853, in New York City. He
had been a hardware merchant in Nontoic, Kansas, before returning to Edmond in 1891.

After selling the Famous in 1908 to Knox & Stout Clothing Co.,
Mr. Lobsitz moved to a new location on the south side of the square
and opened a hardware store with his three sons. He remained in
business there until retiring in 1941 at the age of eighty-seven. Even
then he was on the job each day at the store. When customers came
through the front door, Mr. Lobsitz hustled to greet them with a
handshake and friendly greeting. He had a sparse mane of white

hair, steel-rimmed glasses and a ready smile for all. Jim Lobsitz was an old-fashioned merchant and a gentleman.

Lobsitz Hardware was sold in January 1941 to Frank Oliver of El Dorado, Kansas, and eventually was merged with the Monroe-Lang Hardware Store located next door west. Mr. Lobsitz died of a heart attack five months after retiring. *The Perry Daily Journal* described him as one of the community's most beloved and respected citizens.

# 7

# $A$ FTER THE RUN

For the first several days after the run, efforts were made to organize a local government and to bring order out of utter chaos. An estimated 25,000 people were bumping into each other on a townsite designed for barely 4,000. Hundreds started leaving when the lack of town lots and homesteads became obvious, but for weeks there were far too many people for the facilities available.

By proclamation of the territorial governor, W.C. Renfrow, Perry was declared a city of the first class and a city election was scheduled for October 21, barely one month after the run. Until the election, the city was governed by U.S. marshals, the Interior Department and the Land Office.

Booths were erected around the square to give candidates an opportunity to address the people. John N. Brogan, a grocer, was the Democratic nominee and was elected first mayor of Perry. E. B. Mentz was the Republican candidate. In the election, 1,579 votes were cast, indicating a decided decrease in population since opening day. Judge E.W. Jones estimated the count at 4,500, based on the total vote.

Mayor Brogan was viewed as a wise man with good judgment and he was widely respected. He discharged his duties faithfully and with executive ability. The council adopted a resolution commending the mayor upon his retirement from office, and Brogan Street (now Gene Taylor Street) was named in his honor.

Others chosen in the first city election were A. Duff Tillery, city attorney; George Farrar, treasurer; Alonzo (Lon) Wharton, city clerk; A. Jacobs, police judge; and George Livingston, assessor.

Councilmen elected were C.A. Weideman and J.T. Hill, prominent saloon operators, first ward; J.C. Dulaney and Howard Friend, second ward; Lawrence Drake and Henry Flock, third ward; and J.P. McKinnis and W.T. Cutler, fourth ward. Drake was elected president of the council, a sort of vice mayor. McKinnis was named secretary.

The first meeting of the city council was on October 28 on the upper floor of the Hill Brothers' saloon and gambling house, known as the Buck Horn. Gambling tables were put to a legitimate use by the council and the hired help was given a welcome night off. The first ordinance adopted defined the corporate limits of the city. It was submitted by Drake of the third ward. *The Evening Democrat* was designated the official city newspaper. As one of his first acts, Mayor Brogan appointed William Tilghman town marshal (chief of police) and John Thornhill, George Starmer, "Fatty" Hopkins and H.A. (Heck) Thomas policemen.

Bill Tilghman came to this area as one of 1,000 deputy U.S. marshals appointed to help maintain order. He was among the most noted peace officers of the West and had already won a reputation as a law enforcer in Guthrie. Before coming to Oklahoma Territory he had teamed up with Bat Masterson to bring law and order to Dodge City, Kansas. With Masterson as sheriff and Tilghman his deputy, that wild frontier town was partially tamed. The two may have provided the inspiration for television's fictional Marshal Dillon and his dramatic exploits. Tilghman was killed some thirty years later in Cromwell, Oklahoma, by a bullet fired by a drunken fellow officer.

The first city council faced many serious responsibilities, and its members responded admirably. They set a precedent for the future city by establishing an honest and economical government. Politically, the council was almost totally Democratic; only one Republican won a seat. The members were largely liberal and progressive. They maintained a creditable decorum and steadfastly adhered to high standards.

Mayor Brogan appointed the first city school board on November 1, 1893. Its members were A.J. Gavin and Judge W.M. Bowles, ward one; Dr. O.M. Long and R.E. Bagby, ward two; T.J. Taylor Sr. and J.A. Cruikshank, ward three; and W.H. Dwyre and W.J. Gillette, ward four. Perry had 463 school children enrolled in the winter of 1893. Classes were held in several vacant houses surrounding the square.

The Holmes school building was constructed on a hill east of the city along with the Blaine building in South Perry after bonds totaling $18,000 were approved in the spring of 1894. Both schools were of brick and stone. The Holmes school was destroyed by fire on November 30, 1897. Elements of the Blaine building still stand but they have not been used for public school classes since the mid-1950s.

The first high school building was a frame structure, measuring twenty by sixty feet, on the E Street school preserve. Eleven students were enrolled the first winter with Professors Means and Butcher in charge. It was replaced by a brick and stone building in October 1894, and all grades had classes there that year.

In the spring of 1894, a regular city election was held and William A. Stone was elected mayor, along with a complete new set of city officials. In the meantime, additions to the original townsite had been included in the corporation, creating six wards. This made possible twelve councilmen and twelve school board members.

South Perry addition became part of the town proper, making ward seven, in the spring of 1895, followed by the election of two more council and school board members. Within the next three years the city was redistricted into four wards, with Seventh and D Streets the dividing line.

At the time of the opening, the Perry Post Office was a small frame building on the southwest corner of Government Acre, the courthouse square. Within a few weeks it was moved to the northwest corner. A new stone building was constructed there with subscription funds provided by merchants on the north and west sides of the square. It was leased to the U.S. government for one dollar a year. In 1911 it was donated to the Treasury Department and became government property. While the new Post Office was under construction, the mail service was temporarily moved to a building on the east side of the square. C.P. Drace was the first postmaster.

Grace Hill Cemetery was platted on forty acres of the Hart homestead east of the city in January 1894. Bonds for the cemetery were barely approved, 228-227, in an election on February 21, 1894. Until then, school land adjoining Perry on the west had been used as a cemetery.

The early day water supply was a critical problem. The government had one well dug on the townsite, in the center of Flynn and Brogan Streets. A spring on east A Street furnished water for drinking and laundry purposes, and wells were dug at residences and businesses. Bill Cates did a thriving business supplying water from his well to homes and merchants, making the rounds with his wagon daily.

A city ordinance required each business to have two barrels of salt water and buckets in front for use in case of fire. The fire alarm was given by pistol shot—a six-gun being one of the accessories at nearly all businesses. C.P. Walker had a contract for sprinkling the streets, drawing his water from the pond known as Wills Lake, east of the city.

The first step toward organizing a fire department was taken on March 13, 1894, when the city purchased a hook and ladder wagon for $1,200. Fire protection was badly needed because of the wooden construction used throughout the city. Pabst Brewing Co. of St. Louis presented Perry a hand-drawn hose cart for use during the first winter. Henry Beard, who later became a U.S. marshal, was the first appointed fire chief, followed by John Patterson. He was succeeded by W.W. Keas. Alfalfa was cut in the courthouse park in 1896 to feed the fire department horses. That was before elm trees were planted in the park.

Bucket brigades were often used in fighting fires, but fortunately none of major proportions occurred until the spring of 1895. A portion of the southeast corner of the square, including Lon Wharton's printing office and the Midland Saloon, went up in flames at that time. Another spectacular fire caused major damage when the Donahoe cotton gin in Perry burned on Christmas Eve, 1898.

In December 1893, the city requested bids for a chemical engine, hook and ladder wagon, and fire department fixtures. Mayor Brogan called for an election on February 21, 1894, for $60,000 water works and electric generating bonds and the cemetery. The water and light plant bonds passed easily, 321-101, but the cemetery bonds cleared by only a one-vote margin.

The city engineer drew up plans for a water works system, and on March 28, 1894, a contract for construction was awarded. The bonds were faulty, however, and were not sold. The Howe Pump and Engine Co. of Louisville, Kentucky, then secured a franchise for operating the water and light plant, and on July 20, 1895, the system was completed.

The first county election was held November 6, 1894, and it was then that the name was changed from "P" to Noble County.

Prior to the election county officials had been serving by appointment of Governor Renfrow.

The appointive officers were J.C. Scruggs, sheriff; S.H. Harris, county attorney; Joe Blackburn, clerk; J.L. Haraldson, treasurer; L.L. Talley, superintendent; R.J. Edwards, probate judge; M.A. Mosely, register of deeds; and T.D. Nichols, Emmett Beatty and C.A. Crow, commissioners. The commissioners had their first meeting October 27, 1893. As one of their first acts, they granted licenses for sixty-four saloons in Perry.

The first elective county officers were John A. Hansen, sheriff; Capt. J.R. Wallace, treasurer; M.C. Ford, clerk; S.E. Richardson, register of deeds; A.R. Museller, probate judge; T.H. Seward, county attorney; Dr. C.O. Hood, coroner; and J.H. VanAucken, J.W. Olmstead and W.W. McCullough, commissioners.

County officers were meeting in rooms upstairs and down, all around the square. A courthouse was an obvious necessity but no funds from taxation were available. T.M. Richardson & Sons, lumbermen, came to the rescue and constructed a two-story frame building, seventy by one hundred feet, on the east side of the courthouse park. The building served the county well for twenty years.

A bond issue proposal to build a new courthouse failed by a few votes in 1913, but in the spring of 1915 voters approved bonds in the amount of $100,000 for the construction of a fireproof building, three stories tall with basement. A jail block sat atop the structure. Manhattan Construction Co. began work on October 21 of that year, and the building was accepted by county commissioners in May 1916. The commissioners were J.F. Keeler, Ed R. Martin and J.H. Ledbetter.

When the squatters were driven off Government Acre one month after the run, the five-acre tract was forlorn and neglected. Only the tiny wooden Post Office building, and, for a time, the Land Office, sat upon it. Otherwise it was a windswept and dusty eyesore in the center of Perry. The ground was plowed and sowed to alfalfa in the spring of 1895 to keep down the suffocating cloud of sand and dust.

❧

When Will T. Little came to Oklahoma in 1893, he could stand in the middle of his farm homestead and not see a tree in any direction. He suffered from a severe sinus condition and his life was nearly unbearable when the wind and dust blew on a hot afternoon during those early days.

A nature lover and ecologist several years before the term was coined, Mr. Little devoted his mind and energy to making life more pleasant for future generations by planting trees. He believed that trees "reduced wind velocity, prevented dust storms and increased atmospheric humidity."

In 1896 Mr. Little received permission from the county commissioners to supervise the planting and tending of elm trees in the Perry courthouse park. He proposed to plow up the alfalfa, disc and harrow the ground, and plant 8,600 seedling Wisconsin white elm sprouts in furrows extending east-west.

The sprouts were from six to eight inches long, and apparently each one took root. He agreed to charge nothing for his time if the commissioners would provide funds to purchase the trees and pay for preparing the grounds. Enough trees were sold from this crop to repay the county for all the expense of stock and planting.

Mr. Little also planted a second city park of three acres, plus two school reserves of three acres each. Trees were donated to school districts around the county for planting on school grounds.

Perry's lush courthouse park today is a living memorial to Mr. Little. He was a newspaperman who had homesteaded in Black Bear township. He served as Perry postmaster, became Noble County's representative in the Territorial Legislature and is credited with founding the Oklahoma Historical Society.

Mr. Little also devoted himself to teaching soil culture and publishing *Oklahoma,* a quarterly magazine with advice for farmers about the planting and care of'trees, and about soil and irrigation. A monument in the park takes note of his contribution to beautification of the courthouse square.

ۿ

East-west city streets were named A to L, in alphabetical order starting at the south. In 1928 they were given names with the original initial, using varieties of trees for the most part—Ash, Birch,

Cedar, and so forth. North-south streets always have been numbered, starting at the east.

Rev. Simon P. Meyers, the Presbyterian minister who delivered the first sermon in Perry on September 17, the day after the run, served the First Presbyterian Church here from 1893 to 1895. He became county school superintendent in 1897. Rev. D.J.M. Wood, a Methodist parson from Stillwater, came here during the first winter and held services in a business building at the corner of Seventh and B Streets.

Four weeks after the opening the Roman Catholic congregation had organized with a membership of between ninety and one hundred families. Priests from Guthrie made regular trips here to minister to them. The first mass was said in a room at the rear of Conrad J. Lindeman's store near Seventh and D Streets.

Other denominations quickly established churches in the new community, and their members were faithful in attendance. They had been through a mighty ordeal, one which perhaps deepened and strengthened their faith.

Within the first year after the opening, Perry had thirty-three doctors to provide medical care. Some of them were Dr. Robert Taylor, whose grandson later became a state representative from Noble County; Dr. William B. Brengle and his brother, Dr. D.D. Brengle; Dr. A.S. Moore, Dr. R.W. Southard, Dr. E.E. Doggett, Dr. Cullimore, Dr. Dougan, Dr. Hood, Dr. Hoke, Dr. Love and Dr. Gillette.

More than a hundred attorneys reportedly landed in Perry on September 16, 1893. Some estimates placed the number at 500.

As the dawn of a new century began in Perry, green bermuda grass and young, leafy elm trees were growing in the courthouse park, schools and churches were established and expanding, the initial "shakedown" of businesses and homeowners had been completed, and a stable local government was in place. The signs of civilization and order were everywhere.

A great adventure begins as the Cherokee Strip is opened to settlers on September 16, 1893. Photographer William S. Prettyman made this historic shot that day.

At Orlando, this was the scene moments before the starting signal. It was recorded by A.A. Forbes. (*Cherokee Strip Museum, Oklahoma Historical Society.*)

Waiting to register for the run, five days before the opening.

Seemingly endless lines plagued homeseekers at pre-run registration booths. The photographer captioned this scene "the Orlando farce."

Perry's Land Office was crowded by saloons and other businesses for the first few weeks. They called it "Hell's Half Acre."

Claims were recorded after the run at Land Offices, like this one in Perry. Many waited weeks, even months, for their turn. (*Cherokee Strip Museum, Oklahoma Historical Society.*)

A U.S. flag, near center, was flown by the Buckhorn Saloon in Perry's "Hell's Half Acre," a rough and tumble section in the early days. (*Cherokee Strip Museum, Oklahoma Historical Society.*)

Businesses, including the Hotel Moran, sprang up in Government Acre. But it was reserved for the courthouse and Post Office, and all these enterprises were cleared out within a month after the opening. The view is from 6th Street looking northwest. (*Cherokee Strip Museum, Oklahoma Historical Society.*)

Six weeks after the run, Perry was bustling with construction and commerce. This is identified as C Street and Auction Corner. (*Cherokee Strip Museum, Oklahoma Historical Society.*)

East side of square was taking shape by October 27, 1893. This view looks north from the corner of C Street and 6th. (*Cherokee Strip Museum, Oklahoma Historical Society.*)

West side of square was the first home of the Exchange Bank. Just down the
street was the Bank of Perry. The stone building at left is no longer there.
Streets were unpaved and gas lights were common when this was made.

Pioneer merchant
James A. Lobsitz.

# PART II: 1900 TO 1920

# 8

# *M*ALZAHNS COME TO PERRY

Anna Malzahn, a sturdy German immigrant living in Maple Lake, Minnesota, knew a lot about pain and heartache. At the age of forty-two, she had given birth to seventeen children. Eleven of them died young. Anna wept with her husband, Carl, over each of the small graves through the years.

In 1902, she was severely plagued by asthma. The bitterly cold Minnesota winters caused her great difficulty in breathing, and her doctor recommended that the family move to a milder climate in the Southwestern area of the U.S.

Carl Malzahn was a husky master blacksmith, and Anna's health was of great concern to him and their six surviving children. He agreed they must move. The couple looked at a map, and one of them placed a fingertip on a random location. It was Perry, in Oklahoma Territory.

Next to the wild and woolly Cherokee Strip land rush of 1893, that simple act may have been the single most fateful event in this community's colorful history. The Malzahn family came here as a result of it, and unquestionably Perry can still be found on a map today because Carl and Anna chose it, however casually, for their new home.

Carl Frederick Malzahn set up his blacksmith shop with its anvils and forges in the downtown Perry area, repairing farm machinery and shoeing horses. It was the forerunner of the Charles Machine Works, Inc., the sprawling Perry factory which today manufactures Ditch Witch products for the underground construction industry world-wide, with annual sales topping $100 million. The company, a debt-free phenomenon, is the economic foundation of this community.

Carl and Anna did not live to see the metamorphosis occur, but it came to reality after World War II through the inventive genius of their grandson, Edwin Malzahn, and the patient guidance of his father, Charles, the younger son of Carl and Anna.

Both Carl and Anna were born in Germany but they met in Cleveland, Ohio. He came to the U.S. from Strasburgh in 1880 at the age of twenty-one after five years as an apprentice blacksmith. Carl settled first in Cleveland. There he met and married Anna. She had emigrated to this country when she was nineteen, making the crossing with a brother and heading west to Cleveland.

After their marriage in 1883, Carl and his bride left Ohio for Maple Lake, and it was from there that they came to Oklahoma nineteen years later.

Perry was a busy farm community of some 3,000 residents in 1902. It was just nine years after the opening. Homes, schools, churches, farm and business buildings, roads and streets were being built throughout Noble County, and the entire Cherokee Strip fairly throbbed with activity. Statehood was still five years away.

Carl and Anna had four daughters and two strapping sons when the family arrived here. The Malzahns lived on a farm near Orlando for a time while Carl operated the business in Perry. The older son, Gustave, or Gus, joined his father in the Malzahn Blacksmith Shop at the start. They chose a frame building in the 200 block on the east side of Sixth Street, just south of the southeast corner of the courthouse square.

The other boy, Charles, was born October 26, 1893, in Maple Lake. He was nine years old when the family came to Perry. He "grew into" the business and joined it full-time a few years later. The younger son was just plain Charlie to his family and friends throughout his life. The daughters were Emaline, Irene, Marie and Grace.

Grace, in later years, reminisced about childhood days in Perry. She remembered how diligently her parents strove to protect the four girls from the ways of the world. One particular story concerned Emaline, or Emily:

"She was a beautiful young lady," Grace recalled, "and she didn't know where babies came from. Once while attending a town social, she met a young man, Henry Thiele, who asked to see her home. Some other girls were jealous of Emily and started a rumor that she was pregnant as a result of her friendship with Henry.

"When mother and father heard the rumor, they were furious and insisted upon a wedding. Henry knew he was not the father, for he and Emily 'hadn't done anything.' Besides, he had been in a barroom brawl that left him with an injury rendering him incapable of fathering children.

"However, he did like Emily, and he was willing to 'be the father' if indeed she were pregnant by someone else. He himself had been raised without a father and did not want that to happen to another.

"When it came time for Emily to begin to show and she didn't, Mother began to ask questions," Grace remembered. "When she found out that Emily and Henry had never 'done anything,' even after their marriage, because of his injury, the folks wanted to have the marriage annulled. But, Henry and Emily liked each other and decided to stay together.

"After that, Mother got the rest of us girls together and told us where babies came from," Grace said.

Henry and Emily lived in Moundridge, Kansas. He was a blacksmith and part-time gambler, never too successful at either. Emily worked as a hotel manager and dressmaker. Their desire for children led them to take in a young lady who was pregnant but with no desire to keep the baby. Henry and Emily adopted and raised the child, Florence, as their own.

❧

Carl Malzahn died at the age of fifty-two on July 20, 1913, as the result of a tragic shop accident. While he was sharpening a plow share on an anvil, a sliver of metal from a sledge hammer pierced his abdomen. No serious problem was apparent at the time and a doctor believed Carl could soon go back to work. One week later internal complications developed and he died within twelve hours.

Despite his relatively short period of time in Perry, Carl played a significant role in the development of the community. Farmers relied heavily on blacksmiths to keep their equipment in running order. Cartage services, using teams of horses pulling wagons with wooden spokes and steel rims, hauled freight from the railroad all over the county. Each family had its buggy and stable. The smiths kept all of them going.

In addition to founding a business that evolved into a major industry, Carl Malzahn contributed to the community by serving as a member of the Perry board of education during a time of intense growth and construction. He had just been reelected to a second term shortly before his death. Carl and his wife both were active members of the Evangelical Church.

Anna Malzahn died October 2, 1918, after a short illness. The two are buried here in Grace Hill Cemetery.

After Carl's death, the business was turned over to the sons, Gus and Charlie, and it became known as Malzahn Brothers' General Blacksmithing.

ॐ

Along with many other young Noble County men, Charlie was called up for Army service during World War I. On May 22, 1918, a few days before departing for basic training at Fort Meade, Maryland, near Baltimore, he married Bertha Wolff of Orlando, southwest of Perry. Thus began a lifetime partnership which pervaded both their family and their business affairs.

Bertha's parents also were German immigrants. Her father, George Wolff, was born September 17, 1873, in Alsace-Lorraine, Germany, and came to the U.S. in 1892 with his father, Martin Wolff Sr., from the old country. The family spent about one year in Illinois, another year in Western Kansas, and in 1894 moved to North-Central Oklahoma, settling in Noble County on a quarter-section in Lowe township, four miles from Orlando.

Bertha's mother, Mary Bertha Dorothea Pommerencki, was born November 11, 1881, near Hamburg, Germany. She came to the U.S. in 1887 with her family, and they also lived briefly in Western Kansas before relocating to a farm adjacent to the Wolffs in the Orlando area. There Mary met George Wolff, and on October 26, 1898, when he was twenty-five and she almost seventeen, they were married.

Bertha was born July 17, 1899, at the Wolff family home place. She graduated from Orlando High School before attending Central State Teachers College (now Central State University) at Edmond. Because she and Charlie were married almost on the eve of his departure for Army duty in Maryland, she had to follow him there for a two-week "honeymoon," sandwiched into the schedule as his training permitted.

Charlie was given a course in first aid at Fort Meade, then quickly shipped to France and sent directly to the front lines to serve with Evacuation Hospital 16. This might be viewed as an example of Army cross-training. He had been reared in the family blacksmith shop where horseshoeing was part of the day in, day out routine. The Army at that time still relied heavily on horse-drawn Artillery as well as Cavalry, but this man was assigned to a Medical Corps unit, rather than something where horses were used, under some sort of logic understood only by the military mind of the day.

His unit served in the Meusse-Argonne and Verdun campaigns. Near the Argonne front, he was caught in a deadly mustard gas attack. The residual effects would cause him occasional trouble the rest of his life.

After the armistice was signed on November 11, 1918, ending hostilities, Charlie served an additional nine months as a member of the Allied occupation force in Coblenz, Germany, on the Rhine River, in the homeland of his parents and his wife's parents.

Returning to Perry after discharge from the Army, Charlie plunged back into the blacksmith shop with his brother, Gus. Their services were in demand in the post-war era and the shop was busy. With automobiles fast replacing horses, however, the Malzahns moved more and more into custom machining and welding.

In 1926 they erected a modern brick building to replace the original wooden shop, but on the same location. The name, "Malzahn Brothers," was chiseled proudly in a stone block above the entry. Fate would provide an ironic postscript in just a few years.

# *9*

# *T*HE LIBRARY & OPERA HOUSE

The Cherokee Strip land rush was the principal dramatic feature of the 1893-1900 period in this area. Surely the Grand Opera House and the Carnegie Library were the cultural symbols of the two decades that followed.

Both buildings had their beginnings when Perry was very young. The Grand Opera House was built in 1901 and demolished in 1960 when it was in danger of falling down. The library, built in 1909, still stands proudly in 1991 and is one of the community's most prized possessions.

In a way, the Grand Opera House uniquely represents the spirit of the 1900-20 era. It was a transitory object of the times, serving a contemporary purpose and then vanishing. Wistfully we look back and wish it could have been preserved because of the memories it created and stored. Realistically and practically speaking, the building could not have been saved, but we are left with the lore of its grandeur bequeathed us by earlier generations.

Thankfully we still have the Carnegie Library. Work began in 1990 on a major renovation and expansion project to preserve the building's architectural beauty into the twenty-first century. The workover also will provide more readers with access to its stacks. The library's stately stone entryway columns, sturdy brick and plaster walls and red tile roof have inspired admiring comments from builders of the modern era. Standing regally and serenely on a grassy, shaded corner of the courthouse park, it is a Perry landmark.

### THE PERRY OPERA HOUSE

Some historians say the Old West, the Frontier Days, ended around 1887. The new towns in the Cherokee Strip appeared a few years after that, but they were still reminiscent of the stagecoach stations and cattle drive stopovers of that legendary time.

The earliest Perry buildings were wood frame, some mere shanties to provide temporary shelter until more substantial structures could be built. Brick, native stone and steel beams were coming into general use for many buildings in Perry after the turn of the century. With the new construction there was a clamor for facilities that would bring the community some things of an artistic and educational nature.

The city's first opera house was the Perry Opera House operated by John C. Dulaney on the south side of D Street between Fifth and Sixth Streets. It was destroyed by fire in 1902. The building was described as "magnificent and extravagant," and Mr. Dulaney himself was known as a "genial gentleman of education and refinement."

Touring companies performed at his Opera House, providing the community with the comedy and drama of the theater as well as entertainment by musical artists of the day. The main entrance to the Opera House from the street was spacious and well lighted. A twenty-foot stairway was located in the center and six-foot stairways were on either side. The one on the right led to the gallery and the other to the balcony.

The steel ceiling was handsomely decorated and walls were frescoed with red, trimmed in pink and blue, with flower and scroll design outlined in gold. Two elaborately decorated boxes were on either side of the balcony. Windows on opposing sides of the building provided ventilation, and the glass was stained to harmonize with the interior. There were four aisles on the floor, two leading to the dress circle and one on either side of the boxes.

On stage, the front curtain was painted with a scene depicting a lady in a boat with two white swans playing about. The house was an elegant attraction in itself. *The Noble County Sentinel* suggested that the fire which destroyed the building may have been purposely set, "perhaps to pay the mortgage."

The first touring show that came to town spread its own spacious tent on the courthouse square. It was the Cutler Comedy Company, a family of musicians and performers who had been turned out from Edmond.

An eighteen-year-old performer from Perry named Joe Keaton broke in with this company but his acting was so bad that Mr.

Cutler fired him without notice, knowing that the only applause Joe received was from "a bunch of rounders" brought in by Joe himself.

Joe later got even with Mr. Cutler by marrying his daughter, Myra, and from this union three children were born. The oldest was Buster Keaton, who became one of the most famous comedians of the early silent movies.

### THE GRAND OPERA HOUSE

It was a grand building in every sense of the word. With a majestic brick facade and gracefully arched windows, it dominated the east side of the square for some sixty years. Its spacious stage was trod by Will Rogers and Buster Keaton, and the John Philip Sousa military band performed in concert there. The Grand Opera House was a regal entertainment palace in Perry during the early decades of this century.

The Grand formally opened on May 30, 1901, when Memorial Day services were held there. It was built by J.B. Tate and John Pressler, but Mr. Pressler continued in the business only a few months. In 1902, John Dulaney, former operator of the Perry Opera House, became associated with Mr. Tate at the Grand.

The stage measured thirty-two feet by fifty feet, very generous proportions. It was big enough for a performance by the Polly Circus with a live elephant, five horses and a troop of Shetland ponies. An audience of 800 could be seated comfortably on the main floor level and in the balcony which ringed it above.

The height to the rigging loft above the stage, where scenery was suspended and then lowered into place when needed, was fifty feet. The proscenium arch in front of the curtain measured twenty-two feet by twenty-eight feet, according to records researched by Myrna Stoops. The two-story building was constructed of brick and sandstone. A fire-escape was attached to the north wall and a U.S. flag waved from the front.

In the early 1900s, many towns and cities had opera houses, like the Grand, where touring artists performed. The Overholser Opera House in Oklahoma City was a popular location and drew audiences from as far away as Wichita, one hundred miles north of Perry. The Overholser was closed each Sunday and Monday, but the Grand was open those days, so many from the Wichita area would stop over here en route to Oklahoma City and take in a local playbill. Because of that, the Grand was able to book some major acts.

Perry High School used the theater for graduation ceremonies, class plays and other functions. William Jennings Bryan, the orator and presidential office-seeker, delivered his stirring speech, "The Conquering Nation," to a spellbound audience at the Grand on December 16, 1902. (Oklahomans participated in a presidential election for the first time in 1908, and Bryan was their choice.) Sousa's sixty-five-member band played there on November 19, 1904.

*The Perry Republican* carried a page one advertisement on October 27, 1911, announcing the coming of B.C. Whitney's "piquant musical extravaganza, 'Isle of Spice'," with illustrations of young ladies in military uniforms. The performers were to include "Uncle Sam's Marines and Challenge Beauty Chorus." Ticket prices ranged from twenty-five cents to a dollar and a half.

Another ad in a later edition of *the Republican* described the coming of "the dramatic and social event of the season," with Gilmor Brown starring in "The Tyranny of Tears." Curtain time was eight thirty p.m. and the audience was requested to be in their seats before curtain rises, "as the unusual nature of this play requires an immediate attention."

Attorney Henry S. Johnston had a suite of offices on the second floor of the Grand building, occupying the south half, with windows looking out onto Sixth Street and the courthouse park. His wife, Ethel L., was with him there when a devastating windstorm struck the city in 1912, blowing down the wooden courthouse just across the street. The Johnstons were not injured. He later moved to offices on the south side of the square, over the Famous Department Store.

John F. Tate, cousin of J.B. Tate, operated a portrait photography studio on the second floor of the Grand. Mr. Tate had a selection of pull-down backgrounds to use when customers had their picture taken, but the main piece of equipment was a bulky, boxy camera mounted on a stout wooden tripod.

A black shroud was attached to the back side of the camera, and Mr. Tate would use it to cover his head and shoulders while he peered through the viewfinder to adjust the focus just so. Flash powder in a small open trough topping a hand-held device could be used outdoors when daylight alone was insufficient, but the risk of fire was too great for indoor work, even though the powder could easily light up a room for an eerie instant. Instead, Mr. Tate used a time exposure, requiring the subject to be perfectly still for a matter of several seconds while the lens cap was removed from the aperture. The result was usually a rather stiff, unsmiling portrait.

Mr. Tate was a slight, dignified man whose home in the 700 block of Elm Street was only a few feet from the Presbyterian Church, where he was an elder for fifty years.

Tom Mix, colorful cowboy movie star who spent his early years in Oklahoma, at one time hawked tickets at the Grand, standing on the sidewalk near the box office to entice customers in for a show. He was well acquainted with several Perry residents. Along about the same time he also tended bar in Guthrie.

The Grand was converted into a motion picture theater in 1913, but live entertainment acts were still booked there along with the new film presentations. The first "talkie" in Perry was shown there, although it had only the sound of voices. As the thirty-minute three-reel thriller unwound, six men worked busily behind the screen to provide additional sound effects. Ticket prices were five cents for children and ten cents for adults.

Various businesses, including The Coin ("We Sell Everything") Variety Store, occupied the ground floor of the Grand building until the Annex Movie Theater was built there by the Tate family in 1918. The Opera House continued on the second floor of the building until 1933, offering both film and live entertainment.

The projection booth for the Annex was built into what had been the west rim of the Grand's balcony. Years later the theater's magic lanterns could be seen by kids who climbed the stairs and peered through a narrow doorway into the sound-deadened, extremely hot booth, where Chet Moore was chief operator for years. Just beyond that, still in plain view, were the dusty remains of the Grand's box seats along the side walls.

In 1941 John B. Terry of Wewoka moved to Perry and purchased the town's two movie theaters. The Annex at that time was owned by Henry and Alma Tate, and the other, the Roxy, was owned by Charles and Pearl Wolleson. Both theaters were on the east side of the square, only a few yards apart. Terry announced he would build a large new movie house, the Perry Theater, on Sixth Street in a building formerly occupied by Charlie's Machine Shop, just north of the northeast corner of the square, and that the Annex then would be closed.

The last movie was shown at the Annex in 1942, and the old theater was for all intents and purposes gone. The Perry Theater was larger, cleaner and more comfortable than either of its predecessors. The Roxy continued in operation until the 1950s, when a drive-in theater, the Chief, was built north of town. Like many small towns, Perry now has no movie houses.

The end of the Grand Opera House became obvious the morning of June 14, 1960, when the northeast corner of the old sandstone wall collapsed. The theater portion of the building had been largely unused for nearly twenty years and the second floor had been converted to sleeping rooms and apartments.

In September of that year, the fabled building fell victim to a wrecking ball swung from a crane, demolished because of fears that the other walls also would collapse. The Grand Opera House came down in a cloud of dust, the structure was reduced to rubble and the site leveled. Some say the echoes of famous performers can still be heard on the east side of the square if we but listen.

### BUSTER KEATON

The former Perry resident who undoubtedly achieved the highest level of international fame was Buster Keaton, although many of today's younger generation may never have heard the name. In the roaring twenties and the decade that preceded it, when silent movies and vaudeville were the supreme entertainment mediums, he was a king.

Buster and his father, Joe Keaton, the Cutler Comedy Company washout, performed at the Grand on May 12, 1902, and again ten days later. Myrna Stoops' research indicates that Buster, at the age of seven years, was brought into the act then because his mother, Myra, was ill and unable to go through the act with Joe.

Buster apparently did some stunts, such as riding onto the stage on a broom, that caught the Perry audience's fancy. Because of the enthusiastic response here, his parents kept him in the act. Shortly after the two local engagements, the family played a date in Chicago. Some biographers say that is where Buster made his debut. They are overlooking his performance at the Grand, however.

The Keatons frequently brought their act home to Perry. They were at the Grand again on October 27, 1903, when Buster was eight years old. By that time he had developed some new stunts. In one of these, Joe would appear to bounce his son almost like a rubber ball. It was not child abuse but the kind of acrobatic training that prepared him for a slapstick comedian's career a few years later.

The Keaton family, including Buster's Uncle Bert Keaton, were well known in Perry. When between engagements or otherwise out of work, they spent a great deal of time here. Bert clerked at a local department store.

Buster's grandfather, Joseph Z. Keaton, filed a soldier's declaratory statement on March 14, 1894, and obtained a quarter-section of land northwest of Perry. The claim originally had been staked by W.E. Merry at the opening of the Cherokee Strip in 1893, but Mr. Merry left here shortly thereafter in order to fulfill a teaching contract in Missouri.

The Keaton family later moved into Perry and lived in the first house east of the present Seventh-Day Adventist Church at Seventh and G Streets. Mr. and Mrs. Keaton had three children: Joe, Herbert and Bert. Joe was a good friend of Ralph Treeman and Leo Lobsitz, among others.

Buster Keaton achieved super-stardom and a great deal of wealth as a hapless, stone-faced comic in the silent movies. His pork-pie hat, expressionless face and creative wit were on display in many early film classics, such as "The General," "The Paleface" and "Steamboat Bill Jr." He was regarded as the equal of Charlie Chaplin and Harold Lloyd.

Near the height of his career Buster married Natila Talmadge, sister of Norma and Constance Talmadge, early movie actresses.

The arrival of talking pictures in the 1920s diminished Buster's popularity, although he himself rarely spoke in films, but he continued making movies into the 1950s. Personal problems and his well-publicized unhappy marriage to Miss Talmadge contributed to the loss of his earlier fortune. His fabled talent was never questioned, however.

In 1957, Paramount Pictures produced "The Buster Keaton Story," based loosely on the comic's life and starring Donald O'-Connor in the title role. Also in the cast were Ann Blyth and Rhonda Fleming, two of the studio's most alluring female stars.

Perry was chosen as the site for the world premiere of the movie because of Buster's early days here. When announcement was made that Perry had been so honored, it was an occasion for great celebration and excitement. The Chamber of Commerce was delighted at the prospect of such immense publicity.

Paramount saw to it that the film was heavily promoted. Buster was the subject of "This Is Your Life," a popular NBC network television show hosted by Ralph Edwards. The comedian appeared on the program, impassively of course, while friends, family and colleagues from out of the past were paraded before him. He was a guest on the "Today" show and Ed Sullivan's top-rated CBS-TV Sunday night variety show.

On premiere night, the film was shown first at the Perry Theater downtown, then at the Chief Drive-In north of Perry. It was the biggest box office draw ever at the two theaters, according to Gene McKenna, who was manager of both at the time.

Perry staged a gala day-long celebration to commemorate the event, which was designated an official part of the Oklahoma Semi-Centennial Celebration, marking the fiftieth anniversary of statehood. Buster and his second wife, Eleanor, were here for the entire day. Mr. and Mrs. Fred G. Beers were selected as their host couple by the Chamber of Commerce and saw to it that they made each appointment on time. Ted Newton was general coordinator of the day's events. Mr. and Mrs. H.C. Donahue had a private luncheon for the honorees in their home. A brand-new Oldsmobile was furnished for transportation by Ralph Cooper and Dick Dunford of Cooper Motor Co.

Buster was quiet and reserved during the day, and, in keeping with his stage persona, completely devoid of emotion. He was taken on a brief tour of the city but none of the landmarks were familiar to him. He did visit a home on Grove Street where one of his childhood babysitters still resided. He posed for a photo sitting on her lap, but confessed that his recollection of those early days was hazy, at best.

As another feature of the day, Buster presided over the selection of Bettye Kaye Yahn, teen-age daughter of Mr. and Mrs. Glenn Yahn, as "Miss Perry," in competition at the courthouse park. It thus became her good fortune to act as his official hostess for the three days he spent in Oklahoma, and she traveled with Buster and his wife to Tulsa and Oklahoma City where premieres of the movie also were held.

A walnut plaque bearing a bronze replica of Buster's trademark pork-pie hat was donated by Paramount Pictures to the local Cherokee Strip Museum to mark the occasion.

Despite the revival of interest in Buster's comic genius, few job offers came along for him as a result of the movie. It was commercially successful but not highly lauded by critics. Cable television channels still schedule the film from time to time. Buster appeared in a few TV commercials and did a turn or two in some movies, but the film did not launch him on a career comeback. He died only a few years later.

### THE CARNEGIE LIBRARY

The Women's Christian Temperance Union provided Perry with its first library in 1902, a small reading room and rest room on the north side of the square. The exciting part of Perry's library history was yet to come.

The WCTU struggled hard not only to provide books and decent literature for children and adults of the community, but also for chairs, tables and other furnishings. Members solicited funds and gifts of books from friends for two years, but by 1904 they were about ready to give up the effort. The reading room had only about 400 books at the time, along with some temperance literature.

Rather than see the project fail, the WCTU turned to the three Ladies Literary Clubs of Perry for help. They received an immediate and positive response. During the month of April, a "mass meeting" was held for women of the community to consider the question of organizing a library. As a result of that, the Perry Library Association was formed.

The Ladies Tuesday Afternoon Club, the Perry Progress Club and the Coterie Club provided support in the form of books, magazines and furnishings. To this day, the Progress Club holds an annual benefit to assist the library with gifts of books and money.

Virtually no public funds were available, but the club women organized themselves to guide the project. They elected a board of nine directors, a set of officers and opened the association's membership rolls to anyone interested, men included. Mrs. M.A. Lucy, who later served as librarian, was elected president.

At that first meeting, the group decided to rent rooms on the second floor of Judge Hainer's new building on the northwest corner of the square at a cost of eight dollars per month, including janitor service.

There was no money to hire a librarian, but the women took turns keeping the place open with brief shifts each Wednesday and Saturday. Most books were acquired through donations. Occasional ice cream socials and other benefits also raised funds to add some titles to the shelves.

In September 1904 the board decided longer hours were needed, but this created scheduling problems for the volunteers. They created the position of a salaried person to work for three dollars a week. Hours of operation were from seven until nine-thirty p.m. each Tuesday, Wednesday, Thursday and Saturday evening. Miss Lola Briscoe was appointed librarian in December, and she served for six months.

The association had its eye on a portion of the vacant land in the courthouse park as a building site for a city library, although board members knew that dream was not going to be realized soon. City officials provided the first public funds for library purposes in 1906, a one-mill tax levy over the protests of A.E. Smyser, the mayor of Perry at that time. He felt water lines, sewer extension and fire protection should have priority.

Mrs. H.L. (Lucy) Boyes was appointed in 1908 by the association president, Mrs. B. L. Hainer, to look into the possibility of securing the southwest corner of the square, which was government land, as a library building site. Mrs. Boyes sought the assistance of Congressman Bird S. McGuire, a Perry attorney, in obtaining the land. Within three months, on July 3, 1908, the library board received a patent from the government for the land.

Another major hurdle faced by the women was money for construction. Mrs. Boyes again was the prime mover for this phase. A committee was directed to contact Andrew Carnegie, the Pittsburgh steel magnate and Scottish immigrant who had established a foundation for just such purposes. In 1907 Mr. Carnegie agreed to award the association $10,000. That proved to be the exact amount, to the penny, needed to build the Perry library.

Mr. Carnegie stipulated in his contract with Perry that the building was to be used for no other purpose than a library. He required a resolution by the city council pledging a yearly appropriation of one mill to support the library. The resolution passed unanimously, and Mr. Carnegie promptly placed $10,000 in the Hoboken Trust Co. subject to check of the building committee as the work progressed.

The building committee was headed by Charles Christoph as chairman, plus Mrs. J.H. Bullen, Mrs. H.L. Boyes, Major John Jensen and E.E. Howendobler. A.C. Kreipke of El Reno was the contractor, and architects were Layton, Wemyss, Smith and Hawk of Oklahoma City.

Mr. Carnegie's conditions led to a surprising but bitter standoff just after the new structure was accepted by the building committee on May 21, 1910. James Lobsitz, who then served as mayor, insisted on making the building a city hall as well as a library, but the Library Association would not agree to that because of the original contract made with the Pennsylvania philanthropist.

In an effort to enforce his view and gain possession, the mayor, who operated a hardware store, changed the lock on the library door. This took place after Mr. Lobsitz, a diminutive but determined man of about five feet, four inches, had a confrontation with Charles Christoph, the library board chairman, who towered over the mayor by at least a foot. Each man, convinced that his view was correct, expressed himself forcefully.

Miss Irene McCune (later Mrs. Ralph W. Treeman), the first librarian after the new building was completed, was a young Perry woman of eighteen years who had received professional training in California. It was her first job, but she had only a few months to enjoy the new building before the controversy developed and she found herself locked out of the library.

Library board members located a small unlocked window in the furnace room. It was probably used for a coal chute. They asked Miss McCune to slip into the building that way and resume business. Miss McCune was willing, but her father, L.W. McCune, absolutely forbid it. Her salary of fifteen dollars a month was hardly enough to justify that kind of unladylike behavior, he said.

Because of the dispute, a lawsuit was filed in district court. In the meantime library patrons were able to use the new facility only on a limited basis. A library employee was permitted to sit at her desk, showing possession, but patrons could not enter. Books were passed to them and they were permitted to return books from the outside. The issue eventually was resolved when the Oklahoma

Supreme Court ruled the mayor was wrong, and the library settled into a more peaceful routine.

No one ever questioned the motives of Mayor Lobsitz. He was a dedicated Perry builder, but his point of view differed from those intent upon carrying out the wishes of the philanthropist who made the project possible. Once the court ruling was made, both sides called a truce and got on with the work of improving and developing this city.

Irene McCune, meanwhile, had taken a job teaching school in Red Rock. Throughout her long life in Perry, she maintained an active interest in the Carnegie Library. Likewise, Mr. Lobsitz was supportive of the library after the initial disagreement was cleared up. He had hoped the building could serve several purposes.

Mrs. M.A. Lucy, a library board member, succeeded Miss Mc-Cune as librarian in 1911. Mrs. Lucy reported in a 1910 Perry newspaper article that the library had 1,838 volumes, with 200 more soon to be added. The number was to be evenly divided between juvenile and general fiction. Mrs. Lucy added these comments:

"Naming the many improvements to Perry in the last few years, there are none of more importance than the library building. For in this building will be found the boys and girls of this little city reading and selecting books for home reading. Who can tell what the influences and ambitions for the future may be from the cultivation of the reading habit. If we shall make better citizens, no cost is too great. The future welfare of our commonwealth depends upon the fostering of our public schools and library, for both reach the public at large."

Her remarks are completely relevant to this day as supporters seek to expand and enhance the library.

Mr. Carnegie donated some $40 million for 1,679 libraries in American towns and cities. Oklahoma received nearly $500,000, ranging from $60,000 in Oklahoma City to $6,500 in Ponca City. Many Carnegie libraries have been destroyed and others are no longer in use. El Reno, which received its grant in 1904, and Perry have the oldest libraries still filling that role in Oklahoma.

Rather than attempt to replace its beautiful Carnegie Library with a new building, present-day supporters have chosen to perpetuate and broaden it through the current renovation project. A local anonymous benefactor has agreed to provide a large matching grant with a generosity much like that of the original Carnegie funding.

Mr. Carnegie requested that his libraries be strong and lasting. The one he endowed in Perry has achieved those two goals, and with the forthcoming renovation it will be of even greater value to the community for many years to come.

# 10

# $C$HURCHES, SCHOOLS, HOMES

Early-day Noble County residents kept their priorities in order. When they set about the task of establishing communities, their farms and businesses came first so that they could earn a living, but along with that came the elements of civilization and a social order: Churches to nourish the spiritual hunger, schools to educate the children, and homes to shelter the family.

Schools were organized within the first six weeks after the run. Lack of room and money made it difficult to provide for the education of the large number of children here at that time, so school was held in all kinds of places—dugouts, sheds, shanties and tents, as well as rented business buildings and churches.

Administrators gave teachers considerable latitude during the first few years after the 1893 opening. At Billings, Miss Carr dismissed the primary grades for a week in May 1901 so that she could go to Woodward and maintain residence on her claim. It was part of the government requirements imposed upon those who made the run.

Teachers were paid by popular subscription or by attendance fees. Mrs. M.W. McKinney started the first subscription school in Perry about October 1, 1893. Her husband was among those who made the run but failed to get a townsite lot at the opening. Mrs. McKinney came here to join him from Stillwater, where her parents were living. She solicited students for her school at every encampment where she saw a group of children. In a short time she had enrolled fifteen pupils.

She rented a small one-room frame building at the corner of Eighth and B Streets for six dollars per month. The McKinneys and their infant child also lived in this room. The school remained in session only until December that first year. Soon after, public schools began opening and subscription schools were no longer needed. The subscription school was the last teaching experience for Mrs. McKinney.

The first year, terms were from two to four months, and teachers were paid from $20 to $30 per month.

During the summer of 1894 bonds totaling $20,260 were issued for the construction of a high school and two ward buildings in Perry. Thus, the Blaine and Holmes buildings became the first Perry classroom buildings constructed. The Blaine building, in south Perry, was a separate school for Negroes until court-ordered integration in the mid-1950s, but remnants of the old structure still stand. It has not been used as a school for many years. The Holmes building in east Perry was destroyed by fire in November 1897.

Central High School, a three-story native stone building, was built in 1894, replacing a thirty- by sixty-foot wooden structure. Both were in the same block where the present Perry High School campus is located, on Ninth Street between E and F Streets. The cornerstone for Central was laid October 16, 1894, in ceremonies described by Judge E.W. Jones as "ostentatious." The Masonic Lodge was in charge, and the main address was delivered by Henry S. Johnston, a twenty-three-year-old Perry attorney who would be elected governor of Oklahoma in 1926.

The high school principal received a salary of $70 per month, while teachers were paid from $45 to $60 per month.

The first Perry school census was taken on May 30, 1895, showing 411 white girls and 388 white boys along with fifty-seven black girls and forty-eight black boys, for a grand total school population of 904.

As required by Oklahoma law, separate schools for blacks were built in rural areas, as well as in Perry. An example was Dunbar school, located in Walnut Township. A small cemetery for Negroes was in the same area. Walnut Township, so named because of the timber it contained, was part of Payne County from September 16, 1893, until statehood in 1907, when land records were transferred to Noble County.

By October 1902, Perry schools were crowded and badly in need of more room. Another school building costing $30,000 was added in 1911 in northwest Perry, where the present elementary classrooms are located. Central High School was replaced in 1924 by an $80,000 building on the same site, and in 1928 bonds totaling

$47,000 were approved for an addition to that building, including a gymnasium and auditorium.

The present high school building was erected in the 1960s, a few years after construction of the nearby junior high building. An auditorium and fieldhouse have since been added. The elementary school campus also has had numerous building additions and replacements through the years. Fire destroyed a WPA-era classroom building there in the late 1960s just before the fall term was to begin. Churches and other public buildings were used until a new building could be constructed.

In 1912, County Superintendent R.R. Talley reported that the county had seventy-six school districts with 4,200 school children and 116 teachers, exclusive of Perry. High schools were located in four of the districts: Perry, Billings, Red Rock and Morrison.

The total number of children in the county between the ages of six and twenty-one was reported at 5,066 that year. School houses of the county were valued at $117,725. Total receipts for all districts in 1911 amounted to $76,444.34, while expenditures came to $63,051.67.

Superintendent Talley reported that of the teachers in the county, twenty were male and ninety-six female. The average salary paid the district teachers was $55 per month, but he did not compare the amounts paid to men vs. women as might be expected today. The average school year was "about six and a half months" in 1912.

### THE EARLY-DAY CHURCHES

The Cherokee Strip was fertile ground for Christian missionaries of the day. Several of them arrived with the settlers and at least one, Rev. Simon Peter Meyers, a Presbyterian, staked a claim in the run.

On Sunday, September 17, the day after the run, Mr. Meyers conducted the first worship service held in Perry, preaching in an unfinished hardware store on the north side of the square.He also had been a minister in Stillwater, and his daughter played the reed organ. It was said that Indians of the nearby Iowa tribe frequently attended Sunday services just to enjoy her music. They would file out of the church following the musical portion, when the sermon began, but would return for the closing exercises.

Beer kegs and boards seated Mr. Meyers' congregation for the first two Sundays. He next moved to a grocery store on the west side of the square for some four weeks. By then the flock had raised the price of a tent which was erected at the corner of Eighth and E Streets, where the First Presbyterian Church now stands.

Another Stillwater minister, Rev. D.J.M. Wood, a Civil War veteran, arrived in Perry to preach to the Methodists. Some of their first services were held in a business building at the corner of Seventh and B Streets. Rev. Thomas Wolcott also was here for the Methodists.

The Methodists, after using several temporary store room locations, erected a small frame edifice on the northeast corner of Tenth and E Streets. In 1901 they moved to a frame building at Seventh and E Streets, the present location. A brick building was constructed there in 1930, and it was replaced by a new church in the 1980s.

On October 8, 1893, the first Baptist meeting was held in the Banks & Wade Furniture Store building on the east side of the square between C and D Streets. Rev. J.M. Berry of Stillwater and Rev. T.R. Bozeman of Texas each gave a discourse.

The following week, the group decided to organize a church as soon as enough letters of faith could be procured. Rev. Berry moderated a business meeting the following Wednesday night during which John E. Shanafelt was elected the first clerk. Ten charter members signed the roll on December 17 following services in the district courtroom.

The Baptists built their first church at the corner of Seventh and F Streets, where their present church is located, dedicating the new building on September 2, 1894. A special offering at services that day cleared away the congregation's last $261 of indebtedness on the new church.

E.F. Boggess, a representative of the Christian Church extension board, made the run into Perry from the south border on September 16, 1893. As a site for the prospective First Christian Church, he staked a claim on the southeast corner of Ninth and E Streets, where the junior high school now stands. Because the lot was outside the town proper, and part of the homestead claimed by another party was contested, Mr. Boggess was unable to prove up on the lot and another site was chosen a year later.

However, the congregation he gathered met all that fall at the site which he had claimed. Records do not show that a service was held on Sunday, September 17, the day after the run, but on the following Sunday Mr. Boggess was ready with a tent and his equipment. A Sunday school also was started with Dick T. Morgan, an attorney who later became a congressman, as superintendent.

The tent served until cold weather arrived. Services then were held in Smith's hall and Mr. Morgan's office on West D Street. The church organization was perfected on October 22, 1893. Rev. Powers was the first minister and received $25 per month.

On May 14, 1894, a building committee was named to build "a church house." The building was not to cost over $1,500, and the lot previously selected was at the corner of Eighth and F Streets. The foundation was completed in July 1894. Brother Buzzard, designated "boss carpenter," was to receive two dollars a day providing he would donate three-eighths of that amount to the church. The congregation's frame church was a Perry landmark until 1952, when the present brick edifice at Seventh and Holly Streets was constructed. The frame church then became the new home of the Nazarene congregation, which had been worshiping in a small frame building one block north of there. The Nazarene Church was organized here in February 1922.

In more recent years the Nazarenes have built a brick church at the corner of Ninth and Jackson Streets. The old building at Eighth and Fir gave way to business development in the late 1950s.

The Perry Seventh-Day Adventist Church, now located at Seventh and G Streets, was organized in Perry around 1899, but records of the time are scarce. James Klostermyer, building contractor and operator of the Perry Planing Mill, was lay preacher and a leader in the church for many years.

Services in the early days were held upstairs in the Christoph and Newton building at the southwest corner of the square. Later a frame church was built at Thirteenth and F Streets. After an evangelistic meeting in 1921, the congregation added so many converts that more room was needed. They sold the building on F Street and purchased the old Southern Methodist church at the site of their present church. The present brick building was completed in 1931. A church school for children of the first eight grades was maintained for several years.

A Congregational Church was established near the C Street bridge over Cow Creek in east Perry in the early days. It later became a creamery and eventually was demolished. The Christian Science Church had a small congregation here at the corner of Seventh and D Streets for several years. Some other denominations also arrived and departed during the first few years.

Although several Lutheran families came here at the opening of the Cherokee Strip in 1893, formal organization of Christ Lutheran Church in Perry was delayed until 1900. During the interim, there were two Lutheran missions in the county. One was twelve miles south of Perry, known as Marena, and another six miles east of Perry known as Richburg. These were served by Pastor Julius Huchthausen. Visiting pastors and missionaries led the worshipers in Orlando, Perry, Morrison and other towns of the immediate area.

Since Perry was rapidly becoming a promising city, Pastor Huchthausen was anxious to begin work here. On December 9, 1900, several Lutheran families met in the Free Methodist Church at Seventh and G Streets for the first in a series of services. Pastor Huchthausen was in charge. This led to organization of Christ Lutheran on November 10, 1901, with eleven charter members. The attendance was so encouraging, Pastor Huchthausen immediately moved here. He also continued to serve the Orlando Lutheran church.

The first church was built on the northeast corner of Seventh and Maple Streets, and was dedicated in April 1905. It served the church for forty-five years, surviving a tornado in 1917 and lightning strikes in 1920 and 1943.

Christ Lutheran School was opened immediately after the first worship service, with Pastor Huchthausen as instructor. A hall was rented, and twelve children attended the first day. They were asked to bring two dollars each for their new desks.

In 1907 the church became affiliated with what is now known as the Lutheran Church Missouri Synod, and that relationship continues today. The present church building, an imposing structure of traditional architectural style faced with Silverdale limestone, was dedicated on February 5, 1950. It is located across the street west from where the old church stood. The old church served as a parish hall until 1957, when it was demolished to make way for a new brick school building. The school now offers classes in kindergarten through the sixth grade.

Zion Lutheran Church, five miles east of Perry, was officially organized in 1897 when the Ludwig Ritthaler family donated two acres in a corner of their homestead as a building site. Prior to that, the worshipers had met in various homes. Members provided volunteer labor and the church was built in about one year.

The congregation shared Missouri Synod pastors with other small churches of the area for the first several months. After a split in the congregation developed between 1901 and 1905, Zion church members affiliated with the German Nebraska Synod, which has since evolved into the Lutheran Church in America. From that time until 1960, Zion shared ministers with a sister congregation, Salem, in Stillwater.

The rural Perry church is now recognized as the oldest Oklahoma congregation of the Lutheran Church in America.

The original Zion church was destroyed by a tornado and was replaced in 1917 by a new building. Services were conducted in the German tradition and language for several years. After the arrival of Pastor Edward J. Amend to serve Zion and Salem in 1945, the Perry area congregation began looking to a more modern facility in a more accessible location.

Mr. and Mrs. A.A. Kemnitz donated two acres of their farm, five miles east of Perry on U.S. 64. One year later, the old church building was razed and the lumber moved to the new site. Pastor Amend designed the church and volunteer labor again was used for construction. The congregation began making plans for their own minister in the late 1950s, and in 1960 Rev. David Gieschen was called as Zion's first full-time pastor.

The first Catholic mass was said a few weeks after the opening in a room at the rear of Conrad J. Lindeman's grocery store on the corner of Seventh and D Streets. The priest was Rev. A. Borremans, newly arrived in the U.S. from Belgium. He was unfamiliar with the English language and Western ways, but he succeeded in organizing ninety Catholic families into a "station"—a congregation without a church.

Services were held in various locations until one of the Catholic pioneers, John E. Coyle, offered his large barn as a place of worship. The barn had been used by Mr. Coyle's family for a dwelling while they awaited completion of their home on the corner of Ninth and C Streets. The barn was converted into a church, and mass was celebrated there.

In January 1894, Mr. Coyle deeded the lot with the barn and two adjoining lots to the church. The foundation for a new church building was laid at the end of February, and the structure was completed in August of that year. Volunteers from the congregation contributed considerable labor, working in shifts during the building process.

St. Rose of Lima Church was dedicated on August 26, 1894, just eleven months after the founding of the town. The cost amounted to $1,211. The name of the church, chosen by members of the Altar Society, honors the first canonized saint of America, St. Rose of Lima, Peru.

That building served the congregation until 1923, when the present stately brick edifice was built at a cost of $70,000. Its soaring steeple and bell tower have been prominent on the Perry landscape since then.

A greatly beloved priest, Rev. Willebrord Voogden, took over the St. Rose mission on January 1, 1895, and remained here for thirty-five years. Father Willebrord was a native of Holland. He had served as a missionary in India before coming to this area of the U.S. in 1889, and he had been assigned to five territorial missions prior to becoming the first resident pastor at St. Rose.

St. Joseph's Academy, a full twelve-year school plus "postgraduate" courses, opened for its first term in September 1900. It was a frame two-story building, sixty-four by forty feet, with four classrooms on the south side, a private chapel on the second floor and living quarters for the teaching nuns on the north side. From start to finish, work on the building was completed in two months.

The academy provided an education for many Perry area students, Catholic and non-Catholic. Business courses were offered in addition to traditional studies, but perhaps the outstanding curriculum was in vocal and instrumental music.

The high school was closed in 1935 because of declining enrollment, and the grade school was discontinued in 1968. The old frame building had been replaced by a one-story brick structure, and a parish hall was added to it to provide a meeting place for church and community functions. Property for Mt. Carmel, the Catholic cemetery on the city's south side, was purchased for $200 from Frank Lugert in 1898.

One of the first black congregations in Perry was the Mt. Olive African Methodist Episcopal Church, organized in 1902 at a location in the northwest corner of Ninth and H Streets. A.W. Washington was the founding pastor and remained here until 1906. Members decided to move the church to the present location, 520 Grove Street, in 1909. Several ministers have led the worshipers, but there have been periods when Mt. Olive was without a pastor for as long as two years. Church stewards filled in on such occasions.

The Green Hill Baptist Church also served the black community for a time. Their edifice was at 416 J Street, and Sandy Washington was an early-day pastor.

### WOMEN'S CLUBS FORMED

Women of the community banded together in federated clubs not long after the opening. One of the first was the Ladies Tuesday Afternoon Club, organized on December 4, 1894, in the home of Mrs. J.H. Bullen, 707 G Street. Mrs. L.A. Hudson, whose husband was an attorney, was the first president. Thirteen charter members attended the organizational meeting.

The club has a record of continuous service since then. It became federated in 1898, and now it is one of the oldest federated women's clubs in Oklahoma. Through the years members have promoted many worthwhile community projects. The LTAC was among the first to provide support for the reading room established in 1902 by the Women's Christian Temperance Union. This later became the Perry Carnegie Library.

The club also promoted lyceums and Chautauqua courses, made bandages and gowns for Spanish-American War soldiers in 1898, and petitioned the city council to provide more sidewalks and better crossings at intersections.

Likewise, the Perry Progress Club has an unbroken record of existence since its founding on November 9, 1899. It was federated in May of the following year. Mrs. L.F. Jones was the club's first president. The Progress Club has joined wholeheartedly in efforts to improve the community and its members.

The Carnegie Library is the principal beneficiary of the club's annual service project. Each spring during National Library Week, the Progress Club sponsors a coffee at the library to raise funds for additional books which could not otherwise be purchased. Hundreds of dollars have been raised since this event was started in 1933.

The Perry Study Club was organized in September 1903 and federated in 1912. The original name was the Perry Culture Club, and it was organized for Bible study. The first meeting was at the home of the president, Mrs. M.W. McKinney, 815 Seventh Street. Her husband was a lumberman.

The Study Club's outstanding annual project is a style show. Proceeds are dedicated to community needs and many worthwhile efforts have been bolstered by this means.

### SOME EARLY FINE HOMES

Substantial homes of style and quality began appearing in Perry during the first few years after the run. Two of the most notable were the residences of Mr. and Mrs. Fred G. Moore and Mr. and Mrs. H.A. McCandless on Eighth Street between Ivanhoe and Jackson.

The Moores owned the entire east half of the block and built a sturdy two-story brick home on the south corner. When Mr. Mc-Candless, Mrs. Moore's brother, was about to be married, he purchased the north half as a building site for his home.

The Moores and Mr. McCandless came to Perry from Kansas to establish the Exchange Bank on February 26, 1896. Mr. McCandless later became president of the Oklahoma Bankers Association. Mr. Moore was president of the local bank until 1927, with his brother-in-law as cashier and principal associate during most of that time.

The McCandless home, a two-story frame structure, was built in 1900 with George Byers as contractor. The cost was $3,600. Cypress wood was used, and the brick and mortar foundation walls in the basement are three feet thick. Cypress also was used throughout the interior for trim. The home has been well maintained through the years. In 1951, it was purchased by Dr. and Mrs. Delmar C. Hoot, and Mrs. Hoot still resides there. Her husband died in recent years. Mr. and Mrs. Bert Sparks now own the former Fred Moore home.

Because the Moores and the McCandlesses were for some time the only occupants of the half-block where their elegant homes were located, it was known as "Bankers' Row." Robert McCandless, a son, described the area years later in a letter to Susan Bieberdorf, who was preparing a research paper on the home:

"There was a driveway between the two houses in a semi-circle...and there were beautiful cannas all around the driveway. In the middle between the houses were lots of fruit trees—cherries and peaches."

Mr. McCandless provided a sketch showing two barns, or stables, at the far bend of the driveway, one for each home. A fifty-foot water standpipe tank and windmill also were at the rear of the McCandless home, and each of the two residences had a stone hitching post which can still be seen today.

Two other homes have been built between the original Moore and McCandless homes, but one can picture the half-block as it must have appeared in the early days of this century, with the graceful, flower-lined carriage drive arching between two of the city's finest residences. It was a time of gracious living for some of the pioneer families of this community.

ᕃᕚ

On the corner across the street north from the McCandless home, another Perry banker, John A. Hansen, built a rambling two-story frame residence for his family in 1902. Mr. Hansen was with the Bank of Commerce, located on the northwest corner of the square. His home is now owned by Dr. and Mrs. Edwin Fair. Its many features included leaded glass windows and a water tank on an upper floor filled by a windmill on a well in the backyard.

The W.C. Hartman home at 826 Delaware Street was built on the site of a dugout that was used as a home before the opening of the Cherokee Strip, according to research by members of the Ladies Tuesday Afternoon Club for an historical homes tour of the city. The original home contained a fireplace which was used for cooking and heating, and the fireplace is still in the basement of the present structure. It was a popular rooming and boarding house when owned by the Burlingame family in the early days. Later owners were the Alfred Van Pelts and the John R. Baileys.

One block south was another large rooming house, built by a Mr. Shockley, who was described as "a man of the law." His son, an architect in Kansas City, drew up the plans and had all of the wood precut, assembled in sections and shipped to Perry. Thus, we were introduced to prefabricated housing.

Solid oak was used throughout. The house has fifteen rooms, including five bedrooms upstairs. The furnace in the basement would burn wood, coal or gas. A large brick water tower was in the backyard. An above-ground cistern stored rain water, and beneath it was a well. The Eisenhauer family purchased the home in 1916 and lived there many years. It is now the home of Mr. and Mrs. David Malget.

Mr. and Mrs. Ed J. Coyle built another large, two-story frame house at 411 Eleventh Street in 1902. A professional builder from Kansas was imported for the construction. Mr. Coyle operated a grocery store and meat market in the very early days, but later was in the grain and cotton business here. This is one of the many older homes of the city which have been maintained in excellent condition. Mr. and Mrs. Everett Chaffin bought it in more recent years and reared their four sons there.

C.W. Ransom, an attorney, built his family home at 1013 Elm Street before 1900. The generously proportioned front porch once had rounded corners, but they were later squared off. The H.E. St.Clairs bought the house after the Ransoms, then the G.C. Wollard family lived there many years. Mr. Wollard, a grocer and rural mail carrier, served on the state Board of Affairs during the administration of Gov. Henry S. Johnston.

George Todd was a member of the Perry townsite board. He built a large two-story frame house at 721 Eighth Street before 1900. Later he built the Ponca City refinery, which eventually was sold to E.W. Marland, founder of the present-day Conoco Oil Co. The B.J. Woodruff family owned the house for many years, during which it was enlarged and remodeled. The old stone fence around the front and north side is a part of the earliest history of the house. Sam Ebersole, grandson of the Woodruffs, now lives there with his family.

At the northwest corner of Eighth and Holly, across the street from the former Woodruff home, is a classic example of the type of architecture favored in the early 1900s. The two-story frame dwelling was built by David McKinstry, owner of the Perry Milling Co., where "Pride of Perry" flour was milled. Later the home was owned by Judge William M. Bowles. It is now the residence of Mr. and Mrs. Bill Hodge. A one-time carriage house at the rear of the home now serves as a spacious garage and storage building. It has an opening at the top for a hay loft.

These are just a few of the many interesting homes built by some of the founders of Perry, and still existing today for us to enjoy. They provide us with a visual link to the past.

# 11

# $M$R. HOVEY AND SOME OTHERS

He was enigmatic, even a bit frightening, to some. His quiet demeanor was part of the aura of mystery that seemed to hover over him. Oliver Henry Hovey intrigued people.

Mr. Hovey, and that is how almost everyone addressed him, drove into Perry in 1906 when he was fifty-seven years old. He arrived in the first automobile seen in this young city and of course it caused quite a stir.

Mr. Hovey was a man of many talents—a traveling salesman, printer, musician, photographer and, purportedly, an engineer. In brief, he was an interesting character, and probably a very lonely man. He lived to a ripe old age in Perry with no immediate family or close friends that anyone knew of. He went to work in the printing business here and later acquired a job shop of his own near the west end of the 700 block on C Street, about a block off the southwest corner of the square.

The first thing people noticed about Mr. Hovey was his beard. It covered his face and was long and white, like Santa's, but the resemblance ended there. He was perhaps five feet, five inches tall and very slender. His usual attire was a flat-top black leather cap, black suit and white shirt. It was hard to tell if he wore a necktie because his beard was so long.

He lived alone, almost reclusively, in the small, single-story frame building where his print shop was located. The structure sat back about twenty-five feet from the street, and the front porch was overgrown with ivy-like vines and other vegetation. A small pool for tropical fish was at the front of the building, complete with lily pads, frogs, turtles and very probably some other reptilians. Youngsters strolling by could easily fantasize it as a sinister, mist-shrouded area infested by hungry, man-eating mutants. These existed only in their minds.

A narrow pathway meandered past this daunting region onto the front porch, where a small aviary with a few exotic birds and an occasional caged (and very tame) animal were sheltered by the dense growth.

In the front room was a typically untidy small print shop containing a variety of handset typefaces and a sturdy little press. He resided in the midst of this.

Mr. Hovey made his living as a job printer, but after his death at the age of ninety-one in 1940 evidence was found indicating that he also was the purveyor, if not the author, of some spicy literature. It would be held as exceedingly tame by today's standards, but it was slightly sensational for that day.

Occasionally he printed *The Little Perry News,* a gossip sheet that was published "whenever the circumstances seemed to demand it." It was distributed from the back door of the Post Office and had the additional label of "First Class Male News."

Mr. Hovey was an accomplished organist and frequently accompanied the St. Rose of Lima Catholic Church choir at Christmas mass. He did not have a wife during the thirty-four years he spent in Perry, but he may have been a widower. A daughter, Nellie M. Hovey of Los Angeles, survived him, as did a brother, Charles, of Mantisque, Michigan. Mr. Hovey was a native of Marcellus, New York, where he was born on January 23, 1849.

The automobile that brought him to Perry was a one-cylinder Oldsmobile with bicycle tires inflated by hand pump and no inner tubes. In those days all cars were open and windshields were optional accessories.

He was able to make about eighteen miles an hour at top speed. Mr. Hovey put on some wonderful exhibitions on the dirt streets around the square, according to Judge E.W. Jones in his "Early Day History of Perry," and was often stopped by Police Chief Boright for engaging in dangerous and reckless driving.

The next car brought to Perry was a Ford, purchased by early-day pharmacist Fred W. Beers in 1907 from a dealer in Red Rock. Somebody suggested an automobile race around the courthouse square featuring Mr. Hovey and Mr. Beers for the September 16th Cherokee Strip celebration in 1907. The two men, then owners of the only cars in town, readily agreed. Unfortunately, Mr. Hovey's Oldsmobile broke down a few days before the race and was out of commission, so a dare-devil driver was imported from Oklahoma

City to compete with the twenty-four-year-old Perry druggist in his Ford.

The visitor and Mr. Beers started around the square at the crack of a gun. Judge Jones wrote this account of the race:

"A speed of possibly eight miles an hour was attained, but neither finished the lap. Beers skidded around a corner against the hitch rack after negotiating half the distance and the dare-devil quit, exhausted, coming west up the hill on the north side. For the effort, however, the purse of twenty dollars was divided and the race called a draw."

In later years Mr. Hovey did not drive a car and he was a familiar figure strolling about town. His home/shop was only a few feet from the square, where all the necessities of life—food, medication, apparel—could be obtained. A car nearly did him in on one occasion, however, when he was eighty-one years old. The incident was reported in the March 11, 1930, edition of *the Perry Daily Journal* this way:

"O.H. Hovey was considerably bruised Monday evening when his foot was caught in the rear bumper of a car at the southwest corner of the square and he was pulled for about a block east on Cedar Street (the south side of the square) before the driver of the machine was told of the predicament.

"(Mr. Hovey) was too close to the machine when the car was stopped, and is himself unable to account for the accident other than that his foot was caught and he was unable to release himself. Although he called to the driver, he was not heard and the machine was not stopped until somebody jumped on the running board. Hovey stated that the driver, who was a woman, was in no way to blame, and outside of the bruises and a lacerated hand, was feeling quite well Tuesday morning."

The old gentleman survived that ordeal and continued to run his print shop until a more serious accident shortly before noon on November 26, 1938, when fire damaged the small building where he lived and worked. The rear roof of the house caught fire for some unexplained reason. Mr. Hovey was injured, but fortunately the fire department was located just across the alley and rescuers carried him from the flames and smoke.

Firemen succeeded in checking the blaze before it could spread throughout the building. It was the third fire there within a span of only a few years.

Mr. Hovey's hands, face and feet were burned, and he was taken to Dr. C.H. Cooke's Perry General Hospital on Sixth Street for treatment. At first it appeared he would have a complete recovery, but he spent the rest of his life in a hospital bed. On April 15, 1940, he died there of heart failure, still suffering from complications caused by burns sustained in the fire. Mr. Hovey was ninety-one years old.

### MECHANICS SCARCE

Those who owned the first automobiles in Perry needed to be mechanically adept. For the most part they had to care for their vehicles unassisted. The contraptions were new creations. You could take a lame horse to the blacksmith or the veterinarian. It was not so easy dealing with coughing, sputtering, contrary gasoline buggies and flat tires.

The first automobile mechanics to open a shop in Perry were Charley Collins and Ray Jennes. They came in June 1909 to operate a garage in the Smyser building on South Seventh Street. Jennes stayed for the year and then departed. In a short time, Collins quit auto work and went into the mercantile business. He stayed in Perry many years.

Collins and Jennes drove a two-cylinder Jackson automobile. They were dealers for the Sterling, Pullman, Jackson and Brush autos, some of the very early brands on the market.

After the first two cars made their appearance in Perry, others soon arrived. Dr. Frank L. Keeler had a one-cylinder gas wagon, then Col. John Cordell was about next on the list (according to Judge Jones) with "a big family car that was able to grunt its way around the square, and with a little manpower assistance get back home."

It was customary, and necessary, for many people buying a car in those days to hire a full-time mechanic to ride with them each time they left home. There were few gas stations and fewer people who knew how to repair a breakdown.

Other pioneer Perry autoists included the Catholic priest, Rev. Willebrord Voogden; attorney H.A. Smith and Jack Stone of Everybody's Store. A Perry newspaper of the period reported that Lester Gum of this city gathered up three friends from Billings in his Ramble automobile and took them on a 180-mile tour of neighboring towns at a rate of thirty miles per hour, using eight gallons of gasoline.

At about the same time, the paper stated, Elmer Shank drove his automobile (brand not given) from Ann Arbor, Michigan, to Perry, a distance of 1,400 miles, in eleven days at an expense of one cent per mile.

In 1931, Judge Jones noted that Noble County had more than 4,000 automobiles registered, more than one to a family, and 500 trucks.

"Livery stables and blacksmith shops have given way to garages and feed stores to filling stations," he wrote, "with thousands of dollars the monthly payroll of mechanics and filling station employees."

### EARLY-DAY PHARMACISTS

E.E. Howendobler came to Perry from Wichita shortly after the run to open this city's first drug store. It was located at the east end of the south side of the square, next to the corner lot. He also operated a school of pharmacy here, as he had in Wichita.

Dr. W.D. Brengle, a pioneer Perry physician, was an auxiliary of the Howendobler forces. In the early days he traveled about the county with a highly decorated show wagon, drawn by four to six white ponies. With liveried black drivers cracking the whip, the colorful troupe covered this area advertising the doctor's wonderful catarrh cure. Angus Miller acted as orator, extolling the merits of the elixir in each town visited.

In addition to Mr. Howendobler's firm, drug stores in Perry in the first year after the run included Garnet and English on the west side of the square and Whitney on the east side.

In 1895 Mr. Howendobler sent for Fred W. Beers, one of the young graduates of his previous school in Wichita, to join him here as a pharmacist. Fred was twenty-two years old when he moved down from Kansas. Although he missed the run by two years, he arrived here during a time that was still charged with excitement, the very early stages of growth and development in the community.

By 1903 the young druggist was ready to open his own store. His first location was on the west side of the square, where the Masonic Temple later was built. A spectacular fire destroyed that frame building one night in 1908, but while the embers were still glowing Mr. Beers boarded a train for Kansas City, Missouri, to purchase stock and fixtures for a new store on the north side of the square. This became the City Drug Store, an institution in the city until it was closed at the end of 1940.

Mr. Beers died in 1931, but his wife, Ivy, kept the business operating until it fell prey to the Great Depression. She was assisted most of that time by a nephew, also named Fred W. Beers, who came here from Kansas City to manage the business founded by his namesake.

Ivy Beers' parents were Alfred and Margaret Bucklin. The Bucklin family, including another daughter, Essie, came to Perry February 2, 1902, from Mexico, Missouri, to operate a chili parlor on the north side of the square. The Bucklins' secret chili recipe —lost long ago—was greatly admired by their customers.

Mr. Howendobler served on the city council and the Perry school board. He also was an ardent sportsman and was known as a city builder. He eventually sold his interests here and moved to Tulsa, where he operated a small chain of stores until his death in 1933. Other early-day Perry druggists included Ralph Foster Sr., whose Foster Corner Drug is still located on the east side of the square, owned by Mr. and Mrs. Mike Shannon. Also, Everett Nelson had the Southside Pharmacy in the building now called City Hall. Some years later Charles G. Watson had the Brownie Drug on the west side of the square, and Herb Sanford operated a store just up the street from there at the present location of Chris Cockrum's Pharmacy.

Others have come and gone over the years, but Perry usually has had four or more drug stores, though not always located around the square. Both the Perry Pharmacy, operated by Dennis Thompson at 800 Fir Avenue, and Gene Breshears' Professional Discount Pharmacy at 1401 Fir can trace their genealogy to Monte Jones' Drug, which succeeded Brownie Drug in the mid-1940s.

# 12

# *T*HE FAMOUS STORE

The Famous Department Store was one of Perry's pioneer business institutions. For many years it was Noble County's largest family-owned firm.

James Lobsitz, who made the run on September 16, 1893, founded the Famous. However, the Gottlieb family headed the firm during its most illustrious era.

Mr. Lobsitz was forced to move his newly opened business off Government Acre, the courthouse park, a few weeks after the run. Along with several dozen other would-be merchants, he had been duped into believing that the block was open to settlers. It was not. It was set aside for the courthouse, Post Office and the Government Land Office.

When the order to move was finally enforced by troops, the unhappy merchants scrambled for good locations. Mr. Lobsitz found a spot about a half block south of the southwest corner of the square at 211 Seventh Street, where the Perry Steam Laundry later was located. His partner in the business was Hugh McCredie. Within a few weeks they moved to a small frame building on the south side of the square. Soon after, they realized still more space was needed and moved again, just one door west.

The firm prospered, and in 1898 it was again moved several feet west, this time into a spacious fifty-foot front, two-story brick building where it remained until closing some sixty years later.

Morris Gottlieb, a young Hungarian immigrant with experience in the mercantile business, joined the firm in 1901. Two years later a brother, Sam, came to work for the store in the shoe department. In 1906 another brother, Rudolph, took over the dry goods department. George Gottlieb, the fourth brother, was added to the firm in 1919 after having worked in Chicago and San Francisco.

Mr. Lobsitz headed the business until 1908 when a principal competitor, Knox & Stout Clothing Co., owned by John Knox and Joe Stout, purchased it. The Knox & Stout store was known as "The Clothiers." The founder of that firm was Bethuel Knox, a short, good-natured gentleman and the father of four sons: John, Allen, Philip and Charley.

Mr. Knox began in business here the first week with a push cart and a line of tinware on the south side of the square. He also was an auctioneer. Later he opened a small novelty store and there his sons obtained experience in the mercantile business.

After selling the Famous to Knox & Stout, Mr. Lobsitz entered the hardware business with his three sons, still on the south side of the square, and continued with that until his retirement in 1941.

Morris Gottlieb made the crossing from Europe to the U.S. in 1892, landing first at Hallettsville, Texas. He took a job in Pawnee, east of Perry, in 1901, and came here later that year as a clerk at the Famous. He rented a room at a boarding house on Delaware Street operated by Mrs. Minnie Keith Bailey. Other young bachelors rooming there at the time were attorney and later governor Henry S. Johnston, pioneer dentist Dr. F.C. Seids and R.R. Robinson, high school superintendent.

Morris, Sam and Rudolph Gottlieb gained full ownership of the Famous in 1914 and operated it as a corporation under the name of the Gottlieb Co. Morris was president, George (in later years) was vice president and Rudolph was secretary-treasurer.

Sam Gottlieb died in 1937 and the three surviving brothers continued the business until 1945, when they sold it to Rice-Stix Co. of St. Louis. A subsidiary, the Keller Co., then took it over. In the 1950s the firm was closed by the parent company. A few years later another department store opened in the same location, but shopping habits had changed and the new firm also was forced to give it up.

The Famous probably experienced its greatest period of popularity between 1920 and 1940. It was the anchor firm for the south side of the square and its clientele numbered shoppers from some of the larger cities in this area. The store's decor was quiet and dignified, featuring darkly stained wood trim on shelves and curving, glass-encased counters. It bespoke quality. Familiar brands were offered in lines of apparel and furnishings for the entire family. Large display windows at the front were brilliantly lighted at night, tastefully decorated and always alluring to passersby.

The store survived several disasters, besides the normal ebb and flow of the economy. A frozen water pipe burst one night in December 1902, causing damages estimated at $3,000. Repairs were made and new merchandise was quickly brought in. By 1906 the store was advertising "a square deal for a round dollar."

On July 26, 1931, the store's contents were destroyed by a night-time fire which also threatened the second-floor law offices occupied by former Governor Johnston. The Famous bounced back from each problem and its customers were loyal throughout the inconveniences.

In an editorial comment when the Gottliebs sold the firm in 1945, *the Perry Daily Journal* said the Famous "was recognized as the leading department store of Northern Oklahoma, if not, indeed, the entire state outside the two metropolitan centers."

Many local people were employed at the Famous through the years, and many of them made the store their career. Most were clerks or department supervisors, visible to customers, but two of the most loyal were hidden away in a small room at the back of the store—the alterations department. Mrs. Fannie Hunefelt and Mrs. Olinda Kelley served the trade from that room for many years and they were true artisans with scissors, a needle and thimble.

Some of the other long-time employees included H.A. (Lefty) Cleeton, who became store manager under the new owners, Mrs. Daisy Wylder, Mrs. Ruby Doyle, Mrs. Edna Zeig, Mrs. Edna Edmondson and Mrs. Agnes Tobin. There were many others.

Morris Gottlieb was a civic worker and leader in the classic sense. He was rather stout, with a shock of whitish hair, and a trace of European accent that lasted throughout his life. He was interested in world affairs, but baseball also was a passion. On more than one occasion he spearheaded fund drives to support the local semi-pro team, the Perry Merchants.

Morris also was a staunch member of the Perry Rotary Club, finding its emphasis on international service an outlet for his own concerns in that area. He worked hard for the Boy Scout program, Red Cross, United War Chest drives and the Chamber of Commerce.

In January 1923, he married Madge McCredie, the daughter of Hugh McCredie, James Lobsitz' partner in the original Famous.

Morris and Madge built a handsome two-story red brick home at 703 Jackson Street. They had one daughter, Ann, now of Oklahoma City. The Gottlieb home is now owned by Mr. and Mrs. Robert Bieberdorf.

After the brothers sold the Famous in 1945, Morris and George retired. Rudolph and his wife, Elsie, opened a smart women's ready-to-wear store, Gottlieb's Vogue, on the south side of the square, and operated it for a number of years. Rudolph and his wife, the former Elsie Strauss of Chicago, were married in 1916.

George, a lifelong bachelor, died September 25, 1957, after several months of failing health. A native of Hungary, as were all the brothers, he had lived in this country since 1902. George had no really close friends, but his customers knew him as an honest, friendly man. While serving them, he tried to help them make good, fashionable choices.

Morris died in May 1958. *The Perry Daily Journal* then reprinted an earlier editorial saluting him as "one of Perry's most illustrious citizens." The writer added, "...there are few projects in Perry in the last fifty years in which Morris has not been active. His efforts have shown up in a better community for us all, regardless of who received the credit."

Likewise, Rudolph gave his support to many community efforts through the years until his death in February 1975 at the age of eighty-eight. He and Elsie had sold the Vogue in 1959, and she passed away in 1961. They had two daughters, Edyth Tillman of Oklahoma City and Ethel Maurice Gershon of Stillwater. Rudolph spent his last few years assisting the Gershons in their women's apparel store, known as Bonney's.

A feature story in *the Stillwater NewsPress* in 1973 described Rudolph's joy and satisfaction at having the opportunity to spend sixty-six years in the merchandising business. He had supported the Perry Chamber of Commerce, Lions Club, Eastern Star and Masonic Lodge, and had been chairman of the annual Cherokee Strip Celebration several times.

With the death of Rudolph, the last of the Gottlieb brothers, an era came to an end in this community. Likewise, the loss of the Famous Department Store a few years earlier heralded the demise of a prosperous period in the retail community.

# *13*

# *T*HE CYCLONE OF 1912

Between five and six p.m. on Saturday, April 20, 1912, the Perry area was devastated by a powerful wind. Whether or not it was accompanied by the fearsome funnel of a tornado is not certain, but apparently it had all the other characteristics of that kind of storm. The weekly *Perry Republican* called it a cyclone.

Moving in the classic route usually associated with a tornado, the wind ripped through an area from ten miles southwest of Perry to seven miles northeast of the city. Like a tornado, it hopped back and forth from the earth and into the air, skipping some areas entirely only to land again and wipe out everything in its path. It was accompanied by a slight rainfall and hailstones the size of quail eggs.

Two children were killed and at least twenty other people were injured, some severely. Property loss was estimated at nearly half a million dollars.

The newspaper said the first report of the storm striking the ground was at the Johnson place, ten miles southwest of Perry. Mr. Johnson's home and barn were destroyed. Gary Briggs was badly injured, and he also lost a barn and all his out houses. The John Goright home was struck by lightning and burned to the ground.

The wind followed a course along Cow Creek into Perry. Apparently the storm cell divided and one then meandered along Black Bear Creek. North of Perry the newly formed storm wrecked the barn on Fred Gang's place along Black Bear, traveled on an easterly line to the Fairbanks place, which was wrecked, hit the M. Burke place and finally blew down the Bohemian Hall in that township.

Farm animals, including horses in stables, were killed. Other property damage was reported by Len Barnes, Frank Hejtmanek, Fred Shroeder, Davidson & Quinton, Dr. Doggett and Len Brown, a tenant on the Dingman place near Otoe switch, north of Perry. The Willow Creek School was completely destroyed.

Hardest hit of all, however, was the Will Gerdis home, six and a half miles northeast of Perry. Mr. Gerdis and his father had just returned from Perry. His wife and children were home when the grandfather went in to offer the youngsters some candy. The storm struck the house, totally shattering it. Marguerite Gerdis, three and a half years old, was killed instantly. Her brother, John, who was twelve years old, died of his injuries in a few hours. Mrs. Gerdis also was hurt, but not critically.

Mr. Gerdis, the children's father, had lived on the place three years, and each crop had been a failure. The previous year he lost a team of horses. The storm made his misfortune complete with the death of his children and the destruction of virtually all his worldly possession.

The Perry community immediately started a subscription to benefit the family, and it quickly was met with a willing response from neighbors and others.

Arriving in Perry from the southwest, the storm ripped through the brick Blaine school building as if it were a frail wooden structure, the newspaper reported. It had to be completely rebuilt.

The wind passed over the Frisco Railroad depot and left a mass of debris, including roofing, awnings, porches and telephone and electric lines along Seventh Street. The Farmers' Warehouse, a large galvanized iron building near the depot, was flattened. The Fire Proof Barn at the rear of the Knox & Eisenhauer Pool Room was demolished and its bricks and stonework were strewn along the alley.

The storm swerved east on B Street, where other businesses were unroofed or had siding damage. Two horses were found unharmed under the ruins of a building next to A.E. Smyser's warehouse. Houston Lumber Yard's sheds were destroyed and the roof on the Perry Mill elevator was blown off. Bullen Lumber Yard also was damaged, and going north on Sixth Street the front and roof of the Sunfield building and the Pressler Hotel were missing. The Cook Coal Yard lost all of its coal bins and nearly all its windows.

On the south side of the square, the two-story brick building owned by A. Wilcoxen lost the front and rear of the upper story and the entire roof. The roof and part of the front of the Knox &

Eisenhauer brick building also were gone. The paper said plate glass windows broke like egg shells while heavy iron awning posts and galvanized iron roofing were scattered throughout the business district.

The roof of the Woodruff building on the north side was torn away. The entire front of the Strebel building was demolished. The Gregoire & Houston building at the northeast corner of the square lost its south side. The roof of the Long-Bell Lumber Yard was scattered over the neighborhood, mingling with remains of the Springfield Camp Yard & Feed Barn.

Throughout the south half of the city hundreds of trees, stables, outhouses and other small buildings were blown away. The Presbyterian Church at Eighth and E Streets lost its cupola and chimneys. The smokestack, exhaust pipes and flues of the Miller Cotton Gin were ruined.

The Christensen Feed Yard & Junk Lot was turned topsy-turvy and the junk scattered to the four winds. The Tate buildings on the east side (including the Grand Opera House), the Palovik Grocery and Meshek's Jewelry lost their plate glass fronts. The fronts of the Taylor Transfer Barn and Hovey's Printing Office "embraced each other in the overhead flight," the newspaper account stated.

Electric service lines were a mass of tangles and the city was in darkness that evening, except around the square. Long distance telephone service was cut off. Thus, only meager news could be dispatched or received until later the following week.

Mrs. J.M. Bates operated a restaurant in the Acres building near the northeast corner of the square. She and four customers, who were eating chili, had a miraculous escape when the roof fell on them as the ends and sides were pulled away. A four-foot high icebox caught the falling roof and Mrs. Bates and the others escaped with only slight injuries. Joe Skalenda and Paul Tetik were two of the customers, but the others left without giving their names.

The two-story Kemnitz home southwest of the city was blown away. Will Strub lost his barn. A stranger who stopped in to get out of the storm was badly injured by a heavy timber which struck his back. Fred Schinerling's home, five miles southwest of town, was destroyed by fire after being wrecked by the windstorm. Carl O'Dell, about seventy, of east of Perry, lost his home and suffered a mashed shoulder plus internal injuries "that will probably prove fatal," the newspaper reported.

On the following Monday, the Perry city council held a special meeting to consider the emergency. Superintendent Cornelius estimated damage to the lighting system amounted to $700. The roof of the power house was blown away and lines throughout the town were twisted. Mr. Cornelius was instructed to proceed with repairs.

Fire Chief Brandon reported at least thirty buildings within the city fire limits were dangerous and should be condemned. The street commissioner was ordered to remove them if property owners had not done so within thirty days.

The school board also had a special meeting that night. Members instructed the building and grounds committee to contract for repairs on the old high school building. The county superintendent had charge of the Blaine building and was looking at the use of other buildings to complete the term.

The following Saturday, April 27, heavy rain began falling and continued through the night. A total of 7.03 inches was recorded, the heaviest single-day rainfall in the county's brief history. Houses unroofed by the wind suffered further loss, and the young growing corn in the lowlands was covered with silt, necessitating replanting.

Alfalfa on the Black Bear and Red Rock Creek bottoms was heavily damaged. Black Bear was registering two feet above its previous record mark near Sumner. The Frisco bridge on Cow Creek was washed out, leaving no tracks until the following Tuesday. The city's water works dam contained about thirty feet of water, enough to last the city another eighteen months without further rainfall.

Perry and Noble County felt the storm losses keenly, but were thankful they were not worse. Reports were being received from the Southwest part of the state showing even greater devastation. A cyclone there apparently caused twenty deaths in Kiowa and Jackson Counties, with property losses totaling more than a million dollars.

The howling winds of 1912 apparently were the most damaging ever to strike this immediate area. Residents then had no radio or television warnings and were caught completely unprepared. It was a critical and devastating blow, but the pioneer spirit was still vigorous in the community. They were reeling momentarily, but not knocked out by the forces of nature.

Mr. and Mrs. Carl Frederick Malzahn and their six surviving children came to Perry in 1902. Daughters in front row are Marie (left) and Grace. In back row, from left: Irene, Charles, Emily and Gus.

Charles and Bertha Malzahn in wedding portrait

Grand Opera House, shortly after it opened in 1901. The superstructure visible on roof was a fly loft where sets were hoisted and secured until needed on the theater's stage below.

Memorial Day patriotic program opened the Grand Opera House in 1901. Seats in horseshoe balcony and on main floor were filled. (*Cherokee Strip Museum, Oklahoma Historical Society.*)

Workmen laying foundation for the Grand Opera House (ca. 1900).

J.B. Tate, original owner
of Grand Opera House.

Buster Keaton, "the great stone face," came home to Perry in 1957 for the
world premiere of the movie based on his life. Many townfolk got to meet him.
Here he is with Mrs. Fred G. Beers and daughter, Kathleen (now Mrs. Ron
Lindsey of Leawood, Kansas), during a respite in the day's activities.

Miss Perry (Bettye Kaye Yahn)
was official hostess for movie
great Buster Keaton during the
three days he spent in
Oklahoma in 1957 for the
world premiere of the
Paramount movie telling his life
story. Bettye Kaye is now Mrs.
Gary Evans of Muskogee.

Two-story brick school building with basement gymnasium was at Thirteenth and Ivanhoe Streets. Originally a high school, it later became a grade school. (*Cherokee Strip Museum, Oklahoma Historical Society.*)

Central High School, this imposing structure, was the first high school built in Perry. It was on Ninth Street between E and F. The cornerstone was laid in October 1894. (*Cherokee Strip Museum, Oklahoma Historical Society.*)

O.H. Hovey brought the first automobile to Perry in 1906. (*Cherokee Strip Museum, Oklahoma Historical Society.*)

Pharmacist Fred W. Beers had the first Ford in Perry and raced it around the square for the 1907 Cherokee Strip celebration.

The Famous Department Store was one of Perry's first retail firms. It anchored the south side of the square and was located in this building, constructed in 1898.

Severe wind storm of 1912 wrecked many Perry businesses. This was the north side of the square in the aftermath. Nicewander building at right now houses KRAD-AM and KJFK-FM studios; Chamber of Commerce now occupies frontage where Barton's Book Store is shown. Next to it was Carl Strebel's Tailor Shop, now home of Shelter Insurance; and next door left was Alfred Bucklin's Chili Parlor & Notions Store, now occupied by Northern Oklahoma Butane Co.

East side of square's early businesses are seen in this 1902 photo, made during a
Cherokee Strip celebration. Streets were unpaved and sidewalks scarce. In
lower left, blurred by motion, is a horse-drawn parade float.

North side of square and beyond appear in this 1910 panoramic view. Old
wooden courthouse is in left foreground, surrounded by young elm trees.
(*Cherokee Strip Museum, Oklahoma Historical Society.*)

West side of square appeared in this 1912 postcard. Several wooden buildings remained, and the lot at the north end was vacant. (*Cherokee Strip Museum, Oklahoma Historical Society.*)

South side of square, at least its backside, appear in this photo shot from the roof of the Perry Mill. View is to the northwest. The Famous Store building is just left of center. (*Cherokee Strip Museum, Oklahoma Historical Society.*)

Birds-Eye View, Perry, Okla.

"Bird's eye view" of Perry is provided by this photo, possibly made about 1909 from roof of the Grand Opera House. View is to the northwest. Trees in courthouse park are maturing, streets and curbs are being built around the square, and the residential district is pushing to the northwest.

Two landmarks of the square's east side dominate this view, from a 1908 postcard. The First National Bank is at right, and the Grand Opera House is at left. (*Cherokee Strip Museum, Oklahoma Historical Society.*)

Native stone Post Office was built at northwest corner of the courthouse park shortly after the 1893 run. Mail was brought there from the Santa Fe and Frisco Railroad stations by contract carriers using the driveway at right. A patron's carriage is shown at the west entrance.

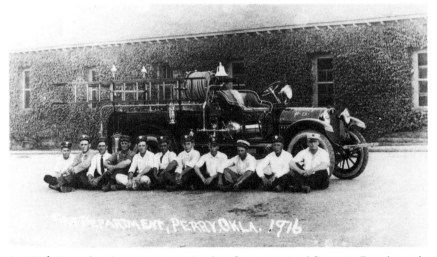

In 1916, Perry fire department received its first motorized fire unit. Regular and call firemen are shown with it on north side of the Post Office. (*Cherokee Strip Museum, Oklahoma Historical Society.*)

Cornerstone for the new Noble county courthouse was set in place in 1916 as dozens looked on. Attorney Henry S. Johnston spoke at the ceremony. (*Cherokee Strip Museum, Oklahoma Historical Society.*)

C.J. Lindeman Grocery was a pioneer Perry firm. It was first located on D Street just west of the square, but when this photo was made about 1917 it had been moved to the south side, near the Famous Store. George Lindeman, a son of the founder, is third from left.

# PART III: THE 1920s

# *L*IFE AFTER WORLD WAR I

In the 1920s, a horse-drawn wagon from the Perry Mill's ice manufacturing plant made daily deliveries to businesses and residences around town. Each home had a golden-oak ice box with cork insulation and a compartment on top big enough to store a one hundred-pound block of ice. The chill that circulated from there throughout the box provided cold storage for the family's perishables. When electric refrigerators became commonplace a few years later, the ice box vanished.

A wagon driver on one of these routes one summer was Norman Jones, son of Paul and Helen Jones. He was a high school student holding down a part-time job that required a great deal of brawn. The blocks of ice were weighty, slippery and clumsy to handle, even with a pair of tongs.

Paul Jones, Norman's father, was in the seed and produce business here. He bore a marked resemblance to President Woodrow Wilson. The family also included another son, Jimmy, the middle child, and a daughter, Pauline, the youngest. Helen Jones was from the Lobsitz family, which played a prominent part in the development of Perry.

The Jones home was a single-story frame dwelling on the northeast corner of Ninth and Jackson Streets, where the Church of the Nazarene now stands. The house had a rambling porch and the entire yard was shaded by a row of large red cedar trees in contrast to the Chinese elms more often seen around homes of that period. The Jones family left Perry in the early 1940s to operate an automotive supply business in Duncan. They were good citizens, reluctant to leave Perry but driven by economic necessity.

Norman's wagon was loaded up early each morning at the plant's ice dock, 614 Birch Street, just a short distance from the south side of the square. The Perry Mill, the city's major industry for years, was situated between Sixth and Brogan Streets and generally faced Birch, adjacent to where the Charles Machine Works, Inc., later built a facility which is still in use today. Appropriately, CMW in time took the Perry Mill's place as Perry's largest employer.

Glistening 300-pound blocks of ice were stacked inside the enclosed van to begin the day's deliveries. With only an ice pick, an experienced iceman could deftly quarter the big blocks, then subdivide them into whatever size was needed.

Customers were furnished with printed cards measuring about 18 inches square. These were hung in the kitchen window or on the back porch, someplace where the deliveryman could read them from the street. The cards were displayed diamond-shaped, with a bold number imprinted in each corner to tell the driver the size of the chunk to place in the ice box—twelve and a half, twenty-five, fifty or one hundred pounds.

The iceman wore a leather sheath on his back, fastened with a buckle in front and with straps crossing his chest like a Sam Browne belt, so he could sling a large block of ice over his shoulders for delivery from the wagon to the home. Sharp-tipped metal tongs were used to pick up and deposit the blocks. The ice looked crystal clear, except for a few striations or stress lines deep inside.

The rear opening of the ice wagon was covered only with a burlap flap. The frozen shards lying on a splintery wooden floor there in the cold, damp darkness were just waiting to be picked up by neighborhood kids who trailed along while deliveries were being made. On a hot summer day, nothing tasted better or cooled quite as much as a mouthful of pure Perry ice, and all icemen, including Norman Jones, were invariably friendly.

It was another of the great, free delights of the age.

"Pride of Perry Flour" was the Perry Mill's major product, but it also had this ice house which supplied virtually every family and business in the city in the decade of the 1920s and beyond. A number of colorful and interesting people were employed there.

Old Mr. Tuttle drove one of the plant's horse-drawn ice wagons for many years. At one point a younger driver was hired to assist him. The young man was assigned to ride with Mr. Tuttle for a few days to learn how things were done. He asked the old gentleman for instructions on handling the route, driving the team and learning where his customers lived.

"If you can read, that's all you need," Mr. Tuttle told him gently. "This team of horses will take you to the first customer's home and you look at the card in their window to see how much ice they want. You make the delivery and the team will meet you at the next house. Just go where the team takes you. These animals know the route."

All a driver had to do was give the team a "giddap" as they left the ice house. Horse sense took care of the rest.

It is said that Mr. Tuttle could chip out a cube of ice weighing exactly twenty-five or fifty pounds from a 300-pound block in a matter of seconds.

Some customers went directly to the ice house, rather than waiting for home delivery. They had to drive around the Perry Mill's landmark one hundred-foot tall tower to reach the ice dock.

One day somebody offered to make a five-dollar wager with Ora Nida, who worked at the dock, that no one could carry a 300-pound block of ice all around the massive base of that tower. The contention was that the feat was humanly impossible, like the four-minute mile. Ora took him up on the challenge—not that he himself would try to do it, but he put his money on a colleague, Bill Pricer. Mr. Pricer was an exceedingly muscular and powerfully built man, a testimony to years of handling those big cakes of ice.

"Bill," Ora said, calling to his co-worker. "Pick up that 300-pound cake and carry it around the tower." No one had ever told Mr. Pricer it could not be done. He grasped his ice tongs, lifted the load onto his leather-sheathed back, and lugged the huge, dripping chunk of ice just as he had been instructed, once around the base of the brick tower, then returned in silence to whatever he had been doing before this little contest came up. Ora collected his money as the challenger rubbed his eyes in disbelief.

Mr. Pricer was the uncle of Billy Pricer, a fireplug-shaped athlete who also demonstrated exceptional strength years later as a state champion wrestler and all-state football player at Perry High School in the early 1950s, later as a varsity wrestler and fullback at the University of Oklahoma under Coach Bud Wilkinson, and finally as a backfield star for the Baltimore Colts in the National Football League.

Perry was rightly proud of its paved streets in the 1920s. The downtown area had brick paving, now lying beneath several layers of asphalt, but a few streets in the most heavily traveled residential areas had been covered with cement and they were carefully tended by city street department employees to protect and preserve them.

Paved streets provided one of the most visible signs of progress in the evolution from frontier life to civilization.

Hot, dry summers and cold, icy winters—the norm in Oklahoma—are hard on cement. As the streets contract and expand, major cracks develop. That is the prelude to potholes, the bain of motorists and street workers alike.

The fissures also invite other trouble. Winter moisture fills them, then freezes and widens the cracks. Seeds from weeds and lawn grass find their way into the openings in the summer months, take root and flourish thanks to moisture stored below the cement surface. As the vegetation thrives, multiplies and sends roots ever deeper, the cracks are made still wider.

Harried homeowners ponder this matter of grass growing in the streets as they perspire each summer, trying to develop a lush cover of grass in their yards. Sometimes it seems so futile.

It's part of Oklahomans' love/hate relationship with Bermuda grass, the type best suited to this climate. They perform rites of fertilization and apply untold tons of nourishment on their lawns to encourage the Bermuda to send out runners, hoping to cover every inch of soil with healthy grass.

At the same time they battle Bermuda furiously with razor-sharp cutting tools and chemicals that sterilize the soil when it encroaches on flower beds, sidewalks and driveways, or other places where it's not wanted.

Many an exhausted lawn warrior has felt defeated at the sight of rich, dark green "volunteer" Bermuda grass blithely demolishing the cement on his driveway while the front lawn turns a sickly yellow and deteriorates despite the most intensive efforts to succor it. Science has not yet found the solution to this paradox.

In an attempt to reduce the problems caused by cracks in the paving, city street department maintenance crews spent many summer days sealing the openings with hot tar.

It was interesting work to watch in progress. Curious youngsters usually gathered around as workmen poured the smelly, black goo from buckets into funnels dangling just above the crevices. The small fry were often rewarded with samples of molten tar which could be rolled around in the palm of a hand until cooled, then made into a ball (like Play-Doh) or popped into the mouth like chewing gum.

Not exactly tasty or recommended by dentists, but it was a kind of adventuresome experience for a kid growing up in Perry during the 1920s.

The decade was a prosperous one for Perry. It seemed the city had matured in many ways. The business district was being enlarged and numerous new homes were under construction. The boys were home from France after victory in the Great War, or the World War. It was a jubilant time throughout the land.

# 15

# $T$*HE MALZAHN BROS.*

Gus and Charlie Malzahn seemed to have a reasonable partnership in the blacksmith shop when they went into business together following the death of their father, Carl, in 1913. They were still on good terms later when they branched into new territory with the machine shop. As the elder, Gus took the lead as manager. Charlie's work uniform invariably was bib overalls; Gus was more often seen in a business suit.

After Gus died in 1928, a rift developed between Charlie and his brother's widow, Helena. Business disputes involved in settling the estate and closing out the partnership created insurmountable differences, and they were never able to reach an amicable settlement. Many family business arrangements have ended in similar fashion.

Henry S. Johnston, the noted Perry attorney who in 1929 was impeached as governor of Oklahoma, had been hired to represent Helena. He pursued his client's interests aggressively, making numerous requests for audits and payments from the business that Charlie could not provide. The economic problems of 1931-32 were severe and all-encompassing.

Unfortunately, such prolonged controversies became commonplace throughout the land. They embroiled many long-time friends and close family members, a product of the doleful business climate of the period.

Charlie finally wearied of what he considered to be continual harassment. "He just walked out and handed the keys to Aunt Lena and Henry S.," recalls Ed Malzahn, Charlie's son.

Charlie had a small nest egg in the Farmers and Merchants Bank on the south side of the square and he planned to use that to start over in business. A few days later President Franklin D. Roosevelt proclaimed a nation-wide "bank holiday," closing all of them for examination. The Farmers and Merchants Bank never reopened. The time was March 6, 1933, before the introduction of the Federal Deposit Insurance Corp. Depositors in many failed banks were devastated.

"The only money my folks had was what they had in their pockets," Ed says. "Times were tough." It did indeed look like the bottom of the barrel.

Aunt Lena, who died September 27, 1979, attempted to continue the machine shop by hiring a manager, but after a few months she sold the business to a local resident, Bert Bolay. Bert's father was a farmer who had been fortunate enough to have a farm in the middle of the newly discovered Lucien oil field, west of Perry. The Bolay machine shop continued in operation for several years.

The Malzahn building at the southeast corner of the square still stands today, perhaps as a monument to a once-thriving business that could not withstand the tragedy of a family squabble. It was a sad episode. No one on either side could have guessed at that time what would evolve as a result.

≥≈

Hoping to erase some of the recent unpleasantness, Charlie gambled on a new life in a different town. He chose Oswego, in Southeast Kansas, only a few miles from the Oklahoma line. He opened a small shop there while the family remained in Perry, waiting to see how things developed. Bertha and the children made occasional weekend trips to Kansas, but that adventure lasted only a few months.

Charlie came back to Perry within a year and started in business all over again in a building at 612 Flynn Street, just west of what was then the Houston-McCune Lumber Co. (now Perry Lumber Co.). A wooden partition divided the building, and he rented the east half. The shop was small, measuring twenty-five by seventy-five feet. It had a large south door, a small lathe, an old drill press, blacksmith tools and a welding machine. Not much, but enough to get things going. There was ample space on the shop floor to pile up the jobs he hoped would soon be arriving.

Charlie was the only employee, and he named it "Charlie's Machine Shop."

He was just getting started in his new blacksmith and machine shop in the dark economic days of the mid-1930s when a cousin, Christ Woyke, arrived in Perry from Minnesota. He moved in with the Malzahn family.

# 16

# *U*NCLE CHRIST

His full name was Christian Paul Woyke, pronounced "Y-key", but he was always known simply as Christ, pronounced to rhyme with "crisp," so most people thought they were calling him "Chris." He was a bricklayer by trade, one of the best around. His wife, Tillie (Matilda), was ill and had to be left behind when he came to Perry in the 1930s looking for work. His skill was needed here. He found plenty of jobs despite the depression.

Until Christ could get his feet on the ground, he lived with his cousin, Charlie Malzahn, in the family home at Ninth and Grove.

"We had only three bedrooms," recalls Ed Malzahn, Charlie's son, "so Christ slept with me. I was fourteen and weighed about 120 pounds. Christ was a large man. I would guess he weighed 250 pounds. The bed we shared was regular size. Queen and king size beds hadn't been invented.

"I spent the winter of '35 hanging to the side of the bed, since Christ took the bed to the slats. He was a heavy beer drinker, took a bath only on Saturday, and slept in his underwear. In spite of these inconveniences, Christ was a very likable person, always joking with Dad and remembering when they were kids in Maple Lake, Minnesota.

"In later years, Christ and Dad were fishing pals. They were both about the same size. The two of them would fill their small flat bottom fishing boat."

Christ worked that winter as a bricklayer on the new division office of the State Highway Department, then under construction on the old U.S. highway in south Perry. He also laid bricks and stone on a lot of houses built in Perry.

"He would take his own sweet time, working by the job, drawing a little grocery and beer money every Saturday," Ed relates. "He usually managed to be drawn up by the time the job was finished."

Years later he laid the brick and stone on a house built by Ed and his wife, Mary, at 1112 Twelfth Street.

"He took so long that Mary and I got tired of waiting and moved in while he was still laying brick," Ed says. "When I would complain to Uncle Christ—it was 'Uncle,' not 'Cousin,' for conversational purposes—he would say, 'Now Eddie, after I'm dead and gone they'll look at this job and say, Christ Woyke did that! They won't know whether it took a week or all winter.'

"Well, it did take all winter, but it was a good job and we soon forgot about the inconvenience."

Christ continued to make his home here, picking up enough jobs to keep from going hungry. After the death of his first wife, Tillie, in 1946, Christ married Grace Garrett and spent the last three years of his life on her farm north of Perry. He died October 23, 1970. Grace died November 22, 1989, at the age of seventy-seven. Christ, Tillie and Grace are buried in Grace Hill Cemetery, southeast of the city.

# 17

# CHARLIE AND BERTHA MALZAHN

To those outside the family, Charlie and Bertha Malzahn seemed to be opposites in many ways. He was large, she was small. His face was usually wreathed in smiles, she was very serious. He was more interested in the nuts and bolts of his machine shop, she was largely preoccupied with business matters. In truth, they complemented one another perfectly.

Both pursued their particular interests with high degrees of intensity. Both were plagued late in life by physical handicaps—Charlie with debilitating illnesses and Bertha with crippling accidents. As a result, pain and disabilities robbed them of some of the fruits of their lifetime of hard work, but no one ever heard them complain. If anything, such burdens seem to have driven them to even higher levels of achievement.

The business was their life. They worked in it side by side, long hours at a stretch, all their adult life, as long as they were able. Their two children were by no means neglected. They inherited their parents' work ethic and passion for productivity in all areas of their life. They were integrated into the family business at very early ages.

The first child born to Charlie and Bertha Malzahn was a son, Edwin, on July 3, 1921. Two years later they had a daughter, Virginia, to complete the family. Edwin, or Ed, is now president of the Charles Machine Works, Inc., successor to the Malzahn Blacksmith enterprises. Virginia died in March 1991.

Charlie Malzahn was a big man, six feet one inch, and weighing 250 pounds. His arms were as big as most men's legs, testimonials to years of handling heavy tools and iron in the blacksmith shop where he grew up.

Ed remembers watching in awe as a youngster when his father grasped a sixteen-pound sledge hammer by the end of the handle.

He would raise it to a horizontal position, hold it straight out at arm's length, raise it upward and slowly let it down to touch his nose, then raise it up again. It was an impressive feat of strength.

"Dad could do about anything with iron," Ed recalls. "I believe he liked blacksmithing best. The heat of the forge and the ring of the anvil brought a smile to his face."

He made his first portable electric welding machine out of an old Dodge automobile engine. For several years it was the only portable welder in town.

Charlie always wore bib overalls and a blue work shirt, with a blue handkerchief hanging out of a back pocket. The handkerchief would come out to wipe the sweat from his brow after each forge heat. It was an extremely hot job in the sweltering Oklahoma summers, but even then he loved it.

Each plow share was laid out on the shop floor for inspection. Charlie carefully checked them all for smoothness and to make certain they were level. It was a matter of personal pride in his workmanship. In his younger days he did shoe horses, but that later became the specialty of another blacksmith shop in town. By the 1930s the number of horses in Noble County had radically decreased and real blacksmiths were on the decline as a result.

Still, blacksmithing was Charlie Malzahn's "private little business," even when he operated a complete machine shop. He ran it on a cash and carry basis. Keeping books consisted of opening a two-compartment, snap-type purse, and dropping in the money. It served as his personal expense account, and sometimes the family grocery money came from there.

Beech Nut chewing tobacco was his weakness. It was something he could do while hammering a plow share or pumping a bellows, things that precluded the use of cigars or cigarets. He usually went through two pouches of the moist, shredded leaves each day. As a youngster, Ed remembers one of the first assignments given him on summer days at the shop was to run to the grocery store early each morning to get his dad's daily supply of two packs of "fresh." Two packs cost a quarter.

A lot of friends and customers also chewed. Charlie always offered them a dip from the pouch in his pocket, because that was the customary thing to do. Ed himself sampled it once at the age of twelve. He got sick, and that was his last experiment with Beech Nut chewing tobacco.

Machinery auctions, not surprisingly, held a special fascination for Charlie. If one was scheduled within a day's driving distance, he would be there. Usually he came home with a "bargain"—a box of mixed bolts, some used drill bits or milling cutters, and even, on rare occasions, a piece of old machinery.

He did engage himself in community activities. Soon after returning from military service he helped organize the local post of the Veterans of Foreign Wars and later served as its commander. He also was an active member of the American Legion, a 32nd degree Mason and a member of the Presbyterian Church. In 1931 he served on the city council. With all this, his first love was his work. It always took priority, sometimes even over his family.

Which is not to say he overlooked the need to teach his children important lessons about independent thinking and upright living. He set correct examples and underscored the points in firm but fair ways.

"We never spent much time together outside the shop," Ed says, "since that's where he was from early morning until late at night, six and sometimes seven days a week. I can't recall his ever doing yard work at home, although he did seem to know a lot about trees and plants.

"In his later years he enjoyed going fishing with Uncle Christ Woyke on Sundays at Lake Carl Blackwell. I can only think of a couple of times that he and I went fishing together.

"I don't recall his ever speaking a cross word to me in all the years we worked together. In fact, I only recall one spanking, when I was about five. I didn't want to go to Sunday school. I did, and still do."

Bertha exerted an even stronger influence on the entire family. She did not need a women's liberation movement or equal rights demonstration to pursue a successful business career. Throughout her adult life she managed the difficult task of combining roles as mother/wife and office manager of Charlie's business.

When there was no money for a bookkeeper in the shop, she kept the books. She negotiated with the bank more often than Charlie did. Bertha called customers to collect delinquent accounts. She never hesitated to speak out if she disagreed with a decision or the progress of work in the shop. She was diminutive in size, but this never proved an obstacle to her in expressing a point of view.

George Wolff's four daughters were unique for their time in that each was well educated. They were professional people and each was the dominant partner in her marriage. They even dominated their two brothers, and in later years their father. All four achieved recognition for leadership in their individual careers.

"Both Virginia and I could credit mother with encouraging and sometimes pushing us to achieve in school and in extra-curricular activities," Ed says. "She and dad sacrificed and did without so that we might have whatever was necessary to complete our education."

In the summer of 1924, Bertha slipped on the front steps of the Malzahn home at Ninth and Grove Streets and cracked her right knee cap. At that time the only recourse was to remove the cap and stiffen her leg. She was twenty-five years old, with two small children and work to do at the shop. The stiff knee was a handicap she carried the rest of her life.

Nor was that mishap the end of it. In January of 1950 when Bertha and Charlie were on the way to Oklahoma City for a physiotherapy appointment, they became involved in a single-car accident. She was driving on a narrow, rain-slick highway, and lost control of the car. Charlie was not seriously injured, but Bertha had multiple fractures of both legs and in the pelvic area. Doctors said she would never walk again. They were wrong. Bertha's self-will and fortitude proved indomitable.

"Mother was plagued with physical problems most of her life," Ed says, "but somehow she would keep pushing herself, right to the very end."

Social groups had no great attraction for her, although she was active in the American Legion auxiliary. She was president of the local unit and also served as the Eighth District auxiliary president. Mrs. Malzahn, often called simply "Mrs. M" by colleagues and friends, was a past worthy matron of the Perry Order of Eastern Star, member of the Perry Business Women's Club, and served on the Presbyterian Church board of trustees.

Around the kitchen at home, Bertha was strictly a meat and potatoes cook. Nothing fancy. When the children were still at home, the Malzahns most often had a "hired girl," a live-in who kept house and did the cooking. It was a common practice in many homes of that day because of the availability of high school-age girls from the rural area who wanted to live in town while completing their education. There were no school buses to deliver farm children to classes in urban area.

For working women like Mrs. Malzahn, it was a very practical arrangement. The experience she acquired as part of the management team in her husband's business was to prove extremely valuable in years to come.

# 18

# *Y*OUNG ED MALZAHN

Bertha and Charlie Malzahn's first child, Edwin, was born in 1921 when the couple were living in a single-story house with a big front porch at the southwest corner of Ninth and Grove Streets. The attending physician was Dr. D.F. Coldiron, who lived just a block south on Fir Avenue.

Two years later a daughter, Virginia, was born to the Malzahns. She graduated from Perry High School in 1940, earned a bachelor's degree in foods and nutrition, a master's in home economics and a doctor of education in home economics, all from Oklahoma State University. She and a son, George Lamb, established a fine restaurant, the Graystone, at Edmond, Oklahoma, in the 1980s. Another son, Charles Lamb, also lives in Edmond. Virginia died in March 1991.

Like her mother, Virginia Malzahn Lamb was happiest when she was deeply involved in challenging projects. Her primary career was in the field of home economics education, but she also wrote extensively on that subject for several publications distributed among professionals in the field. She retired in 1986 as chairman of the home economics department and an associate professor at Central State University in Edmond.

Ed had a natural curiosity about the machines and tools used in his father's machine shop business. His interest resulted in an accident at the shop when he was two years old. He lost three fingers on his left hand in the mishap, but by the time he was ten he was running a lathe, and he was welding at the age of twelve.

He overcame the injury to his hand, but it disqualified him for military service during World War II.

When Ed was in the second grade, Charlie hired a carpenter to rebuild the family's house, adding inside plumbing and a second story, with bathrooms on both levels. The house still stands, looking pretty much as it did in 1928. That period remains quite vivid in Ed's mind.

"Dad made a floor furnace, but it needed a basement," he remembers. "So, they dug dirt out from under the house and made a small room for the furnace and some storage. The room wasn't very tall, and Dad, who was over six feet, continually bumped his head on the floor joists. Because of that, he didn't go down in the basement very often.

"This was my place of refuge. I had a bench with a small wood lathe and a jigsaw made from an old Singer sewing machine, and a stack of walnut lumber that one of Dad's customers gave him to pay a bill. I made table lamps and candle holders, little sailboats and a lot of sawdust.

"Along one wall of the basement were shelves that held dozens of Mason jars of fruits and vegetables, the product of a large pressure cooker that whistled away in our kitchen every summer. It turned the kitchen into a sweat box, even with all the doors and windows open.

"One of the shelves was a catch-all that accumulated some old books that one never throws away. I never had much interest in old books, but somehow I noticed one of them was a doctor's book that had colored pictures of naked men and women. It told about where babies come from and how to keep from having them. Pretty risque stuff for an eleven- or twelve-year-old. Whether the book was there on purpose or by accident, it did answer a lot of questions for an inquisitive mind.

"When Dad allowed me to come to his shop and begin to weld and turn metal on a big lathe, the little shop in the basement became unimportant. And anyway, I thought I had completed my sex education.

"My bedroom was the smallest upstairs. It faced south. That allowed cool breezes to blow across the bed during early summer, until it came time to move out in the yard on those hot July and August nights, to sleep under the stars. I made the furniture for that bedroom, everything but the bedstead, which was one of those standard iron frame things that had six coats of paint and would squeak and rattle every time you turned over.

"I don't know what the neighbors thought about 'that Charlie Malzahn and his kid' always tearing up the yard or hauling something into the garage. One of our bigger projects was a storm cellar built out of the end of a refinery pressure vessel. The tank had been about ten feet in diameter and was made out of 3/8-inch steel plate. We dug a huge hole in the backyard by hand, and lowered the tank end into the hole with a winch truck, ran a concrete floor and stairs, and we had Perry's first and only bomb shelter in 1936.

"Backyard fish ponds were popular in 1936, and the Malzahns had to have one. Of course, it had to be different, homemade underwater lights, three kinds of water lilies, a waterfall with a little water wheel, a couple of ducks (they stayed three days), and great big goldfish. A lot of work, but it sure was fun gathering rocks from all over Pawnee Bill's, the Glass Hills near Woodward, and the Malzahn farm south of town. Now we build swimming pools, not fish ponds. What a loss.

"Most people, when they built a driveway across their yard, used gravel, or concrete, if they were rich. Not the Malzahns. We hauled flat rocks from the country and laid them together in a crazy-quilt pattern. It wasn't any good for roller skating, but it looked pretty and nobody else had one like it. And besides, I was big enough to drive the truck sometimes. The more rock I hauled, the more I got to drive. The summers of '36 and '37 had some great experiences in this teen-ager's life."

### THE FBI PAYS A CALL

When Charlie had introduced Ed to all the machinery in the family business, he gave his son the run of the place. As a thirteen-year-old, he experimented and built all sorts of things.

"I read in a book how to make castings," Ed recalls, "so I tried out my skills by making an impression of a silver dollar in a plaster mold. I poured duplicates with some surplus babbitt (metal lining) left over from bearings Dad had poured.

"Somehow Mom and Dad were not aware of what I was doing, but I sure was popular as I handed out fake dollars to all my friends at school. I must have made a dozen or so.

"I remember the day the FBI agent showed up at Dad's shop and wanted to know where his son was, and did he know what I was doing. Dad and the FBI man stood there as I broke up my molds.

"Not too long after that, I discovered a surplus spotlight that had been around the shop for some time. It was an expensive light, cast out of aluminum, weather tight, and with a great reflector that could be adjusted to shine for blocks. It had a 500-watt bulb.

"I mounted the spotlight on the top of our garage with a remote control so I could shine it around the neighborhood, much to the annoyance of the neighbors.

"At that time, before World War II, student pilots in the Army Air Force were training in night flying at Vance Field, west of here near Enid. One of their 'targets' was Perry. They would circle Perry several evenings a week. I fixed my searchlight to shine up and would try to spot the planes. I wasn't very successful but it was fun.

"After a couple of evenings, the FBI showed up again and wanted to know who was spotting the planes. They thought it might be a spy. That put a stop to the spotlight. I was seventeen at the time."

### POPULAR MECHANICS

Even more than most boys, Ed eagerly pored over each copy of *Popular Mechanics* magazine that came along. Exciting new inventions, far-out ideas and lots of full-color pictures fired his imagination and stirred the latent engineer within him. He still reads the magazine, and recently came across an article that took him back some fifty-five years.

"The article was entitled 'Dirt Boat Wind Races—Landsailing Excitement at 100 mph.' Pictured were sleek fiberglass and aluminum three-wheeled vehicles with tall, computer-designed Dacron sails," he says in recalling the piece.

"As long as I can remember, even before I could read well, *Popular Mechanics* magazines were my 'children's books.' I would keep all the past issues and read them over and over. Occasionally I would attempt to build some of the things I saw on those pages, using spare junk in the garage or around Dad's shop.

"I remember one of those projects was a 'land boat' that I copied from pictures of ice boats. I used wheels from my red wagon, pieces of 2x4 lumber from the wood pile, and some old bed ticking, salvaged from the hamper, for a sail.

"The only place big enough for sailing was the school yard, a block south of our house. Mother wouldn't let me use the road in front of the house. Anyway, I knew nothing about tacking and the wind rarely blew straight down Ninth Street.

"We pushed that boat back and forth across the school yard until the work got to be more than the fun. We never reached 100 mph, but it sure seemed like it sometimes sitting on that 2x4 just six inches off the ground. Store-bought toys were rare things in those days."

### "TODAY I AM A MAN"

The teen-age Ed Malzahn was intrigued by the Boy Scout program. Outdoor living, building camp fires, learning innovative ways of doing things—all these had an appeal. Of course he became an Eagle Scout. As an undergraduate at Oklahoma A.&M. College, he was a member of the honorary Eagle Scout fraternity. Part of the initiation required camping out on the campus for a week in a pup tent. Later in life he spent several years as a Scoutmaster in Perry, imparting his enthusiasm to many youngsters with similar interests.

At his present stage of life, he has made numerous trips to Washington, D.C., but each one still musters a bit of awe and humbling in the adult Ed.

"However," he says, "I suppose I remember more of my first trip there than any of the many that have occurred since then.

"To my knowledge, the first National Jamboree of the Boy Scouts was held in Washington in 1937. It had been delayed for some reason, which I have forgotten, from 1936. The Will Rogers Council of Northern Oklahoma, which included Perry, was invited to send a troop of thirty-two boys to the Jamboree. I was an Eagle Scout by then, so I was chosen to be one of four patrol leaders.

"We boarded the Santa Fe train in Ponca City and connected with the Chesapeake and Ohio in Chicago for the balance of the trip to Washington. All went well with thirty-two excited boys and Mr. Wiles, our Scoutmaster, except the night train from Chicago to Washington wasn't air-conditioned. We left some of the windows open, and the coal-burning engine made for a bunch of dirty boys when we arrived the next morning. Of course, I didn't know it at the time, but Mr. Wiles' son, Bill, who was part of the Blackwell Patrol, was dating Mary (now Mrs. Ed Malzahn). Small world.

"Our camp was on a golf course on an island in the Potomac River. It's still there. From camp we could walk to most of the interesting points in the capital. Our patrol walked the winding stairs to the top of the Washington Monument. We watched the changing of the guard at Arlington Cemetery. From the catwalk we drooled as they printed one-hundred-dollar bills at the Treasury. We heard our voices echo in the rotunda of the Capitol, and we quietly stood in the magnificence of the East Room of the White House.

"We sailed down the Potomac to Mt. Vernon and stood on the front porch where General Washington once surveyed the plantation. A bus ride to Annapolis made us all want to enter the Naval Academy as we stood in the quadrangle and watched the plebes marching in formation to class. We pitched wishing pennies at Sequoyah and stood silently in the chapel.

"My sixteenth birthday was celebrated in Washington. I sent the folks my first telegram. It stated simply, 'Today, I am a man.' The next day, the Fourth of July, we were treated to the biggest fireworks display I had ever seen, rockets and aerial bombs that lit up the whole sky.

"I don't remember a thing about the trip home, but I expanded the horizon of my view of the nation those ten days in that summer of 1937."

### CLASSROOM CAPERS AT PHS

Looking back on his days as a student at Perry High School, Ed realizes the education he received there went a long way in shaping his life. Several teachers inspired or stirred him onward and upward for various reasons.

"For thirty years John Divine was probably one of the best known high school wrestling coaches in Oklahoma, and the entire Southwest," Ed says.

"What may not be remembered is that he also was a good teacher. At least I thought so. John taught chemistry in a laboratory on the third floor of the old (now demolished) high school building.

"In addition to teaching chemistry, John shared the office of principal on the first floor. This required him to be absent from the laboratory for extended periods of time.

"Somewhere in our classroom experiments someone discovered how to make hydrogen sulfide, a colorless, foul smelling gas with an odor like rotten eggs. We later learned it also is poisonous.

"Next door to the laboratory was a classroom used by Mr. Alba Mulkey, the English teacher. We thought he was a little effeminate, and even made fun of him behind his back. High school boys can be very cruel, and looking back I realize he was probably just a lonely bachelor. Between the classroom and the laboratory was the closet where the chemistry inventory was stored, and in the wall separating the two was a small crack.

"Someone (not me) affixed a small glass tube to the top of a flask containing ingredients for hydrogen sulfide. They then hid the whole thing behind some bottles in the closet, with the tube sticking into the crack.

"Soon we heard a lot of coughing and a window opening in Mr. Mulkey's room. Then Mr. Mulkey came into the laboratory to see if the odor was coming from there. By that time, Mr. Divine was back, English class was dismissed, the west end of the top floor was evacuated, lockers were searched, and the odor of rotten eggs was everywhere.

"Mr. Divine finally found the generator, but nobody confessed. We all had to write a theme. I don't remember what it was about, but I'll always remember tall, gangly, Mr. Mulkey, black suit with vest, coming out of that room looking as if he was going to throw up.

"John Divine and Alba Mulkey were two of those devoted teachers who gave so much and tolerated so much at dear old Perry High. Chemistry was fun. I made A's."

# 19

# *H*ENRY S. JOHNSTON

Henry Simpson Johnston was a hungry young attorney when he arrived in Perry a few days after the land run in 1893. He rose to the pinnacle in Oklahoma politics in 1926 when he was elected governor, only to feel the humiliation of impeachment from office midway through his four-year term.

Many then considered him to be the city's most illustrious citizen, the innocent victim of a vicious political struggle. When he motored back to Perry after being ousted from office, hundreds of townsfolk met him in a caravan of autos at the edge of town and escorted him to the courthouse park for a surprise "welcome home" celebration. Some 4,000 filled the park that day.

Still others regarded him as eccentric, cantankerous and manipulative. They were not surprised at his downfall.

Whatever people thought of him, they must have recognized him as a spellbinding orator and a canny lawyer. Those qualities led him to many highs, and lows, in a strange career. His life did not begin and end with the episode in the governor's office.

Most people in this community, both friend and foe, called him simply "Henry S." He came here aboard a Santa Fe train four days after the September 16, 1893, land rush, yielding to an impulse to see the Indian country.

"I had it in my heart to be a pioneer," he later confided, "and this looked to me like the pioneer spot of the world. I put in a week wandering around looking at saloons and tents."

He was tall and slender, with a slightly Roman nose and finely chiseled facial features. His eyes were deep set, piercing and inescapable. A firmness about the mouth and jaw added to the general image of a determined, intelligent man. Offsetting a prematurely receding hairline was a flowing mane that gave him a slightly theatrical appearance. And he could have been an actor, utilizing his melifluous voice and mastery of the English language, and a presence that commanded attention. This was the young Henry S.

By chance he ran across another lawyer, Amos Lapham, whom he had known in Colorado before coming to Perry, shortly after his arrival here. They started a law practice in the new city but Mr. Lapham left after only two weeks. It was estimated that as many as 500 attorneys were here at that time, far more than was needed, and they soon began thinning out.

Mr. Johnston was born December 30, 1867, in a walnut log home near Evansville, Indiana. His parents, Mr. and Mrs. Matthew Simpson Johnston, moved the family to a farm near Erie, Kansas, sixteen months later, and Matthew operated a grocery store. Young Henry S. helped his father in the business until graduating from high school, when he enrolled at Baker University, fifteen miles south of Lawrence.

For two and a half years he took a "general course," but no law studies, until the critical illness of a brother, William, made it necessary for him to return home. William fully recovered and years later became head of the English department at Oklahoma A.&M. College, now Oklahoma State University.

Henry S. headed westward to Denver in 1891 to launch out on his own. He received his education in the law through practical training and tutoring, and was admitted to the Colorado bar later that year. He served as a junior partner in a Denver law firm until the urge to become a pioneer overtook him in 1893.

Mr. Johnston established a successful practice here and immediately became active in the Democratic party. He had offices on the second floor of the Grand Opera House building on the east side of the square for a time, and later moved to a suite of rooms on the second floor of the Famous Department Store building on the south side of the square. That remained his office location until his death in 1965.

In 1896 he was elected to the upper house of the Oklahoma Territorial Council, which was responsible for proposing legislation for Oklahoma Territory. Council members were paid four dollars per day while in session plus four dollars for each twenty miles of travel, he recalled.

In 1901-04 he served two two-year terms as county attorney in Noble County. During this same period he was a leader in the

Knights of Pythias and became the first grand chancellor of the Oklahoma fraternal order in 1906.

When the Oklahoma Constitutional Convention was created in 1906, Mr. Johnston won a seat as a delegate to represent district 17, composed of Noble and Pawnee Counties. He was chosen as presiding officer during the organizational phase of the "Con-Con," as it was called.

Although he was not named permanent chairman of the convention, he never expressed resentment over the fact. His good friend, fellow Democratic delegate and also a future governor, William H. (Alfalfa Bill) Murray, called Mr. Johnston "the smoothest and best parliamentarian in the group."

The delegates consisted of 99 Democrats, twelve Republicans and one independent. Mr. Johnston was elected chairman of the Democratic caucus and as such rapped the gavel that called the convention to order on November 20, 1906, in the Brooks Opera House at Guthrie.

"I uttered the first sentence in organizing the state," he said proudly in reflecting on that moment.

During the 1906 Christmas holidays, an outbreak of smallpox hit prisoners in the city jail, which was located in the basement of the convention hall. When the delegates reconvened, Mr. Johnston fell victim to the disease and was quarantined to his room.

After Oklahoma became a state in 1907, Henry S. was elected to the first State Senate from district 10, consisting of Noble and Pawnee Counties. He served as president pro tempore of the Senate, and later said he believed his work in organizing that body led to his election as governor in 1926.

He ran unsuccessfully for Congress from this district in 1908 and again in 1914. Between those two campaigns, in mid-June of 1909, he married Ethel L. Littleton, a twenty-year-old legislative reporter for the Senate whom he had met while the Legislature was in session in Guthrie. During their long marriage they adopted four children.

Mrs. Johnston was more than a housewife and mother. She was an administrator with leadership qualities in an era before these were expected in women. She was an early leader in the Camp Fire Girls movement and the Red Cross, and later served many years as state secretary of the Order of the Eastern Star, a demanding job requiring detailed record keeping.

She was bright, witty, attractive and charming. She was also a landscape painter of some skill. Like her husband, she was most often referred to simply by her first name and middle initial—Ethel L.

Oklahoma Democrats chose Henry S. as a delegate to their national convention in 1912. He again was elected a delegate to the 1924 convention and many wanted him to seek the chairmanship of the state delegation that year, but instead he resigned his position so that U.S. Senator Robert L. Owen could be added to the group. This was part of some very intricate political maneuvering going on at that time within the state's Democratic party hierarchy, with Governor Martin E. Trapp calling many of the shots. Senator Owen was a Trapp supporter and Mr. Johnston's move gave the governor control of the Oklahoma delegation. It was a time of intense political turmoil.

Some historians view the presidential election of 1924 as the launching pad for the Perry attorney's ascendancy to the governor's office.

Because some felt Mr. Johnston had shown he could effectively oppose Governor Trapp, he was asked to do so again in the 1926 gubernatorial campaign.

Mr. Trapp had been lieutenant governor since 1915 and was filling that position in 1923 when Governor John Walton was impeached from office, and thus succeeded him. Under the Oklahoma Constitution at the time, a governor could not succeed himself.

However, Mr. Trapp was given the green light to file for the office by the Oklahoma Election Board in May 1926. In July the state Supreme Court, by a seven to two decision, held that Mr. Trapp was, in fact, governor and therefore ineligible for election to the post.

Eleven candidates, including Mr. Johnston, were seeking the Democratic nomination. Finally, the Perry attorney won the bid in the primary election by a plurality of 15,000 votes over his nearest challenger. Only 88,000 votes were cast.

In the general election on November 2, 1926, Mr. Johnston led a Democratic sweep and defeated his Republican opponent, Omar K. Benedict of Oklahoma City, by more than 40,000 votes. The Democrats also elected a new U.S. senator and six of the state's eight congressmen that year.

The governor-elect ran into problems with the Legislature even before his term began. For the first time since statehood, the Legislature was organized against the wishes of the governor. It was said that Mr. Johnston proved to be both a poor manager of his political affairs and weak in his dealings with the lawmakers. He alienated many of them through attempted meddling in their concerns.

The Johnston inaugural on January 10, 1927, was a gala affair, but it also provoked dissension over the question of whether dancing should be permitted at the evening festivities. Still, it was considered the greatest state occasion since Oklahoma entered the union in 1907. Some 20,000 persons assembled at the south entrance to the Capitol Building. Many of them were Mr. Johnston's colleagues from the Constitutional Convention. The new governor began his inaugural address with prayer for divine guidance, something not done by his six predecessors.

Political problems began multiplying for Governor Johnston from the earliest days of his administration. One of the most publicized involved his confidential secretary, Mayme Hammonds. She was a former worker in the Democratic party and the women's division of the Ku Klux Klan which itself had been a divisive issue in the election campaign. Mrs. Hammonds met Mr. Johnston during the campaign.

She earned a reputation for shielding the governor from those who wanted to use him for their own interests, but she also earned the wrath of many legislators who were forced to wait, unannounced, when they felt they needed to see him.

The Perry Masonic lodge came to his rescue at one point as the chasm widened between Governor Johnston and the legislature. Dissident Oklahoma Masons started a movement to censure him and remove him from the organization, but the Perry fraternal order, of which he was a respected member, passed a resolution giving him full support.

Bizarre stories cropped up concerning the governor and Mrs. Hammonds. Aldrich Blake, a one-time member of the Walton administration, claimed Mr. Johnston belonged to the Rosicrucian philosophical group, that Mrs. Hammonds "traveled through space" to investigate the character of applicants for public office while still physically at her desk. He also claimed that Mr. Johnston signed legislative bills by the signs of the zodiac and requested Mrs.

Hammonds' aid in consulting with the dead. Mr. Johnston heatedly denied all of these charges, but the story badly damaged his credibility.

During the summer of 1928, work was completed on the new Oklahoma Governor's Mansion a few blocks east of the Capitol Building, and the Johnston family moved into it. They expected to be there for the remaining two years of his term. In the November presidential election, the state went Republican and Mr. Johnston received the blame. His enemies in the Legislature were hard at work with plans to remove him from office.

On January 11, 1929, the House of Representatives appointed an investigative committee to look into grounds for impeachment. Eleven specific charges against the governor were voted on January 18. A charge of general incompetency headed the list. The trial before the Senate lasted through February and March. The transcript of testimony ran more than 5,000 pages, much of it totally irrelevant.

Mr. Johnston's lawyers conceded from the start that all of the charges were true, except for the incompetency article, but they maintained that his actions resulted from poor advice from his associates and other government officials who used him for their own interests without his knowledge. Foes said that fact alone proved incompetency and was sufficient reason for removal.

The Senate agreed that there was no criminal intent on the part of the governor, and on March 20, 1929, found him not guilty on all charges except incompetency. The vote in favor of that article was thirty-five to nine. Mr. Johnston thereupon became the second Oklahoma governor removed from office by impeachment.

"I was impeached because I couldn't be bought off," he said later in discussing the episode. "I feel glorified about that. They couldn't find anything wrong, so they removed me on the grounds I was incompetent."

Some historians have written that Mr. Johnston, as governor, had higher ethical standards than those which seemed to prevail around him. They give him low marks as an administrator, but add that he was unwilling to yield to those who were attempting to make personal profit from state government. At the same time they fault him for placing too much faith in his personal judgment of human character. Governor Johnston was neither a criminal nor a statesman, one observer wrote. His conviction, however, was considered a dangerous precedent.

Mr. Johnston's impeachment differed from Governor Walton's in 1923 in many ways. The Perry attorney was an ardent advocate of prohibition. His political following, slightly less than a majority of the voters, were disappointed when the Oklahoma delegation to the 1927 Democratic national convention accepted Alfred E. Smith as the candidate for President. The Protestant dry voters of the Southwest were opposed to Smith, and the Ku Klux Klan of Oklahoma, together with many advocates of prohibition who were not KKK members but were strongly anti-Catholic, were disappointed in Johnston.

He returned to Perry and was greeted by a large throng of friends and supporters. Mr. Johnston termed that one of the most impressive moments in his career. It was not a time of retirement, however. He continued in the practice of law here and became the principal lawyer for the 101 Ranch during the years of its receivership and bankruptcy. He also continued to be active in Masonic and Pythian fraternal orders.

Mr. Johnston ran unsuccessfully for the State Senate in 1930, but in 1932 he won election to a four-year term in that august body by a 1,700-vote plurality, and served with many of the men who had voted to impeach him. During that same year he placed the name of his friend and fellow delegate, Alfalfa Bill Murray, before the national Democratic convention as a candidate for President of the United States.

March 31, 1939, was a slow news day in Oklahoma, as a story on the front page of *the Perry Daily Journal* illustrated that afternoon. *The Journal* gave the story a three-line, two-column wide headline at the top of the page. The piece read:

Half the state was electrified today by a wild rumor that Henry S. Johnston, former governor of Oklahoma, now a practicing attorney in Perry, was dead, the victim of a heart attack. The rumor evidently started in Oklahoma City and spread to Perry when the Associated Press bureau phoned frantically to *the Perry Daily Journal* for particulars. A *Journal* reporter phoned Mrs. Johnston at their residence and learned that the rumor was untrue, and phoned back to Oklahoma City to relay what Mrs. Johnston had said. "We don't believe it," the AP man said. "We got to have a statement from Henry himself before we believe he isn't dead."

End of item.

In later years, the former governor enjoyed talking about his experiences in shaping Oklahoma's Constitution and its form of government. His mind was clear to the end, though he adopted an interest in some odd areas. For one thing he believed in reincarnation and was convinced that in a previous life he had been an Egyptian nobleman, among other things. Astronomy (not astrology, as his political opponents had claimed) was a lifelong interest.

Mr. Johnston was an honorary pallbearer for his colorful friend, Alfalfa Bill Murray, when the latter died in October 1956. The two men had shared many experiences while developing the form of government and basic laws of this new state in the early days of the century.

Mr. Johnston granted an annual interview to a local reporter on each birthday anniversary as the years went by. These became of general interest to newspaper readers around the state. Mr. Johnston always found something to say that seemed a little unusual. His sense of humor endured throughout his long life.

He died unexpectedly on January 7, 1965, during the noon meal at his family home on Holly Street, at the age of ninety-seven. His death came just one day after the Legislature had taken steps to soften the stigma of his impeachment. His body lay in state at the Capitol Building, followed by funeral services on January 12 in the Perry First Christian Church. His body was cremated and the remains interred at Grace Hill Cemetery.

Many of his office belongings were donated by Mrs. Johnston to the Cherokee Strip Museum in Perry, and still other papers and artifacts were acquired by the Oklahoma State University Library, where researchers have access to them.

The Johnston home and remaining furnishings were sold at auction in 1970, following Ethel L.'s death. The sale attracted antique buyers from a wide area. The house was purchased by the First Christian Church, located next door, and was razed. The church now has a building and parking lot in the general vicinity of the Johnston home.

The Johnston children, Nell, Reba, Gertrude and Robin, have long since scattered to various parts of the country, and the family no longer has any direct connection with Perry.

# 20

# $M$ ANUEL HERRICK

To say that Manuel Herrick was the most peculiar man who ever claimed Perry as a home would be unfair to others who seemingly worked hard to earn that distinction. It all came so effortlessly for Manuel. Nevertheless, it would be difficult to find a more suitable choice.

His career peaked in the zany 1920s when he became a member of the U.S. House of Representatives from Oklahoma's Eighth Congressional District, but he was a well-known figure in the Perry area before that, dating back to shortly before the land run in 1893.

He was ruled insane that year, at the age of seventeen, but was found not subject to institutional care. Eight days later he bungled an attempted train holdup in the Cherokee Strip and as a result was committed to the Oak Lawn Retreat in Jacksonville, Illinois, where Oklahoma mental patients of that time were confined.

By the time he was forty-four Manuel had been sent to Congress from this district as the result of an election fluke after failing repeatedly to win even the most menial county-level office. His bizarre behavior in Washington was thoroughly covered by all the major newspapers and wire services, bringing down waves of derision upon Oklahomans in general. Years later he died alone in a snowstorm on a California mining claim.

How did he get that way?

He may have become confused early in life because his parents earnestly believed him to be the reincarnation of Jesus Christ. Accordingly, at his birth they named him Immanuel, meaning "God with us." They were serious about that.

When the family made a shopping trip from their farm into Perry, Manuel rode on the spring seat in the wagon and the parents sat on straw or a quilt in back. In town, they walked a few steps behind him. It was their way of showing respect. When it was time to eat on these occasions, they would buy cheese and crackers, or perhaps some sardines, and eat together seated on feed sacks in the back of the store.

Manuel's parents were John and Balinda Herrick, both deeply religious people. An earlier biographer found evidence that John may not actually have been Manuel's father, giving rise to the possibility that Balinda, at least, may have considered it to be an immaculate conception. This theory apparently was never investigated. In any event, Manuel was born September 20, 1876, in Ohio, but the family moved to Greenwood County, Kansas, the following year. They came to Oklahoma Territory around 1891, establishing a home near Norman in Cleveland County.

Manuel had little formal education but loved to read. He chose tales of adventure and mystery, and also spent hours studying the Bible and Blackstone. He hired out for farm work in the area and never hesitated to boast that he was a "self-made man."

After being judged insane but not requiring treatment or confinement on June 21, 1893, he was given over to the care of his father. At 3:30 p.m. on June 28, Manuel boarded Santa Fe train No. 408 in Norman. He was carrying a long, bulky package and was wearing boots, overalls and a dirty looking coat. The train was northbound, heading for Kansas.

After the locomotive passed over the Black Bear Creek bridge north of Wharton (Perry), Manuel pulled out a Winchester rifle, buckled a .45 Colt revolver and a Knights of Pythias sword to the belt around his waist, and ordered the conductor, Al Glazier, to pull the bell cord to stop the train. When it came to a halt, he forced Mr. Glazier off the car and followed along behind, walking toward the engine. A young deputy U.S. marshal, Patrick Sylvester McGeeney, was aboard the train and realized what was happening. He also got off the car and approached the conductor and Manuel from behind.

Manuel somehow tripped on his sword, giving Mr. Glazier an opportunity to wrench the rifle out of his grasp. The conductor struck the youth across the face, the rifle in his hand going off harmlessly into the air as he did so. Manuel turned to run away and the conductor fell in the grass as he went after him. The deputy marshal pulled out his six-shooter and ordered the would-be hold-up man to stop, which he promptly did.

At his arraignment on June 30, 1893, in Oklahoma City, Manuel loudly protested that he had been "bullet ordered" by members of the Bill Doolin gang to board the train and assist them in holding it up. Apparently he got the date wrong and boarded one day earlier than the outlaws had instructed him. At any rate, U.S. Commissioner Bowles found his story without merit and committed him to the Oak Lawn Retreat.

The *Daily Oklahoma State Capitol*, published in Guthrie, reported that Manuel "looked foolish" at the hearing, but that he became rather loud as he demanded what he thought should be given to a case of his importance. He was described as being "seventeen years old, with not even a pinfeather sign of whiskers....He is quite good-sized, a narrow forehead and small eyes set close together."

Mr. Glazier received a $300 reward from Wells Fargo for his bravery in the incident and used the money to take his family to the World's Fair in Chicago.

John and Balinda Herrick obtained a claim seven miles southeast of Perry shortly after the September 16, 1893, opening of the Cherokee Strip, although they did not make the run.

Manuel returned to the home of his parents in Noble County after a few months at Oak Lawn Retreat. By this time he was nineteen, weighed almost 200 pounds and was extremely strong. He wore his hair long and had a full beard. He helped his father with farm work, but the Herricks had chosen poor land with thin soil and many outcroppings of rock. Its crop yield was not immense.

Most of their quarter-section was good only for grazing, although a few acres in the south part were suitable for growing corn and other small grain crops. Other farmers in the area wondered how the Herricks eked out a living. They rarely saw Jack or his son working.

The Frank Dvorak family, hard-working Czechoslovakians, had the farm immediately south of the Herricks. Manuel quarreled with them constantly and even built a block house with a porthole for a rifle near his home. From time to time he would herd his parents into the small fortress, take a gun from the shelf and yell: "Hide, hide! The Bohemians are coming!" Needless to say, the two families had a very strained relationship.

Manuel felt called to preach as a youth. He most often could be found speaking in a very loud, high-pitched voice to the open spaces in his backyard. He had a forceful manner and his booming voice was a distinctive characteristic throughout his life. He neither smoked nor drank liquor and condemned those who did.

Manuel was known to rise in place while attending church services, interrupting the preacher to tell his own version of how the congregation should be living. As a result he soon was not welcome at any church in Perry, so the family rarely attended church or Sunday school.

The eccentric farm youth was not well liked around the county but he enjoyed seeing his name in the newspaper. When Oklahoma achieved statehood in 1907, he began running for various political offices, including sheriff, commissioner, and others. Sometimes he ran as a Democrat, sometimes as a Republican, and sometimes as an independent. He never won any of them.

Manuel was contentious and always seemed to be involved in lawsuits with his neighbors. Although he loved to talk with anyone who would listen, he had no close friends. He frequently walked to town, barefoot, and took naps on the grassy lawn of the court-house park. It appeared he was a lonely man. He was the butt of many practical jokes.

During the winter of 1911, on December 9, Balinda Herrick died at the age of seventy. Manuel and his father clothed her in men's underwear and put the body between two feather mattresses in an upstairs room until the ground thawed so that a grave could be dug.

It also was reported that both John and Manuel expected her to be returned to life after three days, and for that reason delayed the burial. A court order was issued requiring them to have the body removed to the Newton Funeral Home in preparation for burial. She was interred on December 16, 1911, near the back door of the family home. The family's native stone home still stands, badly weathered, southeast of Perry. It now shelters only birds and field animals that wander into it.

### MR. HERRICK GOES TO CONGRESS

The Hon. Dick T. Morgan had been elected to Congress for six consecutive terms from this district of Oklahoma and was heavily favored for reelection in 1920 when he died unexpectedly that summer on the Fourth of July. It was one month before the primary election but after the time limit for candidates to file.

That unprecedented set of circumstances automatically gave the Republican nomination to the only other person to file Manuel Herrick of Perry. The general election in November saw a Republican landslide throughout the country, with Warren G. Harding being swept into office as President by a record vote. In normally Democratic Oklahoma, five of the eight congressional seats were filled by Republicans, and one of them was Manuel Herrick.

The story was told that Manuel, the inveterate and unsuccessful county-level office-seeker for years, had been boasting early in 1920 that he would be the next congressman from the Eighth District of Oklahoma. Rep. Morgan, the incumbent, was so popular he was considered unbeatable. When he died, Republicans realized their only candidate was the eccentric Manuel and tried to have the filing period reopened. They were unable to do so. Mr. Herrick had no primary opposition, and despite his reputation he won the general election over Democrat Zaccheus Amos Harris by a comfortable margin. The rest of the story is history. Congressman Herrick soon made Oklahoma the laughing stock of the nation.

Zack Harris had been minister of the First Christian Church of Blackwell for thirteen years but left the pulpit because of throat trouble and became a successful farmer and businessman. He sought the Democratic party nomination for Congress in 1914 but lost in the primary to Henry S. Johnston of Perry.

Rep. Morgan, an able attorney, came to Perry from Guthrie in 1893 and practiced law here until 1901, when he moved to El Reno. Three years later he was appointed by President Theodore Roosevelt to the position of register of the U.S. Land Office at Woodward. That remained his home until the time of his death. He was first elected to Congress in 1908 from the old Second District. The Eighth District was created in 1914, and he continued to serve from there.

Partly as a result of the campaign, Manuel cut his hair and shaved off his beard. He sometimes wore a coat and trousers that matched, and a necktie. Some Republican supporters in Enid were reported to have given him the new clothes. Other party members in Tulsa also bought him a new suit when they realized he would be representing the state of Oklahoma in Washington. Manuel himself set a record by spending only $300 in a successful congressional election campaign.

Addressing a Perry Chamber of Commerce banquet on the eve of his departure for Washington, the congressman-elect said:

"I suppose this should be the happiest moment of my life.... But I want you to know it is not a happy moment for me. If I had attained this position years ago, it would probably have been a happy occasion, but now I am like the beautiful fairy with the golden wand, who was doomed to go through life, bringing happiness to everyone except herself."

Although the remarks were designed to evoke sympathy on his behalf, the imagery was all wrong. Somehow it was too much of a stretch, equating Manuel Herrick with a beautiful fairy.

He distributed this written warning to newspapermen as his last official statement before leaving. The spelling, quotation marks, capitalization and grammar are just as he wrote them:

BEWARE!

February The 22, 1921

"Manuel Herrick Left Today on the 9 O'clock Train To Assume his Duties In washington D.C. Before Leaving he Stated That all news paper Reporters who are wise and value Their good health while The have got It will Stay awa from him ESpecially Those Representing *The Daily Oklahomian* and *Daily news*." Manuel Herrick. "Print this just like I wrote it, capital letters and all, or leave it out of the paper."

Thus ended the congressman's comments for that day.

Rep. Herrick tried to persuade Erle F. Cress of Perry to take a position as his private secretary. He would have been an excellent choice, but young Cress was not interested. He was the son of Mr. and Mrs. P.W. Cress. His father was a prominent attorney and Republican party leader. Erle was a graduate of Kansas University and Harvard, and eventually he became a career officer in the U.S. Army. He served in the Cavalry and later in the new Armored branch when tanks became a major weapon. His brother, Paul Cress, is a retired Perry attorney.

Manuel's two years in Washington were undistinguished, except for his controversial and embarrassing behavior. The first bill he introduced as a member of the House of Representatives would have made it unlawful for anyone other than a member of Congress to conduct a beauty contest. While the measure was still being processed, he became impatient and introduced a beauty contest on his own.

To enlist entries, he wrote a series of letters to some of Washington's fair young maidens. The language he chose was too provocative for newspapers of that day to reproduce. The congressman was chased down the street and hit on the head with a broom by his landlady after her sixteen-year-old daughter received one of the letters. Manuel offered himself as the grand prize for the winner of the beauty contest.

As a result of the contest, Manuel was threatened with a $50,000 breach of promise suit by a Washington matron. She claimed that Mr. Herrick had called on her daughter, a leader in a previous beauty contest. He reportedly told the young woman he was wealthy and that if she married him she would not have to work.

The mother of another contestant asked Washington police to keep Congressman Herrick away from her daughter, claiming he was paying her too much attention.

His whimsical ways were duly reported by the Washington staffs of all the major U.S. newspapers, and Manuel lost his Congressional office in the next primary election. Enid newspaperman M.C. Garber won the Republican nomination in August 1922; Manuel came in third. Mr. Garber went on to become the only Republican congressman elected from Oklahoma that year, and he continued in the office until losing it to E.W. Marland in 1932.

Manuel tried to get the office back, but lost in the primary elections of 1924, 1926, 1928 and, for the last time, in 1930.

When his term in Congress ended, Manuel remained in Washington for a time. On August 12, 1930, word reached Perry that he had been arrested and jailed in Maryland on charges of operating a whisky still, an odd situation for a lifelong teetoaler.

Ethelyn Chrane, a secretary in his office while he was a congressman, carried on a love affair with Manuel. Both of them evidently were willing parties, but trouble brewed.

Mr. Herrick, listing his occupation as a private detective, was charged in a D.C. police court with disorderly conduct on May 3, 1923. Evidence in the case indicated that he had stopped Miss Chrane, who then asked a passerby to bring a policeman. The officer testified that Manuel became profane when the arrest was made. He was convicted of disorderly conduct.

The following month he brought a $50,000 breach of promise suit against Miss Chrane, alleging that she had reneged on a promise to marry him. She was found guilty and Manuel was awarded a judgment of one cent.

It did not end there, however. As a result of Mr. Herrick's statements in the breach of promise suit, Miss Chrane hit him with a $100,000 damage suit, plus court costs. She won the suit and on November 4, 1924, a jury awarded her $7,500 damages. This was later reduced to $6,000. In 1932, Manuel's Noble County farm was sold at a sheriff's auction to satisfy his creditors. It brought only $1,500. Miss Chrane received nothing.

Manuel returned to Noble County and became almost a fixture in the Perry courthouse park, visiting with anyone who strolled by or napping on the grass if the weather permitted. He let his hair and beard grow and once again he donned his comfortable, dirty overalls. Odd jobs and welfare apparently provided him with a meager living.

Sometime during the early 1930s, no one knows just when or how, Manuel joined the Oklahoma migration to California. He settled near Quincy in a hilly region where prospectors looked for gold. His behavior changed little in the new surroundings, and in 1948 he even took a fling at Congress again, cross-filing as both a Democrat and a Republican. He lost badly to the popular incumbent, Rep. Clare Engle, who also cross-filed.

Quincy is located some 150 miles northwest of Sacramento and about eighty miles northwest of Reno, Nevada. Manuel lived like a hermit in a miner's shack a few miles from Quincy, and his life was much as it had been in Oklahoma.

On January 10 or 11 in 1952, Manuel became lost in a snowstorm while trying to walk to his cabin. After several days of effort, searchers found his frozen body on February 29 at the foot of a tall pine tree. He was wearing his familiar overalls, a coat and a large felt hat that completely covered his bearded face. A toboggan was required to bring the body out for return to Quincy.

Manuel was buried in the pauper's section of the Quincy cemetery with a simple granite marker bearing his name, birth and death years, and "Native of Ohio" inscribed on it.

From this perspective of time it is easy to dismiss Manuel Herrick as a certifiable lunatic, and to consider his antics accordingly. Yet there is something very sad about his life, something which might cause us to wonder if he should be more pitied than scorned.

In this present age we seem to accept wild behavior patterns almost as a norm, attributing them to a variety of psychological reasons which few genuinely understand. Medication and therapy often are used to bring some very eccentric personalities under control and to convert them into useful, productive people.

If Manuel Herrick had lived today, his lonely and convoluted path might have been much different. We can only ponder that possibility. Lacking evidence to the contrary, this generation must look back upon him as a pathetic and deranged man who probably was tormented by demons that he alone recognized.

# 21

## $E$DDIE, KATE & THE KUMBACK

Institutions come in many shapes and sizes. One of the most notable in Perry sprang into existence in 1926 as a very small nickel hamburger shop where the owner took the orders, did most of the cooking and greeted every customer with a smile, a wave of the hand and a few friendly words. Come to think of it, perhaps the owner, whose shape was a bit unique, was more of an institution than his homey little restaurant.

Eddie Parker, a soft-spoken teddy bear of a man with a warm smile, presided over the Kumback Lunch on the north side of the square for more than four decades. Unfortunately, he arrived several years too soon for the phenomena of fast food franchising. A nation-wide chain of Kumbacks might have made the grade if there had been enough Eddie Parkers to go around. For Eddie himself was the really distinctive ingredient in the operation.

His ample girth—he weighed 450 pounds when he retired— stood out like a contradiction to the tiny confines of the original Kumback. It was a spartan, no-frills place, occupying a twelve and a half-foot wide masonry building with a double-width window and a single frame door at the front. When summer temperatures made it necessary to keep the door open (in a time long before air-conditioning), the distinctive Kumback aroma drifted tantalizingly over the courthouse square. It smelled just like home cooking, which it was.

❧

Eddie Parker and his twin sister, Ethel, were born July 9, 1901, in Avard, a small community in neighboring Logan County. Their parents were Bert and Minnie Parker. The couple had an unusual multiple-birth family. Their children—thirteen in all—included triplets and two sets of twins.

All of Bert and Minnie's children bore a strong family resemblance. They had a round-faced, cherubic chubbiness, a soft, ready smile and a way of speaking that quickly made you realize they were gentle people. At their family reunions, which continued as the children grew up and produced their own children, there was always a lot of hugging and kissing when younger generations were welcomed into the fold. Total strangers also found themselves wanting to walk up and hug them, for they were appealing people.

One of the triplet brothers, Willard Parker, who now lives southeast of Perry in the Lake McMurtry area, is helping to perpetuate the multiple-birth tradition. His daughter, Mrs. Anna Thompson, a school teacher in Moore, has given birth to triplets and twins. Willard's wife is the former Catherine Schultz, a native of this area.

The other triplet brothers in Eddie's immediate family are Willis and Wilmer. Willard is a "senior" employee at McDonald's Restaurant in Perry, with the special responsibility of making breakfast biscuits. Willis and his wife, Ann, recently celebrated their thirtieth year in the restaurant business at Hennessey, where Willis' homemade pies and cinnamon rolls are regarded as delicacies. Wilmer is retired and lives in Enid. Eddie's twin sister lives in Pueblo, Colorado.

Obviously, the Parkers also had food service careers in their genes.

Eddie went into business for himself at the age of twenty-four on May 3, 1926, when he bought a small building on the north side of the square in Perry and named it the Kumback Lunch. Legend has it that the name came from Eddie's unfailing habit of saying to each departing customer, "Thank you, and come back." The cafe had been built two years earlier by a Mr. Scott, from whom Eddie bought it.

It was a time of great prosperity here and throughout America. Dining out was popular and Perry had a thriving downtown business district. Shoppers, merchants and clerks needed a place to go for coffee, cold drinks and snacks, and the Kumback was the choice for many of them.

Other cafes were located around the square. Eddie once recalled there were twenty-one eating places on the square in the early 1930s. It was a competitive business.

"If it hadn't been for my friends and creditors," he said, "I wouldn't have been able to stay here."

But the Kumback stood out as a favorite for most people. Perhaps it was the compact building, generating a feeling of closeness. More likely it was the genial host himself, Eddie Parker.

≈

The only seats in the original Kumback were six flat top bar stools at a low wooden counter. All the cooking was done on a grill behind the counter. The most popular item by far was the Kumback hamburger, a generously embellished sandwich which Eddie sold for five cents. He did most of the cooking, using the grill as a kind of artist's canvas where thick hamburger patties were deftly flattened with a spatula and an empty Coke bottle.

Despite the trying times of the 1930s depression, the Kumback remained solvent. Eddie was generous and was known to provide handouts for numerous needy neighbors as well as transients, but for the most part it was a cash business. He paid his waitresses and suppliers on time, and still showed a modest profit.

In the 1930s and 1940s, the Kumback was usually open seven days a week from 5 a.m. until 10 p.m. It was a busy place at mealtime and in between. Coffee was a nickel, with free refills, and plate-size cinnamon rolls were a dime. Hamburgers were a nickel and a bowl of chili was a dime. Sunday noon dinners cost one dollar and included a choice of fried chicken or roast beef, plus mashed potatoes with gravy, two vegetables, a dinner roll and a demi-dessert. Cholesterol was unknown and calories were uncounted. They were carefree days.

Deals were made over the Kumback's unadorned tables. Insurance policies were sold, loans negotiated. Occasionally you might see a bit of hand-holding across the table as a young couple used the cafe for flirtatious conversation.

As the Kumback's business grew, Eddie acquired another major asset. He hired Kate Hartung Mewherter to take charge of menu planning, the kitchen and waitresses. She was experienced and capable in all these areas, and that took a great deal of the load off Eddie's back. He still worked behind the counter at the grill.

Kate's gentle manner and pleasant, friendly voice—issuing from a face that always seemed to be sweetly smiling—quickly became part of the Kumback charm.

On May 9, 1944, Kate became Eddie's wife. It was the second marriage for each of them. In due time their customers began calling the Kumback "Kate and Eddie's place," for it truly was a partnership in every sense. Kate was the perfect complement to Eddie.

Kate was born April 27, 1903, in Garfield County, adjoining Noble County on the west, the daughter of early-day settlers Ed and Bessie Hartung. She graduated from Perry High School and spent her entire life in this area.

❧

Dick Foster worked at the city-owned power plant in the southeast part of Perry. He was an early riser by nature, not necessarily by choice. He usually awoke around 3 a.m., and since his shift at the plant did not start until 8 a.m., he had time to kill. Rather than risk disturbing his wife, Lucille, who was a better sleeper than he was, Dick fell into the habit of walking six blocks to the Kumback for breakfast and conversation with other pre-dawn denizens of the business district. It was a ritual still practiced by many.

Dick was usually the first to arrive, even on the bad weather days when it was raining or snowing. Quite often he would be there to help Eddie open the place at 4 a.m., a full hour before customers were admitted. Dick's interest led him to asking questions about kitchen procedures, and soon he began lending a hand with mixing the pancake batter. He became proficient at it and at some point the chore was turned over to him entirely. The job was his for several years. He was never paid for it nor did he expect to be. He loved doing it.

As time went on Dick also helped with the Kumback's cinnamon roll production, taking dough (which had been mixed by the night crew) from the refrigerator and popping it into the oven.

A lot of people bragged on his pancakes. Once his daughter, Penny, who now lives in Illinois, asked Dick to share the recipe so she could try it at home. He had never regarded it as a major industrial secret, but no one had ever asked for it before, so he had to write it down. Penny never got beyond the first line: "Take twenty eggs...." Obviously it was not something to be stirred up in your average housewife's kitchen where just two people were the usual number served.

Even after he retired as a city employee in 1980, Dick still had trouble sleeping past 3 a.m., so he continued as an unpaid kitchen worker at the Kumback for two or three years, until his health failed.

⁊⦿

By 1941 the cafe was prospering but facing a crisis: It was too small to handle all the people who tried to wedge themselves into it each day. Eddie had already built an addition for a few tables and booths at the rear of the building, making it L-shaped. He could see two options: (A) Move to another location, or (B), put his loyal customers on hold while the tiny building was torn down to make way for a new and larger one at the same site. He didn't like either idea.

After carefully considering the problem, he came up with a creative solution: Erect a new building over the old one, then pull the old one out from under it.

Two local contractors, Glen McLimans and Frank Boone, convinced him they could do it, and Eddie decided that was the way to go. The experiment proved successful enough that it was discussed in the "Wake of the News" column on the front page of *the Perry Daily Journal* on June 3, 1941, with this final comment:

"Eddie serves real food and runs a darned good restaurant. More power to him." The community was proud of what he had done.

The new construction featured a gleaming, maroon and cream tile front, replacing the familiar white masonry of the original building. A neon sign was hung outside with the simple message: "EAT," in vertically stacked capital letters. The small dining area at the rear again contained tables and booths to maintain the L-shape design of the previous building. The counter area was considerably longer and wider, more stools were provided, and a sparkling new kitchen at the back of the building contained the latest features to improve and expedite the service to diners.

A grand opening heralded the launching of the new Kumback. Customers approved of the upgraded accommodations, and it seemed a new era had dawned. But, along came World War II. The U.S. was drawn in as an active belligerent on December 7, 1941, and the situation changed radically in a hurry.

The war created shortages of virtually everything needed to operate a business. Emergency controls permeated all aspects of life on the home front. The nation's mighty war effort brought more people into the work force, but many of them left America's small towns, like Perry, for the big city. Young ladies who had been waitresses or kitchen helpers became aircraft riveters and shipyard welders.

Restaurants fought a day to day battle for cooks and waitresses, sugar, eggs and milk—even cooking oil. Every business had unprecedented problems to deal with. It was perhaps a small sacrifice compared to so many others', but that was the reality of their particular struggle.

Eddie, Kate and the Kumback found ways to deal with the emergency and survived. When the war ended in 1945, Eddie announced a welcome home gift for all returning veterans—a free steak dinner. Dozens of former GIs—Eddie estimated at least two-hundred of them—happily accepted as they came home from military service. Life began to resemble its normal self once again.

Fire, the constant threat hovering over any kitchen, caused major damage at the Kumback in 1953. It was a real disaster. The business was shut down while the interior was completely rebuilt and redecorated.

Eddie, always a large man who obviously enjoyed good food, had reached his peak weight by then and that was creating multiple problems for his body. His doctor advised him: "Leave the cafe and find something to do outdoors," or risk the loss of his health.

The first step was finding something he could do, not an easy task for one with his background and physique. The late Gene Luttrell, who at the time operated Perry's Bettye Anne Bakery, was a Kumback supplier and customer and also a friend of Eddie's. He remembers Eddie came to him and asked for a job driving a bakery truck on the daily route to Enid.

"I told him he couldn't handle a job like that," Gene recalled. "It was really hard work, especially for a big man like he was, getting up and down out of that truck, lifting a lot of heavy objects, and so forth. But Eddie insisted he could do it and he really wanted it, so I hired him.

"He only worked for me nine months, but he did a whale of a job. It seemed like he knew everybody in Enid, all the grocers and cafe owners, because he had been in business so long himself. One day, about the time he was ready to give up the route, Eddie and I were talking and he took a pencil that had been behind his ear. He dropped it to the floor and just looked at me. I didn't know what was happening," Luttrell said, "but then he leaned over, picked it up, and held it in my face."

"That's the first time I've been able to do that in thirty years," Eddie told Luttrell, "and it feels great."

He had lost one hundred pounds, several inches around the waist and his health had improved considerably. Eddie still wanted to slim down, so he took up another new career—volunteering as a newspaper carrier for *the Perry Daily Journal.* Walking his route each afternoon was an enjoyable and healthful experience.

"This is fun," Eddie commented while tossing papers onto porches one afternoon. "It lets me visit friends, enjoy the sunshine and absorb some of this good fresh air."

"Best carrier we ever had," one customer said of Eddie.

*The Journal* ran a page one interview and photograph of Eddie after he became a carrier. On July 1, 1968, he chose to fully retire. He sold the Kumback to Kate and turned over the total responsibility for operating the business to her. He concentrated his attention on lawn and garden chores plus a home workshop at their neat white bungalow on Cedar Street. His weight problem was under control.

Kate continued as owner/operator until July 1, 1973, when she sold the landmark Perry restaurant to Tony and Marilee Macias, two young hometown people who grew up knowing of the affection Perry residents held for the Kumback. After more than sixty years, only two families have owned the cafe. It is Oklahoma's oldest cafe in the same location and with the same original name.

ஒ

While Tony Macias was growing up and attending Perry High School in the 1960s, he had a part-time job at the Kumback. Eddie taught him how to trim cuts of meat and many other aspects of restaurant operation. Tony was a natural athlete and became a member of the University of Oklahoma's wrestling team after graduating from PHS. Later, he coached championship wrestlers at the high school and college level in Oklahoma City and on the West Coast.

Marilee Gantt and Tony were high school sweethearts who became husband and wife. They decided to return to Perry and buy the Kumback in 1973, and again the operation has been a joint venture. They have added Mexican cuisine and otherwise expanded the menu to a great extent. Marilee also has been deeply involved in civic projects.

The interior of the restaurant was redecorated in 1974, and the Press Box dining room was added five years later. The old tile front was replaced by a wooden frontier-era facade in June 1981, and a major interior remodeling project was launched in October 1985. A dividing wall between the Press Box and the dining area was removed and the seating capacity was increased by twenty-two when the booth and bar area were rebuilt. A brass and wood carving was designed by Marilee and built by Tony, and the Kumback again stayed open through it all.

Noble County voters approved liquor by the drink in June 1985, and in December that year the Kumback added "Pub" to its name as cocktails and draught beer became available. The Kumback still cuts and grinds all its own meat. Pies, doughnuts, biscuits, dinner rolls and the famous cinnamon rolls are still home baked daily.

Inflation has taken its toll on prices, of course. While Eddie Parker was able to serve his original Kumback hamburger for five cents, the least expensive burger on the 1991 menu is $1.75.

≥●

Kate and Eddie knew several years of relaxation in pursuit of gardening and other hobbies after both had retired. They still enjoyed cooking, and rarely went out to eat. Friends were frequent guests at their dinner table.

Eddie died on August 9, 1986, and Kate passed away in July 1989. Their deaths marked the close of an era in the community which they served in a special way for so many years.

The Kumback itself, however, remains a living institution and a memorial to their unique, gentle ways. They touched many lives.

Because they did, visitors for years to come undoubtedly will still be hearing about Eddie, Kate and the Kumback in Perry, Oklahoma.

# 22

# $W$KL AND THE PERRY JOURNAL

He was not a tall man, perhaps five feet seven inches, and his figure was inclined to be pear-shaped. When he reached middle-age, only a few wisps of hair remained and they were pulled straight back, barely covering the scalp. A cigar was usually clenched firmly in a fist or between his teeth. He was Wesley Kenneth Leatherock, publisher of the *Perry Daily Journal*, and a powerful presence for the better part of two decades in this community.

He signed his personal column in the newspaper with lower case initials, no periods: wkl. To most people he was simply "W.K.," but his employees respectfully called him "Boss" or "Mr. Leatherock." He pretended to be gruff, but his face and chubby waist line had a kind of Winston Churchill cherubic quality that sometimes made the facade hard to believe.

Perry has had at least one newspaper since the day the Cherokee Strip was opened on September 16, 1893. The *Journal* was not here at the beginning, but its ancestry can be traced back to that point.

The first paper distributed here was the *Perry Times*, a daily and weekly publication. Copies were printed in Guthrie and brought here the afternoon of the opening by Bert H. Green, an enterprising publisher.

Also on the first day, Lon Wharton came to Perry from Chandler with the *Perry Sentinel*, which he later changed to the *Noble County Sentinel*. Mr. Wharton was a colorful, fun-loving character who thrived on controversy. In time, the game grew old, he sold his interest and moved to California.

*The Perry Republican* was established in the early days by Arthur Boles and James W. Casey with the backing of Boles' father, Judge A.H. Boles, who had been register of the Land Office in 1889.

Mr. Casey later purchased his partner's interest and published the paper as a daily and a weekly for several years.

Virgil C. Welch and Ed Perry came here in the early days from Alma, Kansas, and began printing the *Weekly Enterprise*. Within a few years they had purchased Bert Green's paper, combining it with theirs to create the *Enterprise-Times*. The *Perry Republican* later absorbed the *Enterprise-Times*.

The *Perry Daily Democrat* was on the streets a few days after the opening, published by Tom Stumbaugh and Bob Galbreath, but apparently it did not last any great length of time.

Others which came and went included the *Perry Populist*, published by Colly and Olds; the *Perry Independent*, published by Sidney Sapp; the *Perry Rustler* and *McKinney Teller,* published by Frank Prouty; the *Oklahoma Herald*, published by Edgar Watkins; the *Populist Independent,* published by Bee Guthrey; the *Perry Democrat-Patriot,* edited by J. Roy Williams; the *Perry Eagle*; and a weekly German-language newspaper, *Oklahoma Neurkerten*, published in the basement of the old First National Bank building at the southeast corner of the square.

The *Perry Daily Journal* was established February 7, 1924, by C.P. Penfield when he consolidated the *Republican* and *Sentinel* weeklies. A two-column announcement on page one of the first edition of the *Journal* gave some details of the new arrangement. Judge E.W. Jones was editor of the *Republican.* Mr. Penfield and E.M. Willett had been owners of the *Sentinel.*

In his farewell statement, Judge Jones concluded: "So the *Perry Journal* is born, offspring of the *Sentinel* and the *Republican.*" The editor also had at one time been county judge here. In 1931 he wrote "Early Day History of Perry, Oklahoma," an interesting and valuable resource document. Judge Jones looked to be a dour little man, but his chronic scowl was more the badge of the aches and pains of advanced age than an indication of his true nature.

The same year Mr. Penfield started the *Journal,* he sold it to Mr. Leatherock, who was twenty-seven years old at the time. Mr. Leatherock operated the *Journal* until 1927 when he left Perry to found the *Clinton Daily News.* While at Clinton he purchased the *Sayre Headlight,* although he never lived in Sayre. After selling his interests in Clinton, Mr. Leatherock moved to Longview, Texas, and operated the newspaper there until 1933, when he returned to Perry. He published the paper here until his death on February 10, 1949.

Mr. Leatherock was the instigator or promoter of many of this community's major civic projects. As a member of a city planning commission appointed by Mayor G.A. Ley when World War II was ending, Mr. Leatherock outlined plans for major improvements in Perry. This ultimately led to a $494,000 bond issue providing funds for sewer extension, water line extension, a municipal hospital and a new white way lighting system for the business district. It was an ambitious, far-sighted post-war program for this city.

In the 1930s he was credited with being the moving force behind construction of the Perry stadium, the present water supply lake and the Perry airport. He was a leader in the American Legion and served in 1941-42 as a district governor of Rotary International. He was a Mason and a member of the Presbyterian Church. Mr. Leatherock and his late wife, Avis, reared two children: A son, Wesley, now of Oklahoma City, and a daughter, Marianne Baker, who died in 1990.

Along with all this he put out a lively daily newspaper. His personal column, "In the Wake of the News," appeared regularly on the front page and contained pithy, witty bits of information, along with his personal opinion on a variety of subjects. His points were always well made; no one had to wonder where he stood on matters of current interest. Although he had little direct involvement with the news content of each day's paper, staff members knew his perspective. Frequent memos from The Boss kept them apprised of his feelings, and they endeavored to reflect that in their coverage.

W.K. was born April 30, 1897, in Cherryvale, Kansas, and volunteered for the Army as an enlisted man in the 35th Infantry Division shortly after the U.S. entered World War I. He was severely wounded in the Battle of the Argonne. After his discharge, Mr. Leatherock purchased a newspaper in Augusta, Kansas, in 1920, and remained there until coming to Perry for the first time in 1924.

After an illness of several months, Mr. Leatherock died February 10, 1949. His successor at the helm of the *Journal* was Milo W. Watson, whom he had hired as advertising manager in 1943.

Milo came here from the *Harper County News* in Buffalo, one of Oklahoma's outstanding weekly papers. He bought an interest in the *Journal* in 1945 and later, after W.K.'s death, he also purchased Mrs. Leatherock's interest. Watson started in the newspaper business as a printer with the *Moran Herald* in Kansas in 1932. He worked in the *Chanute* (Kan.) *Tribune* news department for two years before moving on to Buffalo in 1936.

Milo has been the community's conscience and chief motivator for nearly a half century now. He has supported every worthwhile project undertaken during that time, and he initiated many of them.

Perry is the smallest town in Oklahoma with a daily newspaper. Advertisers and subscribers have made this possible, of course. In return, the *Journal* has always provided the Noble County area with upbeat, thoroughly local news coverage, to the point where it is considered an indispensable part of family life.

Many memorable people, in addition to Milo and Mr. Leatherock, have helped to shape the character of the *Journal.* Managing editors and columnists such as O.B. Campbell, Sam Schwieger, Dick Cheney, Jack Ludrick, Francis Thetford and Jane Schneider; advertising and production experts like Virgil Sherrod, Wendell Gottschall, Boyd Norman, Vivian Skinner and Dale Harms; shop foremen, floormen and typesetters like Harry Jones, Peary Gaskill, Carl Carmichael, Harry Rudolph, Eva Blanche Austin, Buck Lee and Ernie Stoops; circulation managers like Bill Lane, Merl Edwards and Ray Baughman; and bookkeepers like Irene Dolezal and Harry A. DeLashmutt. This would be a far longer list if each worthy were included.

Every newspaper has its own personality. The *Journal's* is a blend of all the staff members who ever occupied its desks, ran its news beats, laid out its advertisements, composed type, loaded its presses, distributed its daily offerings, or otherwise contributed to the production of this perky, small-town chronicle, going back to the days of Bert H. Green and the *Perry Daily Times.* It is quite a heritage.

# *L*IONS AND ROTARIANS

Men's service clubs flourished in small and medium-sized communities throughout the country in the 1920s. Most of them had
their start a decade earlier in large metropolitan centers, but the
era of greatest growth came later.

Perry proved fertile ground for two such organizations, the
Lions Club and Civitan, in 1926 and 1927. The Civitan Club lasted
only briefly and its members soon switched allegiance to the Rotary
Club.

Today neither calls itself a "men's club." Women have been
welcomed into membership by both organizations. The Lions and
Rotarians have maintained a friendly rivalry for members through
the years while contributing greatly to a vast array of civic en-
deavors.

The Lions date their beginning to a meeting on January 8, 1926,
when thirty men turned out at the Carnegie Library to discuss the
possibility of organizing locally. Most of them signed the charter
roll, and others were added six days later when the official charter
meeting was held. In all, the club had twenty-nine charter members.

W.F. Boone was the first president. Other charter members
were Dr. O.W. Boyer, Ross Johnson, Dr. B.A. Owen, Paul Harding,
Bill Fry Jr., Carl Voris, Rev. J.A. Nagle, Ed Coyle, H.L. Johnson,
George Doyle Jr., Charles Collins, Walter A. Bittman, George W.
Clark, Ralph E. Foster, Rudolph Gottlieb, Joe E. Howard, Henry L.
Johnson, Henry S. Johnston, Ivan L. Kennedy, A.C. Lamb, W.A.
Malloch, W.J. McCuiston, Charles Monroe, Walter S. Powers, W.J.
Reckert, W.H. Sheets, L.F. Sowers and L.O. Winters.

From the beginning, Lions have maintained an active interest
and participation in community service projects. Some of these
have reached well beyond the city limits of Perry. The club was

instrumental in establishing the Lions Eye Bank in 1957. This program alone has benefitted hundreds throughout the country.

Perry Lions continue to support the Oklahoma Eye Bank and the Dean A. McGee Eye Foundation in Oklahoma City. Their concern in this area also includes purchasing eye glasses for local area residents who are unable to pay for their own.

The club for many years has contributed five dollars per capita to the IOA Boys Ranch near Perkins. As other needs have been identified, Lions have provided financial support or other means of assistance.

Lions West Park is a favorite recreation center for Perryans of all ages, and the club has made it a top priority. Although it was originally built and equipped by the city as a municipal park, the Lions have been permitted to add a picnic shelter and other facilities which otherwise might not have been possible. The park has two hard-surfaced, lighted tennis courts plus the much-used Municipal Swimming Pool. Club members also have built a picnic shelter at Perry Lake, the municipal reservoir southwest of the city.

In the early years after receiving their charter, the Lions had their Thursday luncheon meetings in the basement of the Carnegie Library. Women from various churches alternated in serving the meals but in the 1940s only one group, the Catholic ladies, was able to continue doing this. As a result, meetings were moved to the St. Rose of Lima Catholic parish hall, then located in the church basement. When the former St. Joseph's Academy was closed, the school building became the church's new parish hall and Lions have been meeting there each Thursday noon for several years.

The nucleus of the Rotary Club was carried over from the Civitan Club, which was organized in the spring of 1927. The Civitans were discontented because there were only two other such organizations in the state, one in Oklahoma City and one in Tulsa. They were hoping for more opportunities for fellowship.

With the help of the Blackwell Rotary Club, several Civitans began exploring the possibility of making a change. The effort was climaxed on July 14, 1927, when a charter night dinner was held by the newly organized Perry Rotary Club in the basement of the First Baptist Church.

Dr. A.M. Crowder was the first president. Other charter members were Bert W. Byerley, Max Chambers, Dr. D.F. Coldiron, Howard R. Cress, H.C. Donahue, Harry Donaldson, H.G. Donley,

Morris Gottlieb, H.A. Hart, Charles Huffman, Harry C. Jackson, Arthur Johnston, Sherman Krisher, Albert Lobsitz, Loren S. Loomis, Bruce R. Lucas, Joe McClellan, McKinley Miller, Henry H. Reynolds, Fred G. Moore, J.A. Samuelson, Rev. G. Frank Sanders, Herbert C. Sanford, Gerald S. Tebbe and Marsh Woodruff.

Like the Lions, the Rotarians met for several years in the basement of the Carnegie Library where meals were served by various church women. When only the Catholic ladies were able to continue this in the 1940s, Rotary meetings were moved to the parish hall in the Catholic Church basement, then to the former St. Joseph's Academy when that building became the parish hall. In more recent years Rotarians have moved their Monday noon meetings to the Cherokee Strip Restaurant.

The Perry Rotary Club has given more, per capita, to PolioPlus, a major world health project conceived by Rotary International, than any club in this district. Proceeds of this project are being used to wipe out polio and other diseases in third world countries and elsewhere around the globe.

Both the Lions and Rotarians contribute to worthwhile projects in significant ways. The youth baseball program, junior livestock show, various support groups in the local schools—these and more have been the recipients of continuing assistance. Both clubs are active in the "adopt a highway" program, clearing litter from stretches of major roads in this area. Both work to make the Cherokee Strip celebration a success each year. Each club has its own unique projects that serve in different ways to improve the local community and beyond.

Similar clubs have come and gone in Perry. A Kiwanis Club had a brief life span, and other groups have investigated the possibility of getting started here. Though not the same orientation, a Toastmasters Club has been active from time to time, and of course the unique Poor Boys Club made an impact during the 1930s and well into the 1940s before disbanding.

Through it all, however, the Lions and Rotarians have provided the community with a continuous flow of dedicated service for more than sixty-five years.

# 24

# $T$ HE WRESTLING CAPITAL

Perry and wrestling are one and the same to many people. The sport is one of the oldest sources of pride in this community for good and valid reasons. Numerous records, fully documented, have been established by individual wrestlers and Perry High School teams down through the years, enough of them that perhaps nowhere else on earth can a little town like this have so much cause to flex its muscles and brag.

Since wrestling was introduced to the local high school in 1922, the Perry Maroons have won twenty-four Oklahoma state team championships, the most by any state team and more than three times the number of the closest competitor in their class. Through 1981, they won eleven consecutive state first place team trophies. In addition, 112 individual Perry wrestlers have won state championships.

The Maroons also earned their first state dual team championship in class 2A in 1991. That tournament, established in 1989, recognizes total team points, rather than individual weight champions. The Perry matmen then qualified ten individuals for the traditional state tournament and won that crown by a decisive 31-point margin.

The record is without equal in Oklahoma and is one of the most remarkable for any sport in the U.S.

Perry has a population of about 4,900 and a three-year high school enrollment of around 300. In the early days of competition, before four divisions were created based on enrollment, Perry competed against much larger schools from Oklahoma City, Tulsa, Ponca City and Enid, and beat all of them regularly. Their enrollments were larger than Perry's by several hundred.

The decade of the 1930s saw the start of the greatest glory years for the Perry Maroons. Jack VanBebber, the most decorated individual wrestler in PHS history, came along in the 1920s, but most of the team honors began accumulating after Coach John Divine, a local boy, was hired in 1931.

In the 1940-60 era, there was a consensus among coaches, fans and sportwriters that the "Big Four" of Oklahoma high school wrestling consisted of Perry, Ponca City, Blackwell and Stillwater, all located within a few miles of each other in North-Central Oklahoma. The rivalry among them led to the creation of a special mid-season tournament that provided some of the greatest thrills the sport has seen in this state. Many of the finest wrestlers produced in Oklahoma have come from those schools. Some of the coaches also went on to greater fame at major universities.

Winning at wrestling is a Perry tradition because the interest starts the moment a little boy arrives upon the scene. Older brothers, uncles, cousins, dads and assorted others begin by show-ing off their own special holds and moves as soon as the youngster develops an attention span of any length, and the training grows more intense day by day.

Championships don't just happen automatically. Hours of sweaty workouts, miles and miles of running and other condition-ing programs, strict dieting to maintain a weight level, plus as-sorted other muscle-building and character-building regimens are required for any boy who sets his goals high in this sport. It is strictly one-on-one when you're out there on the mat. You and the other guy, that's all.

They don't turn out champions with a cookie cutter at Perry High School. Each boy does it on his own, but he does have unusual resources available.

It is true that most adult Perry males, even those who never wrestled at Perry High School or anywhere else, are unusually knowledgeable about the sport. They learn it through a kind of osmosis, or perhaps a radiation process, because they are exposed to it constantly. Then they are more than willing to share this with sons, nephews, even grandchildren and great-grandchildren, or just little friends. The sport has been around that long in this town.

The inevitable and phenomenal result is an entire community wrapped up in the ancient art of wrestling.

The expertise is not limited to the male gender. Many members of the so-called gentler sex know some wrestling pointers and skills which they can teach to a wide-eyed youngster at the drop of a mat.

Long before martial arts became a fad, Perry boys and girls learned about takedowns, pin holds and referee harassment.

Perry is one of the smallest towns in the U.S. with a full-facility YMCA, and one of its most popular programs is the wrestling instruction provided by some of the town's best qualified amateur coaches—former Perry Maroons who still love the sport.

The peculiarity of genetically and environmentally transmitted wrestling know-how was illustrated a few years ago during a certain Perry High School match. The rivalry was intense, and the name of the other team does not matter because that's the condition at all Perry High School matches. The referee was Ocie Anderson of Blackwell, younger brother of Byard Anderson of Perry. Ocie and Byard both were veteran, well-liked school administrators and coaches. Both are now deceased.

Ocie was a seasoned wrestling official and was doing his usual good job that night. However, also as usual, each match produced extremely noisy, sometimes abusive and heated fan reactions in the crowded gymnasium. Finally, after he decided that every call he was going to make would be noisily brought into question by numerous individuals in the stands, a red-faced Ocie marched angrily to the timekeeper's table and slammed down his whistle, the signal and badge of a referee's authority.

"You don't need ME to referee," Ocie told the surprised group at the table. "You've got 5,000 referees in Perry already." He turned and walked directly to the gym exit while spectators watched in an uncharacteristically subdued silence, not really certain what was taking place.

But in a few moments—almost without losing a beat—one of the Perry civilians in the stands was recruited to fill in and the match continued in a rollicking, but orderly, fashion. The substitute referee did not have a striped shirt, but he did perform reasonably well and he stayed on the job until the heavyweights had finished wrestling. No one seriously questioned any of his calls.

The story is true, and in later years Ocie could even smile as he recalled the evening's events.

### JACK VAN BEBBER

Jack VanBebber worked hard to become a champion wrestler, and it paid off for him. Not necessarily in a monetary way, for he lived a modest life, but he accumulated an amazing wealth of honors, awards, medals, decorations and citations. As an Olympic gold medalist, he was the highest achiever yet produced by the Perry High School wrestling program.

In 1932 he won the Olympic gold by defeating the fabled Eino Leino of Finland, who had been a medalist in three previous Olympic games. Perhaps that was the crowning achievement of his collegiate years, but it was not the end of his assault on records and titles. Nor was it the beginning.

Jack Francis VanBebber was born July 27, 1907, the seventh child of Francis Marion and Ila Jeffrey VanBebber. He attended Whipple Grade School in rural Noble County before coming to Perry High School, where his illustrious career in wrestling began. The program was started here in 1922 by Coach Frank Briscoe, who is credited with instilling such a tremendous winning spirit in Jack.

Young VanBebber was undefeated in two years of high school varsity wrestling in 1926-27, winning two gold medals, one silver and one bronze during his prep career; was undefeated for four years as a member of the Oklahoma A.&M. College (now Oklahoma State University) team, won National Collegiate Athletic Association championships in 1929, 1930 and 1931, and national Amateur Athletic Union titles in 1929, 1930, 1931 and 1932, all leading up to the 1932 triumph in the Olympics at Los Angeles. He was the first Oklahoman to win a gold medal in the Olympics. He also won one Pacific Coast and one National Olympic Final in preliminary trials.

He was inducted into the Helms Athletic Hall of Fame in 1962. When the National Wrestling Hall of Fame at Stillwater (the home of OSU) selected its first group of honorees in 1976, Jack Van-Bebber was among them. He was inducted into the Jim Thorpe Hall of Fame at Tulsa in 1978. He is listed in the "Guinness Book of Olympic Records" as a 1932 gold medal winner in the free style welterweight (158 pounds) class. In a 1950 poll among 131 coaches, officials and sports editors throughout the U.S., conducted by *Body Builder Magazine*, he was named one of the ten most oustanding amateur wrestlers in the Western Hemisphere for the first half of the twentieth century.

His coach at Oklahoma A.&M. was the legendary Ed Gallagher, founder of the school's celebrated wrestling program. The 1931 "Redskin," the A.&M. yearbook, had this to say about VanBebber: "The most polished amateur wrestler in the United States is the title conferred on Jack VanBebber, captain of the 1931 all-victorious team."

Nicknamed "Blackjack" in deference to the tough scrub oak trees abounding in Noble County, Jack obviously had a remarkable amateur wrestling career. On several occcasions writers, fans and coaches called him the best ever to wrestle at his weight.

The Olympic year, 1932, produced the high water mark for him with the gold medal win over Finland's Leino. Getting to the Olympics in Los Angeles was a major achievement in itself for Jack, who came from a family of modest means at the time of the Great Depression. No sponsoring organizations were in evidence with funds to help U.S. athletes, even though the summer games were being staged in this country.

VanBebber and a friend, Conrad Caldwell of Miami, Oklahoma, dropped out of A.&M. in January of that year with aspirations of qualifying for the U.S. Olympic wrestling team. Jack lacked only one semester of earning his degree, and he did return to school to complete graduation requirements in 1933.

The story has been frequently told that VanBebber and Caldwell were forced to hitchhike from Oklahoma to Los Angeles to compete. Actually, they only thought about doing that, according to Jack's wife, Julia, who now lives in South Carolina.

"They got as far as Oklahoma City," she relates, "and found someone there who had a car to be driven to Los Angeles, so they took the job and rode the rest of the distance."

Once there, Jack found work in a Safeway Grocery warehouse and lined up the Los Angeles Athletic Club as his sponsor. He won the Pacific Coast welterweight class that summer, while Conrad won the light heavyweight (191-pound) class. In late June the two left for New York City in a model-T Ford provided by a member of the LAAC to compete in an AAU tournament. They stayed in condition by alternately driving and jogging on the cross-country jaunt.

Jack was the only competitor in that summer AAU tournament to pin all eight of his opponents. Although weakened by a kidney ailment, he moved on to Columbus, Ohio, for the final Olympic trials, where he qualified for the U.S. team.

At Los Angeles, VanBebber defeated opponents from Mexico, Denmark and Canada in preliminary rounds of the July Olympics, but faced an unexpected crisis on the day of the final match. He was notified by messenger at the Olympic village that his match had been advanced one hour and no transportation was available to take him on the six-mile trip to the auditorium. The match was to be at 3 p.m., less than two hours away.

Jack put on his wrestling warmup and left the village running in hopes of negotiating the heavily traveled Los Angeles streets in time to make the all-important final match. The August heat was intense as he jogged along the route, trying not to think of his problem. Fortunately, after two miles, an LAAC member recognized him and gave him a ride to the auditorium in time for the match.

His battle with Leino was a classic, matching two fierce and skillful opponents. Jack won a hard-fought decision and claimed the gold for the U.S.

After earning his bachelor's degree in agriculture in May 1933 at A.&M., VanBebber became wrestling coach and assistant economics instructor at Texas Tech in Lubbock. He later took a position with Phillips Petroleum Company and remained with that firm for thirty years, until retiring. He spent three and a half years in the Army Infantry during World War II, serving in Hawaii, New Guinea and the Philippines.

After his retirement, Jack and Julia moved to Perry, and in 1986 he died here after a period of failing health. He contributed much to every community where he lived, working in fraternal orders and in his church, and teaching young men the fundamentals of the sport that brought him international acclaim.

### FRANK BRISCOE AND JOHN DIVINE

Frank Briscoe became Perry High School's first wrestling coach in 1922. Briscoe, son of a pioneer Noble County couple, also coached football and most of the school's other athletic teams. He was a motivator and well qualified in all of them.

Briscoe coached the sport for seven seasons, winning forty-two dual matches, losing six and tying two. Frank learned the sport under the tutelage of Gallagher, the Oklahoma A&M coach.

After leaving the school system in 1928, Briscoe joined his brother, Jack, in a paving company based at Stillwater. They contracted for major jobs throughout the state, and Frank usually was the on-site overseer. His mother lived to a ripe old age at her home in Perry, but Frank faithfully came here each morning to have breakfast with her, often traveling many miles to do so.

According to family friends, it did not matter where the Briscoe company was working—and it could have been in any corner of the state—but Frank would be here bright and early every morning before going to the job. This continued until her death.

The Briscoe home was a one-story red brick structure on Ivanhoe Street next door to Charley Huffman, a grocer with a Will Rogers-like sense of humor. He enjoyed inviting folks up to see "Mr. Briscoe's depot" while the house was being built. Its architectural style evidently reminded him of a train station.

The 1922-23 PHS yearbook, the "Peroma" (a contraction of "Perry" and "Oklahoma"), had this to say: "Mr. Briscoe, our coach, has gained for himself a place in this school that can never be filled by the manager of athletics of future years. He was a good sport and was well liked but the boys seldom 'put one by him.' He placed sports on a standard where they fill an important place in the lives of all classes of students."

Coach Briscoe was powerfully built, slightly barrel-chested and with broad shoulders. He remained trim and looked to be in good condition all his life. His manner was friendly and warm.

Briscoe left PHS at mid-year. Euel Leach, who was to become shop teacher, had been hired to replace him as wrestling coach but found he needed more college credits to qualify for a teaching certificate. His arrival at PHS was delayed.

Kenneth Coldiron, now a retired Perry banker, was the Maroons' team captain in 1928, and Frank asked him to take charge of the team. Kenny gave instructions to his teammates and the younger athletes, and generally did many of the things normally provided by a coach. His team won seven of nine dual matches that season. A faculty member was assigned to be with the team for duals and tournaments. Some of them had never seen a match before that responsibility was thrust upon them.

In 1931 the school hired John Divine to take over the job. Some would say it was a divinely inspired, providential choice. During his long tenure, from 1931 to 1964, Coach Divine's Maroon teams had a peerless dual match record of 241-87-5. His high school teams took the state title in 1951, 1953 and 1961. He coached twenty-six individual state champions and three national champions. Thirty-five of his wrestlers went on to become coaches, and four of them succeeded him at Perry High, including Fred Waltermire, the present PHS coach. Many Divine-coached Perry wrestlers attended college on wrestling scholarships while earning state, national and world titles.

Divine was a local product who wrestled for four years at 135 pounds under Coach Gallagher at Oklahoma A.&M., a feared and powerful wrestling school. John is credited with laying the foundation for the highly successful wrestling program at Perry High School and for building it into a widely acclaimed powerhouse. The school's large fieldhouse was aptly named John Divine Hall when it was built in 1958.

He helped establish the first junior high wrestling tournament in the state. John is past president of the Oklahoma High School Wrestling Association and served on the Oklahoma Board of Control and the National Rules Committee. As a wrestling official for more than 30 years, he participated at the junior high, high school and college levels, officiating for Big Eight and NCAA tournaments.

Divine was the first high school wrestling coach inducted into the Oklahoma High School Coaches Hall of Fame. In 1991 he was chosen by his peers in the OSU Former Wrestlers Club to receive the Edward Clark Gallagher Award. The retired Perry coach said the trophy, which is named for the university's legendary wrestling mentor, was the greatest honor he ever received.

And although he is an Oklahoma State University alumnus, Divine was honored by the arch-rival University of Oklahoma with an "O" letter sweater upon his 87th birthday in 1991. The presentation was made by former OU wrestling coach Port Robertson, a close friend. He called attention to the large number of Perry High School wrestlers who have distinguished themselves on the mat for OU.

As a competitor under Coach Gallagher at Oklahoma A.&M., Divine earned All-American honors and placed second in the 1931 NCAA tournament.

At Perry High School, Divine also taught chemistry, physics, biology, trigonometry, advanced algebra and solid geometry, and in time became high school principal and athletic director, all the while serving as wrestling coach for the entire system.

He earned his high school diploma at what was known as Oklahoma A.&M. Prep School in Stillwater by winning one of two scholarships offered in each county to farm boys achieving the highest scores in a test. His older brother, Joe, had won one of these awards while the family lived in Logan County. John earned his after the Divines moved to Noble County.

He attended classes at A.&M. Prep for three years, working and sleeping in one of the livestock barns as part of his scholarship program. The training was supposed to equip the winners for life on the farm. Instead, Divine taught at Rose Hill, a rural grade school six miles northeast of Perry, for four years, and his first job in Perry was as a bookkeeper for the Perry Mill.

He was part of the Perry school system for thirty-three years. Throughout his career at PHS, John coached all ages, from pre-schoolers through high school, and tried to give equal attention to each one. He used high school wrestlers to assist him in the junior high and grade school programs, but he never had an official assistant coach. His wrestling knowledge and ability to share it, plus patience, made him outstanding.

A mother once called Coach Divine and asked how old a boy must be to go out for wrestling. John said he had never thought about a minimum age, but told her: "He has to be old enough for two things. One is to go to the bathroom by himself, and the other is to mind me." The boy was there the next day, eager to learn all about wrestling.

The first thing Divine taught such neophytes was the art of tumbling. "We didn't have bar bells or weights or things like that," he remembers. He would have the youngsters get down on their knees at the edge of the mat and do somersaults all the way across.

"Some of them couldn't get their rear ends high enough to do it at first," John says, "but you know, by the end of the first week they could all do it and they were on their way. They felt like they had accomplished something. Next thing I'd do was to get about six of the young ones and put them with a high school boy and tell them, 'Now the six of you pin him!' Of course they couldn't do it, but they would give him and themselves a good workout at the same time.

"It taught them how to go for legs or arms and it taught the bigger boy how to defend himself. After going through that, I'd have the high school boy teach them one hold, or a takedown, or some other point. And you know how it is, when you teach somebody something you always learn more than the one you're teaching, so it was good for the older boy and the pee-wee, too."

John is proud of every boy who ever wrestled for him, at any weight and without regard to the number of matches he won or lost. He is still interested in each one of them. Many great coaches have that quality.

The educational opportunities provided for his wrestling prodigies probably gave John his greatest sense of satisfaction. He does not know how many were assisted that way. The University of Oklahoma's 1957 NCAA championship team was dominated by Perry High School graduates.

The number of boys coached by John who went on to successful coaching careers of their own is perhaps legion, but a few examples may be typical.

Herb Karcher, son of Mr. and Mrs. R.E. Karcher, became high school wrestling coach and science biology teacher in 1960 in Lingle, Wyoming. Later he became a successful and prosperous builder. He wrestled collegiately for the Cowboys of the University of Wyoming, where he earned his degree.

E.L. (Junior) Corr, 1952 graduate of PHS, became wrestling coach at Norman High School in 1960 after earning his degree on a wrestling scholarship at the University of Oklahoma. He later became school superintendent at Poteau. His twin brother, Edwin G. (Ed) Corr, also was a varsity wrestler at OU. He is now a U.S. ambassador and has served in Salvador, Peru, Mexico, Colombia, Ecuador and Thailand.

Ed Corr spent the 1989-90 academic year occupying the Henry Bellmon chair in international politics at OU. He is a frequent speaker on Latin American affairs throughout this area. The twins, sons of Mr. and Mrs. Bert Corr, grew up in Perry and were champion wrestlers at PHS.

Bill Luttrell, a powerful heavyweight for Divine's Maroons, was a varsity wrestler for OU and later became a super-successful coach at another of Oklahoma's most renowned wrestling hotbeds, Midwest City High School. He is now in the insurance business.

Leonard Shelton, currently athletic director at PHS, won ten team championships in the 1970s as wrestling coach at Perry. He was another varsity team member at OU. Rex Edgar returned to his hometown after earning NCAA honors for OU's wrestling team and won six team championships in the 1960s. He also coached the Maroon football team. Edgar is now a bank executive in the Oklahoma City area.

Any mention of Perry High School wrestling must include Danny Hodge. As a wrestler his feats are virtually without equal. After compiling an outstanding prep record at PHS, he was a three-time Big Eight Conference champion for Coach Port Robertson at the University of Oklahoma. There he won every one of his forty-six bouts for OU, thirty-six of them by falls, earned three NCAA titles, then served four years in the U.S. Navy.

He was a member of the U.S. Olympic wrestling teams in Helsinki, Finland, and Melbourne, Australia, winning a silver medal in Melbourne. When he later became U.S. Golden Gloves heavyweight boxing champion, he was the first athlete in more than fifty years to win national championships in both sports. Later he had a career in professional wrestling for several years. He is generally regarded as the strongest and one of the greatest collegiate wrestlers of all time, and once was featured on the cover of *Sports Illustrated* magazine. Danny still makes his home in Perry, although he has business interests elsewhere.

Danny Hodge was one of the first inductees into the National Wrestling Hall of Fame on September 11, 1976, along with Jack VanBebber. VanBebber's younger brother, Earl, was an NCAA champion at OSU in 1941.

A list like this could go on an on.

The Oklahoma High School Coaches Hall of Fame has several members with Perry roots. As noted, John himself was the first to be inducted. Others in the Hall include some of his former students —Rex Edgar; Virgil Milliron, ex-PHS star who coached at John Marshall, Midwest City, Oscar Rose Junior College and Auburn University; and Tony Macias, now owner/operator of the Kumback Pub & Cafe in Perry, former PHS state champion, former OU star wrestler and later a coach at Southeast High School in Oklahoma City and in Oregon.

Divine believes he and the late Coach Gallagher may be the only two wrestling mentors who have had fieldhouses named for them. Originally the Oklahoma State University fieldhouse was named Gallagher Hall, but that has now been changed to Gallagher-Iba Arena to include distinguished former basketball Coach Henry P. Iba.

After leaving the Perry school system in 1964, Divine became manager of the local Chamber of Commerce with an office on the north side of the downtown square. He retired from that position in 1980, and now he and his wife, Myrtle, live quietly in their home located just one block from the fieldhouse named in his honor.

Being somewhat removed from the mainstream of activity has its down side, however. John greatly misses the contact with his former wrestling stars.

"When I was in the Chamber of Commerce office," he says wistfully, "hardly a day went by without one of my former wrestlers dropping by to visit or just say hello. I really miss that."

Every wrestling coach at Perry High School since John Divine has carved out a special niche of distinction for himself as head man of the Maroon mat squad. Each also has been a graduate of PHS, giving the sport still another unique facet.

The Perry Maroons' tradition of hard work and dedication continues here, and young men are still learning that such things do offer satisfaction and rewards in due time. It is a lesson all American children should be taught.

Gus Malzahn (left) and brother Charlie formed this business after the death of their father in 1913. Gus died in 1928 and Charlie went out on his own.

Malzahn brothers had a busy blacksmith shop prior to World War I. Two forges were needed. Three employees of the shop are pictured.

Boy Scout projects and many other learning experiences kept young Ed Malzahn well occupied. At this age, he was also finding out how lathes, forges and other shop tools were used.

Future
Governor and
First Lady of
Oklahoma, Mr.
and Mrs. Henry
S. Johnston,
were a young
married couple
when this
beach photo
was made
about 1910.

Henry S. Johnston and his family were first to occupy the newly built
Governor's mansion in Oklahoma City during his term. This was at Christmas in
1928.

After impeachment, Governor Johnston returned to his law practice in Perry.
Many articles from his office are now displayed at the Cherokee Strip Museum
in Perry.

Friends and neighbors filled the Perry courthouse park on a March day in 1929
to welcome home Henry S. Johnston after he was removed from the office of
governor by impeachment. Johnston supporters considered him the victim of a
political battle in the legislature.

Manuel Herrick was sent to
Congress from this district in a
1920 election fluke. Friends
then bought him a suit of
clothes for use in Washington
so that he would not have to
wear his usual mismatched,
threadbare coat and jacket.
(*Photo courtesy Wesley
Aldrich.*)

After his two-year term in Congress ended, Manuel Herrick returned to Perry
and was frequently found napping, or just sitting, in the courthouse park. This
is from a 1924 postcard by the Barney Enright Studio.

Interior of original Kumback Lunch, with only a counter and stools for diners, looked like this in 1926. Owner Eddie Parker is the counterman in foreground.

Major renovation of Kumback in 1941 added booths, tables and more counter space. Eddie and his cadre of waitresses are shown at the grand reopening.

Civitan Club, forerunner to Rotary here, posted this billboard five miles east of Perry in 1927. Front row, from left: Sherman Krisher, Bert Byerley, Al Lobsitz, Marsh Woodruff, Mac Miller, Charles Huffman, Abe Bachman and Howard Cress. Middle row: Herbert Sanford, Bill Fry, Dick Kraemer, Bill Bailey, Rex Hoover, John Samuelson, B.F. Miller and Everett Nelson. Back row: Fred W. Beers, Homer Cody, Ernie Cooper, Max Chambers, E.W. Jones, George Goodnight, Paul Jones, Gerald Tebbe, Jake Seigle, Dr. Gene Osborne, Bruce Lucas, L.D. Hinds, Dr. A.M. Crowder, H.C. Donahue and Loren Loomis.

Open touring cars festooned with colorful crepe paper decorations have brightened many Cherokee Strip celebration parades. This one, turning north at the northwest corner of the square, is believed to have been in the early 1920s.

These were some Perry school faculty members in 1925-26. Front row, from
left: Berniece Hurt, Miss Floyd, Opal Dean, Miss Edwards, Ina Heaton and
Edythe Knosp. Second row: Esther Denton, Wilma Maggard, Ethel Knox, Ethel
Davis, Ruth Mohr, Olive Anderson, Mabel Ringler and Principal R.N. Elliott.
Third row: Loy E. Cook, Mabel Clement, Euline George, Beulah Unzicker,
Cornelia Hughes, Sylvia McCubbins, Eula Shelton, A.L. Mulkey and Leslie Van
Noy. Back row: Eugene Hubbard, Maybelle Howard, Pearlie Mae Acheson,
Esther Nichol, Superintendent W. Max Chambers, Ina Chronister, Beryl
Harbaugh, Margaret Monroe and Olive Means. (*Cherokee Strip Museum,
Oklahoma Historical Society.*)

John Divine joined the Perry
school system in 1931 and
stayed on until 1964.

# PART IV: THE 1930s

# 25

# *F*ACING THE DEPRESSION

The Andy Hardy movies starring young Mickey Rooney began in the 1930s and proved to be one of the most durable, and profitable, film series ever released by MGM Studios. The stories dealt with the joys and trials of a "typical" teen-age male growing up in Carvel, a mythical small town somewhere in America.

The location of Carvel was never made clear, but Perry could have been the setting. Andy/Mickey and the rest of his family, which included his father, stern old Judge Hardy (Lewis Stone), Mother Hardy and Marian, Andy's older sister, were familiar types to anyone living here at the time. Indeed, a very good cast could have been assembled from among the residents of Perry, rather than from the Hollywood studio's stable of stars.

Mickey Rooney actually did make a brief stop in Perry about the time of the first Andy Hardy movie, but that's another story and it comes up a little later.

Or, Perry could have been on the mind of Booth Tarkington when he wrote "Seventeen." Quiet streets lined with elm trees casting gentle shade on the lawns and porches of lovely old gingerbread-trimmed homes gave a character to this little prairie city that was also suggested in Tarkington's novel.

Willie Baxter, the central figure of that book, could have experienced all of his growing-up pains while pushing a clattering lawn mower in the summer heat of Oklahoma, rather than Indiana.

One transplanted Perry lady remarked that her first and recurrent impression of this city was precisely along those lines; it surely must have been lifted directly from Tarkington's classic.

Those fictional fantasies probably never occurred to local residents at the time. They were preoccupied with the bitter reality of a worldwide depression. Oh yes, the previous decade had been mostly whoopee, carefree and prosperous, but alas the 1930s were proving quite different. Each day seemed to bring new, more monumental problems, but life (and death) went on anyway.

A very elderly Perry lady, Mrs. Sarah (Sadie) Green, died on January 16, 1939, in her home at 1310 Elm Street. She was believed to be 121 years old, and was generally acknowledged to be the oldest person in Oklahoma—if not the entire U.S. Newspaper accounts of her passing did not cite any documentation of her age, but apparently her word was good enough. She had lived here since before the turn of the twentieth century. Mrs. Green's mind was still clear in the weeks before her death, and she could recall life during the Civil War, when she was a young woman.

At Perry High School, Miss Pearlie Mae Acheson was the favorite teacher of many. She taught a variety of subjects during her years here but in the late 1930s most of her classes were in geography. Although Miss Acheson utilized some unorthodox methods, her students usually finished the term with an interest in and a grasp of where the countries of the world were located.

One of her techniques was a drill used in second hour social studies each morning. Pairs of students would be armed with wooden pointers and positioned on either side of a large pull-down map of the world. As she called out names of remote countries on some unfamiliar continents, each of the two students would try to be the first to stab the location on the map with his or her stick. The winner was rewarded by being sent to Miss Acheson's apartment some two blocks away to feed her cat, Desdemona. The brief classroom freedom thus afforded was earnestly sought by many students who would not otherwise have cared about Afghanistan and other exotic states.

The depression which began in the previous decade became almost unbearable in the 1930s. The price of oil reached a low of forty cents per barrel in 1933, prompting Governor Murray to issue an executive order declaring that oil could not be purchased for less than one dollar a barrel. Cattle prices fell so low that even the trip to market was not worthwhile. Wheat was bringing twenty-five cents a bushel. Another severe drought made conditions still worse in Oklahoma. Bank deposits in Perry diminished greatly.

Many merchants around the square as well as farmer/stockmen throughout the county had come here when the Strip was opened in 1893. They were tough or they would not have survived that earlier experience. Some of them wondered if they had enough spirit left to make it through this new crisis. Most did, but not all of them. The depression proved too formidable.

Still, it was a time for tempering and growing. The administration of President Franklin D. Roosevelt introduced a series of public works programs as emergency measures to stop the free fall of the nation's economy. Community leaders in this area were astute enough to see these as an opportunity to build parks, replace old school buildings, expand services and otherwise create a better city.

The phrase may not have been coined then, but they were learning how to make lemonade from the lemon that had been handed them.

Perry and Noble County, perhaps even more than the rest of the U.S.A., believed they could thumb their collective noses at the depression and in due time happy days were bound to return. President Roosevelt practically promised that in 1931 during the first of his four successful campaigns.

At times it seemed this decade would never end and that FDR's happy forecast would never be realized.

# 26

# *C*HARLIE'S MACHINE SHOP

In 1932, oil was discovered on the farm of Bertha Malzahn's father (Wolff Estate NW 1/4 Sec. 17). It was the start of the Lucien Field, a major production area. Charlie Malzahn saw the opportunity to expand his machine shop business and decided to make a significant move.

With money borrowed from Grandfather Wolff and the bank, he bought an array of equipment from a bankrupt shop in Three Sands, twenty miles north of Perry. For $10,000, he picked up a used hollow spindle lathe, a shaper, radial drill press and a milling machine. It was a great bargain.

Three Sands had been an earlier oil boom town story. It began before the days of conservation or even what some would call sanity in the oil patch. Drilling rigs were stacked almost on top of one another; no spacing requirements existed. Methods of recovery sometimes resulted in permanent sterilization of the soil. Salt water—the unwanted product of some drilling—was allowed to spill where it drained.

Fortunes were made and lost overnight. Hundreds of oil field workers arrived, earned generous wages, then moved on when new fields called. Businesses supporting the drillers, "roughnecks" and their families appeared on the scene, sprouting up almost overnight, something like the time of the Cherokee Strip Land Run.

When most of the oil had been pumped from known pools in the field, Three Sands quickly became a ghost town. Frame and metal buildings, workers' houses, drill pipe and other paraphernalia of the oil field all were simply left behind to rust and rot, saving the expense of tearing them down and hauling them away. One of these failed businesses provided the basis of Charlie Malzahn's new enterprise.

Because of the additional equipment he acquired from Three Sands, a larger building was needed, so the machine shop was moved a few blocks from Flynn to 627 Elm Street, one block north of the square. It was a fairly spacious building, measuring fifty by 150 feet with an additional twenty-five feet on the east side for junk or scrap material, to be used as needed. Later the building housed the Cooper Oldsmobile agency, and it is now a warehouse for a privately owned collection of second-hand John Deere farm equipment.

Some two years later, the owner of the building raised the rent, so the shop was moved again to 410 Sixth Street, a half-block north of the northeast corner of the square. This building, which later became the home of the Perry Theater movie house, also was fifty by 150 feet. The site is now part of the Exchange Bank drive-through window.

Orlando Walkling operated a market directly across Sixth Street at that time. Ed Malzahn, Charlie's son, remembers trotting over there on summer days when Mr. Walkling would hand crank goat's milk ice cream and sell it at the market. It was not made every day, but a sign in the window announced when it was available. Ed does not remember if it tasted different from regular ice cream, but he says it must have been good because he kept going back whenever that sign appeared in Mr. Walkling's window.

Oil field welding and custom machine shop work kept Charlie and his employees busy during those days. In 1939, the year Ed graduated from high school, another opportunity presented itself, again courtesy the Three Sands boom-bust area.

This time, Charlie purchased an abandoned compressor plant standing forlornly in the old oil field. It was a big steel building, sixty by 240 feet. Malzahn sold half of it to a firm in Tulsa, realizing enough from the transaction to pay for the whole thing.

At the same time, he bought from General Mills Co. a tract on Birch Street, two blocks south of the Perry square. This was the abandoned site of the old Perry Milling Co., where "Pride of Perry" flour was made in the previous decade. Charlie dismantled his half of the Three Sands building and moved it to the newly purchased Birch Street location.

Ed remembers spending the summer of 1939 working on the project.

"It was a lot of fun, building our own shop, one that we owned. No more landlords or cramped quarters," he says. In later years the building was doubled in size. It is still owned and used by the Malzahn company.

By this time, Charlie had taught Ed how to weld and how to run all the machines in the shop, including the threading of drill pipe in the hollow spindle lathe.

Charlie had kept his forge and blacksmithing tools at each of the locations in the 1930s, and he still sharpened plow shares at the new shop. However, this became progressively less important as oil field work gained momentum in the Perry area, and the Malzahns' reputation for good work spread.

The prosperous Noble County farm community was seeing the development of another aspect—a serious oil industry, with all the service-related businesses that follow it. Oil was discovered in this county shortly after 1900, but only minimal drilling took place for the first few years.

Tall wooden derricks erected by skilled specialist rig builders appeared on the landscape in the 1920s and 1930s. Later these were replaced by steel towers. Some of them proved to be dis-covery locations for major subterranean pools of crude oil, such as the Three Sands field. In due time, unrestrained drilling gave way to enforced acreage well spacing and limited production allow-ables, making possible conservation practices.

When drilling was in progress, cumbersome machinery chugged and labored night and day until someone determined that the bit had tapped a producer or, as was often the case, a dry hole. When a derrick came down, pumps were installed to bring up the black gold unless it was a duster, in which case the land was more or less restored to its original condition.

In any event, drilling equipment and pumps occasionally tended to break down, like anything mechanical, and it could happen in the middle of the night as well as in broad daylight. Time lost because of such misfortune was money wasted, so any repair became an emergency in the frenzied life of those in the oil patch. Charlie Malzahn found his portable welder, mounted on a truck, in demand. More significantly, his shop facilities were too.

The new location and the newly erected building allowed for overhaul of the draw works of drilling rigs under roof, the only such place in Northern Oklahoma. This became important and profitable work for Charlie's Machine Shop in the 1940s and 1950s.

During all this, Bertha ran the office, often by herself but on occasion with the help of a part-time or full-time girl. When necessary, she would get in the car and drive to Tulsa or Oklahoma City to collect a bill or pick up supplies.

She would drive to the oil fields day or night to tell her husband or one of the hired welders to go to another job when he was finished with that one. The business was a twenty-four-hour, seven-day a week operation.

Times were still difficult economically, and the Malzahns were usually borrowed to the limit. Bertha normally handled negotiations with the bank. Somehow the family business was able to make it through the period unscathed.

In 1941, the U.S. was caught up in the vortex of World War II. The attraction of helping the war effort prompted Charlie to bid and secure several government contracts for machine parts. An example of this type of work was a pulley device consisting of cast iron parts. Malzahn received a prime contract for 5,000 of these from the U.S. Maritime Commission late in World War II. The intended use of the piece was never disclosed to the Perry company, and work on that contract was completed in 1945.

Though not large contracts by any standard—mostly in the $20,000 to $30,000 range—they were accompanied by reams of paper work and blueprints that occupied a great deal of time for both Charlie and Bertha.

Ed graduated from Oklahoma A.&M. College (now Oklahoma State University) in 1943 with a degree in mechanical engineering. He was an undergraduate instructor in the A.&M. machine shop as a senior, working the midnight to 8 a.m. shift. In that unlikely setting and at that rather dreary time of night, he fell in love. One of his students was Mary Corneil of Nardin, near Blackwell in North-Central Oklahoma. A gifted alto singer, she was preparing for a career in music but financial considerations persuaded her to shelve that ambition temporarily. A.&M. had contracted with Douglas Aircraft to train workers for important wartime military installations in Tulsa and the Oklahoma City area. Mary was hired by Douglas and the company placed her in the college's training program. There she was assigned to Ed Malzahn's class to learn how to operate a turret lathe.

"I was smitten with her the first time I saw her in class," he relates. "I took her to breakfast the first morning, and I knew she was the one for me. She was very adept at learning the lathe, even though as a farm girl she had no background in that area. I realized that when she completed the training Douglas would send her to Tulsa to work at their plant there, so I had to flunk her twice just to keep her around. She understood it was no reflection at all on her skill or ability. I just didn't want to let her get away from me."

The feeling was mutual, and later that year they were married. They moved to Midwest City, home of Tinker Air Force Base, and Ed was employed by Douglas as a machine shop and tooling specialist.

Charlie Malzahn soon sent up a plea for help from the pile of government red tape that threatened to engulf his business. He asked Ed to return to the shop in Perry and assist him in getting out of that difficulty. The pay would be $50 per week, about half the amount Ed was earning at Douglas.

"It was a hard decision," Ed reflects now, "but the pot was sweetened with a promise that I would be a partner. Mary and I thought it over, said 'yes,' and made the move back to Perry in January of 1944."

In addition to regular shop work and oil field welding, Charlie had formed a partnership with Roy Uhl, an old friend and respected former drilling contractor, to do oil field service work. The business was operated as a division of Charlie's Machine Shop. The work consisted of laying pipelines and connecting up tank batteries, principally in the Edmond Field.

Because of the war effort, employees were hard to find in the Oklahoma City area, so several truckloads of men were transported daily from Perry to Edmond for the work. At times thirty-five to forty men were employed in this activity. It was a congenial relationship that did not make a lot of money because of the commuting distance. This lasted from the fall of 1943 to the spring of 1946.

Dewey Moore, a local drilling contractor, approached Charlie in 1945 with an idea for building a portable oil drilling derrick, similar to one he had been using on his rig. Ed spent some time designing and calculating stresses in the proposed derrick and substructure. Together, the three of them invented and produced a new type of portable, telescoping oil drilling rig, one that was much easier to transport than conventional equipment of the day.

Dewey, Charlie and Ed formed a three-way partnership as a division to build the derricks. The first unit was built inside and outside the shop on Birch Street. After that, the partners leased the Noble County Fair exhibit building on East Ivanhoe Street and used that location to manufacture the portable derricks.

The rigs ranged in size from ninety to 120 feet but could be telescoped to forty-five feet in length for highway transport. The derricks sold for $9,000 to $14,000.

The open-frame steel devices were mounted horizontally on the bed of a good-size truck, which could be driven to a drilling site. There the derrick would be raised to a vertical position, stabilized with anchor cables and rigged for drilling. When the job was completed at that site, the derrick would be returned intact to the truck and hauled off to await the next try. No more building and tearing down steel derricks. It was a pioneer industry, just becoming established.

Ten of the portable units were constructed by the partnership during 1946-48. Although the business held great promise, the size and cost of the derricks put a strain on the facilities and working capital of Charlie's Machine Shop, so the Malzahns parted their relationship with Moore and calculated they had about broken even. The derrick was manufactured for a time after that by Oilwell Supply Co., a division of U.S. Steel.

The Malzahns were still searching for the most profitable way to use their equipment, know-how and energy. At that point, the Ditch Witch trencher was not even a gleam in their eye.

# 27

# *M*ARTY, SHORTY AND KIRBY

In the summer of 1939, Charlie Malzahn moved his newly acquired steel building from Three Sands to his newly acquired property on Birch Street. His son, Ed, had just graduated from high school and invited his good friend, Kirby Rider, to spend the summer in the Malzahn home. He was to live with the family and help tear down, move and erect their new oil field machine shop —the biggest in Northern Oklahoma.

"Kirby was a ward of the American Legion home in Ponca City," Ed recalls. "He and a brother had been abandoned when they were small, and they had grown up in the school. It was a practice of various Legion organizations about the state to take one or two of these young people as their responsibility and provide summer vacations in various homes in the sponsoring towns.

"The older kids sometimes had jobs on farms or in businesses. Kirby had spent time in our home during previous summers, and now that we were 'men,' a real job working alongside the other men in the shop was a great experience.

"I remember Marty McQuain and Shorty, an old man named Bill, and Scotty the welder, and trying my first chew of Mail Pouch chewing tobacco. It made me sick, I turned green, threw up, and never chewed Mail Pouch or any other tobacco again. (An earlier, similar experience with Beech Nut tobacco ended the same way.)

"I always looked forward to summers in Dad's shop, first sweeping floors, then being responsible for building a fire in the blacksmith forge, and finally learning to weld, at least my own things. It was a long time before I learned to weld good enough for customers.

"That summer of '39, Dad was busy with the regular shop work in the old building on Sixth Street. He left the moving and erecting of the 'new' building to his crews. Dad checked with us a couple of times a day to make certain all was going well, and that we weren't messing things up too much.

"I particularly enjoyed 'coffee breaks.' The six of us went together to the Corner Lunch Cafe, a half block west of the shop site, for a candy bar and a Coke.

"In 1939 it was oil boom time in Perry. The town was crowded with 'oil people.' You had to stand in line for a meal at all cafes, beer parlors were open twenty-four hours a day, beds in rooming houses were double-used as men worked their tours on the drilling rigs.

"Just west of the shop, on the way to the Corner Lunch, was one of those rooming houses called the 'Cozy Rooms.' It was one of those places where a man could get a bed by the hour, day or week.

"The primary attraction of the Cozy Rooms was the presence of three or four young ladies of the evening, morning, noon, or whenever. The Cozy Rooms were not air-conditioned, but neither was anything else in 1939. So, on those hot July days the young ladies reclined near the open front windows right on the sidewalk. It made for quite a show and a lot of conversation on the way to the Corner Lunch, especially for a couple of 17-year-old small town boys.

"We did not get the building finished before Kirby and I had to go back to school. Kirby, who was a wrestler, went back to high school at Ponca City. You could have a fifth year of high school athletics at that time. I was off to Wentworth Military Academy for a year before enrolling at A.&M.

"I seldom go to the shop on Birch Street that I don't remember that summer of '39, and Marty, Shorty and Kirby, and working without a shirt, and climbing scaffolding, driving a truck and those coffee breaks."

# 28

# CAP SWIFT AND FRIENDS

Cap Swift didn't look much like a psychologist. He almost always wore a cotton cap pulled down tightly on his head, even indoors. He scowled a lot and invariably had a cigaret, sometimes lit, sometimes not, dangling from a corner of his mouth. He had a chronic case of sniffles and dabbed at his leaky nose with a soiled-looking handkerchief. He was a scrawny little man, perhaps five feet five inches, but he brooked no smart aleck talk from any of the kids who hung out at his burger and hot dog stands. His straightforward advice probably kept some of them out of jail.

During the 1930s, '40s and '50s, Cap operated his small business from a series of locations around the square, across the alley from the high school and on game nights at the Perry football stadium. We hadn't acquired the term "juvenile delinquent" then, but we had some troubled youngsters. They were in trouble at home, in the classroom and with the law. Every one of them knew they could unload their problems on Cap's frail, sloping shoulders.

Cap understood them pretty well, not because he had any training as a counselor, but because he had been knocked around by life himself. He had been a featured performer in the 1920s with the Ringling Brothers Circus and later with the internationally known Miller Brothers 101 Ranch Wild West Show, leading a troupe of "Zouaves" in a breathtaking exhibition of wall-scaling acrobatics as part of a pulsating, if offbeat, stage presentation. He was a Zouave captain, and his nickname was derived from that military rank, not the cap he always wore.

The Zouave act had been witnessed and applauded by common folks throughout this country and royalty abroad, but when the Miller Brothers show went belly up in the 1930s, Cap and dozens of cowboys and other performers were stranded at the 101 Ranch north of Perry. Some of them, including Cap Swift, chose to make

Perry their home and were forced to find new ways of earning a living. It was the toughest of times for that. The Great Depression was just settling in all across the land.

Kenneth Coldiron, now a retired Perry banker, was one of several young local men employed by Cap to join the Zouaves during the summers of his college days. He remembers that at its height, the troupe had about twenty men wearing the brightly decorated costumes, fez-like hats and baggy blue trousers, which Cap provided. One size fit all. The original Zouaves, and upon whom this act was based, were members of a French military organization composed of Algerians who wore brilliant uniforms and conducted quick, spirited drills.

At the climax of the act, Cap's 101 Ranch Zouaves would stage an assault on a simulated desert fortress wall, about ten feet high. Through a series of choreographed gymnastic maneuvers performed in precise military fashion, they would climb the barricade and close with an heroic panorama in which one of their number appeared atop the wall waving a flag to signal victory. It was a stirring performance which never failed to elicit applause, whistles and shouts of appreciation from audiences everywhere.

Cap signed about half of his performers from the Perry area and the others from Jackson, Michigan, where he also had lived. Most of them were of college age, in their late teens or early twenties. In addition to Coldiron, some of the Perry Zouave recruits in 1929 were Wilbur Pricer, Harold Hoover, Sam Barnes, Marvin Smith, Byron Bartow, Clarence Bunch, Leo Doyle, Joe Skalenda, Ted Duty, Louis Stanislav, Herman Beasley and Dean Pricer.

"During these years the show traveled in nearly all the major cities and many of the small cities in the North and East United States," Kenny remembers. He was with the show when it went broke in 1931 in Washington, D.C. After days of legal jockeying between the government and Miller Brothers officials, the show was loaded on railroad flat cars and allowed to return to its headquarters at Marland, north of Perry.

"The return trip on the railroad took several days because the defunct Wild West Show from Oklahoma had a very low priority," Coldiron says. "The food supply finally dwindled down to boiled potatoes, but these were sometimes supplemented with roasting ears liberated from corn fields when the train stopped along the way."

Cap came to Perry after that and began operating hole-in-the-wall newsstands from some of the many available locations around the square. Kids were attracted to his place. He wasn't much bigger than many of them and he didn't look strong enough to last long in an Oklahoma windstorm. However, years of shouting Zouave commands on stage and barking at teams of raw young men in intensive training for those performances made him the equivalent of a grizzled Marine drill instructor.

Cap maintained decorum among even the rowdiest in his store. With a crisp "Pipe down!" and perhaps the flip of a wet counter cloth, he could silence a minor disturbance or forestall an incipient teen riot. He had that power. Still, kids crowded into his store after school and after the movies let out. They respected him because he treated them like equals.

He also listened to them when things were going badly in their lives. For all his gruff demeanor and lack of gentility, he was a father figure. But unlike some dads, he heard them out, understood their point of view, and willingly gave advice. Usually it was brief and to the point: "You'd better shape up or you're going to be in serious trouble." They knew he loved them, too.

So the kids listened to Cap Swift and paid attention to what he said, and they had a good time in his little stores.

You could run up a modest tab there. Cap never permitted a flat-broke schoolboy to be embarrassed when he couldn't pay for a date's refreshments. Cap would not let the total get too high, though. Nickel candy bars, sodas, chewing gum, hot dogs and burgers could add up quickly, and Cap operated on a short margin. The only books he kept were in his head or on the back of a scrap of paper in his unpressed shirt pocket, but he knew exactly where each customer stood. Sometimes they had to pay him back with their labor, sweeping floors or cleaning coffee pots.

Cap expanded his enterprises at one point, contracting with the city schools for the right to operate concession stands for home games at the football stadium and for wrestling matches and basketball games at the PHS gymnasium. He hired dozens of kids to help him through the years. He knew those who were honest, trustworthy and diligent. Others found there was no need to apply. His favorite place of business, however, was the little store across the alley from the high school, where school kids congregated. It was converted into a business building from a one-car garage in someone's backyard, and it was snug. When that place closed in the mid 1940s, he again operated from a downtown location.

His last place of business was a small candy store/newsstand adjacent to the Perry Theater on Sixth Street, now the location of the drive-up windows at the Exchange Bank. He rented a modest apartment upstairs in the same small building.

Cap's body was found on his bed shortly after noon on October 15, 1955. Apparently he had died the day before. There were indications that he departed this life partly because of malnutrition. He had never been much concerned about a balanced diet. Friends think he just did not care what he ate, and they knew that sometimes he even forgot to eat at all for days at a stretch. Death was certainly due to natural causes, for he had been in failing health for several months. He was not broke; there was money in his billfold. Cap died at the age of sixty-seven.

At his death, many people learned for the first time that his full name was Richard Vincent Swift. He was buried in the Perry Catholic Cemetery after funeral mass at St. Rose of Lima Church. Cap's official family by that time consisted only of a brother and sister, both residents of Michigan, but those in this community who mourned his passing and loved him like an uncle, brother or father were far too numerous to mention.

# 29

# *P*ROFESSOR RADGOWSKY

Leopold Radgowsky, a royalist refugee from the 1917 Russian Bolshevik revolution, spent the last ten years of his life in Perry. He was adored by his adopted community and became the first recipient of its "Most Valuable Citizen" award. They called him simply "the Professor."

How did the handsome young director of the Imperial Band of Russia wind up as Perry High School's first full-time band director? It was not easy. Enough real-life drama was involved to fill a bookshelf.

Radgowsky, the talented son of aristocratic parents, graduated in 1905 at age eighteen from the Odessa Conservatory, the most distinguished music school in Russia, and soon was appointed conductor of the prestigious Imperial Band of Russia. It was comparable to the U.S. Marine Corps Band. The job was demanding but career-making.

Czarevitch Nicholas, destined to die tragically with his family at the hands of the Bolsheviks, heard the band on several occasions and applauded enthusiastically. In later years, Leopold recalled with a wistful smile that the youthful Czar loved music so much that he would stand breathless while the band played, then ask endless questions and even attempt to blow the French horn.

During World War I, before the revolution, Radgowsky and his band joined the Russian Army artillery and spent four years at the front. During lulls in the fighting, the band traveled up and down the line playing martial music to bolster the soldiers' courage. Most of Radgowsky's family was killed during that conflict. He was never certain how many of his relatives came through the ordeal.

When the Communist-led uprising in November 1917 toppled the Czar and plunged Russia into a dark period of revolutionary violence, Radgowsky fled his native land. He was a "white" Russian with royal heritage, one with access to the Czar's court, and that made him a target of the Bolsheviks. Many others like him were executed before they could escape, and still others were tracked down and summarily assassinated by Marxists around the world. The threat hung over him all his life, although he was never politically active.

His mother, sister and two brothers, Roberto and Joseph, were not so lucky. They were unable to get out of the country, and his mother and sister were killed. The brothers spent the remainder of their lives in Odessa. Leopold was never permitted to communicate with them.

Radgowsky spent the next few years in Turkey, Czechoslovakia and Austria, but he was always reluctant to discuss details of that period of his life. The need for secrecy was understandable. His movements were circuitous and cloaked in intrigue as he dodged the Russian agents. Those who befriended him placed their lives on the line and would have been in grave peril themselves had their names become known.

He left Russia with an ample supply of rubles, and for a time settled in Prague, Czechoslovakia. There he led a comfortable life until his money became worthless because of the change of government in his homeland.

Moving on to Paris, Radgowsky rounded up a number of other Russian expatriates and organized a band. They were playing an engagement in London the following winter when Col. Joe Miller of the Miller Brothers 101 Ranch Wild West Show hired them. They became part of a newly acquired Cossack riding feature.

After touring Europe in 1926 with the Miller Brothers, Radgowsky's band signed a two-year contract with the show and came with them back to Marland, Oklahoma, north of Perry, where the 101 Ranch was headquartered.

Financial problems caught up with the Miller Brothers and in 1928 Radgowsky's band was not rehired. A few of the musicians returned to Europe while others remained here and became U.S. citizens.

Stranded in a foreign land whose language he hardly spoke or understood, with no money to speak of, no job, no passport and no rights of citizenship, Leopold Radgowsky undoubtedly felt his world had come crashing to an end. Still mindful of radical Bolshevik sympathizers lurking in the shadows, he knew his only friends were the cowboys, Indians and other performers left high and dry like himself on the plains of Oklahoma.

Bert Shaw, a barber and fellow musician with the defunct show, persuaded the disconsolate Russian to come with him to nearby Perry in hopes of starting a new life. Radgowsky knew one English phrase: "Howdy-do." Shaw spoke just enough French to communicate with him.

Together, they knocked on doors in Perry and succeeded in lining up eight students willing to pay Radgowsky for private music lessons. He also was hired as the town's first full-time high school band director. He soon added an orchestra and a drum corps. Later the professor organized a civic symphony orchestra which became the talk of the state. Musicians from nearby cities came here to play in the orchestra.

All in all, Professor Radgowsky had a full schedule. He taught from breakfast to bedtime. He taught everything—reeds, brass instruments, violin, percussion; everything.

His English vocabulary was limited but he managed to express himself very well with body language and a few words. Some of his statements took a moment to comprehend. Students who did well were admonished not to become "high in the head," meaning conceited, or "uppity" in the Southwestern vernacular.

Lazy students who performed below his expectations were chastized angrily with "Ai-yi-yi! What you do me!" His deep-set eyes searched the mind and soul of his young pupils. He could devastate them with a fiery glance, a tightly clenched jaw and a fencing-like thrust of the baton, but it was only to challenge them on to new musical heights. They knew that and willingly accepted his disciplined methods. They learned his fabled temper could be cooled with an offering of vanilla ice cream. He dearly loved it.

He was by far one of the most fascinating men ever to set foot in this community. The professor was darkly handsome, with a trim mustache, and a well-tailored dresser. He never married but he set the hearts of many Perry maidens fluttering. He was aristocratic, enigmatic, graceful—even dashing. It was easy to picture him in a Russian Imperial Army uniform. Some say that the uniform he chose as director of the Perry High School band was almost a duplicate of the one he wore while conducting the Czar's Imperial Band years before.

Here was someone who probably saw the Czar daily and sampled the life of Russian royalty vicariously; escaped the fury of the revolution; lived in Paris, then toured Europe and the U.S. with a Wild West show; and finally landed in Perry, of all places, as a high school band director. What stories he could have told, what epic adventures he must have experienced. Sadly, they died untold with him.

In 1934 he was declared Perry's "Most Valuable Citizen" by a landslide in a poll conducted by the Rotary Club. The plaque he received on that occasion was one of his dearest treasures. It was emblematic of the deep, mutual affection that bonded him to his adopted fellow citizens.

At one point it was rumored that the Russians wanted him returned to their country and had asked the U.S. to deport him. Friends got the professor into Mexico long enough for him to qualify for re-entry, legally, into the United States. The process of naturalization then began.

Perhaps the happiest moment of the professor's life was on August 22, 1936, when he was granted his final naturalization papers by Judge Claude Duval at the district courtroom in Perry, making him a full-fledged American citizen.

When he died on April 19, 1938, it was the top news story of the day in the *Perry Daily Journal.* Death came at the home of Mrs. Herman Eisenhauer, 828 Cedar Street, where the professor had rented a sleeping room for many years. He had been seriously ill for a year. Funeral services were held in the high school auditorium where he had taught for ten years and where his bands and orchestras had performed before highly appreciative audiences.

Perry schools were dismissed that day. The superintendent, George Spraberry, and school board members were pallbearers. Two Perry ministers spoke. Floral pieces adorned the large stage from side to side. The service was punctuated by instrumental and vocal music, and his beloved band played. The building was filled with students, former students, musical colleagues from throughout the state, and citizens of this community who considered Professor Radgowsky one of their very own. Burial was in Perry's Grace Hill Cemetery.

Nor has he been forgotten today. In the summer of 1990, members of the Oklahoma Bandmasters Association elected him to their Hall of Fame. The organization is composed of university and high school band directors, many of whom were not even born when the professor died fifty-two years earlier. What he did and who he was captured their fancy, however, much as his story intrigued the citizens of Perry during his ten-year stay with them.

# 30

# *T*HE POOR BOYS CLUB

The Perry Poor Boys Club marched onto the scene in the early 1930s when the Great Depression was at its most oppressive level. After prosperity returned in the 1940s, the club was unable to survive. In between times, the Poor Boys managed to amuse themselves and the citizens of this community on a shoestring.

Perhaps it was inevitable that out of those dreary days would come such an organization, founded on the principle that if you don't take life seriously, fun can be cheap.

A law of physics states that for every action there is an equal and opposite reaction. Surely one of history's most opposite reactions was the Broke and Bankrupt Order of Poor Boys, or BBOPB.

It was a symbolic response, like shaking a fist, at the gloomy economic atmosphere of the time. Young men who could not afford Rotary, Lions or Kiwanis invented an alternative: They started their own club and did away with the payment of dues. It lasted as long as the depression, and it was a lot more interesting.

The club was launched on April Fool's Day, appropriately enough, in 1932. There were fifteen charter members when the original Poor Boys met that first Friday noon for lunch in the basement of the Carnegie Library.

Principal organizers were O.B. Campbell, then managing editor of the *Perry Daily Journal*; Jim Ledbetter, county judge; and Paul Cress, county attorney. Ledbetter died of a heart attack while a young man, but Campbell and Cress still remember the birth pangs of their brainchild, and they chuckle as they tell about it.

"It was in the heart of the depression and young men were seeking fun and civic service opportunities at the least cost," recalls Campbell, now a retired newspaper publisher living in Vinita with his wife, the former Mary Lee Wollard, daughter of the late Mr. and Mrs. G.C. Wollard of Perry. While living here as a bachelor, Campbell roomed at the home of Mr. and Mrs. H.A. DeLashmutt, across the street from the *Journal* office.

"We made Poor Boys a cross between a Junior Chamber of Commerce, a college fraternity, a standard civic club and a fraternal body or lodge," Campbell says.

They limited membership to young men who were born after 1900 and who were at least twenty-one years old. That meant no one past the age of thirty-two could join initially. The main appeal to prospective members was directly related to their pocketbooks: No dues to pay.

Each new member experienced an immediate transformation of sorts. He was given a "Poor Boys name," something that sounded like his real name but just a bit twisted.

Thus, Jim Ledbetter, the county judge, became Dim Bedwetter. Glenn Yahn, a new graduate of Oklahoma A.&M. College, became When Gone, or, sometimes, Wind Gone. Postmaster Ed Bowles was Red Holes and Assistant Postmaster Marion Watson was Clarion Twatson. Pharmacist Fred W. Beers was Sled Gears, or, sometimes, Bed Gears.

Some say they did their most creative work in this area. When Sam Schwieger succeeded Campbell as managing editor of the *Journal,* he joined the Poor Boys and became Dam Jigger.

Schwieger also was editor of the Poor Boys' newsletter, the *Perry Urinal,* which was typeset and printed every now and then by the *Journal* at no charge to the club, although the *Journal* owner may not have known that.

The pages were the size of a standard sheet of typing paper folded in the middle, and the content was irreverent and satiric. Few copies remain in existence, but one or two are in the archives of the Perry Cherokee Strip Museum along with the club's original gavel and a collection of club minutes. They are considered historically significant.

Back to the names: Undertaker/furniture dealer Ted Newton was Bed Pootin. When he was elected mayor of Perry, Poor Boys dubbed him Mare Pootin. County agent Jim Culbertson was Flim Rubbersome. Paul Cress was Paul Mess. Another attorney (the Poor Boys had several, all of them hungry) was Al Singletary, who became Cal Dingleberry.

Bob Coyle, cotton gin operator, was Sob Soil. Wilbur Mouser, oil and gas lease dealer, was Filbur Louser. Perry football coach

Hump Daniels became Pump Handles. Telephone serviceman Jim Baxter was Dim Baxstard (the "x" was silent). Leo Hantz was Peo Pantz. Jay Gaskill was Gay Raskill, and it had a different meaning then. Virgil Sherrod was Gurgle Flarrod. Romaine Powers was Ptomaine Scowers. And so it went.

The club's constitution stipulated that membership was confined to "those self-sustaining, and whose efforts to earn bacon and beans are evidenced by a statement showing indebtedness in some form." In other words, you had to be on your own and in hock to somebody. The club's money, what there was of it, was kept in an actual sock. They did not trust the banks.

No fees, no dues, no fines, and a few laughs. Effective inducements to prospective members, who for the most part were just plain tired from the daily rigors of earning a living in the 1930s.

Officers were the chief pauper (president), chief bill dodger, chief mortgagor, chief bankrupt, keeper of the notes, and chief deadbeat. Together, they constituted the empty cabinet.

In the beginning, the club met each Friday noon in the Carnegie Library basement, where the Rotarians and Lions also assembled on Monday and Thursday noons, respectively. The library did not have a kitchen, only a sink and a gas hot plate. Ladies from various Perry churches alternated in preparing the meals in their church kitchens, then hauling the food and table service to the library each time they served.

Eddie Parker, genial proprietor of the Kumback Lunch on the north side of the square, was a member of the Poor Boys (his club name was Addie Farker) and he served the first BBOPB meals at a cost of twenty-five cents per plate. In due time he had to raise that to thirty cents, and eventually he quit serving altogether. The church ladies took over.

In the mid-1940s, when all but the Catholic ladies had dropped out of the serving rotation, all three clubs switched their meetings to the Catholic Church basement.

The Poor Boys liked symbolism. The official emblem was a corn cob pipe "costing no more than ten cents in lawful money of the United States." The corn cob pipe was chosen because it was an emblem of poverty. Cigars and cigarets were considered pleasures of the well-to-do.

The club colors were black and blue, symbolic of the treatment Poor Boys received at the hands of creditors. "Pride of Perry," a locally milled flour, was designated "the club flower."

While Rotarians and Lions used their meetings to soak up wisdom and inspiration from guest speakers, Poor Boys went to some lengths to avoid anything so meaningful. If some unsuspecting soul accepted a BBOPB invitation to bring a serious program, that person would be forced to watch in dismay as the Poor Boys, one at a time, filed out of the meeting room starting about the time the speaker began a favorite anecdote or attempted to make an important point.

Understandably, it grew increasingly difficult to lure speakers to the meetings. This did not bother the Poor Boys. They never intended to get serious.

On occasion, dignitaries visiting in the community or candidates aspiring to political office were victims of the Poor Boys' exit shuffle. Phil Ferguson of Woodward, then the Congressman from this district, experienced this once—but only once, despite invitations to return. He was there that day as a guest of Ed Bowles, whose job as postmaster was considered quite sensitive politically. Rep. Ferguson was perhaps embarrassed, but Ed survived. The congressman did win reelection.

To fill the void when no sacrificial guest came, which was most of the time, the program was generally devoted to a "reading of the minutes," followed by a relentless harangue of the keeper of the notes (secretary) over petty details of his records.

In some organizations, reading the minutes is a deadly dull point on the agenda. Because the Poor Boys' minutes had nothing to do with reality, the keeper of the notes had a chance to be creative, fanciful and, they always hoped, funny.

Rather than offering up a dry and boring recitation of business transacted at the previous week's meeting, the keeper of the notes was challenged to fantasize. His goal was to invent whatever nonsense he could, describing in a bizarre way things that never happened.

Although some of the minutes were witty gems, depending on the skill of the author, only a few of the real classics have been preserved in the museum's collection or elsewhere. It's this generation's loss. The literary value was questionable, but the minutes did contain worthwhile commentaries on a special period of history.

Some of the surviving minutes may not have as much bite as they did at the time of their origin, but—like the Dead Sea Scrolls —these dusty and decaying fragments suggest the wisdom, style and wit of that time. Unfortunately, some portions were never intended for reading outside a Poor Boys meeting room, so they do contain a few earthy terms. May those portions rest in peace.

Here is a sample of some socially acceptable minutes as written by Jim Baxter, a local Southwestern Bell Telephone Company serviceman who fervently yearned to be a professional writer. He did have a way with words. At the time these minutes were written, the weekly meetings were held each Friday noon in the basement of St. Rose of Lima Catholic Church. This particular meeting was held in October 1945. Here's what the keeper of the notes had to say that day:

"...Very little business was transacted. The members, after their gorging, were content to sit around the edges of the room, glassy-eyed, like frogs around the edges of a pond, and gently burp at one another.

"The Ted Newton-Emmett Rosser wager on a football game has reached a stalemate, with Rosser feverishly searching the law books and Britannica Encyclopedia for proper interpretation of the language of the bet, and Newton maintaining a studied indifference as to the outcome either way. However, Newton, with a fine gesture, has offered to release Rosser from any obligations to him if Rosser will contribute his part of the bet to the club to be placed in the recreational fund.

"I, for one, move that we accept this fine offer from the civic-minded Newton and urge Rosser to be as affable in giving in...."

And a few more:

"...Poor Boys met in regular fashion and after wolfing a sumptuous lunch, proceeded with election of officers. Poor Boy (Jim) Culbertson broke another club record by being present for both his installation and last meeting as chief pauper, missing all in between...." (April 15, 1938; Sam Schwieger.)

"...A fine little group of twenty BBOPB gentlemen assembled for a fine meal. There were also present four lawyers...." (April 29, 1938; Glenn Yahn.)

"...Immediately after the dinner the club went into action and passed an ordinance which provides that no guest may be brought to the club unless first approved by the Guest Committee. Appearance of Preacher Percy Beck and Paul Laird's guest precipitated the motion, which was passed unanimously....A preacher having been present, the report on the fishing trip was postponed and we are reliably informed that some of the debts contracted on that night are still postponed. Everybody finally left...." (May 6, 1938; Sam Schwieger.)

"...The usual good meal was enjoyed by all present, especially the lawyers who do not have a county or city job...." (August 19, 1938; Sam Schwieger.)

"...Minutes of the Poor Boys meetings are becoming more difficult to write, despite the gallant efforts of the Keeper of the Notes to put life into a dead meeting. A resolution was adopted by a unanimous vote asking the Perry board of education to treat the schools for termites for fear they will get into not only students and teachers, but members of the board...." (September 2, 1938; Sam Schwieger.)

The Poor Boys ignored Roberts Rules of Order, but they were ingenious in finding ways to relieve the tedium of the times.

When Campbell moved in June 1932 to Medford, Oklahoma, just a few miles up the highway northwest of Perry, he started another club there. Naturally the BBOPB added "international" to its name, although those were the only two clubs in existence. There are no records documenting when either one formally ceased to exist.

A joint meeting of the two clubs, or "international convention," was held one weekend in Perry. The *Perry Urinal* reported plans for the convention like this:

&

MEDFORD INVITES SELF TO PERRY
Resistance Here Is Finally Torn Down
After a series of invitations extending over a period since the time the Perry club got to them for several meals, the Medford handout boys finally succeeded in getting an invitation to come to Perry, but only after some good lobbying on the part of Paul Mess

who evidently is looking to a little legal business in Grant County, being unable to get any in Perry.

On the sixth ballot the Perry poor house finally voted six to five in favor of accepting the Medford group's own invitation. Some of the boys were eventually won over on the argument that the club have them down and get it over with, at the same time instructing Mess not to get his neck out any more by suggesting anything like a return visit.

The local national champion degree team which astounded the Medford boys with its smooth-working conferring work there at the same time agreed to let the visitors also horn in on this phase of the meeting and will turn over to the invaders Tiny Lang, our newest member, for them to practice on.

A motion made by Mess (he always makes them all) was also passed to force suspension on any member who did not attend the meeting. Some decided they would rather quit the club than entertain Medford. All expressed the hope that the next Poor Boys club organized would be somewhere in Oregon or Washington.

The visiting group was informed that if there were any lawyers in their midst it would be best to keep it quiet or keep them at home as the only trouble in the local club has resulted from its seven lawyers who insist on being themselves.

≥&

When the international meeting with Medford was held in Perry, Glenn Yahn made a point of sending an invitation to Campbell by Western Union telegram.

"I still have a copy of the telegram," Campbell says. "He sent it collect."

The BBOPB served as an antidote to the seemingly unforgiving melancholy of the depression, providing some welcome comic relief for its members and the community at large.

Wilbur Mouser remembers a home talent show put on by the Poor Boys to raise money for some worthy cause. The show was a dramatization of "The Shooting of Dan McGrew," with Poor Boys filling all the roles.

Attorney Judson Pierce had only one line in the play. It came in a dramatic scene when the McGrew character was shot on stage and lay dying on the floor. Pierce, playing a doctor, was to burst in, examine the wounded man and exclaim: "Tell me your name, so I can advise your mother!" McGrew was to gasp in reply: "My mother already knows my name!", then fall back, dead. It was expected to get a big laugh.

Pierce had trouble remembering his line all through the rehearsals, and on performance night he was trembling with stage fright. Standing backstage, he heard his cue and ran out, shouting: "What's your mother's name?"

Not only did that gibberish ruin his own line, it also forced a meaningless ad lib from the befuddled McGrew character and destroyed the entire gag. Some in the audience may not have noticed the flub, but it gave the Poor Boys something to laugh about for years.

Paul Cress has another anecdote. He was pitching for the Poor Boys softball team one night in a town league game on the elementary school playground diamond. The Poor Boys had only recently installed makeshift lights there to enable night games. (It was one of their many worthwhile civic projects.) Cress says they were just galvanized wash tubs mounted on poles, using the brightest light bulbs obtainable. But they did the job.

Cress was on the mound. He was an inveterate pipe smoker and always carried a pouch of tobacco, at least one pipe and a bunch of kitchen matches. As he started to deliver a pitch, he suddenly became aware that the matches in his pocket had ignited and his pants were on fire.

He had no choice but to quickly take off the pants, right there in public under the glare of those bright new lights. Naturally all eyes were focused on him and the small bonfire at his feet. Spectators in cars ringing the field honked their horns and flashed their lights in appreciation as Cress hopped around and struggled to get out of his blazing britches.

Fortunately, he was unharmed, but the pants did not survive. Another pitcher came on in relief.

Mouser tells of another Poor Boy softball game, one night when he was the pitcher and his catcher was druggist Fred Beers. Mouser had just struck out a batter, and there were no runners on base. When the umpire called the third strike, Beers threw the ball to third baseman Sam Schwieger to start a little "pepper ball" around the diamond.

Schwieger had seen the third strike called and turned away momentarily to glance at the stands. The ball caught him smartly in the chest and knocked him sprawling, unconscious. He recovered quickly but it taught him a lesson about concentration which has stayed with him all these years. Schwieger and Beers now live in retirement in Arkansas and Florida, respectively.

Almost in spite of themselves, the Poor Boys contributed some substantially good things to their town. For several years they sponsored homecoming activities at Perry High School, including a parade around the courthouse square with alumni riding decorated floats and an open-top convertible carrying the football queen and her court. Jim Culbertson, wearing a black top hat and tail coat, always marched or rode in the parade, tossing "Dr. Pauper's Pep Pills" (cinnamon red hots) from a doctor's bag into the cheering sea of spectators lining the streets.

Votes for the Perry Maroon football queen were accumulated through the sale of season tickets to the town's adults by each class at Perry High School, and the Poor Boys worked hard at promoting this activity. The school athletic department was most grateful.

In 1933, the Poor Boys purchased a shiny metal crown, decorated with fake jewels, to be used by the PHS football team captains at the queen's coronation. They also built a motorized float topped by an oversized replica of the crown and drove it around the square in the homecoming parade on the day of the big game.

Bessie McBride was the 1933 football queen. Her attendants were Bonnie Dotts, a junior, and Lucille Edgar, a senior. Bessie, who lived here only one year, was the daughter of an oil field worker. In that depression year, he and his co-workers were about the only segment of the population who could afford season tickets.

Bonnie was the daughter of Mr. and Mrs. R.W. ("Mom and Pop") Dotts, of Dotts Hardware. She later married "Ace" Goolsby, who worked in the hardware store for a time after World War II with Bonnie's brother, R.C. "Bus" Dotts. Lucille was the daughter of Clarence and Tillie Edgar. She became the wife of Dick Foster, who retired in 1980 as an employee of the city power plant.

When badminton was a popular backyard sport, the Poor Boys organized a town-wide tournament and had a championship playoff in the armory. Winners received a tin cup with black and blue ribbons attached. Maxine Mugler still has one of these trophies and treasures it.

Long before the United Fund and government welfare programs came to Perry, the Poor Boys sponsored milk and ice fund benefits to assist children in needy families. Sadly, there were many in dire straits then and the assistance was very much needed.

The events usually featured local singers, dancers, musicians and other entertainers on stage at the high school auditorium, with all proceeds going to charity. Packed houses were normal for each performance. The price of admission was kept as low as possible, but many dollars were raised to help some of the destitute in this community.

The end of the depression, spurred by a heated wartime economy in the 1940s, brought an end to the Poor Boys. By 1949, many of the "boys" had become sedate, prosperous, middle-aged Lions and Rotarians anyway.

Somehow it seems too bad that their mildly anti-establishment organization had to pass from the scene. Good-natured fun-poking should never be out of style.

# 31

# *M*ICKEY AND ELEANOR VISIT

Perry is perhaps slightly off the beaten path, so not too many celebrities have visited this city through the years. A few have found their way here, however, and in most cases they were warmly, if sparsely, received.

Two of the biggest names that come to mind are Mickey Rooney and Eleanor Roosevelt. They were here on separate occasions in the late 1930s and the total amount of time required for their stopovers was perhaps less than half an hour.

Eleanor, wife of President Franklin D. Roosevelt, drew the larger crowd of the two, not necessarily because of her greater popularity but primarily because the town knew in advance that she was coming. Her trip to Perry occurred on March 11, 1937.

Mrs. Roosevelt was something of a globetrotting good will ambassador and the author of a well-read, nationally syndicated, daily newspaper column, "My Day." She also contributed thought-provoking topical articles regularly to several major magazines, such as Redbook and McCall's. She represented her country abroad on numerous occasions and was truly an international figure.

The occasion that brought her to Perry was a trip to Alva, some 200 miles northwest of here. Getting there from Washington, D.C., in 1937 was a little complicated. Traveling by train was the preferred mode in those days, but even with all the passenger lines operating then it was still often difficult to get from one point to some others.

In this case Mrs. Roosevelt came to Perry via Santa Fe, but that was as close to Alva as the train could take her. The remaining distance had to be traveled by automobile. The First Lady detrained at the Perry depot. There she was met by a small official caravan to whisk her away for the approximately four-hour highway journey.

Preparations for Mrs. Roosevelt's trip to Oklahoma were well publicized for days in advance. The purpose of her trip to Alva was to speak at the dedication of a new building, honoring Oklahoman Jesse Dunn. From the start, it was known that she would leave the train at Perry. Local dignitaries immediately began making plans for some kind of celebration.

Although she was traveling on a tight schedule, Mrs. Roosevelt graciously consented to make a brief public appearance here. Oklahomans generally were not her husband's most enthusiastic supporters, but, politics aside, the public recognized both FDR and his wife as prominent figures and her coming created a great deal of excitement throughout the state. Perry was honored to be on her itinerary.

Because of the brief time allotted here, the local appearance of Mrs. Roosevelt was limited to a procession of automobiles from the Santa Fe depot, once around the square and then off to U.S. Highway 64 for the final leg of her journey.

As the moment of her train's scheduled arrival approached, hundreds of people lined both sides of the streets around the square. School children were dismissed so they might have an opportunity to see the wife of the President, and the Perry High School band turned out in full uniform under the direction of Professor Leopold Radgowsky.

Once the train was in the station, Mrs. Roosevelt was assisted down the steps of her Pullman car and escorted to a closed black sedan awaiting her there on the brick platform. The band played a salute, then marched smartly to the west, up Delaware Street, the north side of the square, as the caravan followed along behind.

The First Lady leaned forward and waved continuously to the cheering friends and admirers along the half-mile long parade route. The side windows were lowered and she could be clearly seen smiling, waving and nodding her head from the rear seat of the sedan. The general impression seemed to be that she was a friendly, dignified lady. Although never regarded as a handsome person, she nonetheless exuded a charm that endeared her to most people.

What really won the hearts of her Perry crowd, however, was a brief remark overheard by someone in the throng that day. When she heard the music being played upon her arrival at the local train station, she exclaimed, "That is one of the best high school bands I've ever heard!"

Perry citizens were extremely proud of their band, then as now, and her compliment was well received. Mrs. Roosevelt was a good will ambassador of the first magnitude in her brief stopover here.

### MICKEY ROONEY DROPS BY

While Mrs. Roosevelt's trip to Perry was well known in advance, the nation's No. 1 movie box office attraction arrived unannounced.

Mickey Rooney was just beginning his reign at the top of the heap of Hollywood stars when he came to Perry on November 1, 1938. He was king of the hill, the most magnetic name and the brightest star of them all in that magical, glamorous home of movieland. Clark Gable, Jean Harlow and others were megastars, but their names on the marquee did not mean the automatic success that Mickey Rooney's did at that time.

His brief look at Perry almost went unnoticed. By chance, Quine Brengle Jr., a clerk at the local J.C. Penney Co. store, found out that a Santa Fe train bearing Mickey, among others, would be making a routine stop at the Perry station that very day. The telegrapher at the depot apparently was advised that Mickey would be on board when the train pulled in from the north.

Quine, who yearned to be an actor himself—and later became one—heard the news and did his best to let others know. Only about twenty-five Perry folks were on hand for the occasion, however. Mickey came to the bottom of the Pullman car steps, but never really left the train. The stopover lasted perhaps ten minutes.

Betty Munger, a reporter for *the Perry Daily Journal,* was among those on the station platform. She wrote that "while the turnout was small, it made up for lack of numbers by its eagerness to give Mickey, the Judge Hardy series star, a royal welcome."

Although it was known as the Judge Hardy series, the movies were really about teen-ager Andy Hardy, the character played by Mickey. The movies are still shown on cable television stations and Mickey, though getting on in years, performs regularly on Broadway and TV and in touring stage shows. He is a multi-talented actor.

"Mickey looked just like he does on the silver screen," Miss Munger wrote, "and while he answered his questions as though he might have been rehearsed by a press agent, he was very generous. He told a *Journal* reporter that he passed his sixteenth birthday in September, and when little Ronald Brown, son of Mr. and Mrs. A.C. Brown Jr., asked to shake his hand, he seemed glad of the chance.

"Mickey asked the name of the town he was in, and looked out over the faces of the kids that were there to greet him, snap his picture and beg his autograph as though he sort of envied them for not having to live in a 'fish bowl,' open to the public at all times."

Mickey had been in Omaha, Nebraska, to attend a football game before coming here. He was wearing a neat dark suit and necktie, and his reddish hair became slightly disheveled in the Oklahoma wind. He seemed genuinely happy to meet some of his fans in Perry and waved briskly as the train headed down the track, taking him to a formal reception in Oklahoma City.

With his Andy Hardy upbringing and personality, we thought he would have felt right at home in Perry if he could have stayed here.

# 32

# *T*HE EXCHANGE BANK HOLDUP

Y.V. Willett was a handsome man of distinction with a ready smile and a voice that had the resonance of authority. His dark, wavy hair was streaked with gray and his physique was that of an athlete, broad shouldered and muscular. In the summer of 1937, he was president of the Exchange Bank of Perry.

Ray Barker was a twenty-four-year-old engineering inspector working at the State Highway Department's division office in Perry at that time. His features were clean-cut and somewhat boyish. He was not well known in the community. He was married to a young woman whose family lived in a rural area north of Marland, west of Ponca City. Barker had trouble earning enough to support his wife and their three-year-old son.

On a hot August day, the two men's paths crossed in a dramatic way.

It was a difficult but tranquil time for Perry. The Oklahoma weather was characteristically hot and dry, hardly newsworthy, but even so it usually provided the opening comment for casual conversations.

The depression agonized everyone. The government's creative work programs, WPA, CCC and others, provided some relief for the needy and helped to keep their minds off the day to day misery. Perry received its share of these programs, but still people suffered. Crime, a few concluded, was the only possible way to make a living. Some amateurs who had been upright, law-abiding citizens turned to it out of desperation.

Reports of Melvin Purvis and other G-men pursuing the likes of John Dillinger, Pretty Boy Floyd and assorted other professional badmen spiced the national news each day. Some of these notorious outlaws were even reported sighted from time to time in the Perry area, though none was ever captured here. Reading and talking about them provided some diversion from the monotony of the weather and the depression.

Few Perryans dreamed their peaceful little community might itself one day provide the dateline for sensational state and national crime news. That serenity and small town security abruptly evaporated on August 19, 1937.

Shortly before noon on that typically lazy summer day, a nervous and clumsy holdup man invaded the Exchange Bank. Brandishing a small handgun, he visited some of the terror of the era on a few of the city's citizens. Barker, the Highway Department employee, was the gunman. It was the first daylight bank robbery in Perry's history.

The bank, one of two serving Perry, was in a twenty-five-foot front brick building on the north side of the courthouse square. It had a prim marble facade and a large plate glass window that looked out on a broad sidewalk in front. Perry's aging, ivy-covered native stone Post Office building was directly across the street.

A partially paved alley adjacent to the bank's east side linked Delaware and Elm Streets on the north and south. That alley was intersected at the rear of the bank by another east-west alley connecting Sixth and Seventh Streets.

The alleys were often used by shoppers, merchants and deliverymen as shortcuts or for parking their vehicles when spaces around the square were filled.

The holdup man parked his car in the alley at the rear of the bank. This gave him a choice of four directions for a getaway. He evidently was not concerned with the possibility of someone stealing his car; Barker left the motor running and the car unattended while he gathered up some cash inside.

The clock near the front of the bank showed the time to be approximately ten minutes before noon. Mrs. Lillian Hunt, a teller, was on duty along with Willett and his pretty sixteen-year-old daughter, Ruth Esther, who was spending the summer working at the bank. The other employees were at lunch and no customers were in the lobby. Mrs. Hunt and Ruth Esther were at the counter. Willett was at his desk with an Oklahoma City stationery salesman named Fred Platt. There were no others in the bank when the gunman walked through the front door.

Wearing a slouch Panama hat, dark glasses and light-colored trousers, Barker carried a gun concealed in a brown paper sack. He quickly made his way to Willett's desk at the rear of the narrow lobby. Another desk at the front of the lobby, just inside the door, was unoccupied. It belonged to O.R. Hall, cashier, who had finally given in to Willett's repeated entreaties earlier that month and departed on his first vacation in years.

The Hall family, in fact, was returning that very day from a trip to Yellowstone National Park. They had just reached Enid, some forty miles west of Perry, when the robbery was taking place. They probably heard the news on the radio before reaching home.

"This is a holdup," Barker told Willett, taking the weapon out of the sack and pointing it at the banker's head. "I'll kill you if anyone makes a false move or tries to sound an alarm." The gun was cocked.

Barker ordered Willett to call the others to the rear of the lobby. He told the president to ask one of the employees to place all of the cash in a sack for him. The gunman again threatened to shoot Willett first, then each of the others, if anyone made a false move.

While Barker held his cocked revolver on Willett, the banker asked Mrs. Hunt to scoop up the bills on the counter and in the safe and put them in the sack. Barker kept his eyes trained on Willett, but occasionally glanced at the front door.

Ruth Esther was standing in a teller's cage, understandably fearful for her father. She watched the holdup man's every move until he pointed the gun at her, told her to turn around and face the wall or he would shoot her father in the head. He was unaware that even with her back to him, she could still clearly see the robber's face reflected in a mirror on the wall. When he was finally apprehended, the young woman was called as a witness to identify him in a lineup.

Millard Mayfield, a clerk at the City Drug Store just up the street, walked in while the holdup was in progress. He was ordered to sit down at Willett's desk. Mayfield, who had come in to get some change, thought it was a joke until Willett told him in a firm voice, "Sit down. He's got a gun. This man means business." When he realized what was happening, he nearly wet his pants, Mayfield later told friends.

Although there was nothing funny about the situation at the time, later it seemed there was enough material for a good three-act comedy.

Ruth Esther, now Mrs. Anthony Lanza of Colorado, remembers that the stationery salesman was instructed to hide in the kneehole area under her father's desk while the gunman was in the bank. Like everyone else, Platt was frightened because the robber obviously was quite nervous.

Barker's sack was stuffed with all available bills in various denominations, about $11,000. The sack was placed in a wire mesh waste basket. Barker clutched it to his side as he hustled out the front door, turning left down the alley to his car.

Bills fluttered out of the sack as he ran to the car; Barker lost about half his loot. Authorities recovered $5,000 in his wake.

His ordeal wasn't over yet.

The motor in Barker's car, a black 1935 Ford V8, was still running when he reached that part of the alley. The car, which had a Colorado license tag, stalled as he started to drive away. He was forced to get out and rock it back and forth to loosen the starter, according to Allen Merriman, who was a witness though not aware that the man was a bandit.

Merriman, a Perry rural mail carrier, was parked near the robber's car. He was about ready to go over and help the stranger push his car to get it started, but Barker managed to depart unassisted. Merriman wondered why he was in such a hurry to leave.

At the Post Office across the street from the bank, an alarm was triggered when Barker fled. Ed Bowles, postmaster, went to the rear of the Post Office and could clearly see Willett through the bank window, talking on the phone. The postmaster decided they were merely testing the alarm and walked nonchalantly back to his office. A few minutes later he learned that the bank really had been robbed. Willett had been telephoning a report of the crime to the sheriff when Bowles saw him from the Post Office.

Willett was a widely known trap shooter and marksman and he had a gun in his desk at the bank. During the holdup, he kept thinking about that gun and wondering how he could get it out of the drawer. He realized that it would be foolhardy to try while the gunman, obviously very nervous, had a gun pointed at him.

When the robber had his loot and left through the front door, Willett pulled out the gun and went to the back door of the bank, where Barker had parked his car. By that time, the gunman was gone, but Willett did see thousands of dollars in paper currency swirling in the alley where Barker had dropped them in his haste to get away.

It was the first daylight bank robbery in Oklahoma since August 5, 1935, when the Maysville bank was victimized. Depositors in the Perry bank were consoled by the announcement that the entire loss, $11,192, was covered by the Federal Deposit Insurance Corporation. That was no small matter in those depression days.

After the holdup, Barker was described by witnesses as middle-aged, although he was only twenty-four. *The Perry Daily Journal* called it "the most daring daylight holdup that has been effected in Perry," but Barker was said to have appeared extremely nervous. Willett said the robber's voice trembled as he issued orders.

If so, it was not because he was a novice. Barker eventually admitted holding up six loan companies in Oklahoma, Kansas and Texas, all during that same year. Perry officers believed the robbery and subsequent flight from here had been well thought out in advance. The job had the earmarks of a professional, despite Barker's case of nerves.

Once he got his car started again in the alley, Barker drove a half block west to Seventh Street, turned north and disappeared. Officers presumed he was headed toward Ponca City, but he simply dropped out of sight.

The hunt was joined by city police, members of the Noble County sheriff's force and the newly formed Oklahoma Highway Patrol. Unfortunately, radio units were not scheduled for installation in state troopers' cars until September that year, so communication was a major problem. Perry was a district patrol headquarters and was on the list to receive a transmitter.

J.M. Gentry, state safety commissioner who was well known in Perry, lamented the patrol's inability to communicate. "With our radios functioning, we'd have that guy bottled up in thirty minutes," he told reporters. "As it is, we can't coordinate the search."

Officers had little information to broadcast, even if they had access to radios. Reports placed the fugitive at several points. A farmer said he saw Barker in the Otoe Indian country ten miles northeast of Perry. Another unverified report placed him speeding past the 101 Ranch south of Ponca City.

Cars like Barker's were commonplace. There was nothing distinctive about his, except the Colorado license tag, and highways were loaded with touring cars from out-of-state at that time of year. A black Ford V8 was not likely to attract much attention.

Northern Oklahoma and Southern Kansas were scoured by officers of the two states. They were given descriptions of Barker and his car by telephone.

There was speculation that confederates were waiting for the robber outside the city and that he may have changed cars early in the flight. That theory began to fade when no trace of his abandoned getaway car was found.

The gunman had left "one of the coldest trails that has ever been left by a bank robber," wrote *the Perry Journal* reporter the next day. Actually, Barker was never more than a few miles from the scene of the crime.

Although Barker worked at the Highway Department division center located in Perry, he made no great attempt to disguise himself while robbing the bank, other than the dark glasses. No one recognized him. He successfully eluded the manhunt following the robbery and returned to his job within a day or so. Co-workers were unaware of his extracurricular activities. He continued working here until September 10 when he was discharged for economy reasons in a personnel cutback.

Following the holdup, officers found no one who was certain they had seen the black Ford after Barker drove away from the alley behind the bank. It was never definitely established which direction he took from the city.

However, it was the burned wreckage of his getaway car that brought Barker to the attention of lawmen. The car apparently overturned near Wister, in eastern Oklahoma near the Arkansas line, caught fire and was abandoned there. The state fire marshal traced the ownership to Barker ten days after the robbery, and authorities, including the FBI, began their search for more information. At first there was nothing directly linking Barker to the Perry bank holdup, but the car mishap put him under scrutiny. Later developments brought him to justice.

On December 16, 1937, almost four months to the day after the robbery, Barker was arrested peaceably northeast of Marland at the home of his father-in-law. A federal agent, four Oklahoma City detectives and a state Highway Patrol trooper made the arrest. Barker readily admitted the Perry bank holdup and also confessed to the six earlier robberies.

In Barker's signed confession, he said he robbed the bank "to pay bills I owed."

Clinton Stein, chief of the Oklahoma City branch of the FBI, and other federal agents said loan companies which Barker confessed holding up were in Oklahoma City on August 7, $130 obtained; Wichita, June 21, $170; Dallas, June 12, $550; Fort Worth, June 5, $130; Tulsa, May 22, $430; and Wichita, March 7, $100. None of the stickups were major league crimes in terms of dollars taken.

Barker had only about $60 in his possession when arrested. He gave the officers an itemized account of his expenditures.

Authorities said Barker had bought two farms in Missouri. A story circulating locally indicated Barker had buried the bank loot, then dug it up and paid cash for the farms. After being unearthed, the currency had a musty smell, and this caught the attention of bank examiners during a routine check of the Missouri bank where the transaction had been made. That started another search which eventually led to the young robber's downfall.

Barker's arrest rated a bold banner headline in *the Perry Daily Journal,* appearing just under a smaller headline which announced: "Santa Claus Will Be Brought to Perry in Patrol Car." The community was preparing for a joyous holiday season.

"This news was the finest Christmas present that I could ask for," Willett said when he learned of Barker's arrest and confession.

Barker was taken to an Oklahoma County jail following the arrest and was held under $25,000 bond after pleading guilty to the Perry bank robbery. He was held to await indictment at the first 1938 session of the federal grand jury. Barker named an Oklahoma County employee as his accomplice in the Tulsa loan company holdup, but otherwise he worked alone.

On the night after his arrest, Barker apparently became despondent and attempted to commit suicide in the Oklahoma County jail. He knotted a towel around his neck and tied the other end to the bars in his cell, but the effort failed. Eventually he received a twenty-year federal penitentiary term, served his time and apparently was released early for good behavior.

Another bit of local lore adds a final bizarre twist to the episode and perhaps serves as a fitting epilogue. Arthur (Shorty) Hunt, who ran a cattle hauling business operating out of Perry, was attending a livestock sale in Kansas sometime in the 1940s, probably after

World War II. Shorty was visiting with a friendly stranger at the sale and in the course of the conversation mentioned that he was from Perry, Oklahoma.

The other man (apparently Barker) laughingly said, well, he had held up a bank there once years before. It was a remarkable coincidence. Shorty's wife, Lillian, was the teller who scooped up the money for the holdup man on that sultry August day in 1937. Barker had become a law-abiding citizen again. Hunt and the one-time bank robber spent some time reminiscing, but never saw each other again.

ð›

Yeulin V. Willett was a robust man who loved his family, his work, his life and the Perry community. He was a civic leader in every sense, well-liked by the public he served. His death in 1941 at age forty-five shocked this city.

Willett was stricken while on a business trip to Wichita, a hundred miles north of Perry, with Joe McClellan, a close business associate and personal friend. The cause of death was a ruptured artery, an aneurism, near the heart.

It brought to a premature end the life of one of Perry's stalwart builders, a source of stability during the frightening, uncertain depths of the depression. Even while under the gun of a nervous bank robber a few years earlier, Willett was regarded as a symbol of the community's strength and self-reliance.

Willett grew up here, left to enter business elsewhere, then returned in 1933 to become president of the Exchange Bank. He had spent eleven years as president of a bank in Goltry and for a few years before that had been associated with a bank in Douglas. Both communities are a few miles west of Perry. He was well known in Oklahoma banking circles.

His occupation kept him confined to a desk, but he was basically an outdoorsman. Golf, hunting, fishing, trap shooting—these interests tugged at him all the while he transacted the bank's business. Trips to Canada with other Perry sportsmen were special delights. Time just did not permit enough of them.

Willett held positions of responsibility in the Chamber of Commerce, the Country Club, Rotary and the Presbyterian Church. He took them all seriously and worked at every duty delegated to him. He worked hard and played hard, and was good at both activities. Willett's first devotion was to his family, and they were his companions in sports and traveling. After Army service in World War I as a second lieutenant, he married Ruth Fink of Edmond. They had three children—Ruth Esther Lanza, now of Colorado Springs, Colorado; Charles, who died in 1982; and Genevieve Slade, Oklahoma City.

ða

The Exchange Bank of Perry was founded February 26, 1896, by Fred G. Moore, the first president, and his brother-in-law, Harry McCandless. Moore had been educated at the U.S. Naval Academy in Annapolis, and at Princeton University in New Jersey. Mr. and Mrs. Moore and McCandless came here from Kansas.

The Perry bank is among the twenty-five oldest in Oklahoma. Only a handful were chartered earlier than 1896. When opened for business, the bank had a capital of $5,000. Total deposits the first day amounted to $1,008.79. The bank currently shows total assets of approximately $66 million.

The original location was a frame building at the corner of Seventh and Delaware Streets on the west side of the square, where the Masonic Temple later was built. The bank building previously had been Jake Leon's Kentucky Liquor House. One of the bank's first customers was a lady who came to the front door, and with lowered head asked for fifteen cents' worth of whisky. She thought it was still Jake Leon's place.

Looking up, the embarrassed lady saw the cashier, Mr. Mc-Candless, whom she knew, and nervously exclaimed: "My goodness! What are YOU doing here? I was getting this for a sick friend!"

After a devastating fire in 1900 on the west side of the square, the bank moved to a single-story brick building on the north side of the square. The firm remained there until 1963 when the present location at the northeast corner of the square was chosen for a functional new building.

McCandless was elected president of the Oklahoma Bankers Association in the early 1900s.

After many banks failed in 1932-33 because of the depression, President Franklin D. Roosevelt temporarily closed all U.S. banks.

The Exchange Bank was found to be sound and was allowed to reopen in two weeks.

Moore was succeeded as president in 1927 by Joe McClellan, a petroleum engineer educated at Carnegie Tech. He was soon lured away by the expanding oil play in Noble County. Willett, a Perry product, returned here from Goltry in 1933 to become president of the bank succeeding McClellan. Willett continued in that position until his death in 1941.

O.R. Hall, a native Noble Countyan who had been associated with the bank almost continuously since 1909, became president and chairman of the board to succeed Willett in 1941. Hall guided the bank through some turbulent and prosperous years.

Hall was succeeded as president in 1964 by Kenneth K. Coldiron, also a native Noble Countyan who had joined the bank in 1947. Coldiron became chairman of the board after the death of Hall in 1970. At the same time George W. Hall, O.R.'s youngest son, succeeded Coldiron as president. Coldiron retired from active management in 1980 but continued as chairman of the board until February 9, 1982. George Hall then accepted the position of chairman of the board and Robert F. McDaniel, a native Perryan who had been with the bank twenty-eight years, became president. Both men still hold those offices.

# 33

# *T*HE FIRST NATIONAL BANK

Two strong, stable banks provide Perry with a sound financial base, nurturing the economy and encouraging local investments by agricultural interests, businesses and homeowners. Both have assets of well over $60 million. Some communities this size would be thrilled to have just one such institution.

One of them, the First National Bank & Trust Co., emerged from a 1933 depression-era travail to develop into a strong symbol of the city's determination to forge ahead despite adversity. In light of the troubled times experienced by so many of today's U.S. banks and savings and loans, it is interesting to reflect back on the story of this stalwart Perry firm.

The Noble County Bank, a forerunner to the First National, was among the four pioneer Perry banking institutions. It occupied one of the most handsome buildings in Perry, a two-story brick structure at the southeast corner of the square designed by renowned architect Joseph Foucart. The building still stands but is no longer occupied by the bank.

Mr. Foucart himself was an interesting and mysterious figure in early-day Oklahoma. A native of France, he spent only about ten years in this state but he left a timeless imprint with buildings of native-clay red brick and sandstone in Perry, Guthrie, Alva and Stillwater. His trademark was a castle-like design, usually with peaked cupolas.

Mr. Foucart made a particularly indelible mark on Guthrie, the state's first capitol. Recent efforts to restore and uncover the original architectural style of many of that city's historic buildings have revealed anew the beauty of the European designer's classic lines.

A *Daily Oklahoman* article describes Mr. Foucart's "fantasy world of designs reflecting Richardson Romanesque, Baroque,

Queen Anne and Chateau styles with elements of Oriental and German Renaissance features." He arrived in Guthrie two months after the April 22, 1889, land opening in Old Oklahoma, and within six months had helped shape it as a reminder of the Victorian era.

Mr. Foucart was born of French parents but was educated in Belgium. He designed several public buildings in Paris after service in the Franco-Prussian War. He was fifty-one when he arrived in Guthrie, the first of his profession to come to the new territory. During his most productive years he was hired by Dennis Flynn, Perry banker, and associates, to create an appropriate building for the Noble County Bank.

The year was 1902. Mr. Foucart's distinctive structure has been a Perry landmark ever since with its horseshoe arch, flame decoration over the door pediment, peaked turrets and artistic brickwork. The architect vanished soon after completing the job here and was never heard from again.

A full basement is included in the old bank building in addition to the first and second floors. Various tenants have occupied business offices on each level. Lawyers, dentists and physicians were on the second floor; Western Union had a fulltime operator and delivery staff operating from a first floor office at the east end; and at one time a weekly German-language newspaper, *Oklahoma Neurkerten,* was published in the basement to serve a significant segment of the new city's European immigrant population.

The Noble County Bank was successful in developing the rich country around Perry as well as the city itself. The business was incorporated on March 15, 1899, as a state bank by L.C. Parmenter and associates. It was sold the same year to P.A. Janeway and others, and was acquired in 1900 by Chris D. Jensen and associates. During its first two years the capital stock increased from $15,000 to $25,000 and deposits nearly tripled.

The officers then were H.C. Wallerstedt, president; Dennis T. Flynn, vice president; Chris D. Jensen, cashier; and George M. Ellis, assistant cashier. Jensen and his parents had owned controlling interest since he became cashier. Mr. Flynn is well remembered for his leadership in the successful fight to enact a "Free Homes Bill" while serving as a territorial delegate to Congress. The measure saved thousands of dollars for Cherokee Strip homesteaders.

In 1903 business conditions warranted the establishment of a national bank here, and the Noble County Bank soon completed arrangements for its nationalization. Thus, the First National Bank emerged. Jensen was in active charge of the bank by then, and G.A. Foster was president but not actively engaged in the banking business. G.A. Ley was assistant cashier. Dennis Flynn was a stockholder and director.

In 1925 the Bank of Commerce, then located at the northwest corner of the square, consolidated with the First National, bringing deposits for the first time to $1 million. By 1927, however, deposits had dipped below that level. It may have been a precursor of things to come.

The panic of 1929-34 caused a shrinkage of $150 billion in values nationally, thereby reducing the deposit total of every bank in the U.S. It broke many of them.

It was a difficult time. The nation struggled desperately with its most serious and widespread depression. No financial institution was spared from at least a measure of the misery. The First National succumbed to the strain of the period and, after closing its doors for the bank holiday, was unable to reopen for nearly one year.

On February 1, 1934, directors of the reorganized bank elected officers in preparation for the opening of the First National Bank of Perry on February 24. Harry Donaldson was named chairman of the board; G.T. Webber, who came here from Ada, was named president; Fred Mugler, vice president; and L.E. Plumer, cashier.

On the day before the bank's reopening, *the Perry Daily Journal* commented:

"Tomorrow's opening of the new First National Bank of Perry will mark the crowning of noble and untiring efforts which have been extending for the past eleven months by members of the stockholders reorganization committee. This committee was composed of Harry Donaldson, Ira Stout, Adolph Wolleson Jr. and Henry Isham, assisted by P.W. Cress as attorney.

"Very few people realize or have any conception of the work that was necessary to bring to fruition the reorganization of the bank here, which closed its doors with the national holiday on banking last March....To the average depositor of the closed institution, a year is a long time to wait, and expressions of despair and dissatisfaction were not infrequent, but with the announcement by the reorganization group that eighty-five percent of the deposits of the bank would be available at the opening, and the remaining fifteen percent later, criticism is forgotten and they have nothing but praise and respect for the noble work accomplished...."

The newspaper's remarks give an indication of the emotional nature of the event. Perry and the rest of the nation had been experiencing severe economic trials. By reopening the bank, a sense of triumph over the depression was realized. The bad times were not over, but at least there were glimmers of a new day dawning.

Mr. Webber, president of the new First National, said the Perry community wholeheartedly supported reopening of the bank. Mr. Webber came to Perry after lengthy experience with banks in similar predicaments. He had worked with both the Federal Reserve Bank and the Regional Agricultural Credit Association, which he helped organize in Oklahoma.

His background was crucial in launching the bank. He had a simple, but effective, technique: He realized the long-term value of loaning money to depressed farmers and cattlemen in an agriculturally productive area. He believed them the largest potential source of capital for the bank. Among others, he lent to the early agricultural prosperity of Robert S. Kerr and Henry L. Bellmon through the program. Each later became governor of Oklahoma, then a U.S. senator.

Mr. Webber's loans for chickens, cows and many a team of horses enabled farmers to subsist, produce wheat, and reinvest in more grain. Profits circulated back into the bank. Within two years after reopening, all money plus bonuses were repaid to stockholders. Mr. Webber gave full credit to the people of the community.

The newly reopened bank had eighty-four stockholders, making it one of the strongest in the North-Central region of Oklahoma.

Within eight years, a banking foundation was fully re-established. Public confidence and support generated deposits greater than ever before. By August 1942, deposits had climbed past $1 million. It was the first time since 1925 that any Perry bank had reached that mark.

In 1957 the bank directors decided to move from the Foucart building on the southeast corner of the square to the old Davis & Son Furniture building on the northwest corner. Mrs. Charles Malzahn acquired ownership of the building being vacated by the bank. Later it became the home of First Union Life Insurance Co., which extensively remodeled the interior but repaired and preserved the facade without changing its basic lines.

Moving to the new location, the bank thoroughly remodeled the old furniture store to create an open, spacious lobby. Extruded aluminum was used as a veneer to hide the second story windows, and the building emerged with an altogether new appearance both inside and out. The somewhat staid image of the First National suddenly seemed much more contemporary.

Because of failing health, Mr. Webber retired from banking in September 1957. Carl B. Hamm then became managing officer. Mr. Webber was succeeded through chairmanship and inactive presidency by Mr. Donaldson, long-time Perry lumber dealer. Ed Malzahn of the Charles Machine Works, Inc., was elected to the board of directors in 1959 to fill the vacancy created by the death of Ira Stout.

Other changes followed. Mr. Hamm stepped up to executive vice president from cashier in 1965 and L.E. Plumer became senior vice president. Mr. Donaldson died in 1966 and was succeeded as chairman of the board by Mr. Plumer. Mr. Hamm then became active president. Henry Bellmon, a Billings farmer, resigned from the board in 1968 to activate his successful campaign for the U.S. Senate.

Mr. Malzahn was elected chairman of the board in 1975. Mr. Plumer had resigned as senior vice president in 1968 but maintained an office at the bank. He died in October 1975.

In 1976, increased deposits, greater traffic and growth of the community made necessary a completely new 7,500-square foot building. It was to be constructed on the site of the former Davis store building, which dated back to the turn of the century. The cost of the new building was to be $380,000. A 3,500-square foot expansion was added in 1983 at a cost of $325,000.

The 1976 building project was handled in a unique way. Professional planners had recommended that the bank be moved away from the downtown area, but directors vetoed that idea in the best interests of the community's economy. That meant the new building would be erected on the site of the old building, but business had to be carried on in the meantime.

"We decided to design the project in two phases so that the bank could locate in half the new building while the old building was razed and the second half constructed," said Allen Roth of Roth & Brown Architects, Westwood, Kansas.

Stockholders approved plans for the new building on January 13, 1976. Construction started in April on the single story concrete and stucco building. In mid-July, existing teller counters and other equipment were moved into the temporary quarters after closing hours on a Saturday afternoon. The bank was opened for business as usual on Monday morning.

The old building was then torn down to permit construction on the second fifty-foot half. Two temporary drive-up units were set up on the parking lot. The second half was enclosed by September 1, and then began the most hectic phase: finishing the interior.

Daily banking chores were carried on while construction equipment and carpenters went to work. It was a challenge for customers and staff members, but an odd statistic came out of this. The bank had expected business to stagnate, or even decline, during the time of construction. The opposite happened: First National had more than a fifty percent increase in deposits, forty-seven percent increase in assets and twenty-four percent growth in loans.

The bank has charted a steady course of growth since the 1934 reopening, and prospects for the future generally appear bright. Automatic teller machines have been installed for both checking and savings accounts, drive-up facilities have been improved, and computer services have been utilized to facilitate and improve services.

Mr. Hamm continues as president of the bank today, with William J. Baker, Stillwater attorney, as chairman of the board. Mr. Baker's wife, Judy, is the granddaughter of Harry Donaldson, one of those most responsible for reorganization of the bank in 1933-34.

The philosophy of the past fifty-plus years is being continued, assuring customers of courteous, competent and complete service in all areas of banking. Perry and the Noble County area are the winners because of that fact.

The old Noble County Fair exhibit building, looming behind these mounted artillerymen, doubled as Perry's National Guard Armory until a sandstone armory was built by the WPA in the 1930s. The Fair building was destroyed by fire in the 1950s. As an armory, it was the home of Battery C, 158th Field Artillery. Men, equipment and horses of that unit are shown here.

A small lake in the vicinity of the Perry Armory and Lions West Park once provided an auxiliary water supply for the city. This arm was between Fourteenth and Fifteenth Streets and extended north toward Fir Avenue. The Frisco Railroad trestle crosses in the foreground, and the west side of the armory is in upper left. The lake was drained in the 1940s.

It was "Charlie's Machine Works" when the business occupied this building on Sixth Street, between Delaware and Elm, in the 1930s. Charlie Malzahn, wife Bertha and daughter Virginia are standing by the company car, and son Ed Malzahn is at extreme right. This building later became the Perry Theater.

A steel building from the old Three Sands oil field was moved to Perry by the Malzahns in 1939 and erected on Birch Street. The brick office building at left was added after the company introduced Ditch Witch trenchers. Still later, the plant size was doubled with the construction of another steel building attached to this one.

Professor Leopold Radgowsky,
the Russian royalist refugee who
established Perry High School's
band program in 1928.

These were members of the first Perry High School band in 1928. Front row,
from left: Bob Byerley, Robert Elliott, Olin Fitzhugh, Forrest Elliott, Bailey
Render, Charles Wall, Dick Dearborn and Henry Clark. Second row: Charles
Monroe Jr., Merle Johnson, Edwin Martin, Loren Lewis, Donald Rice, Frank Ley,
Bob Donaldson, Regina Gregory and Homer Hill, school superintendent. Third
row: Walter Martin Crowder, Bob Kehres, Charles Lovekamp, Sam Miller,
Ashley Alexander, John Dykes, Bill Elliott and Bob Foster. Back row: Professor
Radgowsky, director; Herman Meyers, unidentified, Mickey Johnson, Harry
DeLashmutt Jr., Harold Dean Victory and Bill Lynch.

"Dr. Pauper's pep pills" were scattered to onlookers around the square by Poor Boys Club members in this 1932 Perry High School homecoming parade. Jim Culbertson, wearing stovepipe hat, was Dr. Pauper. Others identifiable around the Model-T sedan are, from left: Paul Cress, Wilbur Mouser and Judson Pierce.

These were members of the Poor Boys Club in 1933. Front row, from left: Ted Newton, Jim Ledbetter, Henry Mugler, Paul Laird, John Mugler and Glenn Yahn. Middle row: Ned Foster, Ed Bowles, Leo Hantz, Bob Ruggles, Dr. A.M. Evans, Arthur Kretsch, Fred W. Beers, Eddie Parker and Paul Cress. Back row: Burton Hamilton, Sam Schwieger, Jay Gaskill, Bob Coyle, Marion Watson, Keith McQuiston, Romaine Powers and Virgil Sherrod.

Perry High School's 1933 football queen and her attendants rode on this float, provided by the Poor Boys Club, in the homecoming parade. Bessie McBride, the queen, was flanked by Lucille Edgar (left) and Bonnie Dotts. The float was a replica of the queen's crown.

Y.V. Willett, Exchange Bank president in 1937.

Interior of Exchange Bank in about 1937, the year it was robbed. This was the teller's area, and it shows the type of machines in use at that time. O.R. Hall, who later became president and board chairman, is just right of center. Next to him, leaning on counter, is Jack Adams, a long-time bank employee.

H.A. McCandless, first president of the Exchange Bank, was president of the Oklahoma Bankers Association in 1905-06.

Clean lines of design and a gleaming white exterior give the First National Bank a distinctive appearance at the northwest corner of the square. This building was constructed in 1976.

Architect Joseph Foucart designed this building for the Noble County Bank, forerunner to the First National, in 1902. His elegant work left an imprint on Perry, Guthrie, Stillwater and Alva. The old bank building still graces the east side of the square.

The Palace Cafe, operated by Billy and Lucile Reckert, was a popular restaurant for years on the east side of the square. Here it is decorated for Christmas in 1937. Waitresses behind the counter, from left: Oleta (Zep) Clark, Ethel Koch, Juanita Blondell, Mabel Letellier and Myrtle Bennett.

This service station at the southwest corner of the Perry square was built nearly 70 years ago by the Marland Oil Co., forerunner to Conoco, and was only the second in the company's trademark triangular design. Glen Koch, an employee of the station, is standing by the hand-operated gasoline pump on the drive. The St. Louis Hotel is in background at left, and Christoph & Newton Furniture is the building at right.

The 1936 Perry High School homecoming parade was recorded by a Perry Daily Journal photographer. The Maroon band, with Bob Foster as drum major, is in top photo; football queen Mary McClellan and her entourage are next; and the Red Hots pep club are in two lower photos. These were scenes as the procession headed south down the west side of the square.

# PART V: THE 1940s

# *34*

# *T*HE 1940s ARRIVE

Things moved at a different gait as the decade of the 1940s dawned. The dismal 1930s sank slowly in the sunset and few tears were shed in farewell. Hopes were high. There were serious signs that the Great Depression was over and that, at last, President Franklin D. Roosevelt could say "Happy Days Are Here Again" and mean it. Nearing the end of his second turbulent term in office, optimism was abroad in the land.

Never mind the bubbling political cauldron in Europe, where the German-Italian Axis had been officially at war with England and France since September 1939. Observers called it a phony war, something that started barely twenty years after the last shot was fired in World War I—the War to End All Wars. The Third Reich's Hitler sputtered and strutted, Italy's Mussolini behaved like a comic-opera second banana, and both sounded bellicose.

Over here we heard frequent special radio broadcasts relaying the passionate rhetoric of various European leaders, but hardly any shots were being fired. The problems across the Atlantic were far, far away for residents of mid-America. As for the Japanese, they were just mysterious but very polite people from another culture across the Pacific. Great oceans isolated us from all that.

It was a carefree time for a teen-ager growing up in Perry, Oklahoma.

A fellow could take his date to the movies on Saturday night, with two theaters to choose between—the Roxy and the Annex, both located on the east side of the square. The Roxy was operated by Charlie and Pearl Wolleson, with Ted Kimball as projectionist, and the Annex was operated by Henry and Alma Tate, with Chet Moore in the projection booth. Seated in the semi-darkness of one of those two movie houses, watching Fred & Ginger, or Laurel & Hardy, or William Powell & Myrna Loy, plus possibly a Pete Smith specialty, Fitzpatrick Travelogue, Looney-Tune cartoon and the latest newsreel flickering on the screen, he might get to hold her hand.

Neither theater had a concession stand, so, while walking his date home, the young man could suggest stopping at a drug store. Each side of the square had one, and all of them were open until eleven-thirty o'clock seven nights a week. There they could have a soda or scoop of ice cream, plus an exchange of brief salutations with other young people winding up the evening.

A movie ticket was around thirty-five cents and the nightcap at the drug store could run another fifty cents or so. If he was careful, the young man might get by with spending a dollar and a half and be rewarded on his girl friend's front porch with a quick good night kiss. Something to savor, at least until next weekend.

Double-dating was fun if someone in the group managed to borrow the family car for an evening.

Maybe the movie fare was too bland. Plan B could be the Kennedy Roller Rink between Sixth and Seventh Streets on Elm, just a block off the square. About once a month a live band—Bob Wills, Merl (Salathiel) Lindsay, Leon McAuliffe or some other Western musical luminary—was there on a Saturday night for dancers to enjoy. If not, there was skating.

Touring "big bands" from Oklahoma City, Kansas City, nearby college campuses and elsewhere visited the armory periodically. For a while frequent dances also were offered at the Lakeside Club pavilion on Lake Laird, at the north end of Seventh Street in an area where some of the city's nicest homes are now located. Functions at the tar paper-covered Lakeside Club ended abruptly late one night when the building was destroyed by fire, apparently torched by an arsonist. It happened when no one was around, and there were no casualties. The pavilion was never rebuilt.

For the most part, high schoolers were rarely seen at some of the other dance halls in this area—Tom's Hall east of town, Bohemian Hall north of here, the Cottonwood Club at the east edge of Perry and some others that came and went during that time. These were principally for a slightly older clientele.

The Order of DeMolay for Boys and the Order of Rainbow for Girls, two Masonic-related organizations, held dress-up dances periodically at the Perry Golf & Country Club and invited neighboring chapters to join them. These were highlights of the teen-age social season, and they were fine affairs. Young people learned valuable social graces there.

It was still prohibition time in Oklahoma, and no open bars were permitted at dance halls or other public places. The only imbibing was by a few daredevils who knew where the local bootleggers lived. If they tipped the bottle, it was outdoors, in the car. Police dropped by all the public dances.

Saturday night also was a time for high school couples to get together at someone's home for dancing and munching on fudge, cookies or other acne-inducing goodies. (A cake of Fleischman's yeast was supposed to clear up the complexion, according to ads in the Sunday comic section.)

To wind up the weekend, all churches had active Sunday evening youth fellowship groups for both junior high and senior high ages, and it was fun to invite a date to share that experience, also.

What more could a teen-ager ask from life?

This little town still had some economic woes, but most young people were barely aware of that. Mom and dad may have talked around the supper table about unpaid bills and the lack of ready cash, but that's the kind of worries grownups are supposed to have. The depression was a great leveler. Everybody had to deal with less of everything. Few really knew they were having a tough time.

The high school football team, coached by the legendary Harold (Hump) Daniels, was routinely defeating much larger near-by schools, such as Enid, Ponca City and Stillwater. Everyone took great pride in that. The girls were getting prettier and the boys were showing some hopeful signs. It was an exciting period for young people who were just beginning to explore the mysteries of their teen years.

The world, at least what you could see of it from here, had a rosy hue. Maybe some of the older folks (those approaching their thirties) sensed serious developments brewing, but for those 'twixt twelve and twenty it was a wonderful time.

# 35

# *T*HE DITCH WITCH ERA DAWNS

It was a homely piece of machinery. The first Ditch Witch trencher was not designed with aesthetic values in mind. The idea was simply to provide plumbers with a mechanical ditch-digger for water and gas lines in backyards.

Plumbers weren't even much interested at first, but the small trenching machine conceived by Ed and Charlie Malzahn unearthed a huge, untapped market and brought into existence an entirely new industry. Its birth, development and future prospects constitute the kind of story Oklahomans love to tell. It is a bootstrap, Horatio Alger-type saga worth hearing.

The inspiration for the original Ditch Witch trencher occurred one day in 1948 when Ed Malzahn was watching from the rear door of the family business while two men labored with picks and shovels in the backyard of a nearby residence. The men, employees of a local plumber, were hand-digging a shallow trench, fifty feet long and about eighteen inches deep, to replace a broken water or gas line.

In another direction, just a short distance away, Ed could see the Voigt-Frailey Co. equipment yard, where a large wheel-type trenching machine was stored. The self-propelled wheel was used to open large ditches for main lines and oil field pipe lines.

The hand work was laborious and slow in the tightly packed, red Oklahoma clay. It was a hot summer day, underscoring the sweaty, unpleasant nature of their job. Hand digging was not an efficient system, but it was uneconomical and impractical to use the $10,000 wheel trencher for small ditches. It took the men two days with picks and shovels to open the trench.

"There ought to be a better way."

That recurring thought set Ed and his father, Charlie Malzahn, off on a mission to design a compact trenching machine which could operate and maneuver in areas where construction was underway, and priced at a level that would be reasonable for small contractors, such as a plumbing shop in Perry. As they soon found out, there was nothing quite like that on the market. The manufacturers of big wheel trenchers were not interested, preferring to concentrate on the high-dollar units they were already producing.

Another company was making a small trenching device designed to be attached to the rear of war surplus Army Jeeps, which were then readily available. That product never quite succeeded.

The Malzahns had some knowledge and experience in manufacturing with another product, the "Geronimo," primarily used as an oil field safety device, and the portable, telescoping drilling rigs, but by and large Charlie's Machine Shop was doing oil field welding and custom machine work.

"I saw that first trencher," Ed says, "as being a tool for plumbers. I was thinking about the Perry plumber when we started to work."

His first inclination was to make a scaled-down version of the wheel trencher, and he went so far as to build a small wheel. Soon that idea was discarded as impractical and he began work on a self-propelled ladder-type ditcher.

Months of experimentation followed in the Malzahn shop, along with research of U.S. Patent Office files. Charlie and Ed hand-built vertical trencher prototypes. They formed small two-piece buckets with sharp finger-like edges and mounted them on a vertical chain to gouge out chunks of dirt. The buckets were attached in sequence onto an endless moving chain that carried them down a ladder type mechanism to chew out chunks of soil, then upward to dump the "spoil" in neat piles on the ground as they began the downward descent to bring up more dirt. A four-inch wide trench with a digging depth of twenty-four inches was the goal.

The idea was simple but executing it in a practical way provided the challenge. The ditchers would of necessity be working in areas of high dust density, so an engine and power train were required that could operate in extreme conditions for hours at a stretch without impairment. An air-cooled Wisconsin engine, a type already proven in dusty agricultural applications, was chosen. For many years Wisconsin engines were the only type used in Ditch

Witch equipment. Several others, including diesels, now are available.

The operator was seated on a contoured metal seat, facing simple lever controls to raise and lower the digging device. The air-cooled seven-horsepower engine supplying power for the working end also gave the trencher mobility, transferring power through a belt drive. The trencher moved on a welded frame with four small wheels and pneumatic rubber tires, like those used on lawn tractors. Another version had a ratchet drive to utilize the operator's arm and shoulder muscle to go forward or backward.

Although it looked somewhat like a shop-made go-cart, it was not designed to be driven any distance when not digging ditch. It could be loaded on the back of a pickup or a small trailer to be hauled from job to job.

"We set out with the idea of a $500 ceiling, low enough for a small businessman-plumber in Perry to borrow from his local bank for business improvements," Ed says.

After months of experimentation with a half-dozen different models, Ed and Charlie decided to put the trencher on the market but the price tag was in the $750 range. The local plumber, his original target, still did not feel he could afford one.

"I never did sell the Perry plumber," Ed remembers. "But he did borrow one a lot."

By February 1950, after some two years of building up, tearing down, changing this and improving that, Ed was ready to publicly demonstrate his brainchild, which by then had been named "Ditch Witch." It was the first one offered for sale, so it was called the Model A.

"A patent was still pending on the invention," Ed recalls. "We wanted to see if it was a salable item." The answer to that question was soon forthcoming.

In the spring of that year the machine was taken to the Oklahoma Hardware Association trade show in Oklahoma City. A few orders were netted there and others began to come in. Ed towed it behind his car to demonstrate it for plumbing firms. He sold three the first year and about five the next, making them one at a time in the shop. At least the business was up and running, though slowly.

"We found that demonstration was important in introducing our product," Ed recalls, "so we planned to emphasize that, and still do."

Howard Worthington, one of the early Ditch Witch sales managers, signed Russ Sadler of Oklahoma City as the company's first specialist dealer. Russ operated out of his garage at first. He would buy the machines from the Perry company and take them to plumbing firms.

Sales increased sharply until 1956, when they began leveling off. The Malzahns then modified and improved their trencher models and sales started on an upward trend again. After a modest start, the company doubled its production of trenchers every two years while still in the downtown plant.

Meanwhile, the Geronimo safety slide was still being manufactured, and yet another product had been introduced—the Sky Witch, a hydraulic work platform.

Development of the Ditch Witch trencher was a trailblazing operation for the small Perry company. It pumped its resources into research and development of the product. "We pioneered the market," Ed says. "When we decided to get into the market, no others were in it."

By 1955 a marketing organization had been set up. The company placed the machines in a few multiple-equipment line houses where they had to compete for attention with totally unrelated devices. This led to the development of a marketing strategy which entailed the recruitment of individuals willing to become trenching machine specialists, like Russ Sadler, selling only Ditch Witch equipment. That is still a cornerstone of the business.

It became apparent through mail inquiries and foreign visitors at trade shows that interest in the equipment was not limited to prospective users in the U.S. Questions about availability of the little trenchers were being received from throughout the world, including the Soviet Union.

The first dealership abroad, Mole Engineering Pty. Ltd., was opened in Australia in 1958. Today, more than thirty years later, Australia remains the company's largest non-domestic user. Mole Engineering on several occasions has exceeded some domestic Ditch Witch dealers in purchase of equipment on an annual basis. By 1958, dozens of machines were being shipped overseas in wooden crates.

"When I decided to advertise our new trenching machine, I chose the magazine I knew best, *Popular Mechanics*," Ed says. "I had read it since I was ten years old. One-inch ads were popular in that magazine, and besides they weren't too expensive—about $17 or $18.

"I wanted those who saw the ad to get a good impression of the firm, and 'Charlie's Machine Shop' sounded like a small outfit, so I arbitrarily changed the name for the ad to 'the Charles Machine Works.' I then discovered we had to change the letterheads and envelopes, too. We kept the name, but it was a bit confusing until we got all the old office supplies used up.

"In 1958, when we incorporated the business, we registered 'The Charles Machine Works, Inc.' That's how we are franchised to do business today. Dad and I were equal partners in the new corporation. We each owned fifty percent.

"Many people over the years have identified us as 'Ditch Witch.' In fact, sometimes when someone chooses to sue us, the action is filed against 'the Ditch Witch Company.' Since there isn't any such company, it at least gives us a few extra days' grace until they get straightened out. Ditch Witch is a trade name, not the official name of this company."

At one point in the 1940s and 1950s, the Malzahns considered a very broad product line, something like one of today's mini-conglomerates. They did head in that direction for a time with the portable derrick, Geronimo, Ditch Witch trencher, Sky Witch platform and a couple of other products which quickly came and went, the Pump Witch and Hot Witch.

However, Geronimo, Sky Witch and Ditch Witch machines began to overshadow everything else, and by 1960 most of the others had been discarded. By then the company had chosen to offer a vertical, as opposed to horizontal, product line. This meant they would concentrate exclusively on tools for use in the installation of materials underground. Equipment unrelated to that kind of work was to be phased out by CMW.

"We found it was too expensive to set up marketing systems for different products," Ed says. "Instead, we put all our resources and energy into doing what we do well. That is to develop, produce and sell machines that dig trenches."

Trenchers were manufactured at the downtown plant partially on an assembly line basis. Early stages of construction were handled by men with specific jobs to perform, then the units moved on to a paint shop and final assembly.

All the while, Ed recalls, they were trying to improve the product. It was, then as now, a continuous process of refinement. Production capacity by that time had reached 165 trenchers per month.

In seven short years after introduction of the Ditch Witch trencher, the company was forced to double its 6,000-square-foot facility in the downtown location. Another shop building, duplicating in size and configuration the original building brought here from Three Sands, was constructed, adjoining the older building on the west. A brick office building was attached to the front of the plant in 1950. It contained business offices, the marketing department and engineering. More models of equipment were designed and sales were growing.

In 1951, manufacturing accounted for 10 percent of the company's gross business. By 1959 it accounted for 98 percent, and the firm was still doing some oil field equipment repair for the convenience of old customers in the area.

The transitions from blacksmith shop to machine shop to manufacturer were overlapping and gradual. When the oil business came along, Charlie's Machine Shop tooled up to handle it but kept its farm business too. Plow shares were sharpened well into the 1940s. The machine shop business initially had to finance the infant trencher industry.

"It was nights when our new projects were designed," Ed says. "We had to make a living in the daytime. With the trencher we faced two obstacles—we were in a completely new area, developing a completely new product, and we had to do all the pioneering in engineering of that product and then introduce it to our prospective buyers."

It was more than ten years after the first Ditch Witch trencher was built that the decision was made to devote the company's total energy to trenchers.

At the time it seemed a daring vote of confidence in the future for several reasons. Ed Malzahn had been given six months to live after major surgery for cancer, and he made the decision "after surviving those six months," he says.

"We had to decide whether to continue with our oil servicing company or go totally into the manufacturing business," Ed says.

It was not a decision lightly to be made. The family took their time before electing to convert the business exclusively to manufacturing, but that was the ultimate choice. It was an excellent move.

The company borrowed $140,000 from the First National Bank of Perry and the Small Business Administration after deciding to take the big step with a new plant. The loan was used to pay off a previous note and help finance the new plant. The loan was repaid in three years. It was the last capital money borrowed by the Charles Machine Works.

≈

In 1959 the firm obtained 160 acres, mostly in pasture, two miles west of downtown Perry along a bumpy, two-lane, unpaved road, extending off Fir Avenue into a lonely rural area. Interstate Highway 35, now just west of the plant, had been programmed but not yet built. Though it seemed somewhat remote and isolated, the site was chosen for the new home of the Charles Machine Works, Inc., manufacturer of Ditch Witch equipment.

The new building was twice the size of the old downtown facility, containing 24,000 square feet in the plant plus an 8,000-square-foot office complex. The production capacity was estimated at 330 units per month, double the output at the existing plant. Some cynics said it would hold a lot of hay in case the Ditch Witch business failed. Not to worry. It has never even faltered.

The modern new plant and office, representing a $500,000 investment, were ready for occupancy on July 6, 1959. State and local dignitaries were on hand to join Ed, Mary, Charlie and Bertha, the company's fifty employees, and other residents of the community in a joyous ribbon-cutting ceremony. Ed was president and Charlie vice president of the company.

Gov. J. Howard Edmondson sent a letter of congratulations but had to cancel an appearance here at the last minute because of illness. The director of the State Department of Commerce and Industry, Max Genet Jr., represented the governor at the opening and was speaker for a banquet that evening arranged by the Chamber of Commerce to celebrate the historic occasion.

Mayor Harold Scovill proclaimed "Ditch Witch Day" in Perry and also helped with cutting the ribbon. Less than ten years later, Mayor Scovill joined the "family" and became Ditch Witch dealer for the state of Florida. His daughter and son-in-law, Mr. and Mrs. Tony Bjorn, continue to operate that business.

Bob Donahue, chairman of the Chamber of Commerce Industry Committee, proclaimed opening of the plant "the most significant development on Perry's industrial horizon" in modern times.

*The Perry Daily Journal* called the day "one of the greatest demonstrations of community cooperation ever exhibited in Perry." Milo W. Watson, publisher, put out a special edition for the occasion and announced it was the second largest newspaper ever produced in Perry (40 pages vs. 80 pages saluting the 60th anniversary of the Cherokee Strip in 1953).

Ernest Ackerman, minister of the First Presbyterian Church, noted that "the whole Malzahn family not only have been prominently identified with this church but, in the face of repeated circumstances of adversity, have demonstrated a living faith in our Lord Jesus Christ and are a shining witness of His love and power."

The public was invited to tour the plant, offices and grounds, and to watch continuous demonstrations of Ditch Witch equipment throughout the day. Men received free cigars, women were given orchids, and free soft drinks were available for everyone. The Chamber of Commerce dinner that evening climaxed a busy and eventful day for the Perry community.

Charlie Malzahn was in extremely poor health by that time. He was partially blind because of leukemia and diabetes. He also suffered with ulcers. Charlie attended all of the opening ceremonies at the new plant, thereby realizing one of his fondest dreams. He died in October of that year at the age of 75.

"Dad's last years were tough on him," Ed says. "He spent a lot of time in the Veterans Hospital in Oklahoma City. All along the way, even then, he kept encouraging me to go ahead, take the big steps, work hard. He set a good example, and I owe him a great deal for that."

Bertha Malzahn continued an active involvement in the company until she retired in 1969. As part of her estate planning, she sold some of her stock to key employees, set aside some as gifts in trusts to grandchildren, and arranged for some to be purchased by the company as treasury stock.

"It was a well thought-out plan that was typical of Mother's business activity," Ed says.

Following retirement, she spent more of her time supervising her farming activities and oil investments. She also had developed an interest in art. Mrs. Malzahn died at 81 on January 18, 1981.

ॐ

As a sidebar to acquisition of the Fir Avenue building site, a slightly ironic twist might be noted. Mrs. Clara Kadlick was the previous lessee of the property. A widow, she farmed the land and ran a few head of cattle and goats. Mrs. Kadlick was short in stature but she was a no-nonsense, working farmer who handled all the chores herself. She generally wore a broad-brimmed straw hat, bib overalls and a long-sleeved chambray shirt buttoned to the neck.

In 1957 she filed a $25,000 damage suit against Southwestern Bell Telephone Co. in U.S. District Court at Oklahoma City. Mrs. Kadlick, 64 years old at the time, alleged that while phone company workmen were laying a cable on the land she leased, she lost three head of cattle and suffered personal injuries when she fell in a hole dug by the workmen.

No one then knew that two years later the land would become the location of the Charles Machine Works, Inc., builder of equipment for installing phone cable underground without the necessity of opening a trench into which people and cattle could fall.

ॐ

The new facility's greater production capacity also made possible more Ditch Witch models. The Model K, a four-wheel self-propelled rider, enabled deeper and wider trenches. Attachments were invented to be added to basic trenchers. Equipment users found all of them highly usable. CMW's trenchers were priced at from $725 to $3,750, depending on the size of the model chosen.

The company's marketing department at the time developed many basic business strategies which have been continued and refined through the years. Howard Worthington was sales manager and Dwaine Goldsberry, a native of the Hayward area west of Perry, was his assistant. Goldsberry later succeeded Worthington as sales manager.

Other key personnel included Phil Albertson, production manager; J.D. Sadler, office manager; and Bernard Heppler, shop foreman. Ed was in charge of engineering and design functions.

All of them except Ed Malzahn have retired or left the company, but several others who were with CMW at the downtown location are still employed by the firm.

Jim Roth, a 1956 engineering school graduate at Kansas State University, was one of those who joined the Perry company in 1960, a few months after the move to Fir Avenue. Starting as a product design leader, he moved up through the ranks and today is assistant to the president of CMW. Two other early additions to the expanded Engineering Department, Ken Schuermann and Larry Hall, also are still active employees making valuable contributions to the Ditch Witch success story.

Far from being abandoned, the old plant downtown was set aside for warehousing the inventory buildup of Geronimos, Sky Witches and Ditch Witch trenchers expected to be turned out at the shiny new factory. That use never materialized, however. Sales soared, using up everything workmen could produce. There was no surplus inventory. In more recent years the older buildings have been used for some manufacturing and storage.

Seventy U.S. distributors were marketing equipment manufactured by the Charles Machine Works when the company moved to the new plant in mid-1959. In addition, an export firm had been retained to handle sales abroad. Geronimos, Sky Witches and Ditch Witch trenchers were being sold throughout the U.S. and in France, Germany, Australia, New Zealand, Italy and Cuba.

The market also was stimulated at that point by the advent of competition. Chuck Davis, a manufacturer in Wichita, Kansas, began producing similar-size trenchers. The Davis company later was purchased by J.I. Case. Vermeer Manufacturing Co. of Pella, Iowa, moved into the business. Other, smaller operations also emerged.

The net result was a greater consumer awareness that this type of equipment existed. It was still new or unknown to many potential users. As they learned of it through local dealerships, trade shows, advertising media and other sources, a much larger market became identified. Today some ten manufacturers compete for a share of that business.

Ditch Witch equipment historically has dominated the market, accounting for well over half the total number of units sold. That preeminent position has never been seriously imperiled. CMW has enjoyed a good relationship and friendly rivalry with all its competitors through the years.

The Perry plant is located close to the geographic center of the U.S. and is ideally suited to ship its products all over the world. North-south Interstate Highway 35 and east-west U.S. Highway 64 both pass by only a few yards from the Charles Machine Works' loading dock. Two railroad lines go through downtown Perry. Coastal shipping points are easily accessible for distribution abroad. Oklahoma City is seventy miles south of Perry on I-35; Tulsa is about eighty-five miles east on U.S. 64/Cimarron Turnpike. These same features also facilitate the delivery of raw material to the plant from suppliers throughout the world.

With the market rapidly expanding, the Perry company experienced remarkable growth cycles. During the first fifteen years in the new location, sales volume and production facilities both nearly doubled on a three-year cycle. As the market matured, that exciting kind of growth slowed.

CMW had fifty-six employees on the payroll in 1961 and sales that year totaled over $2 million. By 1972 there were 500 employees and a dollar volume in excess of $30 million. If productivity is determined by dividing the number of employees into total sales, the average output per employee nearly doubled during that span.

The company now has approximately twenty-two acres under roof (more than 820,000 square feet) for manufacturing and offices, plus 50,000 square feet for developing new products, plus its own hangar and asphalt cement air strip for fly-in visitors and CMW's corporate aircraft. From the original 160 acres, CMW real estate has grown to include 1,500 acres. The investment amounts to about $50 million, including inventory. Plant and machinery alone total around $20 million. The company has some 800 employees, and the sales chart has topped $100 million while continuing on an upward course.

A list of Ditch Witch customers reads like a Who's Who of American Business. Telephone companies and electric utilities comprise a significant market segment, in addition to plumbers— Ed's original target. Other categories include electrical contractors, cable television, rental businesses, landscape specialists, governmental agencies, the petroleum industry, rural water systems and others.

Ditch Witch engineers are designing equipment to meet today's needs, and also tomorrow's. The company pioneered development of the vibratory plow to install material underground without trenching, and now offers the industry's most complete line of vibratory plowing equipment.

CMW introduced a combination trenching and vibratory plow module, called a "Combo," that gives a single machine the capability of doing both jobs. The company also led the way with the Modularmatic concept: a basic vehicle with interchangeable work modules to do many different underground jobs. Five Modularmatic machines are made, ranging from a thirty-horse-power class through one-hundred-horsepower.

Ditch Witch equipment is sold to users in the U.S. and Canada by a network of some 110 independent specialist dealers. No other manufacturer offers more specialist trenching sales and service locations. International sales now extend into twenty-six countries in Europe, South Africa, the Middle East, Australia and other areas.

New products on the drawing board guarantee that the ultimate plateau has not yet been reached by this unique company. As it digs deeper, wider and better with tools that were not even dreamed about in 1948, its future only looks brighter and more secure.

And that is good news indeed for the Perry community and this entire area of Oklahoma.

# 36

# WHY IS IT "DITCH WITCH?"

One of the most often asked questions by visitors touring the Charles Machine Works plant in Perry concerns the origin of the name "Ditch Witch." Ed Malzahn, who invented the small trencher bearing that name, believes he has shared the answer with every seminar group since the early 1960s, when Ditch Witch almost became a generic name for small trenchers.

It was registered as a trademark by the company with the U.S. Patent Office in the early years of manufacturing to protect it from that very thing.

"Of course, the first trenchers we made didn't have a name," Ed relates. "I just hitched them up on a trailer and went around trying to sell them. It was soon obvious that I needed literature, so I visited with an advertising man in Tulsa, Lewis Brandenburg. He ran a one-man agency out of the basement of his home. I knew him because he had done a piece of literature on the Geronimo for us a couple of years earlier.

"I had taken several Brownie snapshot pictures with me to Tulsa, and we were visiting about what to say in the literature. Lewis asked me what we were going to call it.

"To that point, we had thought about a lot of different names, like 'Ed's Ditcher,' 'Gopher,' 'Mole,' 'Badger,' and others. Lewis liked the idea of an animal name because it fit into a logo that he thought we needed to dress up the machine and literature.

"We spent some time that afternoon thinking about a name. Lewis said it ought to be short and describe what the machine did, so we felt it had to include 'Ditcher' or 'Trencher.'

"I don't remember which of us came up with 'Ditch Witch' that afternoon. It didn't sound like such a great idea at the time. In fact, it sounded a little weird. I guess that's what attracted me to it.

"It got to be suppertime, and I left the problem of the name and the logo with Lewis. The trencher was already painted orange, and the name 'Witch' just naturally led him to come up with the character of a witch riding on a shovel across the face of the moon. Originally it was a full moon, colored green, because the green and black looked good on orange. That became our first logo.

"The first ten years we weren't selling all that many trenchers, so what we called them didn't seem important. We did have the name copyrighted. It has become one of our most valuable assets, and we have to work diligently to preserve our ownership.

"I have jokingly said that one of the smarter things I have done was to go home to supper that evening."

### WHY ARE THEY PAINTED ORANGE?

Another top ten question asked by visitors at the Charles Machine Works is: "Why are Ditch Witch trenchers orange?" Most construction equipment is painted yellow.

Ed Malzahn guesses he has heard the question several thousand times during the past four decades.

"It's a long story," he answers. "It happened by accident and is one of the many good fortune things that happened early in the company life. Truthfully, we have just backed into many of the best ideas we've ever had.

"The color story began in 1946 with the Geronimo. I was painting them red because they were a safety device, and I thought that was the appropriate color, like a fire extinguisher. In the interest of economy, I was trying to cover the black iron with one coat of red paint.

"Red is a semi-transparent color, and I wasn't doing too good a job. I complained to Glenn Yahn, the local lumber yard manager, that the problem was his paint. I was buying it one quart at a time, and after trying his two brands of red without success, he suggested in desperation that I change colors. He handed me a can of orange.

"We have often been accused of adopting the color orange because orange and black are the colors of the school that both Glenn and I attended, Oklahoma A.&M. (now Oklahoma State), and red was the color of the other state school in Norman. The truth is, I was too lazy to go to the extra effort and properly prime before applying a red cover coat. Anyway, the orange worked better on Geronimos.

"When I had completed the first Ditch Witch trencher that I was proud enough to show to someone, I painted it orange because every Friday afternoon was paint time, since it involved preparation time to clean up and sweep the small building adjacent to the shop, and since there would be no further activity to stir up the dust.

"The paint was slow drying, so introducing a second color in the paint room would have been a problem, and anyway I would have had to clean up the paint gun twice. I kind of adopted orange as the company color, because it simplified things. That was the color of the paint that was in the gun.

"After painting the first trencher orange, the second and third just came natural. I really thought that if we ever got into it, I probably would change to yellow, because that was the color of 'Caterpillar' equipment and as far as I was concerned they set the standard."

The bright orange for Ditch Witch equipment survived from 1948 to 1981, when the company changed to a burnt orange color. The change was mandated by an Environmental Protection Agency requirement. The EPA decreed that lead must be removed from industrial paints because of the amount of lead injected into the atmosphere in the painting process, and also because of hazards in the compounding and preparation of the paint.

Most manufacturers who used yellow, red and orange changed their colors, since lead apparently was a basic ingredient in those hues. It would have been possible to continue with the original orange for Ditch Witch equipment with a much more expensive paint, but the company elected to save that money and change colors.

It was only coincidental that Oklahoma State changed to burnt orange a couple of years earlier. Their coach at that time, Jim Stanley, thought the football could be hidden next to a burnt orange jersey, and thus the Cowboys would have an edge in deception.

# 37

# *G*ERONIMO AND OTHER PRODUCTS

An oil field driller working in the Perry area was in Charlie's Machine Shop on Birch Street one day in 1947 and made a chance remark that he was "scared to death" every time he went into the tower for work.

Indeed, one of the most dangerous jobs on a drilling rig is that of the "derrick man." His position is sixty or ninety feet above the ground, depending upon the derrick height. When pipe is being taken out of the hole or put back in, the derrick man maneuvers the top end into position.

In those days, if an emergency occurred on the derrick floor, such as a fire or a blow-out, it was mandatory that the derrick man abandon his position. If his exit down the derrick ladder was blocked, his only alternative generally was to stick it out or jump into the slush pit—a hole containing six to eight feet of mud used in drilling the well. For obvious reasons, neither idea was too appealing.

Someone decided a much safer plan would be to have the derrick man slide down one of the derrick guide wires. Not all derricks had these lines, so a special wire was installed for that purpose.

When an emergency developed, the derrick man would place one leg over the wire and grasp the wire with his gloved hands, then slide rapidly to the ground. Imperfections in the wire, plus damaged hands and legs, made this still a hazardous practice.

Dewey Moore, the local drilling contractor with whom Charlie and Ed Malzahn had developed a telescoping, portable rig, came to Ed with an idea to build a trolley for use on the escape wire. His idea lacked a satisfactory brake and needed some other refinements, but Ed came up with a model that would work. Shaped like an inverted letter T, it gave derrick workers a slide to ground level with a hand-operated brake to control the rate of descent.

"I was convinced that this safety escape device was something every drilling rig needed," Ed says, "so I built several and showed them to our customers as they came into the shop. The word spread and we began to get calls from several oil field supply stores. The selling price was thirty dollars per unit, f.o.b. Perry.

"Within the first several months we decided the slide needed a name. The first and only one we talked about was 'Geronimo,' the battle cry of U.S. paratroopers in World War II when they jumped from their planes. Since this act was similar to bailing out, and the name was catchy and simple, we decided to use it.

"I later learned that the Apache Indian Chief, Geronimo, killed himself by jumping off a cliff. I'm certain our Geronimo saved a lot of lives, so maybe it all balances out in history."

The Malzahns continued to make the Geronimo in their shop from 1947 until 1970. The Ditch Witch business had grown to such proportions by then that the safety device was only a relatively small item. It was being distributed through an entirely different system, to the oil fields. The company sold its inventory and Geronimo fixtures to the Taber Welding Co., another Perry business. The Taber Company later sold Geronimo to another firm and it is still being manufactured.

### THE SKY WITCH

When the Charles Machine Works moved to the new location on West Fir Avenue from the downtown plant in 1959, the company also was making and selling Sky Witch portable scaffolds.

"The idea for Sky Witch did not originate with me by any means," Ed says. "Devices based on the scissor-fold principle were being made early in this century."

In the early 1950s he felt there was a demand for a better quality unit than those then on the market, so he set about designing and manufacturing one. The Malzahns soon had a portable hydraulic lift platform, or scaffold, ready to offer, and by the mid-1950s they were into that business. Production was continued after the company moved to the new plant.

The Sky Witch, which received its name after "Ditch Witch" had been selected for the company's trencher, was produced without patents. The plan was to market a superior product with principles that had been previously proven.

The smallest model was designed to elevate 750 pounds to a height of ten feet, while the largest would lift 2,000 pounds up to twenty-four feet. Prices in the 1960s ranged from $995 to $5,000.

The equipment consisted of a metal framework and platform mounted on a folding frame which could be extended or recoiled by a hydraulic system. Some were mounted on casters, or they could be placed on trailers, truck beds, wheels or skids. Later models were self-propelled. They were used in home construction, installation of heavy fixtures in high factory ceilings, highway bridge construction and to reach high places in a variety of situations. Sky Witches were used in construction of the St. Lawrence Seaway, where they enabled workmen to install equipment and fixtures in high tunnels.

Production facilities in the downtown plant were largely dedicated to Ditch Witch trenchers, but when the move to West Fir was made the company planned to allocate more space to Sky Witch output. However, demand for trenchers became so great that most of the floor space even in the much larger new plant was needed to make Ditch Witch equipment.

The Sky Witch never quite fit into the Ditch Witch product line or distribution system. Because production was severely limited, the platform was unable to dominate its market. CMW had made the commitment to confine its product line to tools for underground construction. Eventually Sky Witch was sold to another company, and it continued to be manufactured for several years.

### THE HOT WITCH

Few remember a product called "Hot Witch," although once it seemed to hold promise of greater things.

When the Malzahns were attempting to build a multiple product line in the 1950s and 1960s, they conceived the idea of a heated roller about sixteen inches in diameter and twenty-four inches long. The roller had a handle attached for moving about and a butane tank for a burner inside the roller.

The idea was to heat the roller and push it over a freshly prepared asphalt patch, thereby sealing it against moisture in hopes of making the patch last longer.

"We never sold many of the rollers," Ed says, "partly because we did not have a sales force calling on people who did this kind of work. Then, too, we never did get a burner that would stay lit on a windy Oklahoma day.

"We made the first roller in 1961 and the last one in 1964. The name again was tied into Ditch Witch, which by then was a well-established brand in the trencher market. We never did bother to patent the Hot Witch. Several other manufacturers have tried it since. They haven't had much luck, either."

# 38

# *C*MW FINDS NEW WAYS

"I suppose," says Ed Malzahn, "if we had a big group of stock-holders who demanded top return on their dollar, we might have to do things differently."

Fortunately, the Charles Machine Works, Inc., which he heads as president, is a privately owned company. The only stockholders are the employees themselves and the Malzahn family. There is no corporate indebtedness and the company manages to show a profit every year.

Operating a modern industrial complex on a pay-as-you-go basis has been viewed as everything from refreshingly American to financially foolish. But, that has been the basic business philosophy of the Charles Machine Works and its forerunners since day one. Obviously it is a system that works well for this company.

"It's really a matter of objectives," Ed points out. "I think our objectives over the years have had a lot to do with the things my grandfather and the other settlers of these areas held in value. They were individualists, independent thinkers. One thing we have been determined to do in this company is not lose the value of the individual. Most of us who have been with CMW any time at all are here because we love it. We try to operate the company so we can go home and sleep at night."

A common factor has been retained at every stage of the development of this company: The goal that the customer's wishes be fulfilled. It goes hand in hand with the basic CMW business philosophy.

"It's just like when I was a kid and my dad, Charlie, sent me out to buy his daily supply of Beech Nut chewing tobacco," Ed says. "If he could shake a quarter out of his coin purse in the morning, he sent me off to the store. If nothing fell out of his purse, he sharpened a couple of plow shares, and then sent me to the store.

That's really our philosophy today. If we need something, we open the purse. If something comes out, we get it. If not, we go do a little more work.

"What we do tomorrow is not dictated by what we do now. We have always been motivated by 'finding a better way.' What we do tomorrow should be dramatically different from today."

It all adds up to a classic American business success story. This company is proof that hard work, thrift, attention to detail and the overriding goal of providing customer satisfaction really do pay off.

Perhaps the restrictions and complications of today would make it difficult to start a new business determined to operate on a pay-as-you-go basis. It would be hard to duplicate CMW's success employing the same methods today. More's the pity.

Loyalty has played a major role in making the company such a stable operation—and that is a two-way street. There is a bond of loyalty between CMW and its customers, its employees, its distributors, its suppliers, and the community of Perry. Through the good years and bad, each has stood steadfastly by the other.

Ed has received several attractive offers to move the company to larger towns, or to sell the business outright for a large amount of money. Loyalty to his hometown and to his hundreds of Perry-area employees always overrode such tempting propositions, and he has never regretted turning any of them down.

The quality of employees found in the Perry area is one of the advantages the company has, Malzahn believes.

"It took a special type of people to settle the Cherokee Strip and Northwestern Oklahoma," he says. "They had to have something special inside them to leave their homelands and come to a new land with nothing more than faith in themselves.

"Now, a few generations later, there still is something of that in people here. For several years I interviewed all new employees. I would ask them what they wanted to do. Quite often they answered by asking, 'What do you want me to do?' They believed they could do anything if they were given the chance. They were right."

Those who work for the Ditch Witch company will tell you, by and large, that they "bleed orange." They are fiercely proud of the trenchers and other equipment produced by the Perry factory. Ed Malzahn never misses an opportunity to tell them and anyone else listening that it is the people who make the product No. 1 in the world.

That fact of superiority was underscored in 1991 by *Fortune* magazine when for the second time in three years it named Ditch Witch trenchers as one of the 100 things that the U.S. makes best. None better are made anywhere, not in Japan, Germany or the country of your choice. That kind of recognition is a morale booster for the people of CMW and it also does a great deal for the independent distributors and the equipment users themselves.

Employees have had a vested interest in the company since profit-sharing was introduced by the Malzahns in 1959. Millions of dollars have been divided by workers at CMW each year since then. Under this plan, the company's board of directors sets aside a percent of the annual profit for dividends and growth capital. All additional profits are split evenly between employees and the company. In most years, bonuses paid to employees have amounted to more than twenty percent of their total annual wages.

An Employee Stock Ownership Plan (ESOP) also was added a few years ago, giving hourly and salaried workers a tangible share of the company. Their holdings grow year by year as long as they stay with CMW. About one-third of the company is owned by employees. The pay rate is comparable to that for similar jobs in Oklahoma City and Tulsa.

These perquisites, making employees part-owners of the business with a positive stake in its profitability, stimulate productivity and efficiency much better than some of the methods tried by management theorists in other companies. The employee turnover rate also is quite low, generally found to be about four percent. This compares with thirty to forty percent in some metropolitan industries.

Additional liberal benefits provided by CMW include fully paid health and accident insurance, production bonuses, competitive basic wages, substantial Christmas gifts for employees and retirees, free hams and turkeys for all at Christmas and Thanksgiving, and coffee on the house for everyone at the 10 a.m. and 3 p.m. coffee breaks.

This type of concern for individuals and involvement of employees in company matters had its beginning with the Malzahns long before the Ditch Witch days. An item on the front page of *the Perry Daily Journal* on February 7, 1928, described "something new in the business field," a banquet for employees and spouses of the Malzahn Brothers Machine Shop in their new two-story brick building on Sixth Street.

The three-course dinner was served in an apartment above the shop with a total of twelve present. The meal was prepared and served by the Cozy Inn, according to the newspaper.

"Following the dinner, many topics of a business nature were discussed by the Malzahn brothers, Charles and Gus, and by their workmen.... The whole evening's discussion centered around the question of serving the public better and endeavoring to serve their needs in a bigger way. The machine shop...is one of the best equipped and the most complete in the Northern part of the state.... They do considerable oil field work...which even shops in larger cities are unable to handle," the article stated.

The company is proud that it has had only one minor experience with layoffs. That came at a point in the early 1970s when a spiraling recession was gripping the country. Only a handful of Ditch Witch people were affected.

Employees find frequent growth opportunities at CMW through internal promotions and creation of new departments to meet specific needs. Training is provided in-house for many basic skills while outside training is encouraged and subsidized by management at all levels.

In years when work requirements permit, numerous Perry area college-age students are hired for summer jobs. The wages paid have financed a full education for countless young people, many of whom returned to Perry as employees of CMW.

First-time visitors frequently comment on two very visible characteristics at the Ditch Witch company—the genuinely friendly people in the office and the plant, and the bright, clean work places found in the manufacturing area as well as in the business offices. This is additional evidence of the sense of pride and high morale demonstrated by CMW people.

Visitors also are struck by the informal attire worn by top executives and all others in the office. None of the men wears a jacket or necktie. Instead it's usually an open-neck sport shirt and slacks. This has been unwritten company policy for decades.

Private offices are scarce. Low dividers segregate most departmental functions, but only a very few have their own offices. An enclosed atrium filled with lush greenery and flowering plants in the center of the main office building is a relaxing coffee break area and meeting room. The garden often is tended by Ed himself.

For years the company has had a series of equipment seminars, or "fly-ins," inviting owners and prospective buyers of their products to come to Perry for a two-day session. Three such events are usually held during the year, with more than one hundred on hand for each. The visitors attend a barbecue, tour the plant and wind up in an informal give-and-take meeting with Ed, CMW engineers and sales department representatives.

Such events serve several purposes, but one of the most significant is to provide a forum where end users of Ditch Witch products can tell the manufacturer face to face how the equipment is working and what kind of changes they would suggest. A number of significant refinements, even including new products, have developed as a result of these fly-ins.

A marketing conference with owners of Ditch Witch dealerships is held each January. These are used to introduce new products, disclose such things as the year's advertising theme, marketing expectations and strategy, and to report on "how we did" during the past twelve months. The conferences are most often held in Oklahoma City and, but on occasion they are moved to a resort area in Florida, Southern California or other warm climate.

Training seminars for sales and service representatives from Ditch Witch dealerships are held at CMW several times each year. Separate service conferences are held for equipment owners.

*୨ଈ*

The Charles Machine Works' Engineering Center is a gleaming, high-tech, two-level building. Built in 1980, it is approximately the size of the entire plant when the company moved to West Fir Avenue in 1959. The center fairly bulges with the latest in sophisticated computer design equipment manned by highly skilled engineers and technicians. Nearby is a separate laboratory building for research and development with its own complete manufacturing facilities.

CMW rightfully prides itself for being on the cutting edge of technology with tools used not only in engineering and design, but throughout the company. The manufacturing plant was among the first users of robotic welders. Equipment in several production centers is automated and tape-operated. Computer-integrated manufacturing is now a fact of life at Ditch Witch, and it is another area in which it has pioneered.

The company's workers produce about a dozen basic models of trench digging machines. Each is somewhat customized for the job it is intended to handle.

"Our concern is the top ten feet of soil and the things that people want to put there," Malzahn says. Output is about 150 machines per week.

A large main frame computer processes data from every segment of the company and is perhaps the nerve center of the entire operation.

The company's sales organization also is different. The U.S. is divided into four geographic regions, each containing several districts. Regional and district sales managers live in Perry but spend about half their time, usually in two-week intervals, in their territories, working with dealers and Ditch Witch owners or prospects. This requires a great deal of travel, but the close personal contact at the factory and in the field pay great dividends in sales and communications in both directions.

International sales are handled in much the same way. The company's sales representatives for export markets also live in Perry, traveling from here to exotic locations all over the world on a regular schedule.

"It works for us," Malzahn says of the slightly unorthodox methods used throughout the business operation. "These things might not be any good anywhere else, but they work for us."

In 1971 former Vice President Hubert Humphrey, then a U.S. senator from Minnesota, headed a delegation from Washington at the Ditch Witch plant to present a Presidential "E" award to the company for excellence in exporting. The award recognized CMW's outstanding contribution to the increase of U.S. trade abroad, according to Maurice H. Stans, President Nixon's secretary of commerce at the time.

The visiting group also included two other U.S. senators—Henry Bellmon of Oklahoma and Carl T. Curtis of Nebraska, and Congressman Happy Camp of this district. They toured the plant and commented that it was an excellent example of the way local industries can stabilize the economy of rural communities.

Numerous other prestigious awards have been earned by the company and by Ed Malzahn himself. He has been inducted into the Oklahoma Hall of Fame; named outstanding regional small businessman by the National Council for Small Business Management Development; member Oklahoma Advisory Council for the Small Business Administration; the Oklahoma State University Alumni Hall of Fame and the OSU Engineering Hall of Fame (he also served on the school's advisory board for education and development).

He was appointed by the governor to serve as director of the Oklahoma Department of Commerce and Industry and chairman of the Oklahoma Industrial Development and Parks Commission; named outstanding engineer in management by the Oklahoma Society of Professional Engineers; chosen Man of the Year by the Perry Chamber of Commerce; and served a term as chairman of the Farm and Industrial Equipment Institute, one of the nation's oldest trade associations.

He served on the board of regents for Oklahoma A.&M. Colleges, which includes OSU, from 1987 until resigning in 1991, when he was vice chairman. With all this, he finds time to teach an adult Sunday school class, sing in the choir and serve on committees at the First Presbyterian Church.

Ed's wife, Mary, has carved out a successful career of her own in the cattle business. She grew up on a farm and has a natural love of all animals, including cattle, horses, llamas, emus, ducks, geese, swans and quail, all of which can be found on the land she cares for. The M&M Purebred Charolais Cattle Ranch, which she manages, is a model of efficiency and progressive methods. Embryo transfers, a selective process for producing improved beef and breeding stock, is the foundation for an expanded high-tech breeding program.

Her Charolais cattle have won major awards at national and regional shows, and the ranch is host each year to one of the breed's most important sales.

Mary was headed for a career in music at the time she and Ed met in 1943 while both were students at Oklahoma A.&M. College. She was a member of the Student Entertainers Bureau and sang as an alto with the Blue Notes trio, a popular campus group. After her marriage later that year she devoted herself to fulltime duties as a housewife and, still later, as the mother of a son and two daughters.

In more recent years, since the children have become adults with families of their own, her energy and efforts have been channeled into the ranch operation. The M&M pastures adjoin the CMW plant, and Mary is a working manager. She has the capable help of full-time, college-trained employees who share her love of the land and animals and assist in overseeing the operation. The ranch is a successful business of 3,000 acres and 500 cattle.

Through the years, Mary has shared her musical gift as a member of the Presbyterian Church choir, which she also directed for 20 years, and she is a member of the church board of deacons. Along with Ed and their three children, she serves on the CMW board of directors.

The M&M Ranch name stands for "Mary Malzahn." Ed's role in that business is more as a cheerleader for his wife's efforts. He shares her pride in what is being accomplished there.

### *MARY'S BENT PROP*

Ed and Mary Malzahn enjoy bringing up moments about one another from out of the past. One of his favorite anecdotes dates from the 1950s when the trencher business was starting to blossom. Frequent airline trips became commonplace for sales people and others at CMW, and commercial flights were proving expensive. The Malzahns decided to purchase a light plane for business travel. Lowell Highfill, one of the company's sales representatives, had been a professional flight instructor and was asked to teach fellow employees how to fly.

After eight hours of dual instruction, the instructor would have the student stop the aircraft on the runway. He would climb out and tell the student, "Take it around the pattern by yourself." That was the first solo flight—a time of pride, shock and sometimes terror, but it always made the adrenalin flow.

"Mary and I started our flying lessons at the same time," Ed says. "Mary was just going to take the ground school so that she would at least know what was going on. Lowell talked her into taking a few rides so that she could better understand the class work. After that, she was hooked.

"The bent prop happened on her solo flight. Lowell had climbed out of the sixty-five-horsepower tandem-seated Piper Tail Dragger, stood by the side of the runway, and motioned for her to take it around. From the very beginning she liked to fly with Lowell doing hoops and spins, but she never did like the landings, and her first one was a doozy.

"Her approach was a little high, and in an effort to get in on the runway she sort of drove it in a little hard—hard enough that the metal prop must have touched the runway. In the embarrassment she didn't notice anything but a hard landing. She taxied up to where Lowell was standing. He stuck his head inside, gave a few reassuring words, and said to try it over again.

"As soon as the airplane was airborne, it began to shake like a bucket of bolts. With luck and a newfound skill, she got back on the ground safely. Sure enough, both ends of the prop were bent in a curve. Anyone else would have quit then and there, while they figured they were ahead. Not Mary. She went ahead and got her license about the same time I did."

❧

Ed and Mary live in an attractive stone home situated on beautifully landscaped grounds just a short walking distance from the CMW plant and office. They have three children: Dr. Don Malzahn, a professor in the Industrial Engineering Department at Wichita State University; Pam Sewell, who operates the Black Bear Angus Ranch northeast of Perry with her husband, David; and Leasa Wilkerson, who operates the Ditch Witch distributorship in the state of Arizona with her husband, Dan. Mary, Don, Pam and Leasa also sit on the CMW board of directors, along with Ed. Four non-family members round out the board.

David Sewell is the son of Mrs. Elva Sewell and the late Joe Sewell Sr. of Perry, and Dan Wilkerson is the son of Mr. and Mrs. Elmo Wilkerson of Perry. His mother, Mary Ann, also is a former Ditch Witch employee. Until retiring in 1990, she was "the voice of Ditch Witch" as the central telephone switchboard operator and main office receptionist for the company. It was said she instantly recognized the voices of hundreds of callers, including many who did not dial the Ditch Witch number all that often. It was a gift that enabled her to route many calls expeditiously.

The Malzahns' example of civic and community involvement seems to be emulated by many of their employees. Ditch Witch people are found at the forefront of numerous worthwhile programs, including the YMCA, library board, community theatre, school activities, churches, city council and various professional associations.

While Ed and Mary meticulously avoid even a suggestion of making Perry a "company town," in which all activities revolve around their business, they are generous donors to worthwhile efforts in the community. Their roles are invariably played out in the background as anonymous benefactors.

ଏ

Competitors know Ditch Witch people as carefree and some-times cocksure individuals. It's not a chip-on-the-shoulder attitude, just something born of knowing they have the world's best product and most of the market for it. They don't rub it in but they surely don't hide their pride in the company and the equipment they represent.

At some of the many national trade shows attended by CMW and competitors, a spirited rivalry often springs up in an effort to make light of each other's displays or booth decorations. Nothing malicious, just industrial-type fun. The "other guys" rarely are able to spring any surprises on the always-alert young sales representatives from Ditch Witch.

A few years ago, at a major outdoor show held on a farm field near Chicago, a crew of sales people from CMW was setting up a large exhibit. When lunch time arrived one of the group quietly made a sandwich using canned dog food as the spread, garnishing it with lettuce and pickles. It was offered to a hungry but unwary colleague, one who was well-known for his extremely weak stomach. After a tentative first bite the victim was told what was in his sandwich. He promptly gagged, as expected.

Somewhat later, he also was able to appreciate the humor in the practical joke, but perhaps not to the same extent as his co-workers.

Word of this got around to a nearby competitor's booth just as some of them were trying to figure out what kind of mischief they could play on the Ditch Witch bunch. The sandwich stunt brought their planning to a halt.

"If those Ditch Witch guys would do that to their own people," one said, "what on earth do you think they would do to us? Let's don't make them angry."

Paul Rogers, now the Ditch Witch sales manager, grew up in Stillwater, just twenty-four miles from Perry. He .remembers with wry amusement a stern warning issued by his father, Murl Rogers, when Paul brought home a poor grade from school one day.

"If you don't study harder," Murl scolded his young son, "you'll wind up as a ditch digger!"

As it turns out, Paul did manage good grades and he couldn't be happier even though he sure enough is in the ditch-digging business.

ஒ

It is reasonable to conclude that Perry would not exist as we know it today if not for the Charles Machine Works, Inc. Agriculture always has been a major enterprise in Noble County and even now it continues to provide a good living for hundreds in this area. However, the business of farming traditionally has been risky at best.

Small acreages can no longer provide enough revenue to enable families to survive in an inflated economy, so they are giving way to bigger operations. Many family farms are being lost in the process, and their property is being added to larger holdings. Farmers must have cash flow, too, to provide the land, seed, cultivating tools, harvest equipment and employees to operate profitably.

About one-fourth of all Ditch Witch employees live on farms in the Perry area, and about one-third of all employees have some interest in agriculture—raising wheat, cattle or otherwise producing crops and/or farm animals. Many of them have children in 4-H Clubs and the Future Farmers of America. Most of the fathers could not earn a decent living today just from the small acreages they tend, but their employment at CMW is making it possible for many family farms to continue.

Women constitute a sizable segment of the work force in the plant, around twenty-five percent. They have achieved excellent work records and many of them provide their family with a second income.

When Ed and Charlie Malzahn began thinking about building a small trencher, the manufacturer of the big wheel trenchers lacked interest because they saw no profitable market in that field. The big trencher maker was chalking up annual sales volumes of around $4 million in 1959 and at the same time CMW's total was about $200,000.

By 1969, ten years after moving into the plant on West Fir Avenue, the Ditch Witch company had sales totaling more than $15 million with its small service line trencher while the big guy was still recording a $4 million annual gross.

Today the Perry company manufactures trenching machines ranging from small units with a nine-horsepower engine to tractors with hundred-horsepower diesels. Vibratory plows range from small handlebar machines to attachments for the largest tractors. Backhoes are among other attachments available for the larger machines.

"The two most important developments for our market," Ed says, "were plastic pipe and improved sheathing for electric lines. Plastic pipe made pipe cheap enough for a lot of people to install water lines that would have been too expensive using iron pipe. The improved sheathing made it possible to lay communications lines underground cheaply."

As long as telephone and utility lines are strung from poles, a future market will exist for Ditch Witch equipment. It appears to be an immense potential at this point.

Good things have happened to the Perry company, but most of them have been the result of prudent planning, creative management, high productivity by workers, and the Malzahn family's genuine concern for individuals. The proper course for the Charles Machine Works, Inc. was set long ago.

# 39

# *A*ROUND THE SQUARE IN 1940

Circling the courthouse square has been a favorite pastime for generations in Perry. Teens of the horse and buggy era probably complained, even as today, that "there's nothing else to do." The scenery changes as different tenants occupy the business district, but the centerpiece, the pleasant courthouse park, remains a constant—restful and beautiful for all to enjoy.

For many years there were no stop signs to impede traffic around the square. Once you got into the pattern there was nothing to slow the flow, except, of course, other people.

When the downtown traffic control system was modernized in 1950 with four-way stop lights on each corner of the square, city officials said they were timed for fifteen miles per hour. Motorists maintaining that speed theoretically could go all the way around on green lights. Many found it impossible to do so, non-stop, on the outer perimeter. The square isn't "square," for one thing; the north and south sides are longer than the east and west.

The solution is to drive clockwise, on the inside route next to the park. Each corner then is a right-hand turn; right turns on red lights are legal, so a careful driver can get all the way around with only a slight hesitation now and then. So, to avoid stopping at each corner, those who are serious about cruising usually choose the inside route.

People enjoyed just walking around the square, as many now do in the big-city malls. Unfortunately, unlike today's enclosed malls, we had no climate control around the square then (or now) so such strolling was (and is) largely a fair-weather exercise. In the 1940s, just looking in the shop windows and speaking to merchants along the way was a rewarding experience in itself. So many great things to see and hear!

A half-century ago, in the early 1940s, most stores were open on Saturday night until at least nine o'clock. On an agreeable evening a lot of folks would park their cars on the square after supper, then just sit back to watch the world pass by. It was an inexpensive kind of live entertainment. Like a kaleidoscope, the images kept moving and reshaping themselves to the endless delight of onlookers. It was a quiet time of simple pleasures.

Sidewalks were busy with leisurely window-shoppers and others, some heading for the drug store fountain before or after a Saturday night movie at the Roxy or Annex Theater. Farm families came to town on Saturday morning to spend the entire day buying supplies, transacting business and visiting.

The courthouse and virtually all businesses and offices in the city were open on Saturday afternoon to accommodate them. Grocery stores stayed open until 9 p.m. on Saturdays. Perry had plenty of them, too—nineteen in the downtown area alone.

Teen-agers changed their favorite hangouts from time to time, but one of the most enduring was Forney's Dairy Store in the Masonic building on the west side of the square. A lot of ice cream cones, burgers and fountain drinks were served at their tables, booths and a long counter with stools.

Still more were carried out to cars parked at the curb and consumed there while patrons young and old watched the passing parade on the sidewalk. Hamburgers and hot roast beef sandwiches sold for ten cents at Forney's, and many working people had lunch there on weekdays. The obligatory nickelodeon, or juke box, played the music of Glenn Miller, Tommy Dorsey, Artie Shaw and other popular big bands of the day at five cents per side on 78 rpm records.

Young people did most of the serving at Forney's, but Charlie and Jennie Forney, the owners, worked right alongside them, as did Don and Stella Kirchner, the store managers. Mrs. C.W. Lynch, who celebrated her 102nd birthday in 1990, also was a long-time employee. She looks remarkably unchanged today and still fondly remembers her days at Forney's.

The business area was prosperous in the early 1940s and looked it, thanks largely to a small oil boom percolating in this part of Oklahoma. Virtually every building around the square was occupied, including the upstairs offices where lawyers, doctors, insurance agents, oil lease dealers and various other professionals

headquartered. Perry was a good place for people-watching in
1940.

To stroll leisurely around the entire square required a lot of
time. There were so many stores, so many friendly and interesting
people to chat with, so much to take in. Some people would just
concentrate on a single side of the square. It was not unusual to
have a decided preference for one side over the other.

Actually, any of them could have served as a complete life-sus-
taining entity for shoppers. Each side had at least one drug store,
grocery store, restaurant and clothing store, plus assorted upstairs
offices containing doctors, lawyers, sleeping rooms and so forth.

You could spend your entire life on just one side of the square
in Perry and have all your basic needs amply filled.

Imagine brick paving all around the square (it still exists there
beneath several layers of asphalt), and a whiteway consisting of
ten-foot poles topped by glowing, yellow, incandescent globes.
The gutters were swept clean almost nightly by old Mr. Johnson,
using a push broom, a wagon and his dilapidated pickup truck.
Every so often the fire department also would flush the gutters at
night to test the fire hydrants, ridding the streets of accumulated
piles of dirt and trash.

Nearly every store had a metal awning suspended across its
front to provide shade and shelter for those passing beneath.

### THE NORTH SIDE OF THE SQUARE

Walking to town from the west in 1940, one might have approached the square on the north side of Delaware Street. Just
across the alley from Frank and Elsie Jones' house (now the location of the First National Bank's parking lot) was the Temple Lunch
(the present location of the bank's drive-up windows). There you
were likely to see Leo Robinson or his teen-age son, Tommy, firing
up an outdoor, heavy-duty barbecue pit for the house specialty—
"Unk's Bar-B-Que."

The Temple, which derived its name from the three-story
Masonic Temple across the street, was a small cafe in a
whitewashed brick building with a counter, stools and four tables.
Jimmy (Sugar) Cain, later a lumber dealer and school board member, worked there for his meals while attending Perry High School.
A schoolboy who told "Shug" about some difficulty he was having
at home remembers the wry counsel Cain offered: "You buttered

your bread, now lay in it!" That stayed with him well into adulthood.

One of the Temple waitresses, along with Leo's wife, Helen, was Kate Hartung Mewherter, who later became the wife of Eddie Parker, proprietor of the Kumback Lunch down the street.

Next to the Temple was one of the two large furniture stores in town, Davis & Son. Fred A. Davis and his son, Farris, were the operators, and Fred's daughter, Virginia, also worked there. They were all plump, cheerful people. Charles Zeig, very slender by contrast, was a salesman, but he was also cheerful. Farris, Fred and Virginia were genuinely devoted to fishing and Farris eventually became a professional fishing guide in Arkansas.

The Davis store carried a decent selection of furnishings, carpeting and appliances for the home. Fred and Farris also were morticians, in keeping with the custom of the time for furniture dealers, and the family opened Perry's first real funeral parlor at Eighth and Elm Streets in the 1930s. Before that, final services were held in churches, at graveside or in the home of the deceased.

Christoph & Newton, operated by George Newton and his son, Ted, had the other major furniture store and also the other funeral home. The furniture store was at the south end of the west side of the square, and the funeral home was toward what was then the north end of Seventh Street. It is now operated by Lloyd Brown as Brown's Funeral Home.

Davis & Son Furniture occupied the ground floor portion of a large, two-story, red brick corner building where the First National Bank now stands. On the second floor were several offices, the principal tenant being Southwestern Bell Telephone Company. The east room of the phone office, just past the top of the stairway, housed a bank of switchboards. Each had an upright backdrop of blinking lights and a maze of lines constantly being connected or, at the end of a call, disconnected, all manually controlled by sweet-sounding female operators.

Visitors were not admitted into that room, but on warm days when doors were left ajar to catch any stray breeze you could get a glimpse of mystifying things. Miraculously, the anonymous "central" at each switchboard linked up callers from throughout the community, or perhaps handled long-distance messages from who knows where.

Seeing that and hearing the operators' fascinating cacophony of modulated voices speaking into horn-shaped tubes draped around their necks, responding to queries or instructions only they could hear through their individual durable-looking headsets, was akin to the feeling one gets today in viewing pictures of Houston's space center engineers flawlessly directing a moon landing. It was the apex of high technology in Perry at the time.

In a small town, most people recognized the voice of the particular telephone operator who asked for their number, please, but the Perry exchange was generally businesslike and not inclined to indulge in idle chatter with the customers. Local telephone numbers were either two or three digits. Party lines also had a letter, either "J" or "W," affixed. If you did not know the number and could not reach a phone directory, the operator would look it up for you. The experienced ones had most of the numbers memorized, anyway.

Depending on the time of day, your operator might have been Marie Booher, chief of the day crew, or Lucille Foster, evening chief. Or it could have been Annabelle Wurtz, Ethel Dunham, Jennie Horn, Sara Kennedy, Dorothy Lampe, Ethel Levy, Rose McLimans or Thelma Gowty, to name only a few who toiled there in the 1940s.

Besides connecting you to the party you were calling, they also would provide numbers and other information on request, including the correct time of day or night, all of it rendered in a pleasant "voice with a smile" and at no extra charge.

Unquestionably, the telephone company was a choice place to work for many young Perry women. It offered job benefits and stability not widely available elsewhere, and it was just an altogether interesting place to be. There was a real sense of pride in belonging to a big, successful company, and at that time it did indeed represent the leading edge of communications technology.

Some of the operators went on to work in the business office, adjacent to the switchboard room. That is where phone bills were paid. In later years, for the convenience of customers who detested climbing all those stairs, the office was moved to ground level, into the Temple Lunch building when the restaurant had gone out of business.

Still later, Southwestern Bell built a modern new office and plant at the corner of Eighth and Delaware. It still houses the automated switching equipment—human operators were eliminated here years ago—but, alas, there no longer is a business office in Perry. Bills are paid by mail to a voiceless, faceless, anonymous computer location at an out of town address.

In addition to the phone company, some of the upstairs offices were occupied by Dr. George Driver, a physician, and Dr. D.F. Croake, a dentist. Dr. Driver and his family had living quarters up there, too, and on sultry summer nights some of them would sleep on pallets spread on top of the metal awnings over Davis & Son Furniture.

Crossing Seventh Street, the corner location on the north side of the square was another two-story brick building. Stone columns flanked a doorway with "Bank of Commerce" carved on the arch above. The bank was long gone by 1940, and the building had been occupied for a time by the office of H.H. (Henry) Reynolds and Howard Cress, real estate and insurance agents.

Mr. Reynolds, who died in the late 1930s, had been a mayor of Perry. He made five of the Oklahoma land runs, including the Cherokee Strip in 1893. Before coming to Perry he had been a mail carrier in "No Man's Land," the Oklahoma Panhandle region. Mr. Reynolds always said the Cherokee Strip opening was the greatest and most spectacular of them all. He was appointed a deputy U.S. marshal shortly after the opening here.

Howard Cress served as Mayor Reynolds' chief of police and went on to become an original member of the Oklahoma Highway Patrol. Jimmy Taylor and his wife, Mary, later operated the agency, calling it Reynolds & Taylor. Mr. Taylor died in the early 1940s.

Some years later the building was occupied by the Oklahoma Tire & Supply (OTASCO) store, operated first by Mr. and Mrs. Wilson Clark, who moved to Colorado, and then by Mr. and Mrs. Gordon Clark, no relation, who numbered triplets among their fourteen children. The building burned down some thirty years later and has been replaced by the modern one-story Albright Title & Trust office.

A stairway between the Reynolds & Cress office and the A.C. Lamb Jewelry, located next door east, led to a second floor honeycomb of sleeping rooms, apartments and professional offices. Virtually all doctors, lawyers and dentists practiced out of second story locations, requiring patients to climb steep flights of stairs. If they were too sick or aged to negotiate the stairway, well, all doctors made house calls.

Dr. J.W. Francis, MD, was one of the second floor tenants on the north side, with a suite over the City Drug Store facing the old Post Office. A lady with an interesting name, Belle Ruff, was the receptionist, and sometimes Dr. Francis' daughter-in-law, Mildred Francis, also worked there. Belle Ruff was the daughter of Dutch Ruff, the county jailer.

Jack Stone was not an employee of Dr. Francis, but served without pay as an unofficial office attendant and telephone answerer. He was a justice of the peace and had his own office in a ground floor location down the street, but he and Dr. Francis were good friends and they enjoyed each other's company.

Jack was small in stature and slender, white-haired and usually smoked a pipe. In earlier days he had operated a prosperous general store called "Everybody's" where Davis & Son later held forth, but by 1940 his personal wealth appeared to have diminished by quite a bit.

Jack was an avid reader of pulp magazine Westerns and detective stories, plus *Collier's, the Saturday Evening Post, Liberty* and *the Literary Digest.* Naturally, Dr. Francis' waiting room had an ample supply of these, none of them current issues. The two men shared an interest in baseball and listened to broadcasts of the St. Louis Cardinals and other major league teams on the office radio when no patients were waiting.

Dr. Francis spoke softly and walked with a slow, loping gait, almost always carrying his black physician's bag. Because of an illness when he was younger, one of his lungs had been removed and his left shoulder drooped perceptibly so that he appeared always to be walking on uneven terrain.

Nothing seemed to ruffle his easy-going nature. He greeted one and all with a cheerful wave of the hand and doffed his hat to each lady. Like his friend Jack Stone, Dr. Francis almost always carried a pipe in his mouth, and it was usually a curved meerschaum.

Once at a Monday evening Rotary Club meeting, several members were asked to tell about the first dollar they earned. Dr. Francis told about his boyhood in Ireland and growing up with a strong yen to come to the U.S., then realizing that goal as a young man by hiring on as a cook's helper on an ocean liner. Once arrived on the golden shore, he went to work in the kitchen of a major

New York City hotel, soon becoming a well-paid chef. By scrimping and saving his wages, he earned enough to enroll in an Eastern medical school and eventually wound up in Perry to begin his practice. It was a fascinating account, embellished with numerous details.

Later that evening one of the Rotarians saw Dr. Francis' wife, Rachel, and told her how much he had enjoyed hearing the story. She smiled gently and tried to hold back laughter, but had to break the surprising news: "Not a bit of that ever happened," she said. "Dr. Francis was born and reared in Arkansas, went to medical school there and emigrated to Oklahoma."

Spinning such absorbing, but totally fictional, stories was just part of his Ozark heritage. He always did it with a straight face.

The two-story brick building where Dr. Francis' office was located bears the inscription "Palmer & Smelser" for the original builders from the early days of Perry. It is now known as the Donaldson building and is owned by Robert Donaldson of Stillwater, grandson of the late Harry Donaldson, Perry lumber dealer.

For many years it was owned by the proprietor of the City Drug Store, Fred W. Beers, who died in 1931. The ground floor had three business locations: A.C. Lamb, jeweler and optometrist, on the west; the City Drug in the middle; and, at various times, the Bon-Ton Bakery, operated by Ben Wiehe; and later the J.L. Barge Grocery & Market, operated by Lester Barge. Walter Weiss was the meat cutter there.

Lamb was a licensed optometrist, the only one here in 1940, but never called himself "Dr. Lamb." Most people thought of him primarily as a watch repairman and a jeweler. Actually he was skilled at all three. His time was divided between working over a watchmaker's table, peering through a jeweler's loupe at tiny gears, springs, ring mountings and the like, and leading patients through an examination to prescribe the correct lenses for their visual problems.

Dr. Lamb's wife, Opal, assisted in operating the store, and their son, Charles, grew up in the business. After World War II, Charles also became an optometrist and practiced for a time with his father at a new location they built on the north side of the square. The elder Dr. Lamb died in 1951. By that time Charles had moved to Seattle, and he is still engaged in the profession there.

The City Drug Store was destined to become a Perry institution from the day it was established by Mr. Beers in 1903 until it was closed by his family in December 1940, nearly ten years after his death. It survived a disastrous fire in 1908 and a few months of "chain store" competition in the 1920s, but the depression of the 1930s was too much for it.

Perry had five drug stores in 1940. Brownie Drug and Hamous & Hopper Pharmacy were on the west side of the square; Nelson's Pharmacy on the south side; Foster's Corner Drug on the east side; and the City Drug on the north side. All had marble soda fountains except Hamous & Hopper. Only Foster's remains today.

On summer evenings, car hops sat in front of the stores that had fountains, ready to jump up and take orders for cold drinks and ice cream from motorists parked at the curb. Trays of refreshments were carried from the fountain and attached to the car door. Tall (twelve-ounce) limeades with a mint leaf garnish were summertime favorites of many people. They cost ten cents. If a scoop of sherbet was added, it came to fifteen cents. Hand-packed Crystal ice cream, the gourmet's delight, was fifty cents a quart. It was decidedly a delicacy and an extravagance.

Like most grocery stores, drug stores provided free delivery service anywhere in the city. You could phone in an order for a ten-cent tin of aspirin, thirty-five cents' worth of chocolate Ex-Lax and a five-cent copy of *Collier's* magazine, and they would bring it right out by car or bicycle, day or night. They really hoped you would order a prescription item, something costing about, say, a dollar and a half, because that's where the profit was. No matter. The delivery service was free for everything they sold.

Drug stores around the square were open from seven-thirty in the morning until eleven-thirty at night seven days a week. They closed only on Thanksgiving and Christmas day. The Fourth of July was a holiday for most folks, but not the drug stores. Most of them sold fireworks, and on the evening of the Fourth young customers would lob cherry bombs, torpedos and other exotic boomers at cars passing by around the square. It was legal. Personal and property damage was surprisingly minimal.

The drug stores were popular hangouts for kids. Teens could talk to one another for hours on end while nursing a nickel Coke, a frosty stein of root beer or a chocolate milk concoction with shaved ice—called a four hundred, for some reason— and most of their friends eventually would appear.

Each of the stores had racks with dozens of popular weekly and monthly magazines, some of them pretty trashy (and well-thumbed). The big-city Sunday newspapers, like *the St. Louis Post-Dispatch, Chicago Tribune* and *the Denver Post,* all of them with bright color comic sections as the outer cover, began arriving here on Thursday. These papers were well-read at the store, but rarely purchased and carried home. They sold for twenty-five cents. Because they were printed so early, most of the news columns were filled with specious articles, comparable to the material now found in supermarket gazettes.

After Mr. Beers died at the age of fifty-seven in 1931, his wife, Ivy, took over operation of the City Drug with the assistance of a twenty-two-year-old nephew from Kansas City, Missouri, who had been attending Oklahoma A.&M. College in Stillwater. He also was named Fred W. Beers, for his uncle. Ivy had two daughters, Jeanice and Gloria, and a six-year-old son who ALSO was named Fred, for his father. Fortunately, his middle name was Gordon, which helped to differentiate him from the other Freds when somebody called for one of them. All three children, Jeanice, Gloria and Fred G., worked at the drug store along with Ivy and her nephew, Fred W.

A.W. Tucker operated a real estate agency in a small office next door east from Barge's Grocery, and the aforementioned Jack Stone also had a desk there. On pleasant summer evenings, Jack would drag a high-back wooden chair across the sidewalk in front of the office, place it in the street so that he could use the curb as a foot stool, and listen to the nightly radio comedy of Amos 'n Andy on NBC. It was an immensely popular show all over the U.S.

Usually the City Drug had a large RCA or Majestic console at the front of the store with sufficient volume to be heard twenty-five feet down the street, where Jack was making himself comfortable. If it was not quite loud enough, Jack would go over and adjust the knobs until it was. The fifteen-minute show came on at six-thirty each weekday evening, and Jack normally had a book or magazine to read as long as the light lasted. His pipe seemed to ward off the mosquitoes.

Elmer V. Davis had a shoe repair shop next door to Tucker's office. Elmer was a handsome, quiet man who worked long hours for years, and lived very frugally. He and his wife, Minnie, had one daughter, Lila Lee, now a teacher in the San Francisco Bay area.

Elmer walked the five blocks from his home to the shop each morning and back again in the evening. Once he had a room-size air-conditioning unit ready to be installed in his shoe shop, but he could never persuade himself that the operating cost was justifiable, so it stayed in the carton. Elmer was a capable shoe repairman, but not an extravagant man.

Perry had four shoe repair shops at the time, one on each side of the square. The others were Ernest Gregory's Perry Shoe Shop, south side; A. W. Christiansen's City Shoe Shop, west side; and William Stopp's East Side Boot and Shoe Shop, east side.

Powers Abstract occupied an office next door to Davis' shop. In addition to Walt Powers Sr., the staff included his oldest son, Bob, and a nephew, Romaine Powers. Walt's daughters, Hazel and Sue, and his other two sons, Jack and Walt Jr., also worked there as time went by. Bob had been severely scarred by burns as a young boy when he and some friends were waging war on an ant den with gasoline, but he continued to operate the abstract business years after his father died in the early 1940s, and real estate people regarded the quality of the agency's work very highly.

Next in line, still moving east down the block, was the Exchange Bank. It was located on the alley in a long, narrow building. The Exchange survived the "national bank holiday" of 1933 and a daylight armed robbery in 1937 to become Noble County's oldest bank in continuous operation.

The other bank in town at that time was the First National, located at the south end of the block on the east side of the square in a building distinguished by its fine example of pre-statehood architecture.

Across the alley from the Exchange was Zorba's Department Store, operated by T. Zorba, his wife, Ann, and their sons, Rudolph and Jack. In 1940 the family had just moved here from Ponca City, and the Zorba store continued in business until the late 1980s when Rudolph closed it upon his retirement. Jack had moved to Stillwater and operated a fashionable men's clothing store there for several years before branching out into other enterprises.

Zorba's was the last full-line, family-operated department store in Noble County. In the 1940s, it was part of a Perry retail community that included Kraemer's Shoe Store on the east side of the

square, the Chic Shoppe and the Famous Department Store on the
south side, the Toggery on the west side, and Walt's Haberdashery
and J.C. Penney Co. on the north side, right next door to Zorba's.
   Above Zorba's and the Penney store were a physician's office
occupied by Dr. J.W. Driver, brother of Dr. George Driver; a
convalescent and maternity center (it was called a "nursing home")
operated by Mrs. Ethel Ryerson, where many Perry babies were
born; and law offices of Henry Dolezal.
   Penney's had a fifty-foot front with large display windows,
showing women's wear on one side and men's apparel on the
other. King W. Montgomery was the local manager in 1940. The
store carried sturdy khaki work clothing, bib overalls and blue
jeans (before they became a fashion statement), along with no-nonsense everyday garments and Sunday attire for the entire family.
One of Penney's biggest attractions, however, was the overhead
cable system put in operation by the clerks when a sale was made.
   J.C. Penney Co. was still a cash-only business then. No charge
accounts, and of course plastic credit cards were unknown. Clerks
received your money, wrote up a two-carbon ticket, and tucked all
of it into a small cylindrical container attached to the cable.
   With the pull of a dangling rope, the device was sent scooting
by a spring mechanism up to a balcony at the rear of the store to
be received by a cashier. The sales ticket was examined and
validated there. If you had change coming, it was dispatched from
the balcony, along with your copy of the ticket, back to the sales
floor by the same cable.
   It was worth a trip to Penney's just to see and hear that
whirring, humming cable system in operation. Somehow it seemed
like a big-city contraption.
   The 1-2-3 Cleaners, owned and operated by Zack McCubbins,
was next to Penney's. It was one of five dry-cleaning shops here
then. The others were Walt Bittman's Art Cleaners, just a few doors
east of Zack's shop; Frank Eby's Economy Cleaners, a half-block off
the north side of the square on Seventh Street; the Martin family's
Perry Steam Laundry, a half-block off the south side of the square
on Seventh Street; and Carrie Denning's Unique Cleaners, between
Fir and Elm where the Shady Lady Tea Room is now located.
   They all operated delivery trucks, but Zack had one advantage:
The name of his shop, 1-2-3, also was his phone number. Pretty
easy for customers to remember.

Judge W.M. Bowles, a distinguished-looking, white-maned member of the Noble County bar and a state Democratic party leader, conducted his law practice from a second-story office above the cleaning shop.

Next door to the 1-2-3 was the combination Mossman Barber Shop and La Grace Beauty Shoppe. Ladies with appointments at the La Grace walked through the barber shop to the back of the building and entered the salon through an entryway of floral-pattern draperies. Ralph and Hubert Mossman, brothers, were the barbers, and Grace La Bord, who later became Mrs. John Hotz, operated the beauty salon. Mrs. Ralph Mossman also worked there as a hair dresser.

The Mossman brothers' father had a barber shop in the same location before the sons took over. Jack Dorl's Barber Shop now occupies the space. No one seems to remember if any other kind of business ever was located there.

The fabled Kumback Lunch was in the next building east. In 1940 owner Eddie Parker had as a business partner Floyd R. Laird, who formerly had been in the clothing business here. Floyd later went to Texas and became an oilman.

The Kumback was just one of fourteen eating places in operation then. Others on or near the square were Babcock Cafe (formerly Pacific Cafe) and Billy Reckert's Palace Cafe, both on the east side; Elite (pronounced "E-light") Hotel & Cafe, operated by the Walt Kehres family, and Helen Folan's Lunch Room, north side; the West Side Cafe on the west side; Wesley Marcy's Gem Cafe, E.V. Hunt's La Fonda Cafe and Ted Workman's U.S. Cafe, all on the south side; H.D. (Speck) Roads' Auto Eat Cafe and Virgil Walkling's Whiteway Cafe, both just off the north side on Sixth Street; the Corner Lunch, just off the south side on Seventh Street; the Temple Lunch, just off the west side on Delaware; and the Seventy-Seven Cafe, part of Daisy Cain's Cain Hotel at Sixth and Fir, on U.S. 77.

The lot east of the Kumback was vacant, except for a billboard frequently used by Kraemer's Shoe Store (an east sider) to advertise Florsheim's Friendly Five five-dollar shoes for men. A. C. Lamb later built his jewelry store and optometry office in that location, moving there from smaller quarters next to the City Drug. Before the billboard was erected, the open lot had been used for touring tent shows and the like, including some amateur and professional boxing exhibitions.

Charlie and Elsie Tucker operated the Western Auto Associate Store east of the Kumback. Charlie was a flying enthusiast. He later left here for the West coast to enter the aircraft industry when wartime demands created tremendous needs. The Western Auto location once had been the site of the Vertz & Vertz Bakery. In two twelve and a half-foot front buildings next to Western Auto were John Julian's Jewelry & Gift Shop and Helen Folan's small cafe. Years earlier, Julian's building was the home of Alfred and Margaret Bucklin's Chili Parlor and Notions Store. Some say their chili was world class, but unfortunately the recipe has been lost.

Next to Mrs. Folan's place, side by side, were the Art Cleaners & Walt's Haberdashery in one building, operated by Walt Bittman; and the Perry Jewelry Co., operated by Dr. Gene Osborne and his son, Forrest, in the other. The city had three jewelry stores and all of them were on the north side of the square. Dr. Osborne also was a veterinarian. Walt Bittman later moved his cleaning shop and haberdashery to the new A.C. Lamb building when it was constructed on the vacant lot between the Kumback and Western Auto.

The lower floor of the building next to Osborne's jewelry was vacant, but the Penney Co. store had been located there before moving up the street, and Harold Scovill later opened C&S Tire & Supply there. The building housed a number of enterprises through the years. F.F. Smith had a grocery store there, a movie theater lasted for a few months, and Cap Swift had one of his numerous little burger stands in the front end of the building at one time. Presently it is occupied by the offices and studios of Perry's two radio stations, KRAD-AM and KJFK-FM.

The second floor of that building was the home of the Arrow Hotel. Moorhead's 1940 city directory listed twelve hotels in Perry, including the Arrow. Seven of them were second-story locations. Those on the north side of the square were B.H. Bowman's, above Bush & Joe's Smokehouse; the Arrow; and the Elite Hotel on the second floor of Walt Kehres' building. On the east side were Anna Marsh's Marsh Hotel and Anna Doggett's Hotel Doggett, both sharing a single, narrow stairway between Foster's Corner Drug and the Roxy Theater; and on the west side, Mrs. Ethel Lamm's Ross Hotel, over George McManess' barber shop.

Hotels off the square included the St. Louis, a half-block off the west side, on Cedar Street, with John Vandenberg as manager; the

Wa-Nee at the west end of the same block; the Standard, above the Public Food Market, two blocks south of the west side, on Seventh Street, operated by J.A. Wolf; Virgil Walkling's Whiteway, just off the north side on Sixth Street, upstairs over his cafe; the Peerless, a block and a half off the north side on Sixth Street, with L.R. Phillips as manager; and the Cain Hotel, operated by Daisy Cain at Sixth and Fir, two blocks north of the square. All have long since vanished.

Across the alley from the Arrow Hotel was the Walt Kehres building, a spiffy-looking two-story buff brick structure that housed the Elite Restaurant on the ground floor, the Elite Hotel upstairs, and two other ground-floor businesses. The Elite Hotel was a popular place for salesmen and others who traveled through here regularly, and it also drew a share of tourists. For years the restaurant was open all night to accommodate hotel guests. Walt built the brick building in 1936. It replaced the last wooden building still on the square. The Elite was a pioneer business, dating its existence back to the run in 1893. The present owners have recreated a statehood era ambience in the hotel rooms and visitors are welcome there.

Also in the Kehres building were Jack's Auto Supply, managed by Harry Elwell, and the Elite Barber Shop, operated by Leo Stieferman.

The two-story building east of the Elite had McLellan's Variety Store on the ground floor and the Donahue & Mugler offices upstairs. Partners in the latter business were H.C. Donahue and John Mugler, and their agency had a broad scope—insurance of all kinds, loans, abstracts and real estate. They eventually branched out into oil and gas interests.

Downstairs, McLellan's crowded an amazing amount of merchandise—it was a five- and ten-cent store—into a twenty-five-foot wide building. The place was a wonderland for kids and adults alike. Toys, gadgets, small items of apparel, toilet articles, sewing supplies, half-sole repair kits for shoes, even a few books, everything stacked high on countertops with little divided trays.

The first thing to catch your attention upon entering McLellan's was the tantalizing fragrance of candy emanating from a long glass-encased display counter on the east wall. They had bulk chocolates, cream and fruit centers, caramels, and of course cherries in thick syrup. There were lemon drops, rock candy, sweet-balls and red and black licorice whips. The aroma of fresh roasted nuts mingled with all this. You could get a small sack nearly filled with any of them for about a dime. Virginia Dufek Jones, Dollie Dufek Bay and Edna Carley Zeig were among the many salesladies who helped make this store successful.

Jess Lee's City Barber Shop, which also was headquarters for H.R. Bittman's taxi stand, was next to McLellan's. Jess was a friendly little man, about five feet, five inches tall, who loved baseball. He may have been too small to play the game, but he understood it better than most people. Perry supported a semi-pro team, the Perry Merchants, for many summers in the 1930s and 1940s, and Jess was one of the numerous unpaid volunteers who put in hours of service to get things done.

He was secretary of the local baseball association, and that meant he was responsible for handling a lot of details. For one thing he was the official scorekeeper. He decided when a player was charged with an error, an important issue sometimes because it might take away a hit from a batter and thereby make his statistics less impressive. It wasn't the big leagues but the players were very concerned about such things. Jess was meticulous at the job. The semi-pro Perry Merchants, some of them muscular young men imported from the college ranks, didn't win any arguments with the diminutive barber.

Jess faithfully delivered box scores to *the Perry Daily Journal* each morning after a game, and patiently explained the mysterious symbols and highlights to a less-knowledgeable cub sports reporter.

Next door to Jess Lee's shop was the Production Credit Association, operated by I.L. (Ace) Levy, who later became clerk of the Noble County Selective Service board when the U.S. was forced to draft men for military duty in World War II. Ace also operated a pawn shop before receiving the government post.

Anchoring the north side of the square at the east end was one of the town's landmarks—Bush & Joe's Smoke House. It was on the corner in a red brick, two-story building, with the Bowman Hotel and sleeping rooms upstairs.

Bush & Joe's Smoke House was a favorite haven for the men of this community for something like fifty years. Many who remember the place still can't believe it's gone. It appeared to be just like many other pool halls or beer palaces of the day, with a row of four or five domino tables along the east wall and five pool tables in a row down the middle of the building. The town had several others like it, but the Smoke House was the choice location for a majority of those who enjoyed that kind of recreation.

Such places were called billiard parlors, but in most of them pool was the main game, using tables with pockets. The domino tables also served for pitch games. Card players grew very serious when a five-point game was underway.

The customers were mostly adult men, but many pubescent teen-age males regarded a trip to Bush & Joe's as a rite of passage. Legally they had no right to be there because 3.2 percent beer, which was forbidden to them by state law, was sold on the premises, but if no one was looking they could slip in for a game of pool and then disappear. "Pool hall" had a certain implication of disrepute at the time and that made the place more tempting to those not supposed to be there.

At the front of the building was a bar of dark stained wood, like mahogany, with a brass foot rail. The counter man dispensed foamy draught beer from kegs at the bar, or bottled beer could be obtained. Toward the front was a curving glass case displaying cigars, cigarets, cans of snuff and a selection of plug tobacco, alongside chewing gum, packets of Sen-Sen breath freshener and a few candy bars.

Incandescent fixtures hanging high above from the embossed tin ceiling eventually gave way to fluorescent lights, but it was never the most brilliantly illuminated business establishment in town. The large plate glass window at the front, facing Delaware Street, was liberally plastered with posters announcing farm sales and advertising matter for El Verso and Roi-Tan cigars, Chesterfield cigarets, Beech Nut chewing tobacco, Old King, Falstaff, Budweiser and Pabst beer, and an assortment of other products.

It was almost impossible for those strolling by to see the interior through the maze of signs. Faint shadows or silhouettes could be made out, moving or sitting in the smoky haze, but little more. The east wall was virtually windowless, except for some at ceiling level. Ceiling fans with wooden blades kept the air moving. An exhaust fan mounted above the back door also helped.

It was a totally male environment, and the ladies let them have it that way, even years later when women's rights were being aggressively asserted elsewhere. Rowdyism was not tolerated.

Pitch players and others who engaged in various games applied themselves with intensity and they would have quickly quelled any noisy disturbances, even if Bush Bowman's and Joe Appleman's house rules were ignored.

Harry Mossman was one of those who worked there for years, alongside the owners, Bush and Joe. Despite a crippled leg, Harry could rack the balls on a pool table with great dispatch, rarely showing any emotion.

Pat Townsend, an Indian who had pitched for the Boston Red Sox (some say he also was once with the old Baltimore Orioles), tended bar at various pool halls around the square, but he preferred hanging out at the Smoke House. He could spin fascinating baseball tales, some of them true. In the twilight of his career, he played for the semi-pro Perry Merchants until his arm gave out. For a time he operated a taxi stand out of Bush & Joe's after retiring from bartending and throwing baseballs.

The Smoke House originally was located on the south side of the square, next door west of the Famous Department Store. Bowman and Appleman built the corner building on the north side of the square in 1909.

When the Smoke House finally closed in the 1950s, marking the end of an era, the location was converted into a fabric shop, which was indeed a turnaround. The walls were painted bright colors, a new floor was installed and the light system was completely redone.

It had a decidedly feminine decor, but they say the smell of tobacco and beer kegs lasted through at least two more tenants. The present occupant is the Roy Morris accounting firm, and the fragrances of the past seem to have finally faded away.

The Perry square and its environs in 1940 were bustling. Business was good and shoppers were attracted here from neighboring communities. Stores provided the kind of merchandise and services customers sought, and they were staffed with friendly, interesting people. Virtually no vacancies could be found at street level or in the second floor office locations.

The north side of the square is remembered fondly. It was only a portion of the business district, but it had a personality and character all its own. This was true even in the years shortly after the run. Judge E.W. Jones, describing the downtown area as it appeared shortly after the turn of the century, wrote this in 1931:

"The north side (of the square) seemed to be more 'gentlemanly' and refined than other districts of the new city. There were few disturbances and few lot contests, and when 'Shorty' (not otherwise identified) moved on there was no saloon on this side for three or four years."

The east, west and south sides of the square had their own appeal and loyal cadre of shoppers. Interesting people operated businesses there, and numerous anecdotes about them could be related. This has been merely an effort to describe some of the people and the places that gave the north side a distinctive character all its own.

# 40

# *T*HE CHEROKEE STRIP MUSEUM

Perry has an excellent museum, one that would be a credit to a town of any size. It is owned and operated by the Oklahoma Historical Society, but all the initiative for creating it was purely local. Like most worthwhile things, it didn't just happen and almost nothing about it was easy.

For years odds and ends of local historic memorabilia found their way into small display cabinets at Perry Carnegie Library. Thankfully, there was always someone who had the vision of a real museum here one day. Contributions were encouraged even if there was no adequate place to display them. Mrs. Henry S. Johnston, among others, preached the importance of collecting artifacts and significant clues to this area's heritage before they disappeared, along with the pioneers.

Eventually one room in the basement of the library was designated a "museum," and it quickly filled up. It could not be attended by the already overburdened library staff and was only open on special occasions, when volunteers could be on hand. The room grew so crowded with exhibits, visitors had a difficult time moving about.

The need for more space and for cataloging the growing quantity of material was obvious. No single organization existed to handle the problem, although many individuals were involved and concerned about it.

One of those most dedicated to the cause of preserving the area's history was Dr. Robert S. Taylor, the son of Guthrie area pioneers. He came to Perry as a chiropractor before World War II. After military service, he returned in 1946 and soon was elected to the Oklahoma Legislature as a member of the House of Representatives from Noble County. At that time, each county had at least one seat in the house.

Through Dr. Taylor's perseverance, a joint House-Senate resolution was authorized to create the "Cherokee Strip Historical Society." The measure was signed by Gov. Johnston Murray on May 12, 1953. It was the result of a suggestion made by Dr. Taylor in *the Perry Daily Journal* before the legislative session began in January.

That was the official founding of the local historical society, which in turn provided the impetus that resulted in construction of the Cherokee Strip Museum in Perry fifteen years later.

First state funding for the museum was made in July 1965 when the Legislature appropriated $30,000 for construction of a "Noble County Cherokee Strip Museum and Henry S. Johnston Memorial." The fund was part of $5.7 million appropriated to the new Oklahoma Industrial Development and Park Commission, the chairman of which was Ed Malzahn of Perry. Henry Bellmon of Billings was serving his first term as the state's first Republican governor.

State Sen. Boyd Cowden of Chandler and State Rep. Ruth Patterson of Guthrie were instrumental in getting the museum portion included. Dr. Taylor was then president of the Noble County chapter of the Cherokee Strip Historical Society. The board had been organized only seven months.

Although greatly appreciated, the $30,000 appropriaton by itself was obviously insufficient to build the type of museum envisioned here. Local leaders considered requesting a county mill allocation on the assumption that a building could be built downtown, possibly on property owned by the city or the county. However, in December 1965 the state attorney general ruled it would be illegal to vote millage for that purpose, so the purchase of an existing building in downtown Perry or elsewhere was proposed.

Among the locations considered were the Springfield corner at the southwest corner of Fifteenth Street and Fir Avenue; school land at the northwest (John Lau) corner of the same intersection; city property east of State Highway Department buildings at the south edge of Perry; Treadway property on the south side of west Fir Avenue; Henry S. Johnston Memorial Road between I-35 and Perry; the courthouse park and the county fairgrounds. Also regarded as a possibility was a five-acre tract owned by Bob Donahue on Fir between I-35 and the Ditch Witch (Charles Machine Works, Inc.) plant.

In an informal poll conducted through *the Perry Daily Journal,* Perry citizens picked the Donahue property as the most appropriate site, and that is where it was built, thanks to a gift from the Donahue family.

The local historical society's executive committee, with Mrs. Charles Malzahn as chairman, kept the project moving. In mid-October 1965, the group saw preliminary drawings presented by Frank Davies, an Enid architect, showing a two-story building with 1,650 square feet on the ground floor and a seven-hundred square foot loft. On the committee with Mrs. Malzahn were Mayor Bill Elliott, Ed Malzahn, Milo Watson and Glenn Yahn of Perry, Mr. and Mrs. Arthur Kerr of Morrison and Gordon Hayton of Billings.

Some two weeks later, on November 3, the Noble County Industrial Foundation was asked by the society's executive committee to turn over the balance of its funds—$9,200—to assist with the museum project. Shortly thereafter stockholders of the foundation voted to transfer $7,766.72 from its treasury for use in construction of the museum. The balance, $1,498.74, was used to liquidate a two-year-old debt to Donaldson-Yahn Lumber Co. for renovation of the Perry armory.

The museum money was designated for access roads, driveways within the park area, parking space, fence, signs, displays and fixtures in the building, fees for architect and engineer, and other details. The transfer depleted the foundation's treasury and effectively marked its demise.

More than a year later, contractors' bids on the museum were opened by the State Board of Affairs and the society's hopes for early construction suffered a blow. The apparent low bidder's base bid came to $54,250. With alternates included, it was $61,530—more than double the $30,000 state appropriation. The local group seemed to have two choices: Find more money or drastically scale down the building plans.

Both strategies were needed. The architect reduced the size to approximately 1,800 square feet, all on one level, with a cost he estimated at $36,000. Rep. Patterson reported that a $15,000 supplemental appropriation was in the mill, and an additional $6,970 was being provided by the state to pay for services of a curator, equipment, maintenance, utilities and supplies.

Mrs. Malzahn, then president of the Noble County chapter of the historical society, said the community already had an investment of $24,366 in the museum as proof to the Legislature that citizens here were serious about the project. The site donated by the Donahues was valued at $10,000. In addition, the building site had been fenced, a sign erected, entrance culvert installed, utilities arranged and grading done for the building and parking lot. All this had been provided locally.

The county historical society already was discussing means of paying for moving the old Rose Hill school, once located northeast of Perry, to the museum grounds. The building, a fine example of the one-room frame schools which once dotted the county, had been stored temporarily on the Perry airport property north of town, awaiting funds for moving it to the museum site and repairs for permanent installation.

A groundbreaking ceremony for the museum was held on March 5, 1967, a cold, windy day. Governor Bellmon, a son of pioneers, used an historic sod plow pulled by a team of mules for the symbolic start of construction. About one-hundred seventy-five people braved temperatures in the mid-30s to witness the event. In addition to Mrs. Malzahn as president of the county chapter, Byard Anderson was chairman of the board of directors. Lawrence Seeliger of Perry was designated building superintendent.

The historic old Perry Land Office building, or at least half of it, was identified about this time as part of a dwelling at 826 Grove Street. The property was owned by John L. Ward, 1018 Cedar Street. For months after the 1893 run, the two-room Land Office building was the hub of activity in this area. It stood on the west side of the square, south of the Post Office, and those who staked their claims in the run went there to register their land or to resolve disputes.

Years later, after it was no longer needed as a Land Office, the building was divided into two equal sections. One half went to Payne County, but the remainder stayed here and eventually was discovered at the Grove Street home. Asbestos shingles covered the original pine board construction. Mrs. Malzahn said the late Mr. and Mrs. John Mount had purchased the building from the government in 1918 and they owned it for several years. After Mrs. Mount's death in 1958, the dwelling was sold.

The historical society completed purchase of the old Land Office building in November 1967 when Dr. Taylor, treasurer, presented a check for $225 to Mr. Ward, the owner. The society previously had paid him $25 in "earnest money." In December the building was placed on jacks, and soon it was moved to a temporary location on the north end of the parking lot at the museum. While construction work on the main building was in progress, the old Land Office was largely ignored. Plans were drawn in July 1968 for moving it to a permanent display site on the grounds and restoration to the original appearance.

Unfortunately, the old building did not withstand the move, and it collapsed. The historical society discussed salvaging usable material for rebuilding, but other priorities prevented that from being undertaken.

Although the ground breaking ceremony was in March 1967, construction of the museum didn't get underway until June. Dedication was set for September 14, 1968, to coincide with the diamond jubilee 75th anniversary Cherokee Strip celebration.

Applications for the position of curator were being received at mid-year in 1967. The pay was to be $210 per month, with a forty-hour work week expected. In July the following year, Mrs. Alice Mae Svelan was hired for the job by the state Industrial Development and Parks Commission.

Mrs. Svelan was a member of a pioneer family and she had been a teacher at St. Joseph Catholic School until it was closed at the end of the 1967-68 term. Her parents operated the Perry Steam Laundry here for many years.

The museum had a contemporary design but the shape was reminiscent of the 1893 prairie schooners, giving it a blend of old and new. The stone exterior was capped by a gently pitched cedar shingle roof, and a small deck on the south end overlooked a wooded area. The building was designed for the addition of a second story loft if that option ever became desirable or practical.

A stream meandered through the property. By selective thinning of trees, a wilderness ambience was maintained. Native grasses carpeted the gently rolling property. Mother Nature had provided a most attractive, undefiled site.

By early December, most exterior work was completed, ahead of the worst winter weather. Detail work on the interior required many months to complete, but finally the building was ready to accept the transfer of all those artifacts from the library basement.

Governor Bellmon gave the dedicatory address on September 14, 1968. He was very close to the project from the beginning. He was one of the original directors of the county historical society and was still a board member at the time of the dedication. Today, a room at the museum houses some of the mementoes from his days as a U.S. senator and governor of Oklahoma. He served two terms in both offices, and thus created some of the history that this museum preserves.

The years of hoping, planning and overcoming obstacles had ended. Perry's Cherokee Strip Museum was a bright, beautiful reality. Civic leaders and the many others dedicated to preserving the area's heritage rejoiced.

In February 1970, priceless antiques were stolen from the museum, and they have never been recovered. Included were some of the items from the room housing material donated by former Governor Henry S. Johnston. As a result of that unhappy episode, the museum began looking at burglar alarms and other warning devices to guard against a recurrence.

Although the old Land Office building disintegrated before it could be restored and made ready for permanent display, no such trouble befell the Rose Hill school. In March 1970 historical society directors made arrangements to move it from the airport property north of Perry to the museum grounds. The building finally was moved—successfully—on July 27 that year.

The school was completely furnished just as it was when the last classes were held there twenty-six years earlier. Student desks and the teacher's desk were in place. A roll-down curtain hung over a platform at the front of the classroom and advertisements for several pioneer local firms were painted on the curtain. A wood and coal stove and an upright piano were in working condition.

Classes were first taught in the Rose Hill school, northeast of Perry, on March 6, 1896, and the final term was held there in 1943-44, when the district consolidated with Perry. The building then became the property of the Perry school district.

Now firmly anchored to a new foundation on the museum grounds, the school still resounds to childhood scuffles, chalk slates and recitations for the teacher. For nine months during the school year, the State Historical Society offers Rose Hill as a learning experience for youngsters throughout the state. A "teacher" dressed in garb of the 1890s is on hand when busloads of children come here from miles away to spend an entire day sampling a typical school day of that period. The boys and girls bring sack lunches and are encouraged to wear clothing appropriate for the period.

The school normally is booked solid for each day of the term. It is a tremendously popular attraction. Teachers find their students have a new appreciation for Oklahoma's pre-statehood history by vicariously experiencing some of it themselves.

Another unique item was lost on the museum grounds in May 1977 when a two-seat surrey, which had been destined to become an exhibit, was wrecked as a horse pulling it bolted, dashed the buggy into a tree and reduced it to a pile of splinters. The surrey was far beyond repair. It had been used by Mr. and Mrs. George Hall several times as an entry in the Cherokee Strip celebration parade, and they were donating it to the museum.

In July 1975, control of the museum was switched to the Oklahoma Historical Society. This was a logical move. The society was the channel for state funds provided for operation of the museum. The society had twenty-eight museums and sites in Oklahoma at that time.

It soon became apparent that the original Perry museum was too small. Virtually no storage space was provided for articles not on display, and the limited exhibit space meant that every piece was stacked close to another. Shades of the old library museum! Relief was granted in July 1977. The just-adjourned legislature had appropriated $25,000 to go with $10,000 from other funds to help finance a major expansion of the museum.

The state funds were to be added to $10,000 left from the previous year and a $20,000 gift from a local anonymous benefactor, making a grand total of $65,000. After receiving the green light from the Oklahoma Historical Society, expansion plans were started.

On May 30, 1978, in a pouring rain, a number of people attended ground breaking ceremonies for a 3,276-square foot addition to the museum. Mr. Bellmon, by then a United States senator, was assisted in the ritual by Mrs. Irene Treeman, also a pioneer, who had taken part in the original museum ground breaking. The addition was to have 1,860 square feet of display space and 1,416 square feet of storage.

Bids on the construction were opened by the State Board of Affairs in September that year, and again there was a serious gap between the amount of money available—$93,839 by then—and the low bid, $189,000. Not until June 1979 did more state funds turn up. The Legislature appropriated $45,000 for the project. A total of $85,000 had been raised locally. On July 6, 1979, *the Perry Daily Journal* reported that $178,365.46 was available to make the expansion possible.

A contract was awarded in November, crews arrived in December, and construction was underway. Early in January 1980, local historical society directors approved a change order to permit completion. Harvey Yost, president of the board at that time, said the contract then totaled $203,000 but sufficient funds were available. Numerous delays plagued the project, but on September 13, 1982, ceremonies were held to mark the grand opening of the new exhibit areas. It was the Diamond Jubilee year of Oklahoma's statehood.

Visitors from throughout the world have signed the guest register at Perry's museum. Since the additional space was created, storage makes it possible to rotate exhibits and to give feature display space to new articles. All this adds a "freshness" to the collection. Repeat visitors find they are constantly seeing objects they missed earlier.

The museum preserves the history and flavor, as well as the pathos, of Oklahoma's biggest land run. An implement building houses tools used by the Strip's early sodbusters, and a deer pen houses two whitetail deer, named Deer Delbert and Deborah Doe by local school children. The animals symbolize the abundant wildlife once found in this area. Picnic facilities are nestled along the small stream on the grounds.

Displays include a general store, the office of Henry S. Johnston, Oklahoma's seventh governor, the Bellmon collection, an early doctor's office, a pioneer dentist's office, and beautiful examples of Otoe-Missouria beadwork to emphasize the Strip's Indian heritage.

Kaye Bond is now the museum curator. She is the daughter of Mr. and Mrs. George Kemnitz and the descendant of early-day area residents.

# 41

# *W*ISTFUL LOCAL LEGENDS

Stillwater, twenty-four miles southeast of Perry, is the home of Oklahoma State University. Ponca City, barely forty miles northeast of here, has the Conoco Oil Co. refinery. Enid, just forty-one miles west of Perry, is the home of Phillips University, Vance Air Force base and one of the world's largest grain storage facilities. Guthrie, thirty-two miles south, once had the state capitol.

Does all this give Perry an inferiority complex? No, at least not a terminal case. Perry is smaller than those nearby neighbors, but we have learned how to hold our own against them in important ways, as in football, wrestling and baseball.

Besides, Perry COULD have been the home of both OSU and Conoco, plus assorted other major industries and institutions, if one is to believe local lore. Sadly, the basis for much of that is not very solid, to say the least.

But it's fun to think about what might have been if all the promises, predictions and dreams for Perry's future had come true through the years.

For one thing, Perry would be the home of the Oklahoma State Prison, which somehow wound up at McAlester instead. We also would be the location of OSU, arguably the state's biggest and best, but neighboring Stillwater won that plum. The Marland Oil Co. refinery, which became Conoco, was another major prize that appeared headed for Perry but wound up in Ponca City. Those jewels all slipped through our grasp—or so legend has it—back in the early days after the run or around statehood in 1907.

With reference to OSU, the story has been told here for ages that Perry was expecting to be the home of that school, but lost out because of a requirement by an early-day city administration that the university pay for electricity, or some such thing. In truth, the school was up and running in Stillwater even before Perry was born.

In Irvin Hurst's book, "The 46th Star," the author states that Stillwater was promised the Agricultural and Mechanical College (which became OSU) in 1890, three years before the Cherokee Strip run. Indeed, the school observed its Centennial year in 1990.

Hurst says that George W. Gardenhire of Stillwater, the lone Populist member of the State Council (or State Senate), was elected council president. As part of the political maneuvering leading up to that, Gardenhire was promised—and got—the Agricultural and Mechanical College for Stillwater. Edmond was promised a normal school—now Central State University—and Norman received Oklahoma University. Thus, the location of OSU, or A.&M., was settled three years before Perry exploded on the scene.

Nevertheless, the story has been repeated here for generations that Perry "almost" became the location of OSU. It is a myth that refuses to die.

Apparently E.W. Marland, founder of Marland Oil Co., which became Continental Oil Co.—Conoco—did select Perry as the location for one of the company's major refineries. In the early days of Oklahoma oil and gas exploration, Noble County showed great promise. Mr. Marland came to Perry because it had two railroads, was at a crossroads of major highways and appeared to be well located in the growing production area.

Perry citizens surprised the oilman by rejecting his offer of a refinery. The basis of their decision is not altogether clear now, because the oil business meant prosperity. Refinery sites created jobs for employees drawing high wages. Oil strikes were multiplying the population of small towns wherever they occurred. Refineries also added smog and pollution, but this was before the era of acute environmental awareness.

Perhaps the early-day Perry leaders were concerned about those problems and chose not to turn this community into a "boom town" of sorts. Whatever their reasons, Perry has grown even without the refinery, and without the industrial waste and pollution associated with such installations.

Attempts have been made to place government institutions in specific cities for political gain since time immemorial, of course, and Perry has fought for its share. The city always has been grateful for the division headquarters of the Oklahoma Department of Transportation, which has been here well over fifty years.

As recently as the 1990 session of the Oklahoma Legislature, politicians were stirring the pot and communities were fighting to get something. Tulsa, the state's second city in terms of population, almost won the state Department of Commerce office away from Oklahoma City. The Legislature had that move under consideration in a proposed switch that was seen by many as punishment for Oklahoma City's powerful morning newspaper, *the Daily Oklahoman*, which has been harshly critical of state lawmakers. Tulsa did manage to secure a branch office of the Oklahoma Corporation Commission.

A story appearing in the March 18, 1990, edition of *the Oklahoman* noted that the war had been going on for a hundred years.

"The first territorial Legislature," said the *Oklahoman*, "convened in 1890, spent one hundred days on the matter of what city would be the capital. Legislators spent ten days on the rest of the public's business. All told, this battle spanned ten years—even before the courts got involved.

"A backroom deal involving territorial capital site selection resulted in the choice of Norman for the University of Oklahoma, Stillwater for what is now Oklahoma State University, and Edmond for what is now Central State University. The deal to award Oklahoma City the capital was vetoed, but Norman, Stillwater and Edmond kept their spoils."

More evidence that Perry never had a shot at becoming the home of OSU, despite local lore.

*The Oklahoman* article continued:

"Married in 1907 to the equally populous Oklahoma Territory, the Indian Territory—having lost its chance at the two major universities—demanded a major share of the new state's payroll. Among the prizes: a penitentiary in McAlester."

That brings up another tale that has been told locally, though it is not as well known as the OSU and Conoco disappointments. It seems Perry once was a sure thing to become the home of the state penitentiary. At least, that was the view of *the Perry Democrat-Patriot,* a local newspaper edited by J. Roy Williams. On February 17, 1897, the paper reported this while the Legislature was in session in Guthrie, the state capitol:

"Perry wants the penitentiary and can offer better inducements in the way of natural advantages than any city in the Territory. If our people go after that Institution right they will get it. There is nothing like living in a town that gets what it goes after."

From an adjacent column, same edition, these headlines:

IS COMING OUR WAY

That's How the Penitentiary
Matter Looks Now

Doyle's Bill to Establish A
Penitentiary at Perry Was
Favorably Reported by A
Majority of the Standing
Committee

Here's a headline from page one of the March 11, 1897, edition of the same paper:

PENITENTIARY BILLS DIE

House Independently Postpones
Legislation of That Nature

Perry Had the Best of It,
But Not Enough to Win

McAlester was awarded the state penitentiary. Who's to say we're not better off without it?

#### 🙠

In later years Perry was wooed by some industries, such as "cut and sew" garment factories, but eventually city leaders became disenchanted when it appeared the prospects had concessions in mind that exceeded any reasonable expectation of profitable return to this community.

Perry civic boosters have danced with several industry prospects, and, in some cases, were willing to pay the piper for the privilege of doing so.

In January 1941, the Chamber of Commerce Industrial Committee recommended to the city council that one year's free rent be given to a McAlester group which proposed to establish a cotton garment factory in Perry. Harry Donaldson was the committee chairman. Other members were Paul Cress, O.R. Hall, King Montgomery, Walt Bittman, Morris Gottlieb, E.E. Nelson, H.C. Galaway, R.T. Scott and W.K. Leatherock. These men represented an impressive and powerful segment of the business community, but the factory never materialized. Fortunately, no local money was lost.

In 1942 Perry was awarded an Army Air Corps landing field, located north of town. The city, lying only a short distance from the giant Tinker Field in Midwest City and Vance Field in Enid, was lucky to get the project.

The Perry field was used by student pilots from Vance for practice "touchdowns." After World War II, the military declared the asphalt landing strips surplus and turned the entire field over to the city of Perry. It serves now as a fine municipal airport. The city even sells hay-cutting rights on parts of the field where incoming or outgoing planes do not pose a hazard. The airport is used daily by private pilots, and the city does a good job of maintenance. A $724,300 federal grant was under Congressional consideration in 1990 for renovation of the main runway. It is probably a much better field than Perry could have afforded on its own.

Approximately twenty-five years ago, a large Air Force bomber (unarmed) made an emergency landing at the city field, skidding off into a wheat field but avoiding major damage. No one was injured, but some thought the pilot looked a bit sheepish about the incident. After repairs were made a few weeks later, the plane was successfully flown out although the airstrip was not designed to handle planes that large.

The Stackhouse Co. was an "outside" industry that did swing into production here in the 1950s, manufacturing a line of athletic equipment—track hurdles and the like. The trade name was Track and Field, Inc. It showed great potential, but the company left here not long after a steel building was constructed on Memorial Drive, or Grace Hill Cemetery Road. Stackhouse also had a plant in Slippery Rock, Pennsylvania, which always sounded interesting.

C.R. Stackhouse, a big, friendly man, was the owner. He and his wife spent a great deal of time in Perry as the operation began, first in a building on the south side of the square where the old Ringler Leather Goods store had been located. The move to Memorial Drive came a year or so later. The Stackhouses designed the new building, and incorporated a residence area for themselves into it.

In November 1959, *the Perry Journal* reported that Stackhouse had just mailed 25,600 copies of a catalog listing products of Track and Field. The mailing, made at the Perry Post Office, went to schools, athletic directors and dealers in North and South America and the Caribbean region.

Tamac Pottery began shortly after World War II in a two-car garage at the Henry Tate home on Cedar Street. Two young veterans—Leonard Tate, who grew up in Perry, and Alan MacAulay, a native New Yorker—invested their creative talents, energy and business skills into a free-form line of dinnerware that quickly caught on. The name "Tamac" was a contraction of the two men's last names. MacAulay left Perry for other interests not long after the business began, and Leonard, son of Henry and Alma Tate, then took over the creative, sales and administrative affairs of the company.

Tate and MacAulay correctly guessed that Americans would be doing more casual backyard dining in the post-war era, and their pottery was designed with that in mind. Flat, tray-like plates came with coffee mugs that replaced the usual handles with tunnel-like appendages into which several fingers could be inserted. The most popular colors were dark green and chocolate brown, both including frosted treatments that suggested a summer-time picnic or barbecue.

Pictures of Tamac pottery appeared in *Life, Good Housekeeping* and other national magazines of the day. The pieces were described as post-war innovative trendsetters.

In time, Tate left Perry and the business was sold to Earl Bechtold, a local businessman. Bechtold had twelve full-time employees, and the retail pottery store at the plant operated seven days a week. The Tamac line was popular with tourists and pottery lovers generally. The kilns and manufacturing facilities were in production five days a week. Bechtold had distribution in forty-eight states.

Mrs. Bob Moore of Mount Hope, Kansas, was the company's owner of record in 1970 and her mother, Mrs. Mary Hladik, was local manager of the plant. The company was filling orders from many parts of the U.S. and even abroad, but finally discontinued operations in the early 1970s. Some of the unique pieces produced by the company are still seen in homes around the country today. Style and quality were never the company's weak points. A lack of outlets probably made the demise inevitable.

乄

Perry's growth expectations were enormous after the run of 1893. Those dreams were not realistic, but the community does have a stable population base and has remained almost constant in size for fifty-some years. Thanks for this is due largely to the Charles Machine Works, Inc., which has its world headquarters here. Indeed, Perry is envied by many towns which used to be this size but have experienced devastating losses as industry migrated to urban centers.

Perry's diverse interests—and no town has more per capita —include a modern YMCA, churches of most major denominations, a first-class hospital, Carnegie Library, solid school system, community theatre, a marvelous museum, and cultural and civic organizations. All of them worry about survival and still struggle daily for financing. And we have a daily newspaper—something rarely seen in a town this size—plus both an AM and FM radio station. Don't forget the two rock-solid banks, another rarity in an era of frequent bank failures.

So, the answer to that earlier question is "no." Perry has no reason to have an inferiority complex, thank you very much.

# 42

# *P*ERRY AT FIFTY YEARS

September 16, 1943, the golden anniversary of the Cherokee Strip land run, found the Perry community earnestly doing its part to support the nation's mighty war effort. The United States was locked in mortal combat with powerful enemies in Europe and the Pacific Ocean. The situation hardly seemed appropriate for a major celebration.

The U.S. became a party to World War II on Sunday, December 7, 1941, when Japanese planes staged a surprise devastating attack on Pearl Harbor. Our losses in terms of human life and equipment were enormous. *The Perry Daily Journal* issued an "extra" that afternoon and it contained names of several area men stationed in Hawaii.

Things were never quite the same after that. Profound changes were underway at home and abroad.

Car dealers and service station owners were among the first to feel the impact of war. New cars were not being manufactured and gasoline was rationed. A forty mile per hour speed limit was authorized to save both fuel and tires, not to mention lives. Consumers and merchants soon became aware of war-imposed shortages in other areas; sugar, meat and shoes were rationed.

At the start of the decade, however, all seemed to be normal. On January 31, 1940, Newt Roads of Morrison retired after thirty-five years of rural mail service in Noble County. During that time, he had worn out twelve head of horses, one motorcycle and seventeen Ford automobiles. In March that year, Kraemer's Shoe Store became the first in Perry to display the newly developed nylon hose for women. Made from coal, air and water, they were to take the place of silk hosiery.

Bartering was not yet outdated. *The Journal* offered a one-year subscription in exchange for twelve and a half dozen eggs, or six months for six and a half dozen. Many farmers paid for their paper that way. Stanislav Grocery & Market, on the east side of the square, advertised a gallon of apricots, peaches or prunes for ninety-nine cents each.

For a benefit dance at the Lakeside Pavilion on Lake Laird, Ellen Butler's orchestra was scheduled to play on a July weekend in 1940, sponsored by Ellis-Jirous American Legion Post. Ellen, daughter of Mr. and Mrs. George Butler, was a talented trumpeter. She performed a fine version of Clyde McCoy's "Sugar Blues," getting the "doo-wahs" and muted notes in all the right places, just like Clyde's popular recording. She had graduated only that spring from Perry High School. The orchestra was made up of nineteen local musicians and four vocalists—Margaret Plumer, Lila Lee Davis, Betty Lee Moore and Lanette Webber.

A federally commissioned modern art mural was installed in the lobby of the Perry Post Office in August 1941. The work, which is now an exhibit at the town's Cherokee Strip Museum, was an oil entitled "Range Branding Down By the Big Tank." The artist, Thomas M. Stell Jr. of Cuero, Texas, came here to direct placing of the linen canvas on the Post Office wall. Mr. Stell also had painted murals for a library in Corsicana, Texas, a Dallas high school, and the Post Office in Teague, Texas. The Perry mural was commissioned as the result of a nation-wide contest sponsored by the government.

A somber and ominous note was sounded on the Cherokee Strip run anniversary date in September 1940. The 45th Division, Oklahoma's National Guard unit, was mobilized for active duty although the U.S. was not yet at war. Perry was the home of Battery C, 58th Field Artillery, a component of the 45th, and many local young men left here that month to begin what was expected to be just one year of training at Fort Sill. Instead, the Thunderbirds remained in federal service until after the end of World War II in 1945.

The 45th Division became one of America's most distinguished and most decorated combat units in Sicily and North Africa during the war.

The road running south from the C Street bridge in Perry past the CCC Park and on to State Highway 51 was officially designated State Highway 86 in March 1941. At that time it was a narrow and dusty country road with washboard surface and jarring potholes.

It was a favorite of young people on date nights and was considered a kind of "back door" route to Stillwater. Although work was delayed by the war effort, the state highway designation enabled a hard surface to be laid down, and it is now a heavily traveled thoroughfare.

After Congress formally declared war on the Japanese, Germany and Italy, mobilization began on the home front. Air raid wardens, like Harold Chace of Morrison, were being appointed in every community early in 1942.

The Noble County Tire Rationing Board was organized on January 4, 1942, with V.K. DeBord as chairman. The county's quota for that month was twenty-one tires and eighteen tubes for passenger cars and motorcycles, and forty-nine tires and forty-one tubes for light trucks and buses. As the war went on, this board also became responsible for administering the rationing of butter, sugar and other goods. In early 1943, loin and round steak were selling for thirty-six cents a pound at the M&W Food Store in Perry.

Lt. Albert J. Mickish, described by *the Perry Daily Journal* as Noble County's greatest war hero, quietly slipped in and out of the county during a week in the fall of 1943 while on leave from the Army Air Force. He wore the Distinguished Flying Cross and the Air Medal with Oak Leaf cluster and was a veteran of twenty-seven operational flights over enemy territory in Europe. He was the son of Mr. and Mrs. Frank Mickish of Route Four, Perry.

Another young Noble Countyan, Lt. Henry Bellmon of Billings, won the Silver Star for gallantry in combat while serving with the Marine Corps in the Pacific. He came home after the war and won election to the House of Representatives in the State Legislature. About the same time he married his hometown sweetheart, Shirley Osborn. He became Oklahoma's first Republican governor in 1962, served two six-year terms in the U.S. Senate, and then was again elected governor. His second term in that office ended in January 1991, after which the Bellmons returned to their farm home at Billings.

Women as well as men were among the hundreds from Noble County in the armed forces at home and abroad. Army Nurse Lt. Mary Frances Render of Perry was based in England for a time and was among those invited to attend an afternoon party with the King and Queen of England at Buckingham Palace. Lt. Render later was to become nursing superintendent at Perry Memorial Hospital in the post-war era.

Although no public announcement could be made, Charlie's Machine Shop in Perry began receiving contracts for the manufacture of war-related items. Charlie Malzahn and his son, Edwin, geared up for the job at their recently built plant on Birch Street, just two blocks off the south side of the square.

Perry experienced a case of the right hand not knowing what the left hand was doing in 1943. Or perhaps it was an illustration of how the failure to communicate can be a problem even in a small town where everyone supposedly knows everyone else's business.

The point of contention was the proposed Perry Airport, which had been started but never completed. A story in *the Perry Daily Journal* on August 31, 1943, reported that the mysterious delay was caused by a City Council resolution passed six months earlier regarding deeds and abstracts. *The Journal* said Army Engineers and the Civil Aeronautics Authority interpreted the resolution to be an indication that city officials desired no further work on the landing field.

Three runways had been completed at the field and it was being used occasionally by Army planes for emergency practice landings. The newspaper estimated $250,000 would be required to complete the job, which had been a top priority of the Chamber of Commerce War Projects Committee.

The committee was unaware that city officials had made an agreement with Army Engineers which did not call for completion of the airport as provided in the original pact. That agreement provided that the city would purchase the land and the Army Engineers would build a modern airport with hard-surfaced runways, administration building, field lighting, control tower, maintenance shops and complete utilities.

All that was to be done with CAA funds and the airport was to be leased by the city to the CAA. The matter was eventually resolved to the satisfaction of the Chamber of Commerce, the City Council, the CAA and Army Engineers, and the project was completed as originally conceived.

Perry wound up owning the airport after the war, and it is now a well-maintained and fairly busy field. It even has been used as an emergency landing field for a disabled Air Force bomber, although the runways are not regulation length for a plane that large.

Polio was ravaging young bodies in the early 1940s, and several Perry families knew the affliction. Iron lungs were frequently used as a life support system, but the cause of the crippling disease had not yet been identified. It was a time of terror throughout the U.S. for parents of young children, who were the most frequent victims.

The war preempted other news on the nation's front pages most of the first half of the decade, but a Perry dateline appeared in many newspapers around the country in September 1944. A 1,900-pound shorthorn bull owned by Harry Gengler, just east of town, climbed to the top of a barn, sat there in contemplation for a few moments, then stood up and slid 16 feet to the ground amidst a flurry of cedar shingles. The unfortunate beast had to be destroyed, but its feat was enough of an oddity that United Press put it on the national wire and editors everywhere provided space for the story. How did the bull get onto the roof? The barn was built into an embankment, on top of which sat a bull pen. The bull broke through a wooden fence and stepped directly onto the crest of the roof. Harry Gengler's son, Bill, then a ten-year-old, was the first to spot the strange sight and still remembers it well.

The community was divided on the issue of student dances being held on school property in the fall of 1943. A poll on the subject conducted by *the Journal* gave these results: 276 in favor of using school facilities for organization dances "and other recreational purposes;" twenty-one opposed to using school facilities for dances. The controversy was ended when the Rotary Club sponsored a Teen Town organization for students in a downtown building.

These were some of the matters occupying the attention of Perry area residents as the fiftieth anniversary of the Cherokee Strip land rush arrived.

The war effort dominated everything, and in 1943 there was no assurance that the Allies were going to crush the Axis. The time called for dedication on the part of men and women wearing military uniforms, and no less by those on the home front. Every age, every social order, every race was affected and deeply involved. It was stressful and tiring, but somehow Americans seemed to know that their cause would prevail in the end. Not in 1943, but at some point they would triumph over the enemy.

Perry had grown up in the half-century since the great Cherokee Strip land rush. The original pioneers were reaching a reflective age and their offspring were now plowing the farms, running the businesses, developing this area into a richer, more exciting place than anyone had thought it could be.

The hardships of the early days, the Great Depression and two World Wars, all these combined could not crush the spirit and determination of those who came to this area during the first fifty years. They met the needs of their times, and Perry survived because of their self-will.

Every decade in Perry since the 1893 land run has been more exciting than the one before. The story did not end in 1943. Nearly another half-century has come and gone since then, and the final chapter of this community is not yet ready to be written.

Given the character of those sturdy early settlers and those who came after them as a base to build on, it is clear that this small prairie city is still learning how to grow. Surely the best is yet to come. What a prospect to stimulate the imagination as we turn from a review of the past to face the challenge of the future.

This aerial view of Perry, made about 1940, looks northeast across the courthouse park. Cars filled most parking spaces around the square on this day.

Street repair job was underway on October 3, 1940, when this photo was made. Most buildings in the background have since been razed. At extreme right was the R.T. Scott Chevrolet dealership; next is the Auto Eat Cafe operated by Harold and Stella Roads; next is the C.T. Talliaferro Grocery; then George Sheets' Perry Plumbing Co.; then came a vacant lot, next door to the Houston & Elliott building, which later housed Charlie's Machine Works and finally the Perry Theater. Awning in left foreground was at Bush & Joe's Smoke House.

First production model of a Ditch Witch trencher is shown being operated by
its inventor, Ed Malzahn, in 1949.

This one-inch advertisement in *Popular Mechanics* helped spread the news
about Ditch Witch in the early days.

First full-time Ditch Witch dealership was Sooner Equipment Co. of Oklahoma City, operated by Russ and Dorotha Sadler. They hauled the trenchers in a pickup truck and on an attached trailer to jobsite demonstrations all over the state.

Two models of Ditch Witch trenchers are shown in this photo from the 1950s at the downtown CMW plant, alongside a newly acquired piece of equipment for the manufacturing process. Ed Malzahn, in work clothes, looks on with a representative of the firm that installed the new equipment.

A new plant and office building became necessary for the Charles Machine
Works, Inc. as the company's line of Ditch Witch trenchers found an
ever-expanding market. This photo was made during construction of the new
facility in May 1959. CMW moved to the location in July that year.

Members of the Malzahn family made an informal inspection tour of the new
Charles Machine Works, Inc. plant and office building on a Sunday afternoon
during early stages of construction. Ed and Mary Malzahn's children are in front,
from left: Pamela, Don and Leasa. Behind them are Mary, Bertha and Charlie
Malzahn. Ed was behind the camera.

Ribbon cutting ceremony on July 6, 1959, formally opening the new Charles Machine Works plant on Fir Avenue, was attended by Perry townsfolk who shared the company's excitement and pride at this significant milestone. Officiating, left to right, were Ed Malzahn; Max Genet, state Department of Commerce and Industry director; Mayor Harold Scovill and Charlie Malzahn.

Broad expanse of open land surrounded the new location of the Ditch Witch factory in 1959. Northwest Perry residences are in background.

Liquid cools metal being turned on lathe in a manufacturing process at the Charles Machine Works, Inc., while operator observes.

Women assembly workers are integral part of labor force in the Charles Machine Works, Inc. plant.

Space age technology is evident throughout the Charles Machine Works, Inc. plant, as this coordinate measuring machine demonstrates. It checks accuracy of parts manufactured by CMW to within 0.0005 of an inch.

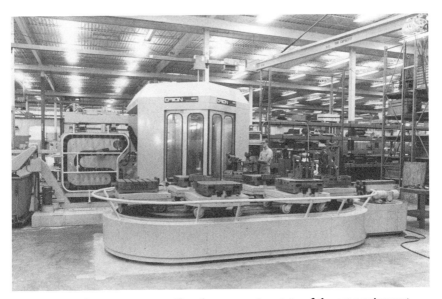

An Orion machining center typifies the progessive state of the art equipment constantly being added to the Charles Machine Works, Inc. manufacturing plant. This sophisticated, automated center is used primarily to produce gear boxes.

A Presidential "E" Award from the U.S. Department of Commerce was
presented to the Charles Machine Works, Inc. in 1971, recognizing sales of
products made in this country to foreign markets. Several dignitaries came for
the occasion. From left: Sen. Carl Curtis, Nebraska; Ed Malzahn; Sen. Hubert
Humphrey, Minnesota; Rep. Happy Camp, Oklahoma; and Sen. Henry Bellmon,
Oklahoma.

Powerful, compact Model 5020 Ditch Witch trencher is typical of products
manufactured today at the Charles Machine Works, Inc. Fortune Magazine
proclaimed the Perry-made equipment among the 100 things the U.S. makes
best.

An Engineering Center with its own research and development facility was added to the CMW complex in 1979. Attractive setting is just a short distance from the main office and manufacturing plant.

Spacious, well-lighted CMW Engineering Center office has two floor levels and is filled with computer-assisted design equipment for the ongoing process of improving the company's product.

Ed Malzahn in a typically casual pose, with one of today's versions of the Ditch Witch trencher he invented in the 1940s.

Mary Malzahn grew up on a farm and fills much of her time today working with Charolais cattle on the M&M Ranch.

Mr. and Mrs. Charlie Malzahn sat for this portrait shortly before the Charles Machine Works, Inc. moved from its downtown location to West Fir Avenue in July 1959. Charlie died later that year, and Mrs. Malzahn died in 1980.

# $\mathcal{A}$PPENDIX[1]

### Directory of First City Officials

| | |
|---|---|
| John M. Brogan | Mayor |
| Alonzo Wharton | City Clerk |
| A. Jacobs | Police Judge |
| A. Duff Tillery | City Attorney |
| George Farrar | City Treasurer |
| George S. Livingston | City Assessor |
| R.R. Talley | School Sup't. |

### Councilmen

| | |
|---|---|
| Lawrence Drake | President |
| J.P. McKinnis | Secretary |

J.C. Dulaney, Howard Friend, C.A. Weideman, W.T. Cutler, J.T. Hill and Henry Flock.

### Police Officials

| | |
|---|---|
| William Tilghman | Chief |
| Heck Thomas | Assistant |

Policemen: J.B. Davis, J.A. Anderson, George Mouser, A.Y. Hopkins, George Stormer, H.S. Miller and W.P. Larabee

### Post Office Staff

| | |
|---|---|
| Charles P. Drace | Postmaster |
| James G. Hillhouse | Assistant |
| Polo Ground | Mailing Clerk |
| C.W. Beaty | Delivery Clerk |
| Frank Thacker | Distributing Clerk |
| Lee Wilson | Delivery Clerk |

### Land Office Staff

| | |
|---|---|
| James E. Malone | Register |
| Joseph H. King | Receiver |
| Thomas W. Steele | Journal Clerk |
| Louis Davis | Chief Clerk |
| Miss Lillie Hickle | Chief Clerk |

Clerks: William H. McCoy, Walter R. Leath, James A. Donagan, Frank Raymond and Frank Keorful.

### Trustees

| | |
|---|---|
| Amos B. Fitts | Secretary & Special Disbursing Agent |
| Timothy McGrath | Chairman |
| DeLong Rice | Chief Clerk |
| Fred L. Bailey | Trustee |

### Perry Business Directory

**Abstract Offices:** Glenn & Koogle, Perry Abstract Co.

**Architects:** Gordon & Raymond, Martin and Nevins.

**Attorneys at Law:** Allen, Roberts & Osborn; Barnes and Cook; Walker Bascom, Boles; Holland and Boles; Brown and White; Brown, Boyd and Milton; Calvert, J.L.; Campbell, Smith and Bonder, Helden; Carr, H.M.; Carter, W.A.; Cheney, O.A.; Clark, Kelly and Travis; Clark and McKnight; Crosby, G.W.; Cone, W.D.; Corrigan and Mahoney; Couch & Webster; Couch, John H.; Cuppage and Sumner; Dodge and McCollum; Drake, Frank; Dulaney, C.J.; Earl, W.E.; Edwards, Price; Friend, H.; Fuller, I.R.; Grant, Bowden; Hanley, Harry; Harland, Barlow and Horn; Herod, Widmer and Bowles; Hodgson and Hodgson; Holt, M.J.; Hofius, Stewart and Sevie; Howie and McMeacham; Hudson, Harris and St.John; Houston, Lanter and Co.; Howard and Howard; Hughbanks and Dean; Howell, D.F.; Hula and Wells; Jarvis and Stukey; Jarvis, M.F.; Jessup, O.G.; Johnson, W.E.; Johnson, Mary; Lyons, James A.; Matt, Edward; Parks, Mrs. Dan; Reighley, J.Q.; Reub Bros.; Sawyers, W.M.; Sherwin, W.B.; Spark and Tauylor, Ward and Rockwood; Wedder, Henrietta; Wells, Mrs. M.L.; Woods, S.; Wolfe, H.; Wisby, Lee; Winn, C.H.

**Auctioneers:** Knox, B., Olson and Markham, Miller and Hirshfield.

**Bakers:** O'Flaherty and Neff; Mullins and Hugo; Reub Bros.; Taylor, Walter; Wagner, Fred; Wilson, Fred.

**Banks:** Bank of Perry, Farmers and Merchants Bank, Richardson and Sons.

**Barbers:** Bond, George F.; Dennis, C.E.; Gulledge and Riley; Kelley, F.M.; Stegall Bros.; Story, Marshall.

**Blacksmiths:** Billingsley, George; Burke, J.Y.; Couch, J.B.; Moyer, Ed F.; Tuller, Bert; Beahoeff, Ira.

**Boots and Shoes:** Globe Shoe Co.

**Carpenters and Builders:** Allison, J.L.; Douglas, W.W.; Gordon and Van Horn; Harwood and Disch; Houghton, R.R.; Lynn and McCune; Johnson, Walker and Stanley; Morris and Johnson; Jones, Southorn and Joes; Kenton, Turner and Baldwin; Kelly and Travis; Kirk and Gilbert; Lafferty, J.T.; Little, A.J.; Lowry, R.A.; Miller & Miller; Miller & Stear; Mier, W.L.; Morgan, Dick T.; Morris, W.S.; Mosley, M.A.; Museller, A. R.; McGinnis, B.J.; Overstreet & Wallace; Palmer and Son; Parish and Mentz; Platt, H.A.; Pursell, George W.; Ransom & Bailey; Rucker, Henry D.; Sapp, Sidney; Sharp, N.E.; Smith, H.A.; Soward & Markland; Stephenson & Bruch; Stone & Doyle; Thomas & Sturdevant; Thompson, C.C.; Tillery & Martin; Turner, R.S.; Tuttle & Gallagher; Van Buskirk & Specher; Walker Bascom; Watkins & Cheney; Whitsett, George P.; Willis & Wells.

**Engineers & Surveyors:** Deloss, R.; Matthews, Richard; Schoel, H.; Jacobs and Lindsay.

**Feed:** Chubb, A.J.; Cotton, D.R.; Darland, F.C.; Deming, R.R.; Drake & Jewell; Fitzgerald, W.W.; Gregorie & Wellingford; Hamill, D.; Jamison and Graham; Joy and Tuttle; Kansas Grain Co.; Larsh, S.P.; Marsley, D.J.; McMichael & Co.; Perry, E.H.; Snow, John C.; Still, L.W.; Walker, S.O.

**Fruit:** Crowles, R.L.; Fitzgerald, W.W.; McDonough, C.F.

**Furnishings:** Cades, A.S.; Denny, E.C.; Lobsitz & McCredie.

**Groceries:** Alcorn, S.T.; Brogan & Jackson; Bowden Groc.; Vadyot, R.J.; Cobb Bros.; Mollett & Lunsford; Martindale Bros.; Neighbors, J.; Ramsey, A.E.; Reddick Bros.; Smith, Edwin; Snider, C.H.; Steele & Matthews.

**Cigar Mfgrs.:** Leininger, C.W.

**Coal:** Bryant & Ely; Caliness, F.M.; Gregg-Henrichs.

**Clothing:** Cole, A.; Vollmer, W.A.

**Confectionery:** Hunt, E.; Kandy Kitchen Bakery; Kretsch, Fred.

**Contractors:** McCracken, W.S.; Mollett & Lunsford; Johnson Perry.

**Crockery:** Chew, & A.H. Co.

**Dentists:** Bagby, A.H.; Purse, W.D.

**Druggists:** Bagby, R.E. & Co.; English, A.H.; Garnett, L.E.; Handley, H.W.; Ingram, C.C.; McNulty, Ed; Perry Drug Co.; Pioneer Drug Co.; Boller, F.A.; Seaton, A.

**Dry Goods:** Boston Store; Spears, T.L.; Smith & Heron; Smith Bros.; VanArsdall, T.J. & Co.; Swain, A.L.; Wells, J.O.; Welch & Faulds; Whitney, G.M.; Woodward & Foster; Wyatt Bros.; Young, J.O.; S.W. & Co.; Zerbe, Frank.

**Furniture:** Bottenfield, J.L.; Ealke Bros.; Dwyer, W.H.; Johnston, J.W.

**Hardware:** Brown, H.; Cogdell & Horner; Collar, J.F.; Davenport Hardware; Farquaherson & Morris; Fleming & Mockley; Hinde, A.C.; Hollingsworth, D.H.; Pattison, W.W.; Perry Hardware & Implement Co.; Parke & Klein; Smyser & McCormick; Welch & Faulds; Wallerstedt, H.C.

**Harness:** Harbaugh, J. Lowe; Klein, Wm.

**Hotel:** Agricola; City Hotel; Evans, Mrs. R.A.; Guthrie & Son; Harris & Clark; Linvolle, Littel, Mrs. N.E.; OK Hotel; Rosenstein, Joseph; Smith, D.A.; Tibbets, Mrs. May; Williams, M.T.

**Insurance:** Allen, W.H.; Bascom, W.; Watkins, J.R.; Smith and Davis.

**Jewelers:** Davis, George; Patterson, E.E.; Russel, Frank; Stansel, P.J.; Thurman, C.F.

**Justices of the Peace:** Clayton, George E.; Holt, O.S.; Brown, A.W.

**Laundries:** City Laundry; Lee, Yee; Lung, Ge; Posey, F.H.

**Liquor, Wholesale:** Cheadle, N.F.; Fellner, Sam; Hill Bros.; Jones, C.R.

**Livery:** Bass, Wm. G.; Bates & Case; Bullock, Ed; Crook, T.H.; Coyle, J.E. & Son; Crum, G.L.; Ellis, B.F.; Fairchild & Jenkins; Gray, F.W.; Hadley & Cox; Henry, L.B.; Hunt, B.F.; Lee, E.A.; Leonard Bros.; Limbocker, C.I.; Lindeman, C.J.; Maine, N.A.; Mitchell, A.; McCubbins, Z.H.; Nelson, A.J.; Norcom, H.S.; Petite, A.D.; Selden, J.W.; Griswold, Robb & Co.; Harmon & Greeley; Primrose & Sons; Red, J.D.; White Star Livery.

**Lodgings:** Lewis, James H.; Strickland, Mrs. M.L.

**Lumber:** Arkansas Lumber Co.; Bullen, H.B.; Chicago Lumber Co., J.F. Elbe, Mgr.; Darlington Lumber Co., Charles L. Wenner, Mgr.; Foster Lumber Co.; McCune, W.C.; Henson & Nims; Long Bell Lumber Co.; Jones, M.T.; McClung, W.E.; Newton Lumber Co., P.C. Palmer, Mgr.; Perry Lumber Co.; Pentecost, F.E.; Primrose & Sons; Richardson, T.M.; Stanley & Frazier; Wentworth, C.D.

**Meat Market:** Abernathy & Olsen; Acers & Co.; Bonewell & Cutting; Bottoms, C.F.; Deal & Mayers; Faust, S.; Hinkle, A.M.; Krater, J.R.; Russell, A. & Co.

**Merchandise, General:** Blythe, J.H.; Cummings, J.J.; Ellis, B.F.; Frace & Lawson; Gerkey & Battenfield; Gray, F.W.; McKinnis, J.P.; Richardson Dry Goods Co.

**Newspapers:** Evening Democrat; Herald Pub. Co.; Morning Sentinel; Perry Evening Times.

**Nursery Stock:** Garnett & VanBuskirk.

**Painters:** Eggleston Sign Works; Hollister, Al; Keas & Parmlee; Oden and Oden; Walker & Beetham.

**Paper Hangers:** Moran, Wm.; Walker & Beetham.

**Police Court:** Jacobs, Alonzo; Jacobs, J.R.

**Physicians:** Baudry, G.; Clanahan, W.M.; Cullimore, J.C.; Dillard, J.W.; Hirsh & Edwards; Hooe, J.C.; Hood, C.O.; Hopkins, W.S.; Jones, Fred F.; Liggett, J.E.; Long & Payne; Nichols, T.D.; Nolder, W.C.; Palmer, J.B.; Patchin, A.W.; Southard, R.W.; Zahn, M.S.; Town & Hitch; Walker, J.D.; Williams, J.R.

**Real Estate:** Beatty, D.R.; Bruce & McClain; Cobb, Wm. M.; Dougherty, E.H.; Fay & Hulin; Flood & Co.; Lanier, W.D.; Hendricks, A.D.; McComb, Wm.; Guthrey & Guthrey; Miller, Russell & Hart; Parker, W.A.; Samuel & Hazel; Shapland, W.G. & Co.; Smith & Jenks; Sumner, Estes & Co.; Walker & Moses; Watkins, H.R.; Wagner & Smith; Williams, C.N.

**Chattel Loans:** Cruikshank, J.A.

**Restaurants:** Alexander Lunch Counter; Blue Star; Bruce and Ireland; Cook, L.R.; Creamery; Crawford & Irwin; Douglas, N.M.; Elite; Emorey, F.; Good Luck; Harvey House; Hardin, Walter J.

**Saloons:** Barash, M.; Big John; Blue Belle; The Cabinet; Buck Horn; Cox; Rowell; Crook, T.H.; Rutler, F.M.; Heath & Hiller; Heim, Ferd Brewing Co.; Hill Bros.; Howe, H.C.; Levy & Co.; Midland; Haley, Ed; Mitchell, R.; Murray & Monroe; The Orient; Rogers, G.W.; Singleton, Mrs. Ella; Sharp & Gates; Shortman & Tise; Stapleton & Co.; Tearney, J.J.; Yates & Roberts.

**Schools:** McCormick, L.L.; Hudley, Miss; McKinney, Mrs.

**Shoes and Hats:** Amos, P.R. & Co.

**Second Hand Stores:** Dulaney, W.M.; Dwyer, W.H.

**Shoe Makers:** Gilbert, A.W.; Kraemer, A.; Zahl, Charles.

**Stenography:** Chapman, Mrs. M.A.; Fairchild, John; Reade, Miss Lena.

**Tinware:** Brion & Beck; Hine, O.O.

**Wagon Makers:** Button, John B.; Tuller, Bert.

**Miscellaneous:** Allen, Blacksmith; Culbertson, J.M.; Martin, J.B.; Ramsey, A.E.; Harwood & Dusch; Shanfelt, J.E., Wells Fargo Agent.

---

1. From notes originally supplied by Edith Taylor for "Perry, Pride of the Prairie," by Robert Cunningham.

# *I*NDEX

## —A—

A.C. Lamb Jewelry, 300, 308.
Acheson, Pearlie Mae, 196, 200.
Ackerman, Ernest, 271.
Acres Building, 103.
Adams, Jack, 255.
African Methodist Episcopal Church, 40.
Alamo, 22.
Albertson, Phil, 273.
Albright Title & Trust, 300.
Alexander, Ashley, 251.
Alva, Okla., 14, 229, 243, 256.
Amateur Athletic Union, 179.
Amend, Edward J., 85.
American Legion, 133, 171.
American Legion Auxiliary, 134.
American Legion Home, 208.
Anderson, Byard, 178, 317.
Anderson, Ocie, 178.
Anderson, Olive, 196.
Annex Theater, 70, 71, 261, 296.
Antrim, Okla., 31.
Appleman, Joe, 312.
Arkansas City, Kan., 9, 12, 14, 15, 17, 18.
Arkansas Valley Railroad, 43.
Army Air Corps Base, 326.
Arnett, Okla., 27.
Arnold, Okla. 31.
Arrow Hotel, 308, 309.
Art Cleaners, 306, 308.
Austin, Eva Blanche, 172.
Auto Eat Cafe, 307, 335.
Autrey, Okla., 31.
Avard, Okla., 31.

## —B—

Babcock Cafe, 307.
Bachman, Abe, 195.
Bagby, R.E., 46.
Bailey, Bill, 195.
Bailey, John R., 89.
Bailey, Minnie Keith, 98.
Baker, Judy, 248.
Baker, Marianne, 171.
Baker, William J., 248.
Bank of Commerce, 89, 245, 300.
Bank of Perry, 58.
Banks & Wade Furniture Store, 82.
Barge Grocery & Market, 302, 304.
Barge, J.L., 302.
Barker, Ray, 233-240.
Barnes, Len, 101.
Barnes, Sam, 211.
Barton's Book Store, 113.
Bartow, Byron, 211.
Bates, Mrs. J.M., 103.
Baughman, Ray, 172.
Baxter, Jim, 221, 223.
Bay, Dollie Dufek, 310.
Beard, Henry, 48.
Beasley, Herman, 211.
Beatty, Emmett, 49.
Bechtold, Earl R., 327.
Beck, Percy, 224.
Beers, Fred G., 73, 304.
Beers, Fred W., (nephew), 96, 195, 304.
Beers, Fred W., (uncle), 92, 93, 95, 96, 112, 220, 226, 252, 302,303, 304.
Beers, Gloria, 304.
Beers, Ivy, 304.
Beers, Jeanice, 304.
Beers, Mrs. Fred G., 110.

Bellmon, Henry L., 185, 246, 247, 288, 315, 317, 318, 320, 321,331, 342.
Bellmon, Shirley Osborn, 331.
Benedict, Omar K., 146.
Bennett, Myrtle, 257.
Berry, Rev. J.M., 82.
Bettye Anne Bakery, 165.
Bieberdorf, Robert, 100.
Bieberdorf, Susan, 88.
Billings, Okla., 30, 31, 37, 79, 81, 94, 315, 316, 331.
Bittman's taxi stand, 310.
Bittman, H.R., 310.
Bittman, Walter A., 173, 306, 308, 326.
Bjorn, Mrs. Tony, 271.
Bjorn, Tony, 271.
Black Bear, Okla., 31.
Black Bear Angus Ranch, 291.
Blackburn, Joe, 49.
Blackwell, Okla., 30, 177, 178, 205.
Blackwell Rotary Club, 174.
Blaine School, 46, 47, 80, 102, 104.
Blake, Aldrich, 147.
Blatt, Rabbi, 43.
Bliss, Okla., 31.
Blue Bell Saloon, 25.
Blyth, Ann, 72.
Boggess, E.F., 82.
Bohemian Hall, 101, 262.
Bolay, Bert, 127.
*Body Builder Magazine*, 179.
Boles, Judge A.H., 169.
Bon-Ton Bakery, 302.
Bond, Kaye, 321.
Bonney's, 100.
Booher, Marie, 299.
Boomers, 9, 31.
Boone, Capt. Nathan, 8.
Boone, Daniel, 8.
Boone, Frank, 164.
Boone, W.F., 173.
Boright, Police Chief, 92.
Borremans, Rev. A., 85.
Bowdenton, Okla., 31.
Bowie, Henry, 22.
Bowles, Ed, 220, 222, 236, 252.
Bowles, Judge W.M., 46, 90, 307.
Bowman Bush, 308, 312.
Bowman, Hotel, 308, 310.
Boy Scouts of America, 99, 140, 190.
Boyer, Dr. O.W., 173.
Boyes, H.L., 18.

Boyes, Mrs. H.L., 75, 76.
Bozeman, Rev. T.R., 82.
Brandenburg, Lewis, 276-277.
Brandon, Fire Chief, 104.
Brengle Jr., Quine, 231.
Brengle, Dr. D.D., 51.
Brengle, Dr. W.D., 95.
Brengle, Dr. William B., 51.
Breshears, Gene, 96.
Bressie, Okla., 31.
Bressie Flats, Okla., 8.
Briggs, Gary, 101.
Briscoe, Frank, 179, 181-182.
Briscoe, Jack, 181.
Briscoe, Lola, 75.
Brogan, Mayor John N., 29, 45, 46, 48.
Brown Jr., A.C., 232.
Brown, Gilmor, 69.
Brown, Len, 101.
Brown, Lloyd, 298.
Brown Jr., Mrs. A.C., 232.
Brown, Ronald, 232.
Brownie Drug, 303.
Brown's Funeral Home, 298.
Bryan, William Jennings, 69.
Buck Horn Saloon, 25, 46.
Bucklin's Chili Parlor and Notions, 113, 308.
Bucklin, Alfred, 96, 113, 308.
Bucklin, Essie, 96.
Bucklin, Margaret, 96, 308.
Bullen Lumber Yard, 102.
Bullen, Mrs. J.H., 76, 87.
Bunch, Clarence, 211.
Burton, Okla., 31.
Bush & Joe's Smokehouse,308, 310-312, 335.
Butcher, Professor, 47.
Butler, Ellen, 330.
Butler, George, 330.
Butler, Mrs. George, 330.
Buzzard, Brother, 83.
Byerley, Bert W. 174, 195.
Byerley, Bob, 251.
Byers, George, 88.

## —C—

C&S Tire & Supply, 308.
Cain Hotel, 307, 309.
Cain, Daisy, 307, 309.
Cain, Jimmy "Sugar," 297.
Caldwell, Conrad, 180.

Caldwell, Kan., 14, 28.
Cameron, Kan., 14.
Camp Fire Girls, 145.
Camp, John N. "Happy," 288, 342.
Campbell, Mary Lee Wollard, 219.
Campbell, O.B., 172, 219, 220, 225.
Carmichael, Carl, 172.
Carnegie Library, 19, 66, 75, 77, 87, 173, 174, 175, 219, 221,328.
Carnegie, Andrew, 75-78.
Carr, Miss, 79.
Case, J.I., 273.
Casey, James W., 169-170.
Caterpillar, 278.
Cates, Bill, 48.
CCC Park, 5, 330.
Central High School, 80, 111.
Central Park, 20.
Central State University, 64, 323, 324.
Chace, Harold, 331.
Chaffin, Everett, 90.
Chaffin, Mrs. Everett, 90.
Chamber of Commerce, 35, 40, 43, 73, 99, 100, 113, 156, 186-187,240, 270, 271, 289, 325, 332.
Chambers, W. Max, 174, 195, 196.
Chaplin, Charlie, 72.
Charles Machine Works, Inc., 4, 6, 61, 122, 131, 247, 268, 270,274, 276, 277, 280, 283-294, 315, 328, 337-343, 346.
Charlie's Machine Shop, 70, 127, 205, 206, 207, 250, 265, 268,269, 279, 332, 335.
Cheney, Dick, 172.
Cherokee Indians, 8, 9, 10, 11, 27.
Cherokee Outlet, 7, 8, 10, 11, 14, 15, 18.
Cherokee Strip celebration, 318, 320.
Cherokee Strip Historical Society, 315.
Cherokee Strip Land, 3, 8, 13, 15, 16, 18, 19, 20, 28, 31, 32,34, 38, 40, 53, 62, 66, 72, 81, 84, 89, 151, 200.
Cherokee Strip Land Run, 11, 12, 35, 39, 41, 61, 153, 169, 202,300, 323, 329, 333.
Cherokee Strip Live Stock Association, 9.
Cherokee Strip Museum, 74, 220, 314-321, 330.
Cherokee Strip parade, 35, 92, 100, 114, 175, 195.

Cherokee Strip Restaurant, 175.
Cheyenne-Araphaho Land Run, 11.
Chic Shoppe, 305.
Chief Drive-In, 71, 73.
Chiquita, Okla., 31.
Chisholm Trail, 8.
Chrane, Ethelyn, 157-158.
Christ Lutheran Church, 84.
Christensen Feed Yard & Junk Lot, 103.
Christian Science Church, 84.
Christiansen, A.W., 305.
Christoph & Newton, 83, 257, 298.
Christoph, Charles, 76.
Chronister, Ina, 196.
Church of the Nazarene, 83, 121.
City Barber Shop, 310.
City Drug Store, 96, 235, 301, 302, 304, 307.
City Hall, 96.
City Shoe Shop, 305.
Civil Aeronautics Authority, 332.
Civil War, 8.
Civilian Conservation Corps, 5, 233.
Civitan Club, 173-174, 195.
Clark, George W., 173.
Clark, Gordon, 300.
Clark, Henry, 251.
Clark, Mrs. Gordon, 300.
Clark, Mrs. Wilson, 300.
Clark, Oleta Zep, 257.
Clark, Wilson, 300.
Clarke, Helen, 10.
Cleeton, H.A., 99.
Clement, Mabel, 196.
Cleveland, Ohio, 62.
Cleveland, Pres. Grover, 10.
*Clinton Daily News*, 170.
Cockrum's Pharmacy, 96.
Cockrum, Chris, 96.
Cody, Homer, 195.
Coin Variety Store, 70.
Coldiron, Dr. D.F., 136, 174.
Coldiron, Kenneth, 182, 211, 242.
Collins, Charles, 94, 173.
Colly and Olds, 170.
Combs, Jack, 23.
Compton, Okla., 31.
Congregational Church, 84.
Conoco Oil Co., 90, 257, 322, 323.
Cook Coal Yard, 102.
Cook, Loy E., 196.
Cooke, Dr. C.H., 94.

Cooper Motor Co., 73.
Cooper Oldsmobile Agency, 203.
Cooper, Ernie, 195.
Cooper, Ralph, 73.
Cordell, Col. John, 94.
Cornelius, Superintendent, 104.
Corner Lunch Cafe, 209, 307.
Corr, Bert, 185.
Corr, E.L. (Junior), 185.
Corr, Edwin G., 185.
Corr, Mrs. Bert, 185.
Coterie Club, 74.
Courthouse, 49, 97, 114, 118.
Cottonwood Club, 262.
Cowden, Boyd, 315.
Coyle, Bob, 220, 252.
Coyle, Ed J., 90, 173.
Coyle, John E., 85, 86.
Coyle, Mrs. Ed J., 90.
Cozy Rooms, 209.
Crane, Jack, 31.
Cress, Erle F., 156.
Cress, Howard R., 174, 195, 300.
Cress, Mrs. P.W., 156.
Cress, P.W., 156, 245.
Cress, Paul, 156, 220, 224-225, 252,
    326.
Croake, Dr. D.F., 300.
Cromwell, Okla., 46.
Crow, C.A., 49.
Crowder, Dr. A.M., 174, 195.
Crowder, Walter Martin, 251.
Cruikshank, J.A., 46.
Culbertson, Jim, 220, 223, 227, 252.
Cullimore, Dr., 51.
Cunningham, Sam, 31.
Curtis, Carl T., 288, 342.
Cutler Comedy Company, 67, 68, 71.
Cutler, Myra, 68.
Cutler, W.T., 45.
Cyclone, 101-105, 113.

—D—

Daily Oklahoman, 21, 27, 156, 243,
    324.
Daily Oklahoma State Capitol, 153.
Dalton Gang, 10, 16.
Daniels, Harold "Hump," 221, 263.
Davidson & Quinton, 101.
Davies, Frank, 316.
Davis & Son Furniture, 246, 298, 300,
    301.

Davis, Chuck, 273.
Davis, Elmer V., 304-305.
Davis, Ethel, 196.
Davis, Farris, 298.
Davis, Fred A., 298.
Davis, Lila Lee, 305, 330.
Davis, Minnie, 305.
Davis, Virginia, 298.
Day, Okla., 31.
Dean A. McGee Eye Foundation, 174.
Dean, Opal, 196.
Dearborn, Dick, 251.
DeBord, V.K., 331.
DeLashmutt, Harry A., 172, 220.
DeLashmutt Jr., Harry A., 251.
DeLashmutt, Mrs. H.A., 220.
Delbert, Deer, 321.
Delma Hotel, 37.
Denning, Carrie, 306.
Denton, Esther, 196.
Dillinger, John, 233.
Dillon, Marshal, 46.
Ditch Witch Day, 270.
Ditch Witch trencher, 207, 250, 264-
    278, 280, 285, 336, 337, 338,342,
    344.
Ditch Witch company, 6, 61, 264-275,
    284, 286, 287, 288, 315,337, 339.
Divine, Joe, 183.
Divine, John W., 35, 141-142, 177, 182-
    186, 196.
Divine, Myrtle, 186.
Dodge City, Kan., 46.
Doe, Deborah, 321.
Doggett, Anna, 308.
Doggett, Dr. E.E., 51, 101.
Dolezal, Henry, 306.
Dolezal, Irene, 172.
Donahoe Cotton Gin, 48.
Donahue & Mugler, 309.
Donahue, Bob, 271, 315-317.
Donahue, H.C., 73, 174, 195, 309.
Donahue, Mrs. H.C., 73.
Donaldson building, 302.
Donaldson, Harry, 174, 245, 247, 248,
    302, 325.
Donaldson, Robert, 251, 302.
Donaldson-Yahn Lumber Co., 316.
Donley, H.G., 174.
Doolin, Bill, 36, 153.
Dorl's Barber Shop, 307.
Dorl, Jack, 307.

Dotts Hardware, 227.
Dotts, Mrs. R.W., 227.
Dotts, R.C. "Bus," 227.
Dotts, R.W., 227.
Dougan, Dr., 51.
Douglas Aircraft Co., 205-206.
Douglas, Okla., 240.
Doyle Jr., George, 173.
Doyle, Leo, 211.
Doyle, Ruby, 99.
Drace, C.P., 47.
Drake, Lawrence, 45, 46.
Driver Dr. J.W., 306.
Driver, Dr. George, 300, 306.
Dulaney, John C., 45, 67, 68.
Dunbar School, 80.
Dunford, Dick, 73.
Dunham, Ethel, 299.
Dunn, Jesse, 230.
Dust Bowl, 5.
Duty, Ted, 211.
Duval, Judge Claude, 217.
Dvorak, Frank, 153.
Dwyre, W.H., 46.
Dykes, John, 251.

—E—

Early Day History of Perry, 23, 92, 170.
East Side Boot and Shoe Shop, 305.
Ebersole, Sam, 90.
Eby, Frank, 306.
Economy Cleaners, 306.
Edgar, Clarence, 227.
Edgar, Rex, 185-186.
Edgar, Tillie, 227.
Edmond, Okla., 12, 42, 43, 136, 206, 323, 324.
Edmondson, Edna, 99.
Edmondson, J. Howard, 270.
Edwards, Merl, 172.
Edwards, Miss, 196.
Edwards, R.J., 49.
Edwards, Ralph, 73.
Eisenhauer, Mrs. Herman, 90, 217.
Elite Barber Shop, 309.
Elite Hotel & Cafe, 307, 308, 309.
Elliott, Bill, 251, 316.
Elliott, Forrest, 251.
Elliott, R.N., 196.
Elliott, Robert, 251.
Ellis, George M., 244.

Ellis-Jirous American Legion Post, 330.
Elwell, Harry, 309.
Emancipation Day, 40.
Enid, Okla., 14, 27, 30, 155, 161, 176, 235, 263, 322, 326.
Enterprise-Times, 170.
Environmental Protection Agency, 278.
Evangelical Church, 64.
Evans, Bettye Yahn, 110.
Evans, Dr. A.M., 252.
Evening Democrat, 46.
Everybody's Store, 94, 301.
Exchange Bank, 40, 58, 88, 203, 233-242, 254, 255, 305.

—F—

4-H Club, 293.
Fair, Dr. Edwin, 89.
Fair, Mrs. Edwin, 89.
Famous Department Store, 33, 42, 43, 69, 97, 98, 99, 100, 113,115, 118, 144, 306, 312.
Farm and Industrial Equipment Institute, 289.
Farmers & Merchants Bank, 18, 126, 127.
Farmers' Warehouse, 102.
Farrar, George, 45.
Federal Bureau of Investigation, 138-139, 238, 239.
Federal Reserve Bank, 246.
Ferguson, Phil, 222.
First Baptist Church, 82, 174.
First Christian Church, 82, 150, 155.
First National Bank & Trust Co., 116, 170, 243-248, 256, 270,297, 298, 305.
First Presbyterian Church, 20, 43, 50, 70, 82, 103, 133, 134,171, 240, 271, 289, 290.
First Union Life Insurance Co., 247.
Fitzhugh, Olin, 251.
Fleming, Rhonda, 72.
Flock, Henry, 45.
Floyd, Miss, 196.
Floyd, Pretty Boy, 233.
Flynn, Dennis T., 10, 244, 245.
Folan's Lunch Room, 307.
Folan, Helen, 307, 308.
Forbes, A.A., 53.
Ford, M.C., 49.
Forney's Dairy Store, 296.

Forney, Charlie, 296.
Forney, Jennie, 296.
Fort Supply, 10.
45th Division National Guard, 5.
*Fortune*, 285.
Foster, Bob, 252, 258.
Foster, Dick, 163-164, 227.
Foster, G.A., 245.
Foster, Lucille Edgar, 163, 227, 253, 299.
Foster, Ned, 252.
Foster, Penny, 163-164.
Foster, Ralph E., 173.
Foster Sr., Ralph, 96.
Foster's Corner Drug, 96.
Foucart, Joseph, 243-244, 246, 256.
Francis, Dr. J.W., 301-302.
Francis, Mildred, 301.
Francis, Rachel, 302.
Free Homes bill, 10, 244.
Free Methodist Church, 84.
Friend, Howard, 45.
Frisco Railroad, 43, 102, 104, 249.
Fry Jr., Bill, 173, 195.
Future Farmers of America, 293.

**—G—**

Gable, Clark, 231.
Galaway, H.C., 326.
Galbreath, Bob, 170.
Gallagher, Edward C., 179, 181, 182, 186.
Gang, Fred, 101.
Garber, M.C., 157.
Gardenhire, George W., 323.
Garfield County, 11, 163.
Garnet and English Drug, 95.
Gaskill, Jay, 221, 252.
Gaskill, Peary, 172.
Gavin, A.J., 46.
Gem Cafe, 307.
General Mills Co., 203.
Genet Jr., Max, 270, 339.
Gengler, Bill, 333.
Gengler, Harry, 333.
Gentry, J.M., 237.
George, Euline, 196.
Gerdis, John, 102.
Gerdis, Marguerite, 102.
Gerdis, Mrs. Will, 102.
Gerdis, Will, 102.

Geronimo safety slide, 265, 267, 273, 276, 277, 278, 279-280.
Gershon, Ethel Maurice, 100.
Gieschen, Rev. David, 85.
Gillette, Dr., 51.
Gillette, W.J., 46.
Glazier, Al, 7, 152.
Goldsberry, Dwaine, 272.
Goltry, Okla., 240, 242.
Goodnight, George, 195.
Goodwin, Okla., 14.
Goolsby, "Ace," 227.
Goolsby, Bonnie Dotts, 227, 253.
Goright, John, 101.
Gottlieb's Vogue, 100.
Gottlieb, Ann, 100.
Gottlieb, Elsie, 100.
Gottlieb, George, 97, 100.
Gottlieb, Madge McCredie, 99, 100.
Gottlieb, Morris, 97-100, 175, 326.
Gottlieb, Rudolph, 97, 98, 100, 173.
Gottlieb, Sam, 97, 98.
Gottschall, Wendell, 172.
Government Acre, 19, 25, 26, 39, 42, 47, 49, 56, 97.
Gowty, Thelma, 299.
Grace Hill Cemetery, 47, 64, 130, 150, 217.
Grand Opera House, 66, 68-72, 103, 108, 109, 116, 144.
Grant County, 11.
Graystone, 136.
Great Western Trail, 8.
Green, Bert H., 169-170, 172.
Green, Sarah, 200.
Green Hill Baptist Church, 87.
Gregoire & Houston, 103.
Gregory, Ernest, 305.
Gregory, Regina, 251.
Gum, Lester, 94.
Guthrey, Bee, 170.
Guthrie, Okla., 16, 25, 28, 46, 51, 70, 145, 155, 169, 243, 256,314, 315, 322, 324.

**—H—**

Hainer, Judge B.L., 75.
Hainer, Mrs. B.L., 75.
Hall, George W., 242, 320.
Hall, Mrs. George, 320.
Hall, Larry, 273.
Hall, O.R., 235, 242, 255, 326.

Hamm, Carl B., 247-248.
Hamilton, Burton, 252.
Hammonds, Mayme, 147-148.
Hamous & Hopper Pharmacy, 303.
Hansen, John A., 49, 89.
Hantz, Leo, 221, 252.
Haraldson, J.L., 49.
Harbaugh, Beryl, 196.
Harding, Paul, 173.
Harding, Warren G., 155.
Harlow, Jean, 231.
Harms, Dale, 172.
Harperville, Okla., 31.
Harris, S.H., 49.
Harris, Zaccheus A., 155.
Harrison, Pres. Benjamin, 9, 10, 32.
Harrison, Pres. William H., 32.
Hart, H.A., 175.
Hartman, W.C., 89.
Hartung, Bessie, 163.
Hartung, Ed, 163.
Hayton, Gordon, 316.
Heaton, Ina, 196.
Hejtmanek, Frank, 101.
Hell's Half Acre, 19, 24, 25, 55, 56.
Helms Athletic Hall of Fame, 179.
Hennessey, Okla., 14, 17, 161.
Heppler, Bernard, 273.
Herrick, Balinda, 152-154.
Herrick, John, 152-154.
Herrick, Manuel, 7, 151-159, 193.
Hetherington, C.N., 31.
Highfill, Lowell, 290.
Hill, Homer, 251.
Hill, J.T., 25, 45, 46.
Hill, Ted, 25, 46.
Hinds, L.D., 195.
Hladik, Mary, 327.
Hodge, Bill, 90.
Hodge, Dan, 186.
Hodge, Mrs. Bill, 90.
Hoke, Dr., 51.
Holmes School, 46, 47, 80.
Honk a Tonk Saloon, 25.
Hood, Dr. C.O., 49, 51.
Hoot, Dr. Delmar C., 88.
Hoot, Mrs. Delmar C., 88.
Hoover, Harold, 211.
Hoover, Rex, 195.
Hopkins, "Fatty," 46.
Horn, Jennie, 299.
Hot Witch, 268, 281-282.

Hotel Doggett, 308.
Hotel Moran, 56.
Hotz, Grace La Bord, 307.
Hotz, John, 307.
Houston Lumber Yard, 102.
Houston-McCune Lumber Co., 127.
Hovey's Printing Office, 103.
Hovey, Charles, 92.
Hovey, Nellie M., 92.
Hovey, Oliver Henry, 91-94, 112.
Howard, Joe E., 173.
Howard, Maybelle, 196.
Howe Pump & Engine Co., 48.
Howendobler, E.E., 76, 95, 96.
Hubbard, Eugene, 196.
Huchthausen, Pastor Julius, 84.
Hudson, Mrs. L.A., 87.
Huffman, Charles, 175, 182, 195.
Hughes, Cornelia, 196.
Humphrey, Hubert, 288, 342.
Hunefelt, Fannie, 99.
Hunt, Arthur "Shorty," 239-240.
Hunt, E.V., 307.
Hunt, Lillian, 234-235,240.
Hurst, Irvin, 323.
Hurt, Berniece, 196.

**—I—**

Iba, Henry P., 186.
Indian Territory, 324.
IOA Boys Ranch, 174.
Iowa and Shawnee-Pottawatomi Land Run, 11.
Iowa Indians, 15, 81.
Isham, Henry, 323.

**—J—**

J.C. Penney Co., 231, 306, 308.
Jack's Auto Supply, 309.
Jackson, Harry C., 175.
Jacobs, A., 45.
Janeway, P.A., 244.
Jennes, Ray, 94.
Jensen, Chris D., 244, 245.
Jensen, Maj. John, 76.
Jewell, Rainmaker, 28.
Jim Thorpe Hall of Fame, 179.
Joe's Smoke House, 37.
John Deere collection, 203.
John Philip Sousa Band, 68, 69.
Johnson, Henry L., 173.

Johnson, Merle, 251.
Johnson, Mickey, 251.
Johnson, Ross, 173.
Johnston, Arthur, 175.
Johnston, Ethel L., 69, 145-146, 150, 191, 314.
Johnston, Gertrude, 150.
Johnston, Henry S., 27, 69, 80, 90, 98, 99, 118, 126, 143-150,155, 173, 191, 192, 319, 321.
Johnston, Matthew S., 144.
Johnston, Mrs. Matthew S., 144.
Johnston, Nell, 150.
Johnston, Reba, 150.
Johnston, Robin, 150.
Johnston, William, 144.
Jones, Chas. "Buffalo," 23.
Jones, Elsie, 297.
Jones, Frank, 297.
Jones, Harry, 172.
Jones, Helen, 121.
Jones, Jimmy, 121.
Jones, Judge E.W., 22, 23, 25, 45, 80, 92, 94, 95, 170, 195,312-323.
Jones, Monte, 96.
Jones, Mrs. L.F., 87.
Jones, Norman, 121, 122.
Jones, Paul, 121, 195.
Jones, Pauline, 121.
Jones, Virginia Dufek, 310.
Jones' Drug, 96.
Julian's Jewelry & Gifts, 308.
Julian, John, 308.

**—K—**

Kadlick, Clara, 272.
*Kansas City Times*, 28.
*Kansas Observer*, 29.
Karcher, Herb, 185.
Karcher, Mrs. R.E., 185.
Karcher, R.E., 185.
Kaw Indians, 8.
Kay County, 11.
Keas, W.W., 48.
Keaton, Bert, 72.
Keaton, Buster, 68, 71, 72, 73, 74, 110.
Keaton, Eleanor, 73.
Keaton, Herbert, 72.
Keaton, Joe, 67, 68, 71, 72.
Keaton, Joseph Z., 72.
Keaton, Myrna, 68, 71.
Keeler, Dr. Frank L., 94.

Keeler, J.F., 49.
Kehres, Bob, 251.
Kehres, Walt, 307, 308, 309.
Keller Co., 98.
Kelley, Olinda, 99.
Kemnitz, A.A., 85.
Kemnitz, George, 321.
Kemnitz, Mrs. A.A., 85.
Kemnitz, Mrs. George, 321.
Kennedy Roller Rink, 262.
Kennedy, Ivan L., 173.
Kennedy, Sara, 299.
Kentucky Liquor House, 241.
Kerr, Arthur, 316.
Kerr, Mrs. Arthur, 316.
Kerr, Robert S., 246.
Kickapoo Country Land Run, 11.
Kimble, Ted, 261.
Kiowa, Kan., 14.
Kiowa-Comanche-Apache Land Run, 11.
Kirchner, Don, 296.
Kirchner, Stella, 296.
Kiwanis Club, 175, 219.
KJFK-FM radio, 308.
Klostermyer, James, 83.
Knights of Pythias, 43, 145, 149, 152.
Knosp, Edythe, 196.
Knox & Eisenhauer Pool Room, 102.
Knox & Stout Clothing Co., 43, 98.
Knox, Allen, 98.
Knox, Bethuel, 98.
Knox, Charley, 98.
Knox, Ethel, 196.
Knox, John, 98.
Knox, Philip, 98.
Koch, Ethel, 257.
Koch, Glen, 257.
KRAD-AM radio, 308.
Kraemer, Dick, 195.
Kraemer's Shoe Store, 305, 307, 329.
Kreipke, A.C., 76.
Kretsch, Arthur, 252.
Krisher, Sherman, 175, 195.
Ku Klux Klan, 147, 149.
Kumback Lunch, 160-168, 194, 221, 298, 307, 308.
Kumback Pub & Cafe, 167.

**—L—**

La Fonda Cafe, 307.
La Grace Beauty Shoppe, 307.

Ladies Tuesday Afternoon Club, 74, 87, 89.
Laird, Floyd R., 307.
Laird, Paul, 224, 252.
Lake Laird, 262, 330.
Lakeside Club pavilion, 262, 330.
Lamb, A.C., 302, 307.
Lamb, A. Charles, 302.
Lamb, Charles, 136.
Lamb, George, 136.
Lamb, Virginia Malzahn, 136.
Lamb, Opal, 302.
Lamm, Ethel, 308.
Lampe, Dorothy, 299.
Land offices, 13, 14, 18, 19, 20, 21, 22, 23, 24, 25, 26, 29, 32,35, 45, 55, 97, 155, 169.
Lane, Bill, 172.
Lang, Tiny, 225.
Langston, Okla., 39.
Lanza, Anthony, 236.
Lanza, Ruth Esther Willett, 234-236, 241.
Lapham, Amos, 144.
Lau, John, 315.
Leach, Euel, 182.
Leatherock, Avis, 171.
Leatherock, Wesley (son), 171.
Leatherock, Wesley K., 169-172, 326.
Ledbetter, James H., 49, 219, 220, 252.
Lee, Buck, 172.
Lee, Jess, 310.
Leino, Eino, 179, 181.
Lela, Okla., 31.
Leon, Jake, 241.
Letellier, Mabel, 257.
Levy, Ethel, 299.
Levy, I.L. "Ace," 310.
Lewis, Loren, 251.
Ley, Frank, 251.
Ley, Mayor G.A., 171, 245.
Liberty, Okla., 40.
Lindeman, Conrad J., 51, 85,, 118.
Lindeman, George, 118.
Lindsay, Merl, 262.
Lindsey, Kathleen Beers, 110.
Lions Club, 100, 173, 175, 219, 221, 222, 228.
Lions Eye Bank, 174.
Lions West Park, 174, 249.
*Little Perry News*, 92.
Little, Will T., 50.

Livingston, George, 45.
LJR Enterprises, 43.
Lloyd, Harold, 72.
Lobsitz, Albert, 175, 195.
Lobsitz, James A., 12, 17, 33, 42-44, 58, 76, 77, 97, 98, 99.
Lobsitz, Leo, 72.
Logan County, 39.
Long, Dr. O.M., 46.
Long-Bell Lumber Yard, 103.
Loomis, Loren S., 175, 195.
Love, Dr., 51.
Lovekamp, Charles, 251.
Lucas, Bruce R., 175, 195.
Lucien oil field, 127, 202.
Lucy, Mrs. M.A., 74, 77.
Ludrick, Jack, 172.
Lugert, Frank, 86.
Luttrell, Bill, 185.
Luttrell, Gene, 165-166.
Lynch, Bill, 251.
Lynch, Mrs. C.W., 296.
Lynn, Henry, 21, 22.

—*M*—

M&M Purebred Charolais Cattle Ranch, 289, 345.
M&W Food Store, 331.
MacAulay, Alan, 327.
Macias, Marilee, 166-167.
Macias, Tony, 166-167, 186.
Maggard, Wilma, 196.
Magnolia, Okla., 31.
Malget, David, 90.
Malget, Mrs. David, 90.
Malloch, W.A., 173.
Malone, J.E., 21.
Malone, John, 22.
Malzahn, Anna, 61, 62, 64, 107.
Malzahn, Bertha Wolff, 64-65, 107, 127, 131, 133, 134, 135, 136,139, 202, 205, 246, 250, 270, 272-272, 3315, 317, 338, 346.
Malzahn Blacksmith Shop, 62.
Malzahn Brothers' General Blacksmithing, 64, 65, 131, 189.
Malzahn Brothers' Machine Shop, 286.
Malzahn, Carl, 61, 62, 63, 64, 107, 126.
Malzahn, Charles, 62, 64, 65, 107, 126, 127, 129, 1311-134, 136,137, 138, 189, 202-203, 207, 208, 250, 264-

271, 279, 283,286, 293, 332, 338, 339, 346.
Malzahn, Dr. Don, 291, 338.
Malzahn, Edwin, 62, 126, 127, 129, 130, 131, 132, 136-142, 190,203-207, 208-209, 247, 250, 264-274, 276-294, 315, 316, 332, 336-339, 342, 344.
Malzahn, Emaline, 62, 63, 107.
Malzahn, Grace, 62, 63, 107.
Malzahn, Gustave, 62, 64, 65, 107, 126, 189, 286.
Malzahn, Helena, 126, 127.
Malzahn, Irene, 62, 107.
Malzahn, Marie, 62, 107.
Malzahn, Mary Corneil, 130, 136, 140, 205-206, 270, 289-292, 338,345.
Malzahn, Virginia, 131, 134, 136, 250.
Manhattan Construction Co., 49.
Maple Lake, Minn., 61.
Marcy, Gay, 307.
Marcy, Wesley, 307.
Marena, Okla., 84.
Marland, E.W., 90, 157, 323.
Marland Oil Co., 90, 257, 322, 323.
Marland, Okla., 30, 211, 215, 233, 238.
Marsh Hotel, 308.
Marsh, Anna, 308.
Martin, Ed R., 49.
Martin, Edwin, 251.
Masonic Lodge, 43, 80, 95, 100, 133, 147, 149, 171, 241, 262,296, 297.
Masterson, Bat, 46.
Mateer, Okla., 31.
Mayfield, Millard, 235.
Maysville Bank, 237.
McAlester, Okla., 322, 324, 325.
McAuliffe, Leon, 262.
McBride, Bessie, 227, 253.
McCandless, H.A., 88, 89, 241, 255.
McCandless, Mrs. H.A., 88, 89.
McCandless, Robert, 88.
McClellan, Joe, 175, 240, 242.
McClellan, Mary, 258.
McClintic, John, 23.
McCoy, Billy, 22.
McCredie, Ann, 100.
McCredie, Hugh, 33, 42, 97, 99.
McCubbins, Sylvia, 196.
McCubbins, Zach, 306.
McCuiston, W.J., 173.
McCullough, W.W., 49.

McCune, L.W., 76.
McCurry, Will, 31.
McDaniel, Robert F., 242.
McDonald's, 161.
McGeeney, Patrick S., 152.
McGuire, Congressman Bird S., 75.
McKenna, Gene, 73.
McKinney, Mrs. M.W., 79-80, 88.
McKinney, Okla., 31.
McKinnis, J.P., 45, 46.
McKinstry, David, 90.
McLellan's Variety Store, 309-310.
McLimans, Glen, 164.
McLimans, Rose, 299.
McManess George, 308.
McManess' Barber Shop, 308.
McQuain, Marty, 208.
McQuiston, Keith, 252.
Means, Olive, 196.
Means, Professor, 47.
Medford, Okla., 18, 224.
Mendota, Okla., 9.
Mentz, E.B., 45.
Merchants Hotel, 20.
Merriman, Allen, 236.
Merry, W.E., 72.
Meshek's Jewelry, 103.
Meyers, Herman, 251.
Meyers, Rev. Simon P., 20, 51, 81, 82.
Mickish, Frank, 331.
Mickish, Lt. Albert J., 331.
Mickish, Mrs. Frank, 331.
Midland Saloon, 48.
Midwest City, Okla., 326.
Midwest City High School, 186.
Miller Brothers 101 Ranch, 31, 149, 210-211, 215, 237.
Miller Cotton Gin, 103.
Miller, Angus, 95.
Miller, B.F., 195.
Miller, Col. Joe, 31, 215.
Miller Jr., George, 31.
Miller, McKinley, 175, 195.
Miller, Sam, 251.
Milliron, Virgil, 186.
Mix, Tom, 70.
Modularmatic machines, 275.
Mohr, Ruth, 196.
Mole Engineering Pty. Ltd., 267.
Monroe, Charles, 173.
Monroe Jr., Charles, 251.
Monroe, Margaret, 196.

Monroe-Lang Hardware Store, 44.
Montgomery, King W., 306, 326.
Moore, Betty Lee, 330.
Moore, Chet, 70, 261.
Moore, Dewey, 206-207, 279.
Moore, Dr. A.S., 51.
Moore, Fred G., 88, 175, 241-242.
Moore, Mrs. Bob, 327.
Moore, Mrs. Fred G., 88, 241.
Morgan, Dick T., 83, 154-155.
Morris, Roy, 312.
Morrison, Okla., 9, 30, 31, 81, 84, 316,
    329, 331.
Morrison, J.H., 31.
Mosely, M.A., 49.
Mossman Barber Shop, 307.
Mossman, Harry, 312.
Mossman, Hubert, 307.
Mossman, Mrs. Ralph, 307.
Mossman, Ralph, 307.
Moundridge, Kan., 63.
Mount, John, 317.
Mount, Mrs. John, 317.
Mouser, Wilbur, 220, 225, 226, 252.
Mt. Carmel Catholic Cemetery, 86.
Mt. Olive African Methodist Episcopal,
    86, 87.
Mugler, Fred, 245.
Mugler, Henry, 252.
Mugler, John, 252, 309.
Mugler, Maxine, 228.
Mulkey, Alba, 1422, 196.
Munger, Betty, 231.
Murray, Johnston, 315.
Murray, William H., 145, 149, 150, 200.
Museller, A.R., 49.

**—N—**

Nagle, Rev. J.A., 173.
Nardin, Okla., 205.
National Collegiate Athletic Associa-
    tion, 179, 183, 185, 186.
National Wrestling Hall of Fame, 179,
    186.
Nelson's Pharmacy, 303.
Nelson, E.E., 96, 195, 326.
Newton Funeral Home, 154.
Newton, George, 298.
Newton, Ted, 73, 220, 223, 252, 298.
Nez-Perce Indians, 8.
Nicewander building, 113.
Nichol, Esther, 196.

Nichols, T.D., 49.
Nida, Ora, 123.
Nix, Marshal E.D., 10.
Nixon, Richard, 288.
Noble County, 8, 11, 20, 26, 48, 51, 62,
    64, 79, 95, 97, 104,132, 144, 145,
    153, 158, 163, 172, 179, 180, 181,
    184, 201,204, 237, 242, 248, 292,
    305, 307, 314, 323, 329, 331.
Noble County Bank, 243-244, 256.
Noble County Fair building, 207, 249.
Noble County Industrial Foundation,
    316.
Noble County Selective Service Board,
    310.
*Noble County Sentinel*, 67, 169.
Noble County Tire Rationing Board,
    331.
Noble, John M., 32.
Norman, Okla., 152, 323, 324.
Norman, Boyd, 172.
Northern Oklahoma Butane Co., 113.

**—O—**

O'Connor, Donald, 72.
O'Dell, Carl, 103.
Oilwell Supply Co., 207.
*Oklahoma*, 50.
Oklahoma A.&M. College, 140, 144,
    179, 183, 205, 220, 277, 289,304,
    323.
Oklahoma Bandmasters Association,
    217.
Oklahoma Bankers Association, 88,
    241, 255.
Oklahoma City, 28, 68, 92, 100, 149,
    167, 174, 176, 205, 206,232, 234,
    238, 239, 241, 262, 266, 267, 272,
    274, ᴓ85, 287,337.
Oklahoma Constitutional Convention,
    145, 146.
Oklahoma Corporation Commission,
    324.
Oklahoma Department of Commerce
    and Industry, 270, 289, 324, 339.
Oklahoma Department of Transporta-
    tion, 324.
Oklahoma Eye Bank, 174.
Oklahoma Hall of Fame, 289.
Oklahoma Hardware Association, 266.
*Oklahoma Herald*, 170.

Oklahoma High School Coaches Hall of Fame, 186.
Oklahoma Highway Patrol, 237, 238.
Oklahoma Historical Society, 319-320.
Oklahoma Industrial Development, 289, 315, 318.
Oklahoma Land Run, 11, 244.
*Oklahoma Neurkerten*, 170, 244.
Oklahoma Society of Professional Engineers, 289.
Oklahoma State Highway Department, 5, 6.
Oklahoma State Prison, 322.
Oklahoma State University, 179, 183, 186, 205, 277, 278, 289,322, 323, 324.
Oklahoma Territorial Council, 144.
Oklahoma Territory, 7, 10, 12, 46, 61, 144, 152, 324.
Oklahoma Tire & Supply Store, 300.
Oliver, Frank, 44.
Olmstead, J.W., 49.
Olympic wrestler, 179.
Order of DeMolay for Boys, 262.
Order of Eastern Star, 43, 100, 134, 145.
Order of Rainbow for Girls, 262.
Orlando, Okla., 10, 12, 14, 15, 17, 18, 20, 25, 39, 42, 53, 54,62, 64.
Orlando Lutheran Church, 84.
Osage Indians, 8, 10.
Osborne, Dr. Gene, 195, 308.
Osborne, Forrest, 308.
Otoe-Missouria Indians, 8, 10, 31.
Overholser Opera House, 68.
Owen, Dr. B.A., 173.
Owen, Sen. Robert L., 146.

**—P—**

Pabst Brewing Co., 48.
Pacific Cafe, 307.
Palace Cafe, 257, 307.
Palmer & Smelser, 302.
Palovik Grocery, 103.
Paramount Pictures, 72, 74.
Parker, Ann, 161.
Parker, Bert, 160-161.
Parker, Catherine Schutz, 161.
Parker, Eddie, 160-168, 194, 221, 252, 298, 307.
Parker, Kate Hartung Mewherter, 162-168 298.

Parker, Minnie, 160-161.
Parker, Willard, 161.
Parker, Willis, 161.
Parker, Wilmer, 161.
Parmenter, L.C., 244.
Patterson, John, 48.
Patterson, Ruth, 315-316.
Pawnee County, 11, 145.
Pawnee, Indians, 8, 10, 15.
Payne, Capt. David, 13.
Pedee, Okla., 32.
Peerless Hotel, 309.
Penfield, C.P., 170.
Peroma, 182.
Perry Airport, 171, 317, 319, 326, 332.
Perry Business Women's Club, 134.
Perry City Council, 43, 104, 332.
Perry Courthouse, 20.
Perry Culture Club, 88.
*Perry Daily Democrat*, 170.
*Perry Daily Journal*, 44, 93, 99, 100, 149, 164, 166, 169-172,217, 220, 231, 237, 239, 245, 258, 271, 285, 315, 316, 321,327, 329, 331, 332, 333.
*Perry Democrat-Patriot*, 170, 324.
*Perry Eagle*, 170.
Perry, Ed, 170.
Perry Fire Department, 117.
Perry General Hospital, 94.
Perry Golf & Country Club, 43, 240, 262.
Perry High School Band, 220-231, 251.
Perry High School, 69, 80, 81, 123, 136, 141-142, 163, 166, 176,177, 179, 183, 185, 186, 187, 216, 227, 253, 2558, 297, 330.
*Perry Independent*, 170.
Perry, J.A., 32.
Perry Jewelry Co., 308.
Perry Lake, 174.
Perry Land Office, 317, 319.
Perry Library Association, 74, 76.
Perry Lumber Co., 127.
Perry Memorial Hospital, 332.
Perry Merchants, 99, 310, 312.
Perry Milling Co., 90, 102, 115, 121-123, 184, 203.
Perry National Guard Armory, 249.
Perry Opera House, 66-68.
Perry Planing Mill, 83.
Perry Pharmacy, 96.

Perry Plumbing Co., 335.
*Perry Populist*, 170.
Perry Post Office, 5, 19, 20, 30, 35, 36, 39, 42, 47, 49, 92, 97,119, 234, 236, 301, 317, 330.
Perry Progress Club, 74, 87.
*Perry Republican*, 22, 69, 101, 169, 170.
*Perry Rustler and McKinney Teller*, 170.
*Perry Rustler*, 170.
*Perry Sentinel*, 169, 170.
Perry Shoe Shop, 305.
Perry Square, 115.
Perry stadium, 5, 171.
Perry Steam Laundry, 97, 306, 318.
Perry Study Club, 88.
Perry Teen Town, 333.
Perry Theater, 70, 71, 73, 203, 213, 250, 335.
*Perry Times*, 169, 172.
Perryman, J.T., 31.
Phillips Petroleum Company, 181.
Phillips University, 322.
Phillips, L.R., 309.
Pierce, Judson, 225-226, 252.
Platt, Fred, 234, 246.
Plumer, L.E., 245, 247.
Plumer, Margaret, 330.
PolioPlus, 175.
Polio, 333.
Polo, 32.
Ponca City, Okla., 77, 140, 176, 177, 208, 233, 237, 263, 322.
Ponca Indians, 8, 31.
Pond Creek, Okla., 18, 27, 28.
Poor Boys Club, 175, 219-228, 252, 253.
*Populist Independent*, 170.
*Popular Mechanics*, 139, 268, 336.
Powers Abstract, 305.
Powers, Bob, 305.
Powers, Hazel, 305.
Powers, Jack, 305.
Powers, Romaine, 221, 252, 305.
Powers, Sue, 305.
Powers, Walter S., 173, 305.
Powers Jr., Walter, 305.
Prather, Charles, 31.
Pressler Hotel, 102.
Pressler, John, 68.
Prettyman, William S., 53.

Pricer, Bill, 123.
Pricer, Billy, 123.
Pricer, Dean, 24.
Pricer, Wilbur, 211.
Pride of Perry Flour, 90, 122, 203, 222.
Prince Hall Lodge, 40.
Production Credit Association, 310.
Professional Discount Pharmacy, 96.
Prouty, Frank, 170.
Pryor Ranch, 31.
Public Food Market, 309.
Pump Witch, 268.
Purcell, Okla., 9.
Purvis, Melvin, 233.

**—R—**

Radgowsky, Joseph, 215.
Radgowsky, Leopold, 214-218, 230, 251.
Radgowsky, Roberto, 215.
Ransom, C.W., 90.
Reckert, Lucile, 257.
Reckert, W.J., 173, 257, 307.
Red Cross, 99.
Red Hots, 258.
Red Rock, Okla., 8, 10, 30, 37, 77, 81, 92, 145.
Redrock, Okla., 32.
Reed, Chas. E., 23.
Regional Agricultural Credit Association, 246.
Render, Bailey, 251.
Render, Lt. Mary Frances, 331.
Rendfrow, W.C., 21, 45, 49.
Reynolds & Cress, 300.
Reynolds & Taylor, 300.
Reynolds, Henry H., 175, 300.
Rice, Donald, 251.
Rice-Stix Co., 98.
Richardson, S.E., 49.
Richberg, Okla., 32, 84.
Rider, Kirby, 208.
Ringler Leather Goods, 326.
Ringler, Mabel, 196.
Ringling Brothers Circus, 210.
Ritthaler, Ludwig, 85.
Roads, H.D. "Speck," 307, 335.
Roads, Newt, 329.
Roads, Stella, 335.
Robertson, Port, 183, 186.
Robinson, Helen, 298.
Robinson, Leo, 297.

Robinson, R.R., 98.
Robinson, Tommy, 297.
Rock Island Railroad, 16, 18, 30.
Rogers, Murl R., 292.
Rogers, Paul, 292.
Rogers, Will, 68, 182.
Rolling, Leroy, 43.
Roman Catholic Church, 51.
Rooney, Mickey, 199, 229, 231-232.
Roosevelt, Eleanor, 229-231.
Roosevelt, Franklin D., 126, 201, 229, 241, 261.
Roosevelt, Theodore, 23, 155.
Rose Hill Grade School, 184, 317, 319.
Ross Hotel, 308.
Rosser, Emmett, 223.
Rotary Club, 99, 173, 175, 195, 217,219, 221, 222, 228, 240, 301,333.
Rotary International, 171, 175.
Roth & Brown Architects, 248.
Roth, Allen, 247-248.
Roth, Jim, 273.
Roxy Theater, 70, 71, 261, 296, 308.
Rudolph, Harry, 172.
Ruff, Belle, 301.
Ruff, Dutch, 301.
Ruggles, Bob 252.
Ryerson, Ethel, 306.

—S—

Sac and Fox Land Run, 11.
Sadler, Dorotha, 337.
Sadler, J.D., 273.
Sadler, Russ, 267, 337.
Salem Lutheran Church, 85.
Samuelson, J.A., 175, 195.
Sanders, Rev. G. Frank, 175.
Sanford, Herbert C., 96, 175, 195.
Santa Fe Railroad, 7, 9, 16, 18, 26, 27, 32, 33, 36, 42, 143,152, 229, 230, 231.
Sapp, Sidney, 170.
Sayre Headlight, 170.
Schinerling, Fred, 103.
Schneider, Jane, 172.
Schuermann, Ken, 273.
Schwieger, Sam, 172, 220, 223, 224, 226, 252.
Scott, R.T., 326.
Scott Chevrolet, 335.
Scovill, Harold, 270, 280, 339.

Scruggs, J.C., 49.
Seeliger, Lawrence, 317.
Seids, Dr. F.C., 98.
Seigel, Jake, 195.
Seventeen, 199.
Seventh-Day Adventist Church, 72, 87.
Seventy-Seven Cafe, 307.
Seward, T.H., 49.
Sewell, David, 291.
Sewell, Elva, 291.
Sewell Sr., Joe, 291.
Sewell, Pamela Malzahn, 291, 338.
Shady Lady Tea Room, 306.
Shanafelt, John E., 82.
Shank, Elmer, 95.
Shannon, Mike, 96.
Shannon, Mrs. Mike, 96.
Shaw, Bert, 216.
Shawnee Indians, 35.
Sheets, George, 335.
Sheets, W.H., 173.
Shelter Insurance, 113.
Shelton, Eula, 196.
Shelton, Leonard, 185.
Sherrod, Virgil, 172, 221, 252.
Shockley, Mr., 89.
Shroeder, Fred, 101.
Singletary, Al, 220.
Skalenda, Joe, 103, 211.
Skinner, Vivian, 172.
Sky Witch platform, 267, 273, 280-281.
Slade, Genevieve Willett, 241.
Small Business Administration, 270, 289.
Smith, Alfred E., 149.
Smith, F.F., 308.
Smith, H.A., 94.
Smith, Hoke, 20.
Smith, Marvin, 211.
Smyser, A.E., 75, 94, 102.
Sooners, 13, 15, 18.
Sorenson, Jacob, 26.
Southard, Dr. R.W., 51.
Southern Methodist Church, 83.
Southside Pharmacy, 96.
Southwestern Bell Telephone Co., 223, 272, 298-300.
Sowers, L.F., 173.
Spanish-American War, 87.
Sparks, Bert, 88.
Sparks, Mrs. Bert, 88.
Sports Illustrated, 186.

Spraberry, George, 217.
Springfield Camp Yard & Feed Barn, 103.
St. Clair, H.E., 90.
St. Joseph's Academy, 86, 174, 175, 318.
St. Louis Hotel, 257, 308.
St. Rose of Lima Catholic Church, 85, 86, 92, 174, 175, 213, 221,223.
Stackhouse Co., 326.
Stackhouse, C.R., 326.
Standard Hotel, 309.
Stanislav Grocery & Market, 330.
Stanley, Jim, 278.
Stans, Maurice H., 288.
Starmer, George, 46.
State Highway Department, 129, 233, 234, 237, 315.
Stein, Clinton, 239.
Stell Jr., Thomas M., 330.
Stieferman, Leo, 309.
*Stillwater NewsPress*, 100.
Stillwater, Okla., 10, 12, 14, 18, 31, 37, 82, 100, 177, 179,181, 243, 256, 263, 304, 322, 324.
Stone, Jack, 94.
Stone, Lewis, 199.
Stone, William A., 47.
Stoops, Ernie, 172.
Stoops, Myrna, 68, 71.
Stopp, William, 305.
Stout, Ira, 245, 247.
Stout, Joe, 98.
Strebel Building, 103.
Strebel Tailor Shop, 113.
Strub, Will, 103.
Stumbaugh, Tom, 170.
Sullivan, Ed, 73.
Sumner, Okla., 32.
Sunfield Building, 102.
Svelan, Alice Mae, 318.
Swearingen, C.W., 31.
Swift, Richard V. "Cap," 211-213, 308.

—*T*—

T.M. Richardson & Sons, 49.
Taber Welding Co., 280.
Talley, L.L., 49.
Talley, R.R., 81.
Talliaferro, C.T., 12, 17, 32, 39-41.
Talliaferro, Lillie, 41.
Talliaferro Grocery, 335.

Talmadge, Constance, 72.
Talmadge, Natila, 72.
Talmadge, Norma, 72.
Tamac Pottery, 327-328.
Tarkington, Booth, 199.
Tate Buildings, 103.
Tate, Alma, 70, 261, 327.
Tate, Henry, 70, 261, 327.
Tate, J.B., 68, 69, 109.
Tate, John F., 69, 70.
Tate, Leonard, 327.
Taylor, Dr. Robert S., 51, 3144-315, 317.
Taylor, Jimmy, 300.
Taylor, Mary, 300.
Taylor Sr., T.J., 46.
Taylor Transfer Barn, 103.
Tearney, Jack, 25.
Tebbe, Gerald S., 175, 195.
Ted Workman's U.S. Cafe, 307.
Temple B'nai Israel, 43.
Temple Lunch, 297, 298, 299, 307.
Terry, John B., 70.
Testerman, Jack, 31.
Tetik, Paul, 103.
The 1-2-3 Cleaners, 306.
*The 46th Star*, 323.
The Clothiers, 98.
Thetford, Francis, 172.
Thiele, Florence, 63.
Thiele, Henry, 62, 63.
Thomas, H.A. (Heck), 46.
Thomas, Rev. David, 43.
Thompson, Anna, 161.
Thompson, Dennis, 96.
Thornhill, John, 46.
Three Sands, Okla., 32, 202, 203, 204, 208, 250, 269.
Tilghman, William, 46.
Tillery, A. Duff, 45.
Tillman, Edyth, 100.
Tinker Air Force Base, 206, 326.
Toastmasters Club, 175.
Tobin, Agnes, 99.
Todd, George, 90.
Toggery, 306.
Tom's Hall, 32.
Tonkawa Indians, 8, 10.
Topeka, Okla., 32.
Townsend, Pat, 312.
Track and Field, Inc., 326-327.
Trapp, Gov. Martin E., 146.

Treeman, Irene McCune, 76, 77, 320.
Treeman, L.D., 18.
Treeman, Ralph, 72.
Tucker, A.W., 304.
Tucker, Charlie, 308.
Tucker, Elsie, 308.
Tulsa, 155, 174, 176, 203, 205, 274, 276, 285, 324.
Tuttle, Mr., 122, 123.

## —U—

U.S. Cavalry, 9.
U.S. Golden Gloves, 186.
U.S. Marit ne Commission, 205.
U.S. Steel, 207.
Uhl, Roy, 206.
Unique Cleaners, 306.
United Fund, 228.
United War Chest, 99.
University of Oklahoma, 123, 167, 183, 185, 186, 277, 333, 324.
Unk's Bar-B-Que, 297.
Unzicker, Beulah, 196.

## —V—

VanAucken, J.H., 49.
VanBebber, Earl, 186.
VanBebber, Francis Marion, 179.
VanBebber, Ila Jeffrey, 179.
VanBebber, Jack F., 176, 178-181.
VanBebber, Julia, 180.
Vance Air Force Base, 322.
Vance Field, 326.
Vandenberg, John, 308.
Van Noy, Leslie, 196.
Van Pelt, Alfred, 89.
Vermeer Manufacturing Co., 273.
Vertz & Vertz Bakery, 308.
Veterans of Foreign Wars, 133.
Victory, Harold Dean, 251.
Voigt-Frailey Co., 264.
Voogden, Rev. Willebrord, 86, 94.
Voris, Carl, 173.

## —W—

Wa-Nee Hotel, 309.
Walker, C.P., 48.
Walkling, Lavinia, 36.
Walkling, Orlando, 12, 17, 32, 33-38, 203.

Walkling, Virgil, 307, 309.
Wall, Charles, 251.
Wallace, J.R., 49.
Wallerstedt, H.C., 244.
Walnut Township, 80.
Walt's Haberdashery, 306, 308.
Waltermire, Fred, 182.
Walton, Gov. John, 146, 149.
Ward, John L., 317.
Washington, A.W., 87.
Washington, Sandy, 87.
Watkins, Edgar, 170.
Watson, Charles G., 96.
Watson, Marion, 220, 252.
Watson, Milo W., 171-172, 271, 316.
Webber, G.T., 245-247.
Webber, Lanette, 330.
*Weekly Enterprise*, 170.
Weideman, C.A., 45.
Weiss, Walter, 302.
Welch, Virgil C., 170.
Wellington, Kan., 28, 30.
Wells Fargo, 10, 153.
Wentworth Military Academy, 209.
West Shawnee Trail, 9.
West Side Cafe, 307.
Western Auto Associate Store, 308.
Western Union, 244.
Wharton, Alonzo, 45, 48, 169.
Wharton, Okla., 9, 10, 26, 27, 32, 36, 40, 152.
Whipple Grade School, 179.
Whiteway Cafe, 307.
Whiteway Hotel, 309.
Whitney, B.C., 69, 95.
*Wichita Eagle*, 28, 29.
Wiehe, Ben, 302.
Wilcoxen, A., 102.
Wiles, Bill, 140.
Wilkerson, Dan, 291.
Wilkerson, Elmo, 291.
Wilkerson, Leasa Malzahn, 291, 338.
Wilkerson, Mary Ann, 291.
Wilkinson, Charles "Bud", 123.
Wilkinson, Lt. James B., 8.
Willett, Charles, 241.
Willett, E.M., 170.
Willett, Ruth Fink, 241.
Willett, Yeulin V., 233-241, 254.
Williams, J. Roy, 324.
Willow Creek School, 102.
Wills Lake, 48.

Wills, Bob, 262.
Winters, L.O., 173.
Wister, Okla., 238.
Witherspoon Ranch, 31.
Wolcott, Rev. Thomas, 82.
Wolf, J.A., 309.
Wolff, George, 64, 133, 202.
Wolff Sr., Martin, 64.
Wolff, Mary Pommerencki, 64.
Wollard, G.C., 90, 219.
Wollard, Mrs. G.C., 219.
Wolleson Jr., Adolph, 245.
Wolleson, Charles, 261.
Wolleson, Pearl, 261.
Women's Christian Temperance Union, 74, 87.
Wood, Rev. D.J.M., 51, 82.
Woodruff, B.J., 90.
Woodruff, Marsh, 175, 195.
Woods County, 11.
Woodward, Okla., 14, 79.
Woodward Building, 20, 103.
Woodward County, 11.
Workman, Ted, 307.
Works Project Administration, 5, 233, 249.
World War I, 4, 64, 171, 189, 214, 241, 261, 334.
World War II, 5, 61, 139, 171, 181, 205, 280, 310, 314, 326, 327, 329, 333, 334.

Worthington, Howard, 267, 272.
Woyke, Christian Paul, 128, 129, 130, 133.
Woyke, Grace Garrett, 130.
Woyke, Matilda, 129, 130.
Wurtz, Annabelle, 299.
Wylder, Daisy, 99.

**—Y—**

Yahn, Bettye Kaye, 73, 110.
Yahn, Glenn, 73, 220, 223, 224, 252, 277, 316.
Yahn, Mrs. Glenn, 73.
YMCA, 178, 291, 328.
Yost, Harvey, 321.
Young, J.W., 20.

**—Z—**

Zeig, Charles, 298.
Zeig, Edna Carley, 99, 310.
Zion Lutheran Church, 85.
Zorba's Department Store, 305, 306.
Zorba, Ann, 305.
Zorba, Jack, 305.
Zorba, Rudolph, 305.
Zorba, T., 305.
Zouave act, 210-211.

*Favorite Fairy Tales*
# TOLD IN ENGLAND

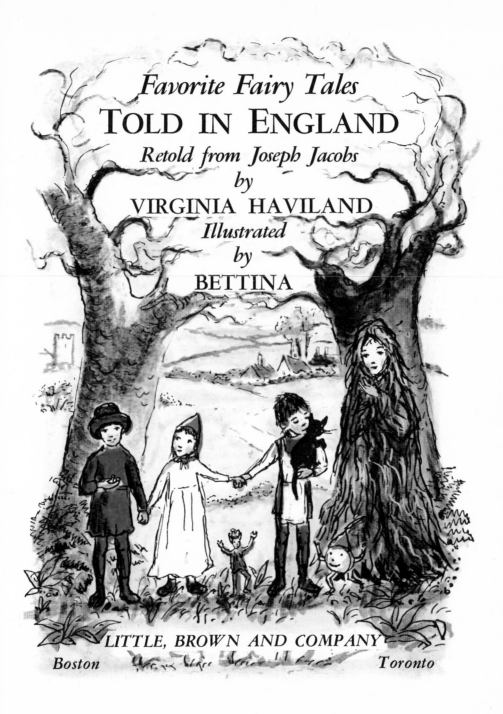

*Favorite Fairy Tales*
# TOLD IN ENGLAND
*Retold from Joseph Jacobs*
*by*
## VIRGINIA HAVILAND
*Illustrated*
*by*
## BETTINA

## LITTLE, BROWN AND COMPANY
*Boston*                    *Toronto*

These stories have been retold from *English Fairy Tales* collected by Joseph Jacobs (originally published 1892 by G. P. Putnam's Sons).

*Published simultaneously in Canada*
*by Little, Brown & Company (Canada) Limited*

PRINTED IN THE UNITED STATES OF AMERICA

# Contents

JACK AND THE BEANSTALK 3

JOHNNY-CAKE 22

TOM THUMB 30

MOLLY WHUPPIE 44

DICK WHITTINGTON AND HIS CAT 56

CAP O' RUSHES 76

6507

*For Margery*
*my youngest reader*

*Favorite Fairy Tales*
# TOLD IN ENGLAND

# Jack and the Beanstalk

ONCE UPON A TIME there was a poor widow who had an only son named Jack, and a cow named Milky-white. All they had to live on was the milk the cow gave every day. This they carried to the market and sold. But one morning Milky-white gave no milk.

"What shall we do? What shall we do?" cried the widow.

"Cheer up, Mother! I'll go and get work somewhere," said Jack.

"We've tried that before, and nobody would take you," said his mother. "We must sell Milky-white and with the money start a shop."

"All right, Mother," said Jack. "It's market day today. I'll soon sell Milky-white. Then we'll see what we can do."

So he took the cow's halter in his hand, and started off. He had not gone far when he met a

funny-looking old man who said to him, "Good morning, Jack."

"Good morning to you," said Jack, wondering how the man knew his name.

"Well, Jack, and where are you off to?" said the man.

"I'm going to market to sell our cow."

"Oh, you look the proper sort of chap to sell cows," said the man. "I wonder if you know how many beans make five."

"Two in each hand and one in your mouth," said Jack, as sharp as a needle.

"Right you are," said the man, "and here they are, the very beans themselves." He pulled out of his pocket a number of strange-looking beans. "Since you are so sharp," said he, "I don't mind trading with you—your cow for these beans."

"Go along!" said Jack.

"Ah! You don't know what these beans are," said the man. "If you plant them at night, by morning the stalks will be right up to the sky."

"Really?" said Jack. "You don't say so."

"Yes, that is so, and if it doesn't turn out to be true you can have your cow back."

"Right," said Jack. He handed over Milky-white's halter and pocketed the beans.

Back home went Jack. It was not dusk by the time he got to his door.

"Back already, Jack?" said his mother. "I see you haven't got Milky-white, so you've sold her. How much did you get for her?"

"You'll never guess, Mother," said Jack.

"No, you don't say so! Good boy! Five pounds? Ten? Fifteen? No, it can't be twenty!"

"I told you you couldn't guess. What do you say to these beans? They're magical—plant them at night and . . ."

"What!" said Jack's mother. "Have you been such a fool as to give away my Milky-white for a set of dry beans? Take that! Take that! Take that!" and she gave him three hard slaps. "As for your magic beans, here they go out of the window. Now off with you to bed. Not a drop shall you drink and not a bite shall you swallow this very night."

So Jack went upstairs to his little room in the attic. Sad and sorry he was, to be sure.

At last he dropped off to sleep.

When he woke up, his room looked very strange! The sun was shining, yet the room seemed dark and shadowy. Jack jumped up and ran to the window. What do you think he saw?

Why, the beans his mother had thrown out of the window into the garden had sprung up into a big beanstalk. It went up and up and up till it reached the sky. The old man had spoken the truth after all.

The beanstalk grew close to Jack's window and ran up beyond like a great ladder. So Jack jumped onto the beanstalk, and began to climb. He climbed, and he climbed, and he climbed, and he climbed, and he climbed, and he climbed, and he climbed. At last, through the clouds, he reached the sky. When he got there he found a long, broad road going on as straight as an arrow. So he walked along, and he walked along, and he walked along till he came to a great tall house. On the doorstep there was a great tall woman.

"Good morning, mum," said Jack, quite polite. "Could you be so kind as to give me some breakfast?" For he hadn't had anything to eat the night before, you know. He was as hungry as a hunter.

"It's breakfast you want, is it?" said the great

tall woman. "It's breakfast you'll *be* if you don't move off from here. My man is a giant, and there's nothing he likes better than boys broiled on toast. You'd better be moving on or he'll soon be coming."

"Oh! Please, mum, do give me something to eat, mum. I've had nothing since yesterday morning, really and truly, mum," said Jack. "I may as well be broiled as die of hunger."

Well, the giant's wife was not half so bad after all. She took Jack into the kitchen, and gave him a chunk of bread and cheese and a jug of milk. But Jack hadn't half finished these when — *thump! thump! thump!* — the whole house began to tremble with the noise of someone coming.

"Goodness gracious me! It's my old man," said the giant's wife. "What on earth shall I do? Come along quick and jump in here." She bundled Jack into the oven, just as the giant came in.

He was a big man, to be sure. At his belt he had three calves strung up by the heels. He threw them down on the table and said, "Here, wife, broil me two of these for breakfast. Ah! What's this I smell? . . .

*"Fee-fi-fo-fum,*
  *I smell the blood of an Englishman!*
  *Be he alive, or be he dead,*
  *I'll grind his bones to make my bread."*

"Nonsense, dear," said his wife. "You're dreaming. Or perhaps you smell the scraps of that little boy you liked so much for yesterday's dinner. Here, go wash and tidy up. By the time you come back your breakfast will be ready for you."

Off the giant went. Jack was just going to jump out of the oven and run away when the

woman told him not to. "Wait till he's asleep,"
said she. "He always has a nap after breakfast."

The giant had his breakfast. After that he went to a big chest and took out of it two bags of gold. Down he sat and counted till at last his head began to nod. He began to snore till the whole house shook again.

Then Jack crept out on tiptoe from his oven. As he passed the giant, he took one of the bags of gold under his arm. Off he ran till he came to the beanstalk. He threw down the bag of gold, which of course fell into his mother's garden. He climbed down and climbed down till at last he got home. He told his mother what had happened and showed her the gold.

"Well, Mother," he said, "wasn't I right about the beans? They *are* really magical, you see."

They lived on the bag of gold for some time, but at last they came to the end of it. Jack made up his mind to try his luck once more at the top of the beanstalk. So one fine morning he rose early and got onto the beanstalk. He climbed, and he climbed, and he climbed, and he climbed, and he climbed, and he climbed. At last he came out on to the road again and up to the great tall house he had been to before. There, sure enough, was the great tall woman standing on the doorstep.

"Good morning, mum," said Jack, as bold as brass. "Could you be so good as to give me something to eat?"

"Go away, my boy," said the great tall woman, "or else my man will eat you up for breakfast. But aren't you the boy who came here once before? Do you know, that very day my man missed one of his bags of gold!"

"That's strange, mum," said Jack. "I dare say I could tell you something about that. But I'm so hungry I can't speak till I've had something to eat."

Well, the great tall woman was so curious that she took him in and gave him something to eat. But he had scarcely begun munching it, as slowly as he could, when—*thump! thump! thump!*—they heard the giant's footstep, and his wife again hid Jack in the oven.

Everything happened as it did before. In came the giant, roaring "Fee-fi-fo-fum," and had his breakfast of three broiled oxen. Then he ordered, "Wife, bring me the hen that lays the golden eggs."

So she brought it. Her husband said, "Lay," and the hen laid an egg all of gold. But then the giant began to nod his head, and to snore till the house shook.

Now Jack crept out of the oven on tiptoe and caught hold of the golden hen. He was off before you could say "Jack Robinson." This time, the giant woke—because the hen gave a cackle. Just as Jack got out of the house, he heard the giant calling, "Wife, wife, what you have done with my golden hen?"

And the wife said, "Why, my dear?"

But that was all Jack heard, for he rushed off to the beanstalk and climbed down in a flash. When he got home he showed his mother the wonderful hen, and said, "Lay!" to it. It laid a golden egg every time he said, "Lay!"

Well, Jack was not content. It wasn't very long before he decided to try his luck again up there at the top of the beanstalk. One fine morning he rose early, and stepped onto the beanstalk. He climbed, and he climbed, and he climbed, and he climbed, till he came to the very top. This time he knew better than to go straight to the giant's house. When he came near it, he waited behind a bush till he saw the giant's wife come out with a pail to get some water. Then he crept into the house and hid in a copper tub. He hadn't been there long when he heard *thump! thump! thump!* as before. In walked the giant and his wife.

"Fee-fi-fo-fum, I smell the blood of an Englishman!" cried out the giant. "I smell him, wife, I smell him."

"Do you, my dear?" said his wife. "Well then, if it's the little rogue that stole your gold and the hen that laid the golden eggs, he's sure to have got into the oven." And they both rushed to the oven.

But Jack wasn't there, luckily. The giant's wife said, "There you are again with your fee-fi-fo-fum! Why, of course, it's the boy you caught last night that I've just broiled for your breakfast. How forgetful I am! And how careless you are not to know the difference between alive and dead, after all these years."

So the giant sat down to his breakfast. Every now and then he would mutter, "Well I could have sworn..." And he'd get up and search the larder and the cupboards and everything. Only, luckily, he didn't think of the tub.

After breakfast, the giant called out, "Wife, wife, bring me my golden harp." So she brought it and put it on the table before him. "Sing!" he ordered, and the golden harp sang most beautifully. It went on singing till the giant fell asleep, and began to snore like thunder.

Jack now got out of the tub very quietly and crept like a mouse over to the table. Up he crawled, caught hold of the golden harp, and dashed with it towards the door. But the harp called out quite loud, "Master! Master!"

The giant woke up just in time to see Jack running off with his harp.

Jack ran as fast as he could. The giant came rushing after, and would soon have caught him, only Jack had a head start and knew where he was going. When he got to the beanstalk the giant was not more than twenty yards away. Suddenly Jack disappeared. When the giant came to the end of the road, he saw Jack below climbing down for dear life.

Well, the giant didn't like to trust himself to such a ladder. He stood and waited, so Jack got another start.

But the harp cried out again, "Master! Master!"

The giant swung himself down onto the beanstalk, which shook with his weight. Down climbed Jack, and after him climbed the giant.

Jack climbed down, and climbed down, and climbed down till he was very nearly home. Then he called out, "Mother! Mother! Bring me an ax, bring me an ax!" His mother rushed out with the ax in her hand. When she came to the beanstalk, she stood stock-still with fright. There was the giant with his legs just through the clouds.

Jack jumped down, took the ax, and chopped at the beanstalk, almost cutting it in two. The giant felt the beanstalk shake, so he stopped to see what the matter was. Then Jack chopped again. The beanstalk was cut in two. It began to topple over. Down crashed the giant, and that was the end of him!

Jack gave his mother the golden harp. With the magical harp and the golden eggs, Jack and his mother became very rich. Jack married a Princess, and they all lived happily ever after.

# Johnny-cake

ONCE UPON A TIME there was an old man, and
an old woman, and a little boy. One morning
the old woman made a johnny-cake, and put it
in the oven to bake. "You watch the johnny-
cake," she said to the little boy, "while your father
and I go out to work in the garden."

The old man and the old woman went out and
began to hoe potatoes, leaving the little boy to
tend the oven. But he did not watch it all the

time. Suddenly, when he was not watching, he heard a noise. He looked up and saw the oven door pop open. Out of the oven jumped Johnny-cake. He went rolling along end over end, towards the open door of the house.

The little boy ran to shut the door, but Johnny-cake was too quick for him. He rolled through the door, down the steps, and out into the road long before the little boy could catch him. The little boy ran after him as fast as he could run, crying out to his father and mother. They heard the uproar and threw down their hoes and chased Johnny-cake, too. But Johnny-cake outran all

three and was soon out of sight. The little boy
and his father and mother, out of breath, had
to sit down on a bank to rest.

On ran Johnny-cake. By-and-by he came to
two well-diggers.

They looked up from their work and called
out, "Where ye going, Johnny-cake?"

He said, "I've outrun an old man, and an old
woman, and a little boy, and I can outrun you
too-o-o!"

"Ye can, can ye? We'll see about that!" said
they. They threw down their picks and ran after
him. But they couldn't catch up with him. Soon
they had to sit down by the roadside to rest.

On ran Johnny-cake. By-and-by he came to two ditch-diggers, who were digging a ditch.

"Where ye going, Johnny-cake?" said they.

He said, "I've outrun an old man, and an old woman, and a little boy, and two well-diggers, and I can outrun you too-o-o!"

"Ye can, can ye? We'll see about that!" said they; and they threw down their spades, and ran after him too. But Johnny-cake soon was way ahead of them, also. Seeing they could never catch him, they gave up the chase and sat down to rest.

On ran Johnny-cake, and by-and-by he came
to a bear.

The bear said, "Where ye going, Johnny-cake?"

He said, "I've outrun an old man, and an old
woman, and a little boy, and two well-diggers, and
two ditch-diggers, and I can outrun you too-o-o!"

"Ye can, can ye?" snarled the bear. "We'll see
about that!" He trotted as fast as his legs could
carry him after Johnny-cake, who never stopped
to look behind him. Before long the bear was left
so far behind that he saw he might as well give up

the hunt first as last. He stretched himself out by
the roadside to rest.

On ran Johnny-cake, and by-and-by he came
to a wolf. The wolf said, "Where ye going,
Johnny-cake?"

He said, "I've outrun an old man, and an old
woman, and a little boy, and two well-diggers,
and two ditch-diggers, and a bear, and I can outrun you too-o-o!"

"Ye can, can ye?" snarled the wolf. "We'll see
about that!" And he set into a gallop after
Johnny-cake, who went on and on so fast that the
wolf saw there was no hope of overtaking him.
He too lay down to rest.

On went Johnny-cake. By-and-by he came to a fox that lay quietly in a corner of the fence.

The fox called out in a sharp voice, but without getting up, "Where ye going, Johnny-cake?"

He said, "I've outrun an old man, and an old woman, and a little boy, and two well-diggers, and two ditch-diggers, and a bear, and a wolf, and I can outrun you too-o-o!"

The fox said, "I can't quite hear you, Johnny-cake, won't you come a little closer?"—turning his head a little to one side.

Johnny-cake stopped his race for the first time, and went a little closer. He called out in a very loud voice, *"I've outrun an old man, and an old woman, and a little boy, and two well-diggers, and two ditch-diggers, and a bear, and a wolf, and I can outrun you too-o-o!"*

"Can't quite hear you! Won't you come a *little* closer?" said the fox in a feeble voice. He stretched out his neck towards Johnny-cake, and put one paw behind his ear.

Johnny-cake came up close, and leaning towards the fox screamed out: "I'VE OUTRUN AN OLD MAN, AND AN OLD WOMAN, AND A LITTLE BOY, AND TWO WELL-DIGGERS, AND TWO DITCH-DIGGERS, AND A BEAR, AND A WOLF, AND I CAN OUTRUN YOU TOO-OO!"

"You can, can you?" yelped the fox, and he snapped up Johnny-cake in his sharp teeth and ate him in the twinkling of an eye.

# Tom Thumb

IN THE DAYS of the great King Arthur, there lived a mighty magician called Merlin. He was the most skillful wizard the world has ever seen.

This famous magician, who could take any form he pleased, was once traveling about as a beggar. Being very tired, he stopped at a poor cottage to rest, and asked for some food.

The countryman who lived there made him welcome. The man's wife, who was a very kind woman, brought him some milk in a wooden bowl and some coarse brown bread on a platter.

Merlin was much pleased. But he could not help seeing that the man and wife seemed unhappy, although everything was neat and snug in the cottage.

When Merlin asked them why they were so sad, the poor woman said, with tears in her eyes, "It is because we have no children. I should be the

happiest person in the world if I had a son. Even though he were no bigger than my husband's thumb, I would be satisfied."

Merlin was so amused by the idea of a boy no bigger than a man's thumb that he decided to grant the poor woman's wish. In a short time, the farmer's wife had a son. And he was not a bit bigger than his father's thumb!

One night while the mother was admiring her child the Queen of the Fairies came in at the window. The Fairy Queen kissed the boy and named him Tom Thumb. She then sent for some of her fairies, who dressed him as she ordered:

"*A cap of oak-leaf for his crown;*
*A jacket woven of thistledown;*
*A shirt of web by spiders spun;*
*His trousers now of feathers done.*
*Stockings of apple-peel, to tie*
*With eyelash from his mother's eye;*
*Shoes made up of mouse's skin,*
*Tanned with the downy hair within.*"

Tom never grew any larger than his father's thumb, which was only of ordinary size. But, as he grew older, he became very clever and full of tricks. When he was old enough to play marbles with other boys he sometimes lost all his marbles. Then he would creep into the bags of his playmates to fill his pockets. Crawling out without being noticed, he would again join the game.

One day, as he was coming out of a bag of marbles, where he had been stealing as usual, the boy to whom the bag belonged saw him.

"Aha! my little Tommy," said the boy, "so at last I have caught you stealing my marbles. You shall be punished for your trick."

He drew the string of the bag tight around Tom's neck and gave the bag such a shake that poor little Tom was in great pain. He cried out, and begged to be let free. "I will never steal again!" he said.

A short time later his mother was making a batter pudding. Tom, being anxious to see how it was made, climbed up to the edge of the bowl. Then his foot slipped and he fell into the batter. His mother had not seen him. She stirred him into the pudding, and put it in the pot to boil.

The batter filled Tom's mouth and prevented him from crying. But he kicked and struggled so much as the pot grew hot that his mother thought the pudding was bewitched. Taking it out of the pot, she threw it outside the door.

A poor tinker who was passing by picked up

the pudding. Putting it into his bag, he walked off with it.

Tom had now got his mouth cleared of the batter, and he began to cry aloud. This frightened the tinker so much that he flung down the pudding and ran away. The pudding string broke. Tom crept out covered all over with batter, and walked home. His mother was very sorry to see her darling in such a state. She put him into a teacup and washed off the batter. Then she kissed him, and laid him in bed.

Soon after this, Tom's mother went to milk her cow in the meadow, and took Tom along with her. Lest the high wind should blow him away, she tied him to a thistle with a piece of fine thread. But the cow saw Tom's oak-leaf hat. She liked the looks of it and grabbed poor Tom and the thistle in one mouthful.

Tom was afraid of her great teeth and roared out as loud as he could, "Mother, Mother!"

"Where are you, Tommy?" asked his mother.

"Here, Mother, in the red cow's mouth."

His mother began to cry. But the cow, surprised at the odd noise Tom was making in her throat, opened her mouth and let Tom drop out. Luckily his mother caught him in her apron as he was falling down, or he would have been dreadfully hurt.

One day Tom's father made him a whip of a barley straw so that he could drive the cattle. Out in the field Tom slipped. He rolled over and over into a steep furrow of earth. A raven, flying over, picked him up and carried him out to sea. There it dropped him.

The moment Tom fell into the sea, a large fish swallowed him. Soon after, this very fish was

caught, and was bought for the table of King Arthur. When the cook opened the fish in order to cook it, out jumped the tiny boy!

Tom was happy to be free again. The cook carried him to the King, who made Tom his

special dwarf. Soon he grew to be a great favorite at court. By his tricks and fun, he amused the King and Queen, and also all the Knights of the Round Table.

The King quite often took Tom with him when he rode out on his horse. If it rained, Tom would creep into the King's pocket and sleep till the rain was over.

One day King Arthur asked Tom about his parents. The King wished to know if they were as small as Tom and whether they were well off. Tom told the King that his father and mother were as tall as anyone about the court, but rather poor. The King then carried Tom to the room where he kept all his money and told him to take as much as he could carry home to his parents. Tom, full of joy, at once got a purse.

But it would hold only one silver piece. Even this he could hardly lift.

At last he managed to place this load on his back, and he set forward on his journey home.

After resting more than a hundred times by the way, in two days and two nights he reached his father's house.

Tom was tired almost to death. His mother carried him into the house.

During his visit Tom told his parents many stories about the court. One day, however, he decided he must return to the King.

Back at court, the King noticed how much Tom's clothes had suffered from being in the batter pudding and inside the fish, as well as from his journey. So the King ordered a new suit made for him. And he had Tom mounted on a mouse, like a knight, with a needle for a sword.

It was great fun to see Tom in his new suit, mounted on the mouse. When he rode out hunting with the King and his knights, everyone was ready to laugh.

The King was so pleased with Tom that he had a little chair made, also, so that Tom might sit upon his table. Then to live in he gave him a little palace of gold, with a door an inch wide. There was a coach, too, drawn by six small mice.

This way Tom was happy for a long time, and his parents were pleased with his success.

# Molly Whuppie

ONCE UPON A TIME a man and his wife had too many children. They could not feed them all, so they took the three youngest and left them in a wood. The three little girls walked and walked, but never a house could they see. It began to be dark, and they were hungry.

At last the little girls saw a light and headed for it. It shone from a house. They rapped on the door, and a woman came, who said, "What do you want?"

"Please let us in and give us something to eat."

The woman answered, "I can't do that, as my man is a giant. He would kill you when he comes home."

"Do let us stop for a little while," they begged, "and we will go away before he comes."

The woman took them in. She set them down before the fire and gave them bread and milk.

Just as they began to eat, a great knock came to the door, and a dreadful voice said:

*"Fee-fi-fo-fum,*
*I smell the blood of some earthly one—*

"Who's there, wife?"

"Eh," said the wife, "it's three poor lassies, cold and hungry. They'll go away. Ye won't touch 'em, man."

The giant said nothing. He ate up a big supper, and ordered the girls to stay all night. He had three lassies of his own, he said, who would sleep in the same bed as the three strangers.

Now the youngest of the three girls was called Molly Whuppie, and she was very clever. She noticed that before they went to bed the giant put straw ropes round her neck and her sisters', and round his own daughters' necks he put gold chains. So Molly took care not to fall asleep, but waited till she was sure everyone was sleeping sound.

Then Molly slipped out of bed. She took the straw ropes off her own and her sisters' necks, and took the gold chains off the giant's lassies. She then put the straw ropes on the giant's daughters and the gold ones on herself and her sisters, and lay down.

In the middle of the night up rose the giant, and he felt for the necks with the straw. It was dark. He took his own daughters out of bed, and carried them out to a cage where he locked them up. Then he lay down again.

Molly thought it was time she and her sisters were off and away. She woke them and told them to be quiet, and they slipped out of the house. They all got out safe, and they ran and ran.

They never stopped until morning, when they saw a grand house before them.

It turned out to be a King's house, so Molly went in and told her story to the King. The King said, "Well, Molly, you are a clever girl. You have managed well. But—you can manage better yet. Go back and steal the giant's sword that hangs on the back of his bed, and I'll give your eldest sister my eldest son to marry."

Molly said she would try. So she went back. She managed to slip into the giant's house and to hide under his bed.

The giant came home, ate up a great supper, and went to bed. Molly waited until he was snoring. Then she crept out and reached over the giant and got down the sword. But just as she got it out over the bed, the sword gave a rattle. Up jumped the giant!

Molly ran out the door, and the sword with her. She ran, and the giant ran, till they came to the "Bridge of One Hair." She got over, but he couldn't; and he cried, "Woe unto ye, Molly Whuppie, if ye ever come here again!"

But Molly replied, "Twice yet I'll come to Spain."

So Molly took the sword to the King, and her sister was wed to his son.

Well, the King said: "You've managed well, Molly. But you can do better yet. Go back and steal the purse that lies below the giant's pillow, and I'll marry your second sister to my second son."

Molly said she would try. So she set out for the giant's house and slipped in and hid again under his bed. She waited till the giant had eaten his supper and was sound asleep snoring.

She crept out then. She slipped her hand under the pillow, and got out the purse. But, just as she was leaving the giant wakened, and ran after her.

She ran, and he ran, till they came to the
"Bridge of One Hair." She got over, but he could-
n't; and he cried, "Woe unto ye, Molly Whuppie,
if ye ever come here again!"

But Molly replied, "Once yet I'll come to
Spain."

So Molly took the purse to the King, and her
second sister was wed to the King's second son.

After that the King said to Molly, "Molly, you are a clever girl. But you can do better yet. Steal the giant's ring that he wears on his finger, and I'll give you my youngest son for yourself."

Molly said she would try. So back she went to the giant's house and hid under the bed. The giant wasn't long in coming home. After he had eaten a great supper, he went to his bed, and shortly was snoring loud.

Molly crept out and reached over the bed. She took hold of the giant's hand. She pulled and she pulled at the ring on his finger. But just as she got it off the giant rose up, and gripped her by the hand. "Now I have caught ye, Molly Whuppie! Well, now—if I had done as much ill to ye as ye have done to me, what would ye do to me?"

At once Molly said, "I would put you into a sack. I'd put the cat inside with you, and the dog beside you, and a needle and thread and shears. And I'd hang you up upon the wall. Then I'd go to the wood, and I would choose the biggest stick

I could get. I would come home and take you down and bang you till you were dead."

"Well, Molly," said the giant, "I'll do just that to ye."

So he got a sack, and put Molly into it, and the cat and the dog beside her, with a needle and thread and shears. He hung her up upon the wall. Then he went to the wood to choose a stick.

Molly sang out, "Oh, if you saw what I see!"

"Oh," said the giant's wife, "what do ye see, Molly?"

But Molly never said a word, only, "Oh, if you saw what I see!"

The giant's wife begged Molly to take her up into the sack so she could see what Molly saw. So Molly took the shears and cut a hole in the sack. She took the needle and thread out with her, and jumped down and helped the giant's wife up into the sack, and sewed up the hole.

The giant's wife saw nothing, and began to ask to get down again. But Molly never minded. She hid herself behind the door. Home came the giant with a big tree in his hand. He took down the sack and began to batter it. His wife cried out, "It's me, man, it's me, man!" But the dog barked so, and the cat mewed so, that the giant did not hear his wife's voice.

Molly came out from behind the door. The giant saw her and ran after her. He ran, and she

ran, till they came to the "Bridge of One Hair."
She got over, but he couldn't; and he said, "Woe
unto ye, Molly Whuppie, if ye ever come here
again!"

But Molly replied, "Never more will I come to
Spain."

So Molly took the ring to the King. She was
married to his youngest son, and she never saw
the giant again.

# Dick Whittington and His Cat

MANY YEARS AGO there lived a little boy whose name was Dick Whittington. Dick's father and mother died when he was very young. As he was not old enough to work, he was very badly off. The people who lived in his village were so poor that they could spare him little more than the parings of potatoes, and sometimes a hard crust of bread.

Dick had heard many strange things about the great city called London. The country people thought that folks there were all fine gentlemen and ladies. They believed that singing and music were heard all day long and all the streets were paved with gold.

Time passed till one day a wagoner was driving a large wagon through Dick's village on his way to London. Dick asked if he might walk with him by the side of the wagon. When the man learned that poor Dick had no father or mother, and saw by his ragged clothes that he could be no worse off than he was already, he told him he might go. So they set off together.

Dick got safely to London and ran off as fast as he could to look for the streets paved with gold. He ran until he was tired. At last, when it was dark and he had found every street covered with dirt instead of gold, he sat down in a corner and cried himself to sleep.

The next morning he got up and walked about, asking everybody he met to give him a coin to keep him from starving. Only two or three people gave him any money, and he was soon weak from hunger.

At length Dick laid himself down at the door of Mr. Fitzwarren, a rich merchant. Here he was found by the cook, who had a very nasty temper. She was busy getting dinner for her master and mistress, so she called out to poor Dick, "What business have you there, you lazy boy? If you do not take yourself away, we'll see how you'll like a sousing of dishwater. I have some hot enough to make you jump!"

Just then Mr. Fitzwarren himself came home to dinner. When he saw the dirty ragged boy lying at the door, he said to him, "Why do you lie here, my boy? You seem old enough to work. I am afraid you are lazy."

"No, indeed, sir," said Dick. "I would gladly work, but I don't know anybody, and I'm sick for lack of food."

"Poor boy, get up. Let me see what ails you."

Dick tried to rise, but had to lie down again, for he had not eaten in three days. The kind merchant then ordered him to be taken into the house and given a good dinner. He was to stay, to do what work he could for the cook.

Dick would have lived very happily with this good family if it had not been for the ill-natured cook. She would scold him, and beat him cruelly with a broom. At last her bad treatment was reported to Alice, Mr. Fitzwarren's daughter, who told the woman she would be turned away if she did not treat Dick more kindly.

The cook's behavior became a little better, but Dick suffered another hardship. His bed stood in a garret, where there were so many holes in the floor and walls that every night rats and mice ran over him. One day when he had earned a penny for cleaning a gentleman's shoes, he thought he would buy a cat with it.

He saw a girl with a cat, so he asked her, "Will you let me have that cat for a penny?"

The girl said, "Yes, that I will, though she is an excellent mouser."

Dick hid his cat in the garret, and always took care to take part of his dinner to her. In a short time he had no more trouble with rats and mice, but slept soundly every night.

Soon after this, one of Mr. Fitzwarren's trading ships was ready to sail. It was the custom for all his servants to share in the profits of a voyage, so he called them into the parlor and asked them what they would send out to trade.

They all had something that they were willing to send, except poor Dick. For this reason he did not come into the parlor with the rest. But Miss Alice guessed what was the matter and ordered him to be called in. "I will lay down some money for him, from my own purse," she said.

But her father told her, "This will not do. It must be something of his own."

When poor Dick heard this, he said, "I have nothing but a cat which I once bought for a penny."

"Fetch your cat then, my lad," said Mr. Fitzwarren, "and let her go."

Dick went upstairs. With tears in his eyes, he brought down poor Puss. Giving her to the ship's captain, he thought, "Now again I'll be kept

awake all night by the rats and mice." But Miss
Alice, who felt pity for him, gave him money to
buy another cat.

This kindness shown by Miss Alice made the cook jealous of poor Dick. She began to treat him more cruelly than ever, and always made fun of him for sending his cat to sea.

At last poor Dick could bear it no longer. He thought he would run away. So he packed up his few things and started off, very early. He walked as far as Holloway, and there sat down on a stone to think about which road he should take.

While he was considering this, the bells of Bow Church began to ring, and seemed to say to him:

*"Turn again, Whittington,*
    *Thrice Lord Mayor of London."*

"Lord Mayor of London!" said Dick to himself. "Why, to be sure, I'd put up with almost anything now—to be Lord Mayor of London, and ride in a fine coach, when I grow to be a man! Well, I will go back. I'll think nothing of the

cuffing and scolding, if I'm to be Lord Mayor of London."

Dick did go back and was lucky enough to get into the house and set about his work before the cook came downstairs.

Now we must follow Puss to the coast of Africa. The ship, with the cat on board, was a long time at sea. At last it was driven by the winds to a part of the coast of Barbary. The Moors who lived here came in great numbers to see the sailors, and treated them politely. After they became better acquainted, the Moors were eager to buy the fine things that the ship carried.

When the captain saw this, he sent examples of the best things he had to the King of the country. The King was so pleased that he invited the

captain to come to the palace. Here they sat on
carpets woven with gold and silver, as was the
custom. Rich dishes were brought in for dinner.
However, a vast number of rats and mice rushed
in too. These ate all the meat in an instant!

The captain learned that the King would give
half his treasure to be freed of the rats and mice.
"They not only destroy his dinner," he was told,
"but they attack him in his chamber, and even
in bed. He has to be watched while he is sleeping."

The captain was delighted! He remembered poor Whittington and his cat, and told the King that he had an animal on board ship that would do away with all these pests at once. The King jumped so high for joy that his turban dropped off his head.

"Bring this animal at once," he said. "Rats and mice are dreadful! If she will do as you say, I will load your ship with gold and jewels in exchange for her!"

Cleverly, the captain set forth the merits of Puss. He told the King, "It is not very convenient to part with her, for, when she is gone, the rats and mice may destroy the goods in the ship. But, to oblige Your Majesty, I will fetch her."

"Run, run!" said the Queen. "I'm impatient to see the dear creature."

Away went the captain to the ship, while another dinner was made ready. He put Puss under his arm, and arrived at the palace just in time to see the table again covered with rats. When the

cat saw them, she did not wait for orders, but jumped out of the captain's arms. In a few minutes almost all of the rats and mice were dead at her feet. The rest of them scampered away to their holes in fright.

The King was happy to get rid of the plague so easily. He was pleased, too, to learn that Puss's kittens would keep the whole country free from rats. So he gave the captain ten times as much for the cat as for all the rest of the cargo.

The captain now could take leave of the court and set sail for England.

Early one morning Mr. Fitzwarren had just sat down to his countinghouse desk, when he heard somebody—*tap, tap*—at his door.

"Who's there?" said Mr. Fitzwarren.

"A friend," answered the other. "I come to bring you good news of your ship, the *Unicorn*.

The merchant opened his door. Whom should he see waiting but his captain and his agent with a cabinet of jewels! He looked at their report of the trading, and thanked Heaven for giving him such a prosperous voyage.

He heard the story of the cat and saw the rich gifts that the King and Queen had sent to poor Dick. He called out to his servants:

*"Go send him in, and tell him of his fame;*
*Pray call him Mr. Whittington by name."*

Mr. Fitzwarren proved he was a good man. Some of his servants said that so great a treasure was too much for Dick. He answered them, "God

forbid I should deprive him of the value of a
single penny."

Dick was at that time scouring pots for the
cook, and quite dirty. He wanted to excuse himself from coming into the countinghouse, but
the merchant ordered him to enter.

Mr. Fitzwarren had a chair set for him. Dick
began to think they were making fun of him and
said, "Don't play tricks with me. Let me go back
to my work, if you please."

"Indeed, Mr. Whittington," said the merchant, "we are all quite in earnest. I rejoice in the news that these gentlemen have brought you. The captain has sold your cat to the King of Barbary. In return for her you have more riches than I possess in the whole world. I wish you may long enjoy them!"

Poor Dick was so full of joy he hardly knew how to behave. He begged his master to take any part of the treasure that he pleased, since he owed it all to his kindness.

"No, no," answered Mr. Fitzwarren, "this is all yours. I know you will use it well."

Dick next asked his mistress, and then Miss Alice, to accept a part of his good fortune. But they would not. Dick was too generous to keep it all to himself, however. He gave presents to the captain, the agent, and the rest of Mr. Fitzwarren's servants—even to the ill-natured old cook.

After this, Mr. Fitzwarren advised Dick to

send for a tailor and have himself dressed like a gentleman. He told him he was welcome to live in his house till he could provide himself with a better one.

When Whittington's face was washed, his hair curled, his hat cocked, and he was dressed in a fine suit of clothes, he was as handsome as any young gentleman who visited at Mr. Fitzwarren's. Miss Alice, who had once been so kind to him and thought of him with pity, now looked upon him as fit to be her sweetheart. Whittington thought always of how to please her, and gave her the prettiest gifts he could find.

Mr. Fitzwarren soon saw that they loved each other, and proposed to join them in marriage. To this they both readily agreed. Their wedding was attended by the Lord Mayor, the court of aldermen, the sheriffs, and a great number of the richest merchants in London.

Mr. Whittington and his lady lived on in great splendor and were very happy, with several chil-

dren. He became Sheriff of London and thrice
Lord Mayor, and from the King he received the
honor of knighthood. Each time he became Lord
Mayor, he recalled the sound of Bow Bells:

*"Turn again, Whittington,*
   *Thrice Lord Mayor of London."*

# Cap o' Rushes

ONCE UPON A TIME there was a very rich gentle-man who had three beautiful daughters. He thought he would see how fond they were of him.

He asked the first, "How much do you love me, my dear?"

"Why," said she, "as I love my life."

"That's good," he replied.

He then asked the second, "How much do *you* love me, my dear?"

"Why, better than all the world," said she.

"That's good," he answered.

He turned then to the third, who was clever as well as pretty.

"How much do *you* love me, my dear?"

"Why, I love you as fresh meat loves salt!"

My, but he was angry! "You don't love me at all," he said, "and in my house you shall stay no longer." So he drove her out there and then,

and slammed the door after her.

She went away, on and on till she came to a swamp. In that low, marshy place she gathered some rushes and wove them into a kind of cloak with a hood, to cover her from head to foot and hide her fine clothes. Then she went on and on till she came to a great house.

"Do you need a maid?" she asked.

"No, we don't," they said.

"I have nowhere to go," she said, "and I ask no wages. I'll do any sort of work."

"Well," they said, "if you like to wash pots and scrape pans you may stay."

So she stayed, and she washed the pots and scraped the pans and did all the dirty work. Because she did not tell them her name, they called her "Cap o' Rushes."

One day there was to be a great dance nearby. The servants were allowed to go and look on at the grand people. Cap o' Rushes said she was too tired to go, so she stayed at home.

When they were gone, she took off her cap o' rushes and cleaned herself. And away she went to the dance, for she loved to dance. No one could dance more beautifully. And no one there was so finely dressed as she.

Now who should be there but her master's son! And what should he do but fall in love with her the minute he set eyes on her! He refused to dance with anyone else.

But before the dance was done, Cap o' Rushes slipped away home.

When the other maids came back, she was pretending to be asleep with her cap o' rushes on.


Next morning they said to her, "You did miss a sight, Cap o' Rushes!"

"What was that?" she said.

"Why, the most beautiful lady you ever did see, dressed right rich and gay. The young master, he never took his eyes off her."

"Well, I should like to have seen her," said
Cap o' Rushes.

"There's to be another dance this evening; perhaps she'll be there."

But, when evening came, Cap o' Rushes said
she was too tired to go with them. Still, she re-

membered the young master, who danced so well. When the others had gone, she took off her cap o' rushes and cleaned herself. And away she went to the dance.

The master's son had counted on seeing her. He danced with no one else, and never took his eyes off her. But, before the dance was over, she slipped away, and home she went. When the maids came back she pretended to be asleep with her cap o' rushes on.

Next day they said to her again, "Well, Cap o' Rushes, you should have been there to see the lady! There she was again, right rich and gay. The young master, he never took his eyes off her."

"Well, there," she said, "I should like to have seen her."

"Good," they said, "there's another dance this evening. You must go with us, for she's sure to be there."

Well, at evening Cap o' Rushes again said she was too tired to go. But when the maids were gone, she took off her cap o' rushes and cleaned herself. And away she went to the dance.

The master's son was full of joy to see her. He danced with no one else and never took his eyes off her. When she wouldn't tell him her name, nor where she came from, he gave her a ring. He told her that if he didn't see her again he would die.

Well, before the dance was over, she slipped away, and home she went. When the maids came home she was pretending to be asleep with her cap o' rushes on.

Next day they said to her, "There, Cap o' Rushes, you didn't come last night. Now you won't see the lady, for there's no more dances."

"I should like to have seen her," said Cap o' Rushes.

The master's son tried every way to find out where the lady had gone. But go where he might, and ask whom he might, he never heard anything about her. And he felt worse and worse for love of her till he was so ill he had to take to his bed.

"Make some gruel for the young master," they said to the cook. "He's dying for the love of the lady." The cook set about making it when Cap o' Rushes came in.

"What are you doing?" she asked.

"I'm going to make some gruel for the young master," said the cook, "for he's dying for the love of the lady."

"Let me make it," said Cap o' Rushes.

Well, the cook wouldn't allow her at first. But

at last she said yes, and Cap o' Rushes made the gruel. When she had made it, she slipped the ring into it before the cook took it upstairs.

The young man drank it. Then he saw the ring at the bottom.

"Send for the cook," he said.

So up she came again.

"Who made this gruel?" he asked.

"I did," said the cook, for she was frightened.

"No, you didn't," he said. "Say who did it, and you shan't be harmed."

"Well, then, 'twas Cap o' Rushes."

"Send Cap o' Rushes here," he said.

Cap o' Rushes came.

"Did you make my gruel?" he asked.

"Yes, I did," she replied.

"Where did you get this ring?"

"From him that gave it me," she answered.

"Who are you, then?" asked the young man.

"I'll show you," she said. And she took off her cap o' rushes, and there she was in her beautiful clothes.

Well, the master's son—he got well very soon. And they were to be married in a short time. It was to be a grand wedding, with everyone invited from far and near. Cap o' Rushes's father was invited, too, but she never told anybody who she was.

Before the wedding, Cap o' Rushes went to the cook and said, "I want you to prepare every dish without a mite of salt."

"That'll be plain nasty," said the cook.

"That doesn't matter," she replied.

"Very well," said the cook.

The wedding day came, and they were married. And after they were married, all the company sat down at the feast. When they began to chew the meat, it was so tasteless they couldn't eat it. Cap o' Rushes's father tried first one dish and then another. Then he burst out crying.

"What's the matter?" asked the master's son.

"Oh!" he said, "I had a daughter, whom I loved very much. When I asked her how much she loved me, she said, 'As much as fresh meat loves salt.' I turned her away from my door, for I thought she didn't love me. Now I see that she loved me best of all. And she may be dead, for all I know."

"No, Father, here she is!" said Cap o' Rushes. And she went up to him and put her arms around him.

And so they were happy ever after.